Buddhism

Buddhism

Edited by
Peter Harvey

CONTINUUM
London and New York

Continuum
The Tower Building, 11 York Road, London SE1 7NX
370 Lexington Avenue, New York, NY 10017-6503

First published 2001

British Library Cataloguing-in-Publication Data
A catalogue record for this book is available from the British Library.

ISBN 0-8264-5351-1 (hardback)
0-8264-5350-3 (paperback)

Library of Congress Cataloging-in-Publication Data
Harvey, Peter, 1951–
Buddhism / edited by Peter Harvey.
p. cm.—(World religions, themes and issues)
Includes bibliographical references and index.
ISBN 0-8264-5351-1—ISBN 0-8264-5350-3 (pbk.)
1. Buddhism. I. Title. II. Series.
BQ4012 .H37 2001
294.3–dc21

00–052342

Earlier versions of chapters appeared in the following books in the *Themes in Religious Studies* series, edited by Jean Holm with John Bowker and published in 1994 by Pinter Publishers: *Sacred Writings; Human Nature and Destiny; Picturing God; Worship; Rites of Passage; Making Moral Decisions; Women in Religion; Attitudes to Nature; Myth and History; Sacred Place.*

Typeset by YHT Ltd, London
Printed and bound in Great Britain by TJ International Ltd, Padstow, Cornwall

Contents

Illustrations and tables

The contributors

Martin Boord currently lives quietly as an independent scholar/translator with his family in Oxford. Supported by the Stein-Arnold Exploration Fund, he has done field research on the sacred history and geography of Sikkim, India from local oral and Tibetan literary sources. Rev. Dr Boord's particular interest is in the Northern Treasures (*Byang-gter*) revelationary tantric teachings of the rNing-ma school of Tibetan Buddhism. Among his published works are: *The Cult of the Deity Vajrakīla* (Institute of Buddhist Studies, Tring, 1993) and (with Losang Norbu Tsonawa) *Overview of Buddhist Tantra, Panchen Sonam Dragpa* (Library of Tibetan Works and Archives, Dharamsala, 1996). He has written on the mythology of Tibet and Mongolia, produced catalogues of Tibetan manuscripts and Tibetan art, and helped edit the works of Hugh Richardson on Tibet. His latest work on the *Phur 'grel 'bumnag* (*The Black 100 Thousand Words Commentary on Vajrakīla*) is to be published in 2001 by Wisdom Books, London.

Rita M. Gross is the author of two prize-winning books on Buddhism, *Buddhism After Patriarchy: A Feminist History, Analysis, and Reconstruction of Buddhism* (State University of New York Press, 1993) and *Soaring and Settling: Buddhist Perspectives on Contemporary Social and Religious Issues* (Continuum, New York, 1998). She is also the author of *Feminism and Religion: An Introduction* (Beacon, 1996) and co-editor of the classic *Unspoken Worlds: Women's Religious Lives*, which has just been released in its third edition. She is a frequent contributor to inter-religious exchanges, especially Buddhist–Christian dialogue.

Ian Harris was educated at the universities of Cambridge and Lancaster. He is a Reader in Religious Studies at St Martin's College, Lancaster and co-founder (with Peter Harvey) of the UK Association for Buddhist Studies. The author of *The Continuity of Madhyamaka and Yogacara in Early Mahayana Buddhism* (E. J. Brill, 1991) and editor of *Buddhism and Politics in Twentieth Century Asia* (Pinter, 1999), he has written widely on Buddhism and environmental ethics. He is currently working on a study of Buddhism in Cambodia, to be published by the University of Hawaii Press in 2001.

Peter Harvey is Professor of Buddhist Studies at the University of Sunderland, and co-founder, with Ian Harris, of the UK Association for Buddhist Studies (1995). His research is in the fields of early Buddhist thought and the ethical, devotional and meditational dimensions of Buddhism. He is author of *An Introduction to Buddhism: Teachings, History and Practices* (Cambridge University Press, 1990), *The Selfless Mind: Personality, Consciousness and Nirvana in Early Buddhism* (Curzon, 1995) and *An Introduction to Buddhist Ethics: Foundations, Values and Issues* (Cambridge University Press, 2000). He has also published articles on the *stūpa*, *paritta* chanting, 'signless' meditations and the nature of the *tathāgata*. He is a Theravāda Buddhist and a teacher of Samatha meditation.

Christopher Lamb is Head of the Centre for Inter Faith Dialogue and Senior Lecturer in Religious Studies at Middlesex University. He is the Joint General Editor, with M. Darrol Bryant, for the series *Issues in Contemporary Religion* published by Continuum, and the Joint General Editor, with Edward Bailey, for the series *Faith and Society* published by Middlesex University Press. He is the co-editor, with Dan Cohn-Sherbok, of *The Future of Religion: Postmodern Perspectives – Essays in Honour of Ninian Smart* (Middlesex University Press, 1999) and co-editor, with M. Darrol Bryant, of *Religious Conversion: Contemporary Practices and Controversies* (Cassell, 1999).

Stewart McFarlane is Everton Research Fellow and International Adviser at Liverpool Hope University College and Visiting Professor in Buddhist Studies at the Chung Hwa Institute of Buddhist Studies in Taiwan. He is the author of *The Complete Book of Tai Chi* (Dorling

Kindersley, 1999) and wrote and presented the four-part series *Shadow Boxing on the Path to Nirvana*, broadcast on the BBC World Service in 1998.

Ulrich Pagel is Lecturer in Language and Religion in Tibet and Middle Asia at the Department of the Study of Religions, School of Oriental and African Studies, University of London. Dr Pagel's research interests include the *bodhisattva*-ideal, (early) Mahāyāna *sūtra*s, the *Kanjur*, Buddhist bibliography and history, and Buddhism in Central Asia. In addition to several articles in journals and edited collections, he is author of *The Bodhisattvapiṭaka: Its Doctrines, Practices and Their Position in Mahāyāna Literature* (Institute of Buddhist Studies, Tring, 1995).

Pronunciation guide

Both Pāli and Sanskrit have more than 26 letters; so to write them in the roman alphabet means that this needs to be expanded by the use of diacritical marks. Once the specific sounds of the letters are known, Pāli and Sanskrit words are then pronounced as they are written, unlike English ones. It is therefore worth taking account of the diacritical marks, as they give a clear guide to pronunciation. The letters are pronounced as follows:

a is short and flat, like the *u* in 'hut' or 'utter'
i is short, like *i* in 'bit'
u is like *u* in 'put', or *oo* in 'foot'
e is like *e* in 'bed', only pronounced long
o is long, like *o* in 'note' (or, before more than one consonant, more like *o* in 'not' or 'odd').
A bar over a vowel makes it long:
ā is like *a* in 'barn'; ***ī*** is like *ee* in 'beet'; ***ū*** is like *u* in 'brute'.

When there is a dot under a letter (*ṭ*, *ḍ*, *ṇ*, *ṣ*, *ḥ*, *ṛ*, *ḷ*), this means that it is a 'cerebral' letter. Imagine a dot on the roof of one's mouth that one must touch with one's tongue when saying these letters. This produces a characteristically 'Indian' sound. It also makes *ṣ* into a *sh* sound, and *ṛ* into *ri*. But *ḥ* after a vowel represents a slight pulse of breath.
ś is like a normal *sh* sound.

Aspirated consonants (***kh***, ***gh***, ***ch***, ***jh***, ***th***, ***dh***, ***ph***, ***bh***) are accompanied by a strong breath-pulse from the chest, as when uttering English consonants very emphatically. For example: ***ch*** is like *ch-h* in 'church-hall', ***th*** is like *t-h* in 'hot-house'; ***ph*** is like *p-h* in 'cup-handle'. When

aspirated consonants occur as part of a consonant cluster, the aspiration comes at the end of the cluster.
c is like *ch* in 'choose'.
ñ is like *ny* in 'canyon'; ***ññ*** is like *nnyy*.
ṃ is a pure nasal sound, made when the mouth is closed but air escapes through the nose, with the vocal chords vibrating; it approximates to *ng*.
ṅ is an *ng*, nasal sound said from the mouth, rather than the nose.
v may be somewhat similar to English *v* when at the start of a word, or between vowels, but like *w* when combined with another consonant.
Double consonants are always pronounced long; for example, ***nn*** is as in 'unnecessary'.
All other letters are pronounced as in English.

ō is used to denote a long *o* in Japanese (as in 'note', rather than 'not').
Tibetan words are generally given in both their full transliteration, including silent letters, and their form when pronounced, e.g. *bKa'-'gyur* and *Kangyur*.
Chinese words are transcribed according to the classical Wade-Giles system of romanization rather than the more recent pinyin system.

Introduction

Peter Harvey

This work explores the rich Buddhist tradition from a number of interlocking perspectives, so as to gain a better understanding of it. In doing so, it places more emphasis on the ways in which the Buddhist visions are put into practice than do many other books on the religion. While it does not include much material on classical forms of meditation, it helps put these into their context within traditional Buddhism.

The work draws together the ten contributions on Buddhism to Pinter Publishers' 1994 series *Themes in Religious Studies*, edited by Jean Holm with John Bowker, which explored selected themes across world religions. Here, the papers have been re-edited, provided with certain supplementary material and further notes, cross-referenced and extensively indexed, and had additional items of further reading added, particularly as regards books post-dating the original series. This Introduction giving a historical overview of Buddhism has also been added. Each contribution originally had the title 'Buddhism' in its respective volume, but here they have been given individual titles.

While the chapters of this book can be read separately, they are given in a sequence which is designed to unfold in a helpful way. Chapter 1 covers Buddhism's textual sources, which comprise a key basis for much in the following chapters. Chapter 2 outlines key aspects of Buddhist doctrine, as a useful framework within which to set what follows. Chapter 3 focuses on aspects of doctrine, and related myth and iconography, concerning beings and levels of reality beyond the human realm. Chapter 4 then explores how humans relate to these through devotion. Chapters 5 and 6 explore other aspects of Buddhist practice relating to rites of passage and ethics. Chapter 7 focuses on ethical issues relating to gender. Chapter 8 explores doctrinal, mythic and ethical aspects of Buddhism's attitude to nature. In doing so, it helps to provide some background for Chapter 9's broader exploration of Buddhist cosmology. Chapter 10 builds on this to explore ideas of outer and inner sacred space.

Accordingly, the material in this work can be seen to relate to Ninian Smart's well-known seven 'dimensions of religion',[1] which provide a useful framework for understanding any religious tradition:

1 Doctrinal and philosophical dimension

2 Narrative and mythic dimension

3 Ethical and legal dimension

4 Practical and ritual dimension

5 Experiential and emotional dimension

6 Social and institutional dimension

7 Material dimension

'The sacred writings of Buddhism' covers some key sources for most of the dimensions, with the physical form of sacred texts themselves being part of the material dimension.

'Buddhist visions of the human predicament and its resolution' relates primarily to dimension 1.

'Portrayals of ultimate reality' relates to 1, 2 and 7, and other chapters relate as follows:

'Devotional practices' to 4, 2 and 5; 'Rites of passage' to 4 and 6; 'Making moral decisions' to 3, 6 and 1; 'Women in Buddhism' to 3, 6, 1 and 2; 'Attitudes to nature' to 1, 3 and 2; 'Cosmology, myth and symbolism' to 2, 1 and 4; 'Sacred space' to 7, 2 and 4.

Amongst the languages important for an understanding of Buddhism, probably the two key ones are Pāli and Sanskrit, two closely related Indian languages. The first is the scriptural and liturgical language of Theravāda Buddhism, and the second the language in which many Mahāyāna texts were recorded, prior to their translation into Tibetan or Chinese. It is normal to use Sanskrit terms in discussing Mahāyāna Buddhism, but practice varies as to whether Pāli or Sanskrit is used for Theravāda Buddhism or early

Buddhism, of which the Theravāda school is the only extant variant. In this work, a number of the chapters mostly use Sanskrit versions of names and terms, but this Introduction and Chapters 2–4, 6 and 8 use Pāli when appropriate, except for certain key terms now best known in their Sanskrit form: *nirvāṇa* (Pāli *nibbāna*), *karma* (Pāli *kamma*), *bodhisattva* (Pāli *bodhisatta*) and *stūpa* (Pāli *thūpa*). The index of this work includes guidance on which Pāli and Sanskrit terms are equivalent. Note that both Pāli and Sanskrit often form compound words. Wherever reasonable, this work separates out the components of such compounds by hyphens, to aid recognition of individual words.

Buddhism and its spread

Buddhism, Christianity and Islam are the three great missionary religions of the world, for each has sought actively to spread its message and practice beyond the culture where it originated, and their membership is not confined to any specific ethnic group. Admittedly the missionary style of these religions has varied; on the whole Buddhism has sought to make available an invitation to try out its way. Indeed it describes its teachings and path (Pāli *Dhamma*; Sanskrit *Dharma*) as 'come-see-ish', and monks have traditionally not been allowed to teach to a new audience unless they have been invited to do so, having first established a presence in an area.

The drive to spread the Buddhist message goes back to a time in the Buddha's life when his disciples had come to include 60 monks who were *arahats*,[2] like himself: people who had fully experienced *nirvāṇa* and destroyed all attachment, hatred and delusion. He sent out these enlightened disciples saying:

> Walk, monks, on tour for the blessing of the manyfolk, for the happiness of the manyfolk, out of compassion for the world, for the welfare, blessing and happiness of gods and humans ... Teach the *Dhamma* that is lovely in the beginning, lovely in the middle, lovely in its culmination.[3]

In time, Buddhism spread throughout India and then beyond, becoming the main form of Indian religion for export and often spreading literate culture as it went. Hinduism also spread to parts of Southeast Asia, but more slowly. Today, there is no country in Asia that has not had a strong Buddhist presence at some time, including such lands as currently Islamic Afghanistan and Indonesia. Even where living Buddhism is now absent, or minimal, the artistic heritage of Buddhist civilization is part of the landscape in Asian countries.

As it spread, Buddhism was quite happy to live alongside other religious traditions, whether well-developed text-based ones such as Confucianism and Taoism in China, less developed ones such as Shintō (Japan) and Bon (Tibet), which it came to heavily influence, or local cults worshipping various nature deities. There has perhaps never been a state with *only* Buddhism as its religion: a parallel to a 'one-party state' in politics. Buddhism has been happy to have an open frontier with other religions, which it related to with critical tolerance, always making clear its invitation into the various different levels of Buddhist commitment and practice.

The Buddha taught men and women and people of all social backgrounds. Many of his more committed followers became monks (Pāli *bhikkhu*; Sanskrit *bhikṣu*) or nuns (Pāli *bhikkhunī*; Sanskrit *bhikṣuṇī*), following a way of life designed explicitly to enhance spiritual progress. Many remained as lay-people, though, providing material support for the monks and nuns, who in turn gave them teachings and advice. This relationship of mutual giving lies at the heart of many continuing forms of Buddhism. Lay practice has tended to focus on developing qualities of generosity and moral restraint, and more devotional forms of practice, including the more devotional forms of meditation. Monastic practice has developed higher levels of restraint, and provided greater time for study and a range of meditations, though the more committed lay practitioner has also partaken of these within the time constraints of lay life.

The Buddha in his cultural context

Many books give the dates of the Buddha as 566–486 BCE ('Before the Christian Era'), though recent scholars, by re-assessing the evidence, think that more likely dates are around 484–404 BCE. The person who became known as 'the Buddha' (Awakened or Enlightened One) was Siddhattha Gotama (Pāli; Sanskrit Siddhārtha Gautama), known to Theravāda Buddhists as Gotama Buddha and to Mahāyāna Buddhists as Śākyamuni – sage of the Śākyans – Buddha, and to both as *Bhagavan*: the 'Blessed One', 'Fortunate One' or

'Lord'. He lived his life in a religious context in which an early form of Hinduism, generally known as 'Brahmanism' or 'Vedic religion', was of considerable influence. The teachings of Gotama shared certain basic ideas with Brahmanism, for example *karma* and rebirth, the goal of liberation from this, the existence of gods, yogic practices, and the valuing of spiritual insight. Nevertheless, his ideas on these were different from that of the brahmin priests, and he clearly differed from Brahmanism in that he did not accept certain key features of their world-view. He did not accept their scriptures as at all authoritative and also did not accept: the religious efficacy of sacrifices to the gods and the killing of animals involved in this; the idea of a divinely-ordained social system of four *varṇa*s, which became the basis for the later system of many castes; and the idea that a person contains a permanent, fixed Self. Even where he shared ideas, such as *karma* and rebirth, he did not simply accept these from the existing culture. For one thing, they were relatively new ideas, and were challenged by some of the renunciant (Pāli *samaṇa*; Sanskrit *śramaṇa*) communities that rejected Brahmanism and which in some ways resembled early Greek philosophical movements. Amongst these were the Jains, and the Buddhists themselves, both of which accepted some form of *karma* and rebirth doctrine; but the Materialists rejected *karma* and rebirth, the Sceptics were agnostic on them, and the Ājīvakas were fatalists who believed that one's rebirth was determined by a blind impersonal Fate, not one's freely chosen *karma* (action). For another thing, Gotama felt that his meditative experience gave him direct evidence of past lives, in the form of memories, and of the way in which the quality of a person's *karma* affected his or her future rebirth. Thus it would be wrong to see Buddhism as 'arising from Hinduism', both because of what has been said already, and because what we now call 'Hinduism' is a culmination of various changes arising from Brahmanism drawing on a variety of popular cults. Moreover, Hinduism was in part influenced by ideas drawn from Buddhism, which was a rival religion in India.

Early schools of Buddhism

After the death of the Buddha, the monastic community or *saṅgha* (Pāli; Sanskrit *saṅgha* or *saṃgha*), the heart of Buddhism, remained unified for around 86 years, until the 'first schism' took place at Pāṭaliputta (Pāli; Sanskrit Pāṭaliputra). This was very probably not over any matter of doctrine, but on points of monastic discipline. As the monks followed an agreed code of discipline, the development of variants in this meant that different communities could not carry out official *saṅgha* activities together. As a result of the schism, the *saṅgha* split into two fraternities, those of the Theravāda, 'The Ancient Teaching', and the Mahā-sāṃghika, 'Belonging to the Universal *Saṅgha*'. The first were probably a group of reformists who wanted to include certain aspects of developing monastic practice into the formal code, to ensure proper training of new recruits. The second group, which was larger at the time, preferred to keep to the existing formal code. In time, these two fraternities themselves split into other fraternities. As certain doctrinal positions became associated with particular fraternities, in time schism was sometimes based on doctrinal rather than monastic matters. By around the beginning of the Christian era, there were around eighteen of these different fraternities or schools. Today, the only ones that survive in any way trace themselves back to the Theravādins of the first schism:

- a school which retained or reclaimed the name Theravāda, which survives as a full tradition in Sri Lanka, Thailand, Myanmar (Burma), Cambodia and Laos;
- the Sarvāstivādins, once a very influential school in India: the monastic code of the Mūla-Sarvāstivādins is still in use in Tibet, and the *Abhidharma-kośa-bhāṣya* is a mostly Sarvāstivādin text which is quite often cited by the Mahāyāna Buddhists of Tibet, China, Vietnam, Korea and Japan;
- the Dharmaguptakas, whose monastic code is the one used in China, Vietnam and Korea.

The schools that trace their origin to the Mahā-sāṃghikas of the first schism have not survived in any institutional sense. Nevertheless, when the Mahāyāna movement developed (see below), the ideas it drew on may have come more from developments among Mahā-sāṃghika-related schools than Theravāda-related ones, and the former were then more open to subsequent Mahāyāna developments.

The contribution of Emperor Asoka

During the reign of the emperor Asoka (*c.* 268–239 BCE), Buddhism spread widely, reaching most of the Indian sub-continent and also beyond, thus becoming a 'world religion'. The Magadhan empire which Asoka (Pāli; Sanskrit Aśoka) inherited included most of modern India except the far south: the largest in the sub-continent until its conquest by the British. Asoka adopted the social ethic of Buddhism as the guiding principle of his rule, and has been seen by Buddhists as the model of a compassionate Buddhist ruler. The most important sources for our knowledge of him are his numerous edicts, as promulgated on rocks and stone pillars in a variety of languages, including Aramaic.

At the start of his reign, Asoka seems to have been content to carry on the policy of his forebears, which saw it as the duty of a ruler to expand his realm by force, according to a 'might is right' philosophy. While Asoka had already become a nominal Buddhist around 260 BCE, the full implications of his new faith do not seem to have hit home till after his bloody conquest of the Kaliṅga region, in the following year. In an edict after this episode, he evinced great remorse at the carnage he had caused, and expressed the desire to govern, please and protect his subjects according to *Dhamma*, in the sense of what was compassionate and just. He now felt that it was his duty to improve the quality of his subjects' lives, so as to provide a sound framework for their following a moral and religious way of life, Buddhist or otherwise. He inaugurated public works such as wells and rest-houses for travellers, supported medical aid for humans and animals, and gave aid for the fostering of such measures in regions beyond his empire. *Dhamma*-officials were appointed to encourage virtue, look after old people and orphans, and ensure equal judicial standards throughout the empire. While Asoka retained some judicial beatings, he abolished torture and, perhaps, the death penalty. Released prisoners were given some short-term financial help, and encouraged to make good *karma* for their future lives.

Asoka's concern for the moral improvement of his people was partly expressed in legislation, but more often in attempts to persuade people to live a better life. A prime value encouraged in his edicts was *ahiṃsa*, or 'non-injury': a key emphasis of both Buddhism and other Indian traditions. While he kept his army as a deterrent to invasion, Asoka gave up conquest. Hunting trips, the sport of kings, were replaced by pilgrimages to sites associated with the Buddha. In time, the large royal household became completely vegetarian. Brahmanical animal sacrifice was banned in the capital, and a wide range of non-food animals, birds and fishes were protected. Generosity towards *samaṇa*s, brahmins and the aged was urged. Respect for these and parents, good behaviour towards friends and relatives, and good treatment of servants was praised. Mercy, truthfulness, sexual purity, gentleness and contentment were recommended.

Asoka gave Buddhism a central place in his empire, just as the Roman emperor Constantine did for Christianity. Nevertheless, he supported not only Buddhist monks and nuns, but also brahmins, Jain wanderers and Ājīvaka ascetics, in accordance with a pattern that later Buddhist and Hindu rulers also followed. At a time when different religions were in competition for converts, he urged mutual respect and tolerance. His Twelfth Rock Edict says:

> King Priyadarsi honors men of all faiths, members of religious orders and laymen alike, with gifts and various marks of esteem. Yet he does not value either gifts or honors as much as growth in the qualities essential to religion in men of all faiths.
>
> This growth may take many forms, but its root is in guarding one's speech to avoid extolling one's own faith and disparaging the faith of others improperly or, when the occasion is appropriate, immoderately. The faiths of others all deserve to be honored for one reason or another. By honoring them, one exalts one's own faith and at the same time performs a service to the faith of others. By acting otherwise, one injures one's own faith and also does disservice to that of others. For if a man extols his own faith and disparages another because of devotion to his own and because he wants to glorify it, he seriously injures his own faith.
>
> Therefore concord alone is commendable, for through concord men may learn and respect the conception of *Dhamma* accepted by others.
>
> King Priyadarsi desires men of all faiths to know each other's doctrines and to acquire sound doctrines.[4]

During Asoka's reign, Buddhist missionary activity was considerable. Theravādin sources record that the monk Tissa Moggaliputta sent out parties of monks to a number of 'border areas'. Asokan edicts also record that the emperor sent out embassies to a number of foreign lands; for he wished to spread the ideals he followed: a 'conquest by *Dhamma*' rather than a military conquest. To the north-west, embassies were sent as far as Syria, Egypt and Macedonia, though there is no record of their having arrived there. To the east, they went to 'Suvaṇṇa-bhūmi' (the Golden Land), probably the Mon country of lower Burma or central Thailand. To the south, they went to south Indian kingdoms and also to the island of Ceylon (now known, as a country, as Sri Lanka). The relationship between the missions and the embassies is not clear, but monks could well have accompanied the embassies, and in the case of Sri Lanka, there was clearly co-operation. Here, in around 250 BCE, a mission headed by Asoka's own son, the *arahat* monk Mahinda, was very successful in implanting the Theravāda school of Buddhism.

The origin and development of the Mahāyāna movement[5]

Some time between 150 BCE and 100 CE, a new movement in Buddhism gradually began to arise as the culmination of various earlier developments. Its origin is not associated with any named individual, nor was it uniquely linked to any one early fraternity and school. It emerges into history as a loose confederation of groups, each associated with one or more of a number of new *sūtra*s: texts attributed to the Buddha. As no one had heard of these texts before, many were sceptical about them, but the Mahāyānists saw them as revealed to them by a heavenly form of the Buddha, or as his once secret teachings previously hidden in another world, or as arising from the same transformative wisdom as had been the source of the Buddha's teachings. Those who accepted the new teachings were part of the new movement, those who did not remained outside it. Mahāyānists continued to respect the early schools' records of the Buddha's teachings while re-interpreting and adding to them. In this there is perhaps a parallel to Christianity's use of early Jewish texts. The Mahāyānists remained a minority among Indian Buddhists for some time, though by the seventh century CE perhaps half of the monks had accepted the new texts and their orientation.

While scholars once thought that the Mahāyāna was developed by lay-people 'chafing at the pretentions of aloof monks', recent scholarship has shown that it was probably developed by monks, though they did encourage higher levels of practice and commitment amongst the laity.

The key ingredients of the Mahāyāna perspective were as follows. Firstly, a new cosmology arising from visualization practices devoutly directed at the Buddha as a glorified, transcendent being. Secondly, a new formulation of the path, centring on the figure of the *bodhisattva*. Thirdly, a new philosophical outlook. In the first of these, the Buddha was seen to still exist in a heavenly form, one among countless heavenly *buddha*s spread throughout the cosmos, and to be contactable by prayer; earlier forms of Buddhism saw him as in final *nirvāṇa*, beyond existence as an individual being. While earlier forms of Buddhism generally saw the historical Buddha as a recently enlightened *bodhisattva*, the Mahāyāna came to see him as having been a manifestation on earth of his heavenly counterpart, who had already been a *buddha* for countless ages. However, he attained his state in the past by the long path of the *bodhisattva*, a being-for-enlightenment. Various early schools had outlined the details of the *bodhisattva*-path that led to becoming a perfect *buddha*, one who rediscovers the liberating *Dhamma*-truth after previous generations had forgotten the teachings of a previous *buddha*. The Mahāyāna saw this path as not just for the rare spiritual hero, but as the path that most should tread, to the goal of buddhahood, not just arahatship.[6] This path was seen as longer than the Ennobling Eightfold Path to arahatship, and to be motivated by strong compassion, expressed in the aspiration to develop such a wealth of spiritual qualities, including deep wisdom, that countless other beings could be helped towards liberation.

Accordingly, the Mahāyānists came to see their way as the Mahā-yāna, or 'Great Spiritual Vehicle' in contrast to the 'Hīna-yāna' or 'Lesser Spiritual Vehicle' of those content with the goal of arahatship. They thus used the disparaging term 'Hīnayāna' for the various non-Mahāyāna schools. A more neutral, and thus acceptable, term that they also used was 'Śrāvakayāna': the spiritual vehicle of *śrāvaka*s, or 'disciples' who sought their own liberation as *arahat*s by developing insight into the four Ennobling Truths, as taught by a *buddha*. In the Mahāyāna, *arahat*s were respected, but seen as falling short of the true goal, buddhahood, and as leaving the round of rebirths as soon as they could for final *nirvāṇa*. For the Mahāyānists, once a *bodhisattva* was advanced enough, he or she reached a point where the round of rebirths could be transcended, but, by choice, the *bodhisattva* remained in it so as to be able to continue, in the form of a heavenly *bodhisattva*, to help beings, until finally becoming a heavenly *buddha*, who would attain final *nirvāṇa* after a huge length of time.

In this new perspective, a number of heavenly *buddha*s and

bodhisattvas were picked out for special attention, and became the objects of devotional cults. Notable among them are Avalokiteśvara, the *bodhisattva* 'Lord who looks down' in compassion to help any being in need who calls out to him, and the *buddha* Amitābha or 'Infinite Light', who in certain Indian texts, and then in Chinese and Japanese schools which followed these, became a grace-full saviour-being who saved all who had faith in him by drawing them to be reborn in his paradise-like 'Pure Land', where the conditions for attaining enlightenment were seen to be ideal.

A key Mahāyāna idea is that of 'skilful means' (*upāya-kauśalya*), according to which liberating truth might be framed in a great variety of ways to suit the character and tendencies of those in need of it. In practice, in the Mahāyāna this meant that a great range of teachings, sometimes apparently contradictory, came to be expressed.

The Mahāyāna developed new philosophical perspectives, as articulated in particular schools of thought. The Madhyamaka[7] school built on early teachings that no permanent Self can be found in anything. This was extended to mean that everything, mental or physical, is 'empty of' any inherent nature or essence. Nothing can exist apart from its relation to other things, which can exist only through their relation to other things which support them, and so on to infinity. The nature of anything came to be seen as 'emptiness' (*śūnyatā*), a word indicating this radical inter-relatedness of things. Emptiness was seen as something that could not really be captured in words, and so came to be seen as no different from *nirvāṇa*, which was also beyond words and had always been seen as known through deep insight into things as being empty of Self. This meant that, in the Mahāyāna, *nirvāṇa* was seen as none other than the everyday world, but as seen by the eye of deep wisdom. In the early schools it tended to be seen as radically different from the world, and known by deep insight which let go of attachment to anything in the world.

The Yogācāra school (also known as the Cittamātra, or Mind Only, school) focused all its attention on immediate experience: on how it functions in unenlightened beings and how it can be transformed so as to realize *nirvāṇa*. The common-sense 'objective' world was seen as a projection arising from people's misinterpretation of the flow of their experiences. Thus the idea of an external, physical world was regarded as either a complete delusion or only a dubious postulate for which we have no direct evidence.

An important line of thought focused on the idea of the *tathāgata-*

garbha, the *buddha*-potential hidden within all beings that was seen either as a seed of perfection waiting to be matured, or as full-blown perfection waiting to be uncovered. The idea was not the subject of a formal school in India, but its idea of a *buddha*-nature came to be of pervasive influence in the Buddhism of East Asia and, to a lesser extent, Tibet.

The Vajrayāna perspective

A new perspective within the Mahāyāna arose in India from the sixth century CE. It sought to speed up the long Mahāyāna path by potent methods of practice that were based on texts known as *tantra*s which described complex ritual-meditative systems. This approach came to be known as the Vajrayāna, the vehicle of the adamantine thunderbolt, or the Mantrayāna, the vehicle of *mantra*s, sacred words of power. It used *mantra*s to evoke the visualization and presence of a range of heavenly *buddha*s, *bodhisattva*s, and other holy beings. Such beings were seen both as existing separately from the practitioner, and also as represented by potencies latent within his or her mind. By the contemplative visualization of such beings, and the chanting of their *mantra*s, it was felt that their qualities could be awakened in the heart, so as to produce accelerated progress along the path. The visualized holy beings might be either male or female, and were sometimes portrayed or visualized in sexual union, symbolizing the perfect union of the spiritual qualities of wisdom (seen as female) and compassionate skilful means (seen as male). The holy beings were also sometimes portrayed as wrathful, as an aid to understanding qualities such as anger and transforming them into their opposites.

Such potent means were seen as dangerous if not used correctly; so it was emphasized that a practitioner needed the guidance of a *guru* (*bla-ma*, pron. *lama*, in Tibetan), a spiritual preceptor and guide whom he could completely trust. In Vajrayāna Buddhism, such *guru*s were just as likely to be lay adepts as monks or nuns.

The decline of Buddhism in India

Just as Christianity now hardly exists in its birthplace, so with

Buddhism in India. From the fourth century CE, Indian Buddhism existed alongside an increasingly resurgent Hinduism, which borrowed some of its ideas while criticizing and sometimes persecuting it. Tantric forms of Buddhism and Hinduism also seemed superficially similar, which helped dilute the distinctiveness of Buddhism. From the late tenth century, Muslim Turks invaded India, and in 1198 they toppled the last royal defender of Buddhism, in the north-east, and destroyed there a key stronghold of Buddhism, Nālandā monastic university. In any case, while Hinduism encouraged a martial spirit, at least for its warrior-noble class, Buddhism did not. In a struggle between Hindus, who identified strongly with Indian culture and fought in its defence, and a foreign ideology and force, Buddhism got squeezed out in the middle. It struggled on around the fringes, perhaps surviving as late as the seventeenth century in the far south of the Indian sub-continent. By then, it had long spread beyond India, taking many Indian values with it.

The Buddhist world today

Buddhism today is often divided into Theravāda and Mahāyāna Buddhism, referring respectively to:

- the form of Buddhism transmitted via Sri Lanka, based on one of the ancient, pre-Mahāyāna schools that came to identify itself with the Theravāda of the first schism and which uses Pāli as its scriptural and liturgical language, its key textual corpus being the Pāli Canon; and
- the form of Buddhism transmitted via Tibet or China that takes the Mahāyāna *sūtra*s as authoritative, and that has extensive canons in Tibetan and Chinese based on parallels to the Pāli Canon and later texts generally translated from Sanskrit originals.

In the past, these were sometimes known as 'Southern' and 'Northern' Buddhism, from the first being predominant in Sri Lanka and Southeast Asia, and the second in Tibet and areas to the east of there. Nevertheless it seems more useful to recognize the different nature of the Tibetan and Chinese transmissions of Mahāyāna

Buddhism, however much they have in common, by dividing the Buddhist world in Asia into three cultural areas: Southern, Northern and Eastern Buddhism. Southern Buddhism encompasses primarily Sri Lanka, Thailand, Myanmar (Burma), Cambodia and Laos. Its Buddhism is Theravāda, with a few influences from the classical and Vajrayāna forms of Mahāyāna, which in the past had an active presence in these lands. Northern and Eastern Buddhism are both Mahāyāna in form. Northern Buddhism is found primarily in Tibet, Mongolia, parts of north-west China between these two lands, Bhutan, Nepal (alongside Hinduism), Ladakh in the far north of India, and in the exile Tibetan community in India. In many ways it has continued late Indian Buddhism and its mix of classical Mahāyāna and its Vajrayāna variant. For Eastern Buddhism, China has been the key transmission route, from where it spread to Korea and then Japan, and also to Vietnam. In Eastern Buddhism, a form of the Vajrayāna is one small strand alongside several more influential developments. A number of these have been touched by aspects of Chinese culture more strongly expressed in Confucianism and Taoism. While Southern and Northern Buddhism retain the flavour of Indian culture, Eastern Buddhism has in fact been strongly influenced by Chinese culture. Southern and Northern Buddhism broadly inculcate a gradualist approach to enlightenment, of progress along a spiritual path, and value the training of the intellect. In Eastern Buddhism, Zen seeks to go beyond gradual developments in instantaneous flashes of insight, and can be impatient with analytic training of the intellect, while the Pure Land school sees faith as a way of short-cutting the gradual development of what it sees as too difficult a path. These have been more popular than the T'ien-t'ai and Hua-yen schools, which accorded more role to the intellect in their complex philosophies.

As well as these three main cultural areas of Buddhism, there are areas now lost to Islam: Afghanistan, Pakistan, Bangladesh, Indonesia and Malaysia (though the latter contains a sizeable number of Chinese Buddhists). In India itself, Buddhism exists around the fringes, amongst some ex-'untouchables' who have converted since the 1950s to help improve their life situation, and among the exile Tibetan community, headed by the Dalai Lama.

Southern Buddhism[8]

Of the existing Buddhist countries, Sri Lanka is the one where Buddhism has existed longest, from the time of Mahinda's mission. Sri Lankans are very proud of this, and see themselves as the preservers of the ancient Buddhist tradition. Buddhist chronicles tell of the history of Buddhism on the island, and the pious deeds of many Buddhist kings, who in time came to be seen as *bodhisattva*s. The form of Theravāda introduced by Mahinda in time came to develop certain variant monastic fraternities, some of which were open to Mahāyāna developments from the sub-continent, though these were re-unified by a king in the twelfth century under the umbrella of the most orthodox Theravāda monastery, the Mahā-vihāra, or Great Monastery.

Sri Lanka preserved and transmitted the Theravāda Canon of texts from India, in the Pāli language. This consists of the Pāli Canon:

- the *Vinaya-piṭaka*: the 'Basket of Monastic Discipline': four texts in six volumes (in their modern printed version);
- the *Sutta-piṭaka*: the 'Basket of Discourses (of the Buddha)': nineteen texts in 36 volumes;
- the *Abhidhamma-piṭaka*: the 'Basket of Further Teachings': seven texts in thirteen volumes.

The 55 volumes of this are far longer than the Bible, partly reflecting the fact that the Buddha's teaching career lasted 45 years, from his enlightenment at the age of 35.

The texts state that the contents of the first two 'Baskets' were recited at a council held just after the Buddha's death. Their content differs only in minor respects from the surviving fragments or translations of other early canons. The *Abhidhamma-piṭaka* contains early systematizing texts of the Theravādins, in the form of detailed analysis of mental and physical states and their relationship: the world's first systematic psychology (along with the *Abhidhamma*s of other Buddhist schools). It is formally attributed to the Buddha, but can be seen to have developed from building on the approach of certain very analytical *sutta*s.

The above texts were transmitted by communal recitation at first, as writing was little used in India, and a learned person was 'much heard' rather than 'well read'. The texts were first committed to writing around 80 BCE in Sri Lanka, at a time of war and famine when it was feared that sections of the texts would be lost with the deaths of the monks who recited them. The commentaries developed by the Theravādins in India were said to have been brought to Sri Lanka by Mahinda and his companions along with the Canon, all in their memories. Later the commentaries were translated into Sinhala, and in the fifth century CE the monk Buddhaghosa came to Sri Lanka to seek access to these and work on them. To prove his worthiness for this task, he wrote the *Visuddhimagga*,[9] a masterly survey of Theravāda doctrine and meditation methods. He was then allowed to translate the commentaries back into Pāli, edit them, and add certain thoughts of his own. Through these activities, he became the major spokesman of Theravāda orthodoxy.

While Theravāda Buddhism may have existed from the time of Asoka in the Mon region of what is now Myanmar (Burma) and Thailand, other forms of early Buddhism, as well as Mahāyāna Buddhism and Hinduism, later came to be influential. From the eleventh century, though, much of Southeast Asia became predominantly Theravādin, through the actions of certain kings, missionaries from the Mon region, and the influence of Sri Lankan Buddhism. Theravāda became dominant in Myanmar in the eleventh century, stimulating missionary activity which started to spread it. The Theravāda became dominant in Cambodia from the twelfth century, with the thirteenth century seeing its dominance in Thailand and the fourteenth in Laos. The passing on of an orthodox ordination line, going back to the Buddha, has been treated as a precious heritage – in the eleventh century, the monks' ordination line had to be re-imported from Myanmar to Sri Lanka, as wars had led to a decline in discipline in Sri Lanka. The nuns' ordination line, though, was not re-introduced, and died out in Sri Lanka at that time (surviving in Myanmar until at least the thirteenth century).

Sri Lanka was the first Buddhist country to be affected by Western colonial powers. The Catholic Portuguese (1505–1658), then the Calvinist Dutch (1658–1796) controlled certain lowland regions. The British finally brought an end to the highland kingdom of Kandy in 1815, so as to rule the whole island. While only the Portuguese had persecuted Buddhism, each colonial power tried to transmit its own brand of Christianity to the islanders. The British controlled Myanmar from 1885, and the French controlled Cambodia and

Laos, along with Vietnam, from 1893. Thailand managed to remain independent, by skilfully playing off the British and French against each other. In this, a number of gifted Buddhist monarchs played an important role, especially King Mongkut (1851–68), an ex-monk poorly portrayed in *The King and I*, and his son Chulalongkorn (1868–1910), who both did much to modernize the country.

Southern Buddhism retains an emphasis on the teachings emphasized in Pāli *sutta*s, such as *karma* and rebirth and the Four Ennobling Truths. In expressing devotion to the *buddha*s, the key focus is Gotama, with some attention paid to past *buddha*s and Metteya, the *bodhisattva* who will be the next *buddha*, in some thousands of years' time. Southern Buddhism values monasticism highly, with the lands of Southeast Asia, but not Sri Lanka, having developed a system where many young men ordain for a period of a few months, sharing the life of the long-term monks. As the ordination line for full nuns (*bhikkhunī*s) has died out, some committed women live a semi-monastic life following eight or ten precepts, rather than the 311 for full *bhikkhunī*s, though there are moves to try to re-establish the *bhikkhunī* ordination line from Chinese nuns.

While the Theravāda school of Southern Buddhism has little formal divisions within it, apart from monastic fraternities with slightly different traditions, there is a range of differences as regards intellectual approach and practices. The majority of monks live in towns and villages and share in a life of keeping the monastic discipline, common chants and some practice of meditation. Beyond this they may put particular emphasis on study, chanting or other rituals for the laity, or helping the laity in areas such as reforestation, drug addiction or development projects.

Those who specialize in meditation are the minority, and are generally known as 'forest monks', because they either live in the forest, an ideal setting for meditation, or are related to teachers or key monasteries that are. They tend to strongly emphasize monastic discipline as well as meditation, but to spend little time on study.

Some monks, and laity, could be seen as 'Ultimatist', in that they de-emphasize practices such as making good *karma* by giving, and devotion, to focus on the central meditative aspects of the Buddhist path to *nirvāṇa*. A good example is the Thai monk Buddhadāsa.[10]

In Thailand, the government and leading monks have encouraged the involvement of monks in government-led rural development efforts, and this has roused debate over the proper role for monks in modern society. The twin dangers which are seen as necessary to avoid are:

1 Becoming irrelevant to the needs and priorities of modern society.
2 Through inappropriate 'socially relevant' activity, undermining the unique contribution of monks to the rest of society.

In certain respects, Christians face a similar dilemma.

From the late nineteenth century in Sri Lanka, a modernist version of Buddhism developed among some urban, British-educated laity. As these were influenced in certain ways by the Protestant Christianity they came to oppose in a Buddhist resurgence, they are sometimes known as 'Protestant Buddhists'. They are reformists who emphasize the early texts, and advocate a greater role for the laity and more social activism for monks. A current example of this trend is the Sarvodāya Shramadāna village development movement in Sri Lanka. This is a lay-led movement, also involving monks, and influenced by the Hindu Mahātma Gandhi's emphasis on village awakening. It seeks to put Buddhism into practice in the villages by waking people up to improve their economic, social and natural environment. A more recent term for such activist-Buddhism is 'Engaged Buddhism', of which there are both Theravāda and Mahāyāna examples.[11]

Northern Buddhism[12]

Buddhism reached mountainous and inaccessible Tibet in the seventh century, and started to put down firm roots in the eighth century. The indigenous religious tradition, which came to be known as Bon, centred on the cult of dead kings, spirit-possession, magic, and the exorcism of demons and vampires, though it shared a belief in rebirth with Buddhism. In time, Bon was influenced by Buddhism, and Buddhism allowed it to continue alongside itself. The Tibetans' love of magic, though, meant that the form of Mahāyāna which took root there was a mix of Vajrayāna mysticism and ritual and monastically-based Mahāyāna scholasticism. The key eighth-century figures in the transmission process were Śāntarakṣita, representing the latter trend, and Padmasaṃbhava, representing the former. Padmasaṃbhava is said to have successfully exorcized the site of Tibet's first Buddhist temple and also bound a number of Bon deities into becoming protectors of Buddhism.

Of the four main schools (*pa*s) of Buddhism that developed in Tibet, that which sees Padmasaṃbhava as its founder is the Nyingma-pa (rNyingma-pa). This has a strong emphasis on tantric practice and magic, has many non-monastic adepts as teachers, and claims to have gradually recovered a number of texts that Padmasaṃbhava had hidden for later rebirths of his disciples to rediscover and teach to later generations.

The other three schools, with roots in an eleventh-century renaissance in Tibetan Buddhism, are 'reformed' in that they reject some of the Nyingma texts as inauthentic, and place more emphasis on celibate monasticism. The reforms were sparked by Atīśa, an Indian monk-professor who taught in Tibet. He founded the Kadam-pa (bKa'-gdams-pa) or 'Bound by Command (of Monastic Discipline) School', which also influenced two other new schools: the Kagyu-pa (bKa'brgyud-pa) or 'Whispered Transmission School' and the Sakya-pa (Sa-skya-pa). The former emphasizes the secret transmission from master to pupil of guidance in a complex system of yoga; the latter emphasizes scholarship.

A later reformer, Tsong-kha-pa (1357–1410), founded what was to become the most dominant school, the Geluk-pa (dGe-lugs-pa) or 'Virtuous School', on the basis of the old Kadam school. He emphasized the study of logic and the Mahāyāna teachings on emptiness, monastic discipline, reduction of magical practices, and the postponement of certain tantric practices until practitioners were well prepared to use them.

While Tibetans introduced (Sakya-pa) Buddhism into Mongolia in the thirteenth century, these later lapsed from it. The introduction of Geluk-pa Buddhism there in the sixteenth century was more successful, and a Mongol ruler gave the title 'Dalai (Ocean (of Wisdom)) Lama' to the Geluk-pa leader who did so. He also became recognized as the second reincarnation of Tsong-kha-pa's nephew, who was retrospectively regarded as the first 'Dalai Lama'.

Lama is the Tibetan term for a respected spiritual teacher, equivalent to Sanskrit *guru*. Of the many monks in Tibet, some are also *lama*s, but respected lay practitioners can also be *lama*s. Amongst *lama*s, around three hundred are seen as *tulku*s (*sprul-sku*s). This means that they are seen as one of a line of repeated incarnations of an advanced *bodhisattva* or *buddha* that are not reborn by the force of *karma*, like most beings, but by choice. The Dalai Lamas came to be seen as incarnations of Avalokiteśvara, the *bodhisattva* who embodies compassion, and the present Dalai Lama is seen as the fourteenth of these.

The system of recognized reincarnations is peculiar to Northern Buddhism, as is the system of rule of a country by monks and monasteries, which developed in Tibet in the thirteenth century, and again from the seventeenth, at a time when secular political power collapsed and the Mongolians wanted their spiritual leaders to rule Tibet.

From the 1950s, Tibet was taken over and colonized by Communist China, leading to the present Dalai Lama fleeing to India in 1959, where he heads a government in exile. During the 1960s and 1970s, the Chinese destroyed many monasteries, and much of the artistic and literary heritage of Tibet, though since then they have eased up their persecution to a level sufficient to repress the political ambitions of Tibetans to control their own country and culture. The Chinese colonization of Tibet has led to a diaspora of Tibetans and many of their religious leaders, spreading first to India, then to other parts of Asia and to the West. The Chinese Communists have thus inadvertently been an important impetus to the spread of Tibetan Buddhism in the West.

The Dalai Lama is probably the best-known Buddhist in the world. Widely respected by both Buddhists and non-Buddhists, his formal position is as (a) the current head of the Tibetan government-in-exile, (b) the most respected figure, if not the formal head, of the Geluk school, (c) a person whom Tibetans see as a recognized incarnation of previous Dalai Lamas, each of whom is also seen as an incarnation of Avalokiteśvara. The Dalai Lama himself, though, often refers to himself as 'a simple monk'.

The Dalai Lama emphasizes such notions as 'universal responsibility' in the social and environmental spheres, and is supportive, for example, of Tibetan nuns, who follow the ten precepts of a novice, gaining higher ordination from nuns of the Chinese tradition. In recent years, a discordant note in Tibetans' universal respect for him was sounded by supporters of the deity Dorje Shugden, whose followers in the West have founded what they call the New Kadampa Tradition. While the Dalai Lama sees Dorje Shugden as a worldly deity lacking in enlightened intentions, his supporters see him as a true Buddhist guide, and as a champion of the Geluk school against syncretism with the teachings and practices of other Buddhist schools, which they see in the Dalai Lama's ecumenical approach.

Eastern Buddhism[13]

Buddhism spread to China via the 'silk road', an international trade-route passing from north-west India to Central Asia, north of Tibet, and on to northern China. Buddhism was spread along this by Buddhist merchants and accompanying monks. It reached China by around 50 CE, and by a century later Chinese interest had led to the start of the vast project to translate the many Indian Buddhist texts into Chinese, which was in full swing by the start of the fifth century.

While most of the countries that Buddhism spread to in Asia did not already have a developed literate culture, this was not the case in China. It had a unified empire with a bureaucracy run by scholar-gentlemen schooled in the texts of Confucianism. Confucianism emphasizes respect for parents and ancestors, proper and harmonious social relationships, and in the past saw the emperor as the mediator of the right relationships between Man, Earth and Heaven, the latter being seen in somewhat impersonal terms. While Confucianism sought social harmony, the parallel tradition of Taoism sought harmony with nature through meditation and free-flowing spontaneity of action, following the example of the Tao or 'Way' which was seen to run through and sustain the whole of reality.

Over time, Buddhism became, with Confucianism and Taoism, one of the three religions of China. At times it was the dominant tradition, occasionally it was persecuted by the state. From the twelfth century, Neo-Confucianism, which had borrowed certain aspects of Buddhist philosophy, gradually undermined the prestige of Buddhism among the educated, while leaving it strong at the popular level. The marginalization of Buddhism by Neo-Confucianism followed in Korea, too, reaching its height in the sixteenth century.

When Buddhism spread from Korea to Japan in the sixth century, though, it brought much of Chinese civilization, including Confucianism, with it. Buddhism was soon associated with centres of state power, and was a major force in the development of Japan as a unified state with a literate culture. Buddhism was never overshadowed by Confucianism in Japan, but worked alongside it and the indigenous tradition of Shintō, which was focused on worship of a range of nature deities, auspicious places and people. Only during Japan's nationalistic phase from 1868 to 1945 did a form of Shintō come to marginalize 'foreign' Buddhism and Confucianism.

While Buddhists helped develop the first form of written Japanese, in China Buddhism was closely associated with the invention of printing. Woodblock printing was used in the eighth century to reproduce Buddhist chants and then whole texts, with the world's oldest extant printed book, dating from 868 CE, being a copy of the *Vajracchedikā Sūtra*, a text on the idea of 'emptiness'. The entire Buddhist Canon (which even includes some material on Nestorian Christianity) was printed between 972 and 983, using over 130,000 printing blocks.

In China, a variety of schools of Buddhism developed. Some were imported versions of Indian schools of Mahāyāna philosophy, such as the Madhyamaka and Yogācāra. One was a form of Mantrayāna Buddhism, the Chen-yen or 'Mantra' school. While of relatively minor importance in China, it became more important in Japan, where it is known as Shingon.

Two Chinese schools sought to synthesize the great range of Mahāyāna teachings emerging from India as more and more texts were translated. The Hua-yen (Japanese Kegon) school saw the totality of reality as a vast web of inter-related factors which mutually supported each other – a view now becoming popular among those with both environmental and Buddhist sympathies. The T'ien-t'ai school emphasized the idea of the *buddha*-nature as a potential, or even hidden actuality, inherent in all beings, and in the transcendent nature of the heavenly *buddha* and his 'skilful means' in teaching and helping beings in a range of ways suitable to their capacities. The Japanese form of this school, the Tendai, was the dominant one there from the ninth to the twelfth centuries.

The most popular forms of Buddhism, though, were those that came to focus on a particular form of practice and a small number of texts. In China, the Ch'an (Japanese Zen), or 'Meditation', school developed from the late fifth century.[14] Focusing its energy on meditation practice, it gave relatively little attention to texts, but accorded great importance to the words and actions of a series of masters who were seen to have come to know and express their *buddha*-nature through meditative quieting and probing of the mind. Taoist ideals of spontaneity were influential and deep awareness of simple natural events was seen to offer a window on the mysterious 'suchness' that was the fundamental 'empty' nature of reality. Insight into reality also came to be developed by the meditative contemplation of *kōans*, enigmatic questions such as 'what is the sound of one hand clapping?' or 'who is it who recites the name of the Buddha?'

These are intended to drive the mind beyond conceptual thinking so as to access the intuitive insight of the *buddha*-nature.

In China, Korea, Vietnam and Japan, Ch'an/Zen became the most influential school among artists, intellectuals and many monks and nuns. Alongside it, a greater impact was made at the popular level by the Pure Land school, which also originated in the fifth century. While Ch'an saw enlightenment as coming from within, the Pure Land school looks to the heavenly *buddha* Amitābha (Japanese Amida), 'Infinite Light', as the source of salvific power. The three basic texts of this approach were composed in India.[15] They portrayed Amitābha as a *buddha* who had vowed to save all that called to him in faith, drawing them, at death, to be reborn in his Pure Land known as Sukhāvatī, 'Happy Land', where the conditions for attaining enlightenment are ideal, and where everything is pleasant and uplifting. In China, Pure Land teachers taught that theirs was the 'easy path' of reliance on 'other-power', not the 'path of the saints' which used 'self-power' (as in Ch'an), as this was 'too difficult' for the ordinary person at a time when humankind was seen to be declining in morality and self-discipline. Pure Land practice puts a premium on faith, a short chant of devotion to Amitābha, *Nama Amida Butsu* in Japanese, and the practice of compassion. One form of the school, the Japanese Jōdo-shin, or 'True Pure Land' school, saw even faith as coming from Amitābha, and in effect sees liberation as coming from reliance on the grace of Amitābha alone.[16] Thus its founder Shinran (1173–1263) came to abandon monastic celibacy, seeing it both as too difficult and as wrongly suggesting that humans can help save themselves, and he even came to see the approach he advocated as the difficult, not easy, path: it is hard to *totally* rely on Amitābha. He also emphasized the 'sinful' and corrupt qualities of unaided human nature, a concept at odds with the outlook of most other schools of Buddhism.

A school of Buddhism unique to Japan is the Nichiren school, which developed in the thirteenth century, around the time when Zen and Pure Land were also becoming popular there. Like the Pure Land school, Nichiren Buddhism emphasizes faith, but it places this not in Amitābha Buddha but in the liberating truth of the *Lotus Sūtra* (the text seen as the supreme one by the Tendai school) and in Śākyamuni Buddha as the eternal being who teaches and is embodied in this. Like Zen, it seeks to uncover and manifest the *buddha*-nature, through a form of self-power, but this is to be done through active reform of society and the devout chanting of *Na-mu myō-hō ren-ge-kyō*, 'Honour to the *Lotus Sūtra* of the True *Dharma*'. The founder of the school, Nichiren (1222–82), was the nearest thing in Buddhism to an Old Testament prophet, for he denounced other Buddhist schools to the government, forthrightly criticizing them for neglecting what he saw as the central teaching of Buddhism and sapping the fibre of Japanese society.

The Ashikaga period in Japan (1333–1573) saw a prolonged time of conflict between rival war-lords and the collapse of a unified state. In such violent times, many of the Buddhist schools took to arms to defend themselves or the peasants that supported them, and they sometimes fought with each other. In the sixteenth century, the Portuguese brought Christianity to Japan. Some rulers had favoured it as a foil to the power of Buddhist monasteries, and propagated it with violence. In the Tokugawa period (1603–1867), however, Japan was unified and closed its doors to all but a few traders from the outside world. During this time, the country's military leaders ruthlessly persecuted Christianity as a possible conduit of foreign influence.

In the twentieth century, Chinese Buddhism underwent something of an intellectual renaissance in the Republican period (1912–49), an ideologically more open period free of Confucian dominance, partly in response to well-organized Christian missionaries. The Communist victory of 1949 brought suppression and manipulation in mainland China (not Taiwan), with the 'Cultural Revolution' of 1966–72 being especially destructive. Things have eased up somewhat since then, though. While the 738,200 monks and nuns of 1930 were reduced to 28,000 by 1986, these are likely to be the more committed and active.

In Korea, Japanese colonization of the country between 1910 and 1945 brought the previous Confucian-dominated era to an end and allowed a revival in Buddhism, though under influence from Japanese forms. After the defeat of the Japanese in 1945, and the end of the Korean war in 1953, Buddhism in South Korea has speeded up its revival, while remaining repressed in Communist North Korea. In the rapidly modernizing South, Buddhism is now faced, though, with a rising Christian population. The Christian conversion drive is weak on subtlety and this has meant that a number of Buddhist temples have been burnt down by over-zealous converts. While some Christian leaders have spoken against this, Christian leaders' portrayal of Buddhism does little to discourage such acts of small-minded aggression, an unfortunate resurfacing of Christian intolerance of past ages.

In Japan, the rush to modernize and catch up with the West ushered in the Meiji era in 1868. At first it spurred on Japan's imperial adventure in Asia, leading to wars with Korea, Russia, China and then America. Since Japan's defeat in 1945, modernization has gone on apace, but with a peace constitution. Buddhism has continued alongside Shintō, with people often drawing on elements of both. Traditional forms of Buddhism have had to reorientate themselves in Japan's fast-changing urban landscape, but a host of New Religions have come to develop. Among the most successful is the Sōka-gakkai, a lay-led form of Nichiren Buddhism which has been very active in seeking converts in the West.[17]

Challenges and opportunities for Buddhism in the modern world

In recent centuries, Buddhism has been buffeted by a number of winds blowing from the West:

- Colonialism: which undermined political structures associated with Buddhism, but also led to Western scholarship on Buddhism and so helped the spread of it to the West.
- Christianity: missionaries' early studies of Buddhism helped spark the interests of more objective Western scholars. Christians' criticism of Buddhists was one element in stimulating increasing Buddhist social activism. In South Korea and the Republic of China, Christianity and Buddhism are currently rivals for people's commitment.
- Communism: a wet blanket on Buddhism in China (currently including Tibet), North Korea, Vietnam and Laos. Recently escaped from this are Cambodia and Mongolia, though a repressive Marxist-nationalist regime is still in power in Myanmar (Burma). While some Buddhists, including the Dalai Lama, have seen more humanistic aspects of Marxism as containing something of value, Communism's tendency to encourage hatred is at clear odds with Buddhism.

- Capitalism: like Christianity, originally brought with colonialism, though Japan developed its own capitalism as a foil to Western colonial threats. This has brought some greater prosperity but also undermined traditional value-structures.
- Consumerism, a particularly virulent form of capitalism, is currently perhaps the greatest corrosive force undermining Buddhism in such lands as Thailand and Japan. Its commodification of life and emphasis on possessions has heightened elements of greed in human nature and encourages a reorientation of values accordingly.

On the other side of the coin, increasing globalization and ease of information transfer means that a mass of information on Buddhism is now available world-wide through books, the Internet and other media, as well as ease of travel. Buddhism is putting down firm roots in many Western countries and starting to enter into dialogue with Western philosophy, psychology and environmentalism.

Buddhism in the West

Of the Asian forms of Buddhism, those most successful in the West are Theravāda, the various forms of Tibetan Buddhism, Zen, and the Sōka-gakkai. In America, Pure Land Buddhism is strong among people of Japanese descent. Using the Chinese idea of 'self-power' and 'other-power' (see above), we might compare these as follows:

Zen: self-power through knowing and showing one's innate *buddha*-nature;

Theravāda: mainly self-power through the cultivation of morality, meditation and wisdom, but also drawing on the other-power of the Buddha through his preserved teachings and their power to bless and protect when chanted;

Sōka-gakkai: self-power through devout chanting and social activism, but also drawing on the saving truth-power of the *Lotus Sūtra*;

Tibetan Buddhism: a mix of self-power, by activating inner potentials, and other-power, by drawing on the help of heavenly *buddha*s and *bodhisattva*s who correspond to these potentials;

Pure Land: other-power through faith in the saving grace of Amitābha Buddha.

Thus the central thrust of Buddhism, which seeks the awakening of the human mind so as to overcome suffering in both oneself and others, has been expressed and developed in a variety of complementary ways.

Notes

1 For example N. Smart (1996) *Dimensions of the Sacred*. London: HarperCollins.
2 The spelling *arahat* is the Pāli form that appears in compounds, for which the Sanskrit is *arhat*; the Pāli stem-form *arahant* is also in common use in works on Buddhism.
3 I. B. Horner (trans.) (1951) *The Book of the Discipline*, vol. 4. London: Luzac, p. 28, with some small changes.
4 N. A. Nikam and R. McKeon (1959) *The Edicts of Asoka*. Chicago: University of Chicago Press; Midway reprint (1978), pp. 51–2.
5 For further details, see P. Williams (1989) *Mahāyāna Buddhism: The Doctrinal Foundations*. London: Routledge.
6 A classical outline of the *bodhisattva* path is given in the *Bodhicaryāvatāra*, an inspiring poem of the eighth-century Śāntideva: see K. Crosby and A. Skilton (1996) *Śāntideva: The Bodhicaryāvatāra*. Oxford: Oxford University Press.
7 A follower of which is called a Mādhyamika.
8 For further details on India and Sri Lanka see R. Gombrich (1988) *Theravāda Buddhism: A Social History from Ancient Benares to Modern Colombo*. London: Routledge and Kegan Paul; on Southeast Asia see D. K. Swearer (1995) *The Buddhist World of Southeast Asia*. Albany: State University of New York Press.
9 Translated by Bhikkhu Ñāṇamoli (1975) *The Path of Purification* (3rd edn). Kandy, Sri Lanka: Buddhist Publication Society; and (1976; 2 vols) Berkeley, CA: Shambhala.
10 For examples of Buddhadāsa's writings, see *Me and Mine: Selected Essays of Bhikkhu Buddhadāsa*, ed. D. K. Swearer (1989). Albany: State University of New York Press.
11 See C. S. Queen and S. B. King (eds) (1996) *Engaged Buddhism: Buddhist Liberation Movements in Asia*. Albany: State University of New York Press.
12 For further details see D. Snellgrove and H. Richardson (1968) *A Cultural History of Tibet*. London: Weidenfeld; also S. Batchelor (ed., trans. and intro.) (1987) *The Jewel in the Lotus: A Guide to the Buddhist Traditions of Tibet*. London: Wisdom.

13 For further details see K. K. S. Chen (1964) *Buddhism in China: A Historical Survey*. Princeton, NJ: Princeton University Press; also J. M. Kitagawa (1966) *Religion in Japanese History*. New York: Columbia University Press.
14 See H. Dumoulin (1988) *Zen Buddhism – A History: India and China*. London: Collier Macmillan. The term *ch'an* is derived from the Sanskrit *dhyāna* (Pāli *jhāna*), meaning a state of deep meditation.
15 Luis O. Gomez (1996) *The Land of Bliss: The Paradise of the Buddha of Measureless Light (Sanskrit and Chinese Versions of the Sukhāvatīvyūha Sutras) – Introductions and English Translations*. Honolulu: University of Hawai'i Press.
16 See A. Bloom (1965) *Shinran's Doctrine of Pure Grace*. Tucson: University of Arizona Press.
17 See R. Causton (1988) *Nichiren Shōshū Buddhism: An Introduction*. London: Rider.

1. The sacred writings of Buddhism

Ulrich Pagel

The sacred writings of the Buddhists form a collection of literature of astonishing magnitude. The spiritual fountainhead of all Buddhist scriptures is the Buddha, or to be more precise, the doctrine (*Dharma*) that was taught by him. Most scholars would agree that the teachings of the historical Buddha are recorded in the scriptures of the Theravāda school – the Pāli Canon.

Broadly speaking, the religious texts of Buddhism fall into three categories. First, there is a large body of early canonical writings. Preserved in the Pāli *Tipiṭaka*, their contents are generally accepted to have come from the lips of Śākyamuni Buddha. Secondly, there is a smaller collection of paracanonical works. Chronologically, these texts followed closely on the canonical writings, but failed to find their way into the early canon by the time it became fixed. Thirdly, we have a large number of pseudo-canonical and non-canonical texts. From the historian's point of view, these include the *sūtra*s of the Mahāyāna, the *tantra*s of the Vajrayāna and a large body of commentarial literature that sprang up around the canon. In their own traditions, however, both *sūtra*s and *tantra*s enjoy canonical status as they too are attributed to the Buddha. The commentarial works were mostly composed by prominent Indian scholars and exegetists discussing the contents of canonical writings. Taken together, the three categories of writings build up to a collection of several thousand individual works. The length and scope of all these texts vary greatly, ranging from writings of only a few lines to works comprising many thousands of pages.

The divisions of Buddhist scriptures

Overwhelmed by the magnitude of its literature, Buddhist tradition drew up several modes of scriptural classification. The most common is that into three baskets (*tipiṭaka*), i.e., *Vinaya-piṭaka, Sutta-piṭaka* and *Abhidhamma-piṭaka*.[1] Tradition has it that this threefold classification was established at the communal recitation (*saṅgīti*) held soon after the demise of the Buddha. However, since there is only one late reference to someone 'knowing the three *piṭaka*s' in the canon itself, this classification was probably introduced *a posteriori* to sanction the lineages of transmission evolving from the *saṅgha*'s division of labour in scripture memorization.

Most other divisions recorded in Buddhist writings have only theoretical value, since they do not correspond to any true classification. The division that is most frequently cited refers to nine/twelve branches (*aṅga*) of literary genres present in the canon. These are the *sutta* (prose), *geyya* (recitation of prose and verse), *veyyākaraṇa* (prophecies), *gāthā* (verse), *udāna* (solemn utterances), *itivuttaka* (discourses prefixed: 'Thus has been said by the lord'), *jātaka* (birth stories of the Buddha), *abhutadhamma* (descriptions of feats) and *vedalla* (analysis and elaboration). Although books called *Jātaka*, *Udāna* and *Itivuttaka* are included in the Pāli Canon, it is unlikely that their namesakes among the *aṅga* refer to them, but are examples of the types of literature that had gained prominence in Buddhist circles – not specific texts.

The northern Sanskrit tradition of Buddhism augmented the nine branches with three further genres. These are the *nidāna* (short introductions giving the circumstances in which the discourse was delivered), *avadāna* (biographic, faith-inspiring accounts of elders contemporary with the Buddha) and *upadeśa* (explanatory literature on the contents of *sūtra*s). While it is generally correct to associate the twelvefold division with the Mahāyāna, it is important to note that the twelve *aṅga* are also found in Sanskrit works of Śrāvakayāna schools (see p. 10).

Following the fragmentation into schools (third/second century BCE), the division into three baskets was amended to include new sets of writings. The Bahuśrutīya school, for instance, divided its body of scriptures into five categories to comprise, besides the traditional *Vinaya-*, *Sūtra-* and *Abhidharma-piṭaka*, a *Saṃyukta-* and *Bodhisattva-piṭaka*. Mahāsāṃghika followers devised a similar division, only replacing the *Bodhisattva-piṭaka* with a *Dhāraṇī-piṭaka*. The Dharmaguptaka reportedly possessed four baskets of writings, adding a *Bodhisattva-piṭaka* to the established *Tripiṭaka*. Since these collections are not preserved, it is impossible to ascertain the exact contents of the additional baskets.

In translation, the organization into baskets was only partially implemented. Tibetan translations of the Buddhist canon are divided into two categories, the *bKa'-'gyur* (pron. *Kangyur*) and *bsTan-'gyur* (pron. *Tengyur*). The *bKa'-'gyur* contains only those texts that are attributed to the Buddha himself. It consists of well over 100 volumes and is subdivided into five major groupings comprising works of the *Vinaya*, Mahāyāna *sūtra* collections, *dhāraṇī* texts, independent Mahāyāna *sūtra*s (augmented by several pre-Mahāyāna works) and a selection of *tantra*s. In the *bsTan-'gyur*, totalling over 220 volumes, the compilers of the Tibetan canon included translations of works belonging to the Indian Buddhist commentarial tradition. Although these writings are non-canonical by Indian standards, they enjoy great authority in Tibet and are regularly studied in conjunction with *bKa'-'gyur* material.

The Chinese Buddhist tradition divided the scriptures from a different viewpoint. First, it included not only works of Indian origin, but also a great number of indigenous Buddhist writings. Secondly, it amended the traditional threefold division by introducing other criteria. Issues such as the author's country of origin, a text's doctrinal orientation (Śrāvakayāna or Mahāyāna), the epoch in which it was translated and the degree of authenticity granted were all considered. What is more, the criteria varied from period to period. Thus, depending on the epoch in which they were drawn up, catalogues show quite different organizations. Today, the Japanese Taisho Shinshu Daizokyo edition of the Chinese canon (subdivided into 24 sections and itself based on Korean and Ming readings) is generally used as standard reference work by scholars.

The process of canonization

Tradition has it that immediately after the demise of the founder, steps were taken to safeguard the accurate preservation of the Buddha's teachings. For this purpose, Mahākāśyapa,[2] a prominent disciple of the Buddha, reportedly convened a council in Rājagṛha,[3] the capital of Magadha. He appointed 500 *arahat*s (accomplished monks free of all attachment) to decide on the authenticity of the teachings that were submitted to the council. For the doctrine he called on Ānanda, the Buddha's personal attendant known to have heard most sermons, to recite all the discourses (*sutta*) he remembered. For the monastic code or *Vinaya*, Mahākaśyapa summoned Upāli, a great expert in this, and asked him to relate all monastic rules that he heard from the Buddha's lips. Before a discourse or precept was formally authenticated, it was subjected to careful scrutiny and required unanimous approval by all 500 *arahat*s. Whenever in doubt, the assembly refused admission out of fear that they might unwittingly alter the Buddha's teaching.

Assessment of the scripture's authenticity followed a set of guidelines drawn up by the Buddha himself. Recognizing the threat false claims of authenticity could pose to his teaching, he advised his disciples to confirm in every case that a newly introduced text stemmed either directly from his own lips or from that of elders (*thera*s) of a formally constituted *saṅgha* and that it conformed to the spirit of both the *Dhamma* and *Vinaya*. Any text that did not match these four principal 'authorities' was to be rejected as bogus.

Several sources included also the recitation of the *Abhidhamma-piṭaka* in their accounts of this council – some attributing it to Ānanda, others to Mahākaśyapa himself. The scholastic nature of the *Abhidhamma-piṭaka* cast doubt on this claim, although we know that the systematization of *sutta* material began already very early.

Research by modern scholarship has introduced serious reservations about the claims found in the accounts of this council. It is highly questionable whether the monks who were present at the council had access to all the sermons of the Buddha. The texts themselves speak of disciples who refused to endorse the sermons as recalled by Ānanda, preferring instead to adhere to the form in which they had memorized them. There must have been many monks in India who, although remembering genuine discourses, either failed to gain admission to the council, or did not reach it in time to have them considered. Furthermore, the earliest version of the account conspicuously lacks a description of the canon whose authenticity it proposes to establish. What is more, the various schools do not agree on the contents of their canon, showing differences in the distribution of the texts and the presence of an *Abhidhamma-piṭaka*. Had there been an early codification, it would undoubtedly have been adopted as a common basis by all sects. The claim of codification is further dented by the late composition of some of the *Abhidhamma* works and the enduring controversy surrounding the composition of the *Khuddaka-nikāya*. In view of these objections, one cannot help but conclude that the traditional account of the Rājagṛha council lacks historical foundation. One suspects that while a gathering of scriptures probably took place soon after the demise of the Buddha – for a collection like the Buddhist canon does not come about by chance – the information we are given on this event perhaps reflects how the council was perceived by the order in later times.

The circumstances in which the 'true' gathering of teachings took place are not known. It is widely believed that the collecting of texts was begun already during the lifetime of the Buddha. Progress of the compilation is implicitly documented in the accounts of a second Buddhist council that was held about 70 years after the Buddha's death at Vaiśālī.[4] At that council, a group of monks was rebuked for practices deviating from the monastic code. Their conduct was condemned on the basis that it contravened what was then regarded as canonical tradition. For this condemnation to be convincing, the majority of the order had to have a very clear idea of what constituted inviolable scripture, at least as regards the monastic code. Wishing to authenticate their version of the canon and to give the community a body of scriptures that would hold authority in future dissidence, the Rājagṛha account might have been inspired by the proceedings at Vaiśālī.

Contents of the Buddhist canons

THE PĀLI CANON

Division of the early scriptures into three baskets represents fundamentally an organization of writings according to contents: the *Vinaya-piṭaka* lists the rules and precepts governing monastic life, the *Sutta-piṭaka* contains discourses of the Buddha on the doctrine (*Dhamma*) and the *Abhidhamma-piṭaka* consists of scholarly treatises analysing material taken from the *sutta*s.

The *Sutta-piṭaka* is the main source for the doctrine of the Buddha. Buddhaghosa (fifth century CE), our chief authority on the division of the early Buddhist canon, speaks of the *Sutta-piṭaka* as being divided into five groups (*nikāyas*) of texts. These are the *Dīgha-nikāya* (collection of long sayings), *Majjhima-nikāya* (collection of middle-length sayings), *Saṃyutta-nikāya* (collection of works grouped together according to their contents), *Aṅguttara-nikāya* (collection of *suttas* characterized by numerical groupings of items treated) and *Khuddaka-nikāya* (collection of minor texts).[5] The discourses of the first four *nikāyas* are, for the most part, in prose punctuated with verse. The teaching proper is invariably preceded by a short introduction (*nidāna*) giving the circumstances in which the *sutta* was delivered, starting with a phrase supposedly uttered by Ānanda at the first council: 'Thus I have heard, at one time the lord was dwelling at . . .'. The names of the *nikāyas* reflect to some extent the length of the *suttas* they contain, although there is evidence that in some cases the size increased through interpolation. Their present length is thus not necessarily a guide to their original contents. There are several *suttas* that appear in two or more of the five *nikāyas*. This applies especially to the *Khuddaka-nikāya* (but also to the *Saṃyutta-* and *Aṅguttara-nikāya*), which contains much material from the other four *nikāyas*. The order of the *nikāyas* reflects generally the order of the *suttas*' age and authenticity, though attempts to disentangle the chronological strands amongst the *suttas* bore little fruit.

The *Dīgha-nikāya* contains 34 independent *suttas* which deal with various aspects of the doctrine. In the *Brahmajāla-*, *Sāmmaññaphala-* and *Mahā-parinibbāna-sutta*, it includes several of the most important early Buddhist writings. Apart from containing detailed accounts of the spiritual training of monks, descriptions of ascetic practice and important doctrinal expositions, the *suttas* of the *Dīgha-nikāya* are a valuable source for life in ancient India in general. Several of its *suttas* also provide information on the biography of the Buddha – legendary and historical – that is not found elsewhere in the canon.

In the *Majjhima-nikāya*, some 150 *suttas* of medium length are loosely grouped together according to subject matter and title. Like the *Dīgha-nikāya*, the *Majjhima-nikāya* shows little cohesion in content. Its *suttas* deal with almost all aspects of the Buddhist doctrine, ranging from monastic life, asceticism, morality and meditation to the Four Noble Truths and the Eightfold Path. Variations in depicting the Buddha suggest substantial differences in the *suttas*' time of composition. The latest strand is probably found in the *suttas* of the penultimate group (*vagga*) which foreshadow the trend to systematizing typical of the *Aṅguttara-nikāya* and later *Abhidhamma* works.

The *Saṃyutta-nikāya* includes almost 3,000 mostly shorter *sutta*s that are arranged according to their contents. It is subdivided into 56 collections (*saṃyutta*s) arranged into five *vagga*s, each of which looks at particular aspects of the doctrine or shares the interlocutor to whom its *sutta*s are addressed. This arrangement rests unmistakably on an editorial intervention stemming from a conscious selection of material. Like those of the preceding *nikāya*, the *sutta*s of the *Saṃyutta-nikāya* deal with a broad spectrum of topics. The majority of texts display a slight shift away from the early, 'primitive', method of teaching towards a more scholastic way of exposition. This applies particularly to those *sutta*s that deal with numerical subjects where there is some notable overlapping with the topics treated in the *Aṅguttara-nikāya*.

The *Aṅguttara-nikāya* consists of over 2,000 individual, short *sutta*s. Unlike the *Saṃyutta-nikāya*'s subject-oriented approach, the *Aṅguttara-nikāya* lists its *sutta*s according to numerical criteria, arranged serially in ascending order. It is subdivided into eleven sections (*nipāta*s) organized in about 160 *vagga*s. Typically, each *nipāta* contains *sutta*s that deal with subjects in a similar fashion and are connected to the number of the section. Most *sutta*s are devoid of narrative elements but employ technical, stereotyped patterns of presentation. Their scholastic propensity ties the *sutta*s of the *Aṅguttara-nikāya* to the *Abhidhamma* books of later centuries, and facilitated the interpolation of additional material in the appropriate *nipāta* up to the period of its fixation.

The material that is included in the *Khuddaka-nikāya* is not recognized as canonical by all schools. It includes the 'lesser' texts that remained outside the four *nikāya*s, because they were perceived to be of doubtful authenticity. It is the longest collection of the *nikāya*s and comprises fifteen books of varying subjects, contents and character, most of which are written in verse. The titles of these books are (1) *Khuddaka-pāṭha*, (2) *Dhammapada*, (3) *Udāna*, (4) *Itivuttaka*, (5) *Sutta-nipāta*, (6) *Vimāna-vatthu*, (7) *Peta-vatthu*, (8) *Theragāthā*, (9) *Therīgāthā*, (10) *Jātaka*, (11) *Niddesa*, (12) *Paṭisambhidāmagga*, (13) *Apadāna*, (14) *Buddha-vaṃsa* and (15) *Cariyā-piṭaka*.

Of all five *nikāya*s, the *Khuddaka-nikāya* was always the most fluctuating collection. Even in the Sinhalese (Sri Lankan) tradition, its exact composition was long subject to controversy. Although, in its present form, doubtless the most recent part of the canon, several of its originally independent works are of great antiquity. Some of its texts are used as sources for the first four *nikāyas* and most have correspondents in Prākrit[6] or Sanskrit. Conceived as poetic works intended to arouse interest in Buddhism, they are not methodical treatises of scholarly stature, but won acclaim for their inspirational value. As a body of literature they are of considerable interest in themselves and they played an important role in the popularization of Buddhism.

The next[7] basket of the *Tipiṭaka*, the *Vinaya-piṭaka*, contains the rules of conduct that were drawn up by the Buddha in response to misbehaviour by his disciples. As a communal law, the *Vinaya*'s prime objective was to guarantee the smooth running of the Buddhist order. For this purpose, it decrees various sets of sanctions meted out in response to violations of accepted parameters of behaviour, and lays down the guidelines for the functioning of the order. Since each rule was formulated in response to an actual offence, the *Vinaya* shows a high degree of realism. The majority of rules address ethical concerns intended to maintain the community's moral standard. More often than not, these rest on ancient Indian conventions of morality complemented by rules that serve the particular requirements of the Buddhist order.

There is, however, more to the *Vinaya* than the dimension of legality and morality. Its precepts are not meant to be followed uncritically, but intended to create an inner awareness of the nature of one's action. Changes in the rules in adjustment to new surroundings suggest that they were primarily seen as a preventive force designed to control the environment of the monks as well as their actions in relation to it. The sanction that is meted out to the offender varies in line with changes in the circumstances relating to the intent and degree of completion of the wrongdoing.

> If (the monk) thinks it is trading when it is trading there is an offence of expiation involving forfeiture. If he is in doubt as to whether it is trading, there is an offence involving forfeiture. If he thinks it is not trading when it is trading, there is an offence of expiation involving forfeiture. If he thinks it is trading when it is not trading, he is guilty of wrong-doing.[8] If he is in doubt as to whether it is not trading, he is guilty of wrong-doing. If he thinks that it is not trading when it is not trading there is no offence. (*Vinaya*, II, 111–12)

Hence, the precepts become a finely tuned set of indications revealing blemish in the monks' mental state. When fully implemented in intuitive observance, they become the ideal representation of the teaching of the *Dhamma*.

The *Vinaya* is furthermore the principal means for the Buddhist *saṅgha* to legitimate its status as successors to the Buddha. It sustains the identity and purity of the order as a whole, and holds in balance the delicate relationship to its lay supporters.

As it is known today, the Pāli *Vinaya* is divided into three major categories. First, there is *Sutta-vibhaṅga*, whose core consists of the 227/311 *Pāṭimokkha* rules for monks and nuns. It always maintained an elevated position in Buddhism and underwent little change. Conceived as a casuistic law, the *Pāṭimokkha* does not decree broad principles, but lists individual cases as they were decided by the Buddha. The rules themselves fall into eight classes, enumerating the transgressions in descending order of gravity. Governing social behaviour and cultural conventions as well as spiritual concerns, the *Sutta-vibhaṅga* gives insight into many aspects of life in ancient India and represents a valuable historical source in its own right.

The second portion of the *Vinaya*, the *Khandhaka*, introduces a new wider circle of *Vinaya* rules that complement the *Pāṭimokkha* precepts. Most of them concern the collected acts of the order and address discord in the communal life. They govern the procedures for major monastic ceremonies and propose a mechanism to resolve the threat of schism. Although largely cast in the context of Śākyamuni's biography, the *Khandhaka* deviates from the order of events because it classifies the rules by subject matter.

The third section of the *Vinaya*, the *Parivāra*, is a collection of auxiliary works of varying dates that sprang up around the *Vinaya* in the centuries following the Buddha's demise. Singling out material from the bulk of *Vinaya* texts and reducing them to surveyable portions, it is used by novices to facilitate the task of mastering the *Vinaya*. Although of canonical status, the *Parivāra* is little more than an appendix to the *Vinaya*.

The *Abhidhamma-piṭaka* is later than the *Sutta-* and *Vinaya-piṭaka*. Yet, it figures among the earliest known Indian philosophical treatises which reason by means of sets of established logical techniques to establish their propositions. The themes of analysis are always taken from the discourses of the *Sutta-piṭaka*. This work of categorization started during the lifetime of the Buddha, when it was mostly entrusted to Śāriputra.[9] Initially, the systematization consisted of little more than drafting sets of headings (*mātikās*) to serve as notes on the doctrine. This method was retained and most *Abhidhamma* works propose a *mātikā* at the beginning of the treatise as a table of contents on which they then expand. The *Abhidhamma* of the Theravāda tradition consists of seven separate *Abhidhamma* books. Other schools drew up different sets of *Abhidhamma* treatises.[10] In subject, spirit and methodological approach, however, they all belong to the same scholastic tradition.

The works included in the three *piṭakas* came into existence early enough to attain canonical status. That is to say, they had gained sufficient influence and standing to be considered by the time the canon was closed. Besides these texts, Buddhism recognizes several other early works of paracanonical or early post-canonical status. For the *Vinaya*, these are the *Pāṭimokkha-sutta* and the *Kamma-vācanā*. For the *Sutta-piṭaka*, the best known of these texts are the *Peṭakopadesa, Nettippakaraṇa* and *Milindapañha*. While the first works are essentially exegetical treatises aiding scholarly analysis of *sutta* material, the *Milindapañha* also shows many strands of popular Buddhism, and it enjoyed great repute among lay followers for its enlightened dialogues:

> Milinda asked: 'Is it through wise attention that people are freed from further rebirth?' 'Yes, that is due to wise attention and also to wisdom and the other wholesome *dharmas*.' 'But is wise attention not the same as wisdom?' 'No, O king. Attention is one thing and wisdom is another. Sheep and goats, oxen and buffaloes, camels and asses possess attention, but wisdom they lack.' 'Well put, Nāgasena!'
>
> Milinda asked: 'Which is the characteristic of attention and which is the characteristic of wisdom?' 'Reflection is the characteristic of attention – cutting off is that of wisdom.' 'Why? Please provide a simile.' 'You supposedly know what barley reapers are?' 'Yes, indeed.' 'In which fashion do they reap barley?' 'With the left hand they take hold of a bushel of barley, in the right hand they hold a sickle and then they cut the barley with the sickle.' 'Likewise, O king, the yogin gathers his thought with attention and cuts off defilements by means of wisdom.' (*Milindapañha*, 32–3)

Such was its popularity that the *Milindapañha* gained canonical status in the Burmese tradition and was included alongside the

Peṭakopadesa, Nettippakaraṇa and *Sutta-saṅgaha* in the Burmese *Khuddaka-nikāya*.

Round about the beginning of the Christian Era, the *sutta*s of early Buddhism began to be supplemented by new works. For those who subscribed to their doctrines and religious ideas, these new texts superseded the old established writings. Like the early *sutta*s, they too claimed the authority of the Buddha. Seen as miraculously emerging from the underworld where they had been hidden for several centuries, they trace their origin to sermons allegedly preached by Śākyamuni in places that were inaccessible to the *śrāvaka* (disciples of the historical Buddha). Hence, they escaped attention at Rājagṛha. Starting out with a few scattered texts, the literary output of this new tradition grew swiftly to immense proportions, turning out scriptures of unseen magnitude and philosophical depth.

MAHĀYĀNA *SŪTRA*S

Unlike their counterparts of early Buddhism, Mahāyāna scriptures are not organized in a methodical classification, but fall into two broad categories. That is to say, they are either part of one of the scriptural collections of the Mahāyāna or belong to the large body of independent *sūtra*s.

The *sūtra* collections of the Mahāyāna are four, viz., the *Prajñā-pāramitā, Mahā-ratnakūṭa, Buddhāvataṃsaka* and *Mahā-saṃnipāta*. With the exception of the *Prajñā-pāramitā*, little is known about the period in which these collections came into existence or the circumstances that gave them their present form.

The *Prajñā-pāramitā* (Perfection of Wisdom) is doubtless the earliest and doctrinally most influential of the Mahāyāna collections. Its founding texts, the *Ratnaguṇa-saṃcaya-gāthā* and the prose version thereof, the *Aṣṭasāhasrikā*, represent the earliest strands of the Mahāyāna. Their philosophical visions served as inspiration for many generations of Buddhist thinkers after them. There is probably not a single text among the hundreds of Mahāyāna *sūtra*s whose religio-philosophical thinking they did not affect.

The period of composition of *Prajñā-pāramitā* texts lasted well over 1,000 years. It began in the century before the Christian Era and came to a close in the twelfth century CE. During the first period, extending roughly from 100 BCE to 100 CE, the basic texts containing the original impulses were elaborated and systematized. In the second period (100–300 CE), these were then expanded to produce new, much larger versions. In the period from 300 to 500 CE, scholars set out to reformulate the basic doctrines of the founding works in short *sūtras* and versified summaries. In the *Vajracchedikā* (Diamond-cutter) and *Hṛdaya* (Heart) *Prajñā-pāramitā*, this period produced some of the most outstanding examples of Buddhist philosophical writings.

> 'O Subhūti, is there any doctrine that was taught by the Tathāgata?' 'No, indeed, O lord, there is no doctrine that was taught by the Tathāgata.' 'O Subhūti, when you ponder the number of particles of dust in this world system comprising one thousand worlds, would they be many?' 'Yes, O lord, because that which the Tathāgata taught as dust particles, he declared "non particles". Thus, they are called particles of dust. And this world system the Tathāgata declared a "no system". Thus, it is called world system.' 'O Subhūti, what do you think, can the Tathāgata be perceived through the thirty-two marks of the great being?' 'No, indeed.' 'Why?' 'Because the thirty-two marks of the great being that were taught by the Tathāgata are, in reality, "no marks". Thus, they are called the thirty-two marks of the great being.' (*Vajracchedikā*, 13b–d)

After 600 CE, the creative phase of *Prajñā-pāramitā* literature came gradually to a halt. Its teachings were increasingly influenced by ritual-emphasizing manifestations of tantric thought and lost much of their philosophical appeal. *Prajñā-pāramitā* doctrines were compressed in brief magical spells whose exact meaning was revealed only to a few chosen ones. At an even later stage, *Prajñā-pāramitā* became conceptualized as an independent spiritual force. It was given a place in the pantheon of Buddhist deities and declared worthy of veneration.

The *Mahā-saṃnipāta*, as given in the Chinese canon, consists of seventeen *sūtras* of little religio-philosophical cohesion. Because they share so little apart from a certain preoccupation with magic, scholarship has thus far failed to ascertain the rationale behind their grouping into a single collection. The earliest reference to the *Mahā-saṃnipāta* goes back to the second century CE, but it does not reveal the composition of this early version. Today, as a group of texts, the *Mahā-saṃnipāta* is preserved only in Chinese, although its *sūtras* do appear individually in the Tibetan canon. Information on an Indian prototype of the *Mahā-saṃnipāta* is very scarce indeed. Judging by this lack of references, its composition might have been a local affair that never attracted much attention – if indeed it originated in India.

The *Mahā-ratnakūṭa* collection as it stands today was edited at the beginning of the eighth century in China by Bodhiruci, a South Indian *Tripiṭaka* master. Before Bodhiruci, the history of the collection is obscure. Little conclusive can be said about the earliest phases in the formation of the 'original' *Ratnakūṭa* collection. It seems certain that the *Ratnakūṭa* was shaped in Central Asia where it grew out of a small collection of informally assembled *sūtra*s. This group, which may have comprised as many as twenty or more *sūtra*s, was rendered into Chinese in the third century by Dharmarakṣa. It is probable that by the time Hsüan-tsang visited India in the seventh century CE, they had assumed the shape of a formal collection entitled *Mahā-ratnakūṭa*. However, since most Indian exegetists seem ignorant of it, one suspects that in India this collection never gained the prominence it achieved in Central Asia.

The earliest references to a collection of *sūtra*s bearing the name *Mahā-ratnakūṭa* are found in fifth-century Chinese translations of Indo-Buddhist commentarial literature. There we find several references to a *Mahā-ratnakūṭa* collection, consisting of at least five works from among those presently included. The translations themselves were executed in Chinese Central Asia, suggesting that there the *Ratnakūṭa* was a well-known body of scriptures, possibly as early as the fourth century CE. Five of its *sūtra*s belong to the earliest Mahāyāna texts ever translated into Chinese, among them the influential *Kāśyapa-parivarta*. On the *bodhisattva*, the *Kāśyapa-parivarta* says:

> O Kāśyapa, there are four [means] to attain the great treasure of *bodhisattva*s. Which four? He rejoices at the presence of the Buddha; he hears the six perfections (*pāramitā*); he meets *Dharma* teachers without malevolent prepense and delights unremittingly in the practice of seclusion.
>
> O Kāśyapa, there are four things that help the *bodhisattva* to transcend all evil. Which four? He retains the thought of enlightenment; he harbours no ill-feeling towards sentient beings; he discerns mistaken views and he despises no one.
>
> O Kāśyapa, there are four things that enable the *bodhisattva* to accumulate roots of virtue. Which four? He takes genuine delight in seclusion; he holds on to the four means of conversion without expectation for reward; he pursues the Doctrine unfettered by concern

for body or life and he accumulates roots of virtue without satiety.

O Kāśyapa, there are four adornments of immeasurable merit. Which four? He teaches the Doctrine with a pure mind; he shows great compassion for people of low character; he imparts the thought of enlightenment to all beings and he bears with those who are languid. (Stael-Holstein (ed.) §§ 17–20, pp. 37–43)

Philosophically, the *Kāśyapa-parivarta* attracted much attention for the exemplary transparency with which it expounds the Doctrine of Emptiness:

O Kāśyapa, things are empty not because one thinks of them as empty (*śūnya*) – they are empty in themselves. Things are signless not because one thinks of them as signless – they are signless in themselves. Things are wishless not because one thinks of them as wishless – they are wishless in themselves. Things are unaccumulated, unborn,[11] unarisen and without own-being not because one thinks of them as such – they are so in themselves. Furthermore, O Kāśyapa, emptiness does not rest on the disappearance of the existence of individuality (*pudgala*). Individuality itself is emptiness and this emptiness is emptiness in itself, absolute emptiness. . . . O Kāśyapa, take refuge in emptiness – not in individuality. But those who seek refuge in emptiness through the perception of emptiness using the senses, these I declare hopelessly strayed from my Doctrine. O Kāśyapa, it is better to subscribe to the belief of the substantiality (*ātmadṛṣṭi*) – even if it is as large as Mount Sumeru – than to subscribe arrogantly to the view of emptiness (*śūnyatādṛṣṭi*). Why? Because to those who adhere to the belief of the substantiality, emptiness is liberation – but how is one liberated from the view of emptiness? (Stael-Holstein (ed.) §§ 63–4, pp. 94–5)

The 49 *sūtra*s now comprising the *Ratnakūṭa* cover the complete spectrum of (early) Mahāyāna thought. Indeed, the impression gained is that the collection may have been compiled as part of an early conversion activity, with the aim of providing a well-balanced cross-section of Buddhist thought. Such a motive for its compilation would account for the almost complete absence of evidence on the formation and existence of an Indian *Ratnakūṭa* collection. Moreover, it would intrinsically link its formation with those Central Asian areas where the earliest traces of the *Ratnakūṭa* literature have been discovered.

The *Buddhāvataṃsaka* is extant in two Chinese recensions, consisting respectively of 34 and 39 chapters. Most of the chapters came into existence as separate *sūtra*s that circulated independently for many centuries. The period in which they were gathered together to form a greater collection is not known. The dating of Chinese translations has shown that two of its texts are very early indeed and might go back to the beginning of the Christian Era. However, the first reference to a collection of texts called *Buddhāvataṃsaka* does not appear before the beginning of the fifth century CE. It was in China that the collection attained most attention, eclipsing even the *Mahā-ratnakūṭa* and *Mahā-saṃnipāta*. Favoured by a shift towards Yogācāra[12] thinking, of which several of its texts are fervent exponents, the *Buddhāvataṃsaka* gained great popularity during the last quarter of the first millennium CE. The best-known and doctrinally most important works of the *Buddhāvataṃsaka* are the *Gaṇḍa-vyūha* and *Daśa-bhūmika-sūtra*. Judging by the dating of its earliest translation, the *Daśa-bhūmika* is likely to have preceded the *Gaṇḍa-vyūha*. Its exposition of the ten stages grew into a landmark for the *bodhisattva* doctrine that affected all later developments in the organization of the *bodhisattva* path. In contrast, the contribution of the *Gaṇḍa-vyūha* rests on its value as literary masterpiece. Conceived as a balanced work of art, it combined convincingly the literary dimension with innovative philosophical thought. Embellished by similes, elaborate descriptions and figurative language, the *Gaṇḍa-vyūha* guides the reader through a maze of narratives without ever neglecting its vision of universal interpenetration or inter-relationship. Although often held to display the idealist view of the early Yogācāra, the *Gaṇḍa-vyūha* carefully avoids statements that would affirm such a position.

The independent Mahāyāna *sūtra*s share with the texts of the four collections a common interest in the *bodhisattva* and Mahāyāna ontology. Taking this interest as point of departure, they set out in many different ways to elaborate, interpret or expand on these themes.

The *Saddharma-puṇḍarīka*, often referred to as the *Lotus Sūtra*, is generally regarded to have arisen alongside the early *Prajñā-pāramitā*. Almost certainly a composite work, its doctrines touch on many subjects central to Mahāyāna thinking. Above all, it became famous for its treatment of skilful means (*upāya-kauśalya*) as the supreme expedient effectuating liberation for all sentient beings. Enlaced in its picturesque language and mythological setting is a fervent criticism of the *śrāvaka*'s (see p. 10) limited aspiration. Owing to the *Saddharma-puṇḍarīka*'s immense popularity and its propagation of the 'cult of the book', the *Saddharma-puṇḍarīka* is extant, besides the customary Tibetan and Chinese translations, in numerous Sanskrit redactions.

Another early Mahāyāna *sūtra* of great influence is the *Vimalakīrti-nirdeśa*. Doctrinally, it stems from the same philosophical movement as the earliest known recensions of the *Prajñā-pāramitā, Mahā-ratnakūṭa, Buddhāvataṃsaka* and *Mahā-saṃnipāta*. Composed at the beginning of the Christian Era, the *Vimalakīrti-nirdeśa* became a major source for the ontological thought of the Madhyamaka school. Its greatest contribution to Buddhist thought was, however, its authoritative discussion of the ideal of the lay *bodhisattva*. By ascribing the role of the protagonist to a lay *bodhisattva* and crediting him with an erudition second to none, the *Vimalakīrti-nirdeśa* firmly established the lay *bodhisattva* in the fold of Buddhist saints.

Fine examples of the many philosophically accomplished works are the *Laṅkāvatāra* and *Saṅdhi-nirmocana*. Both texts contain highly abstract, ontological thought that played a major role in shaping Mahāyāna philosophy. Unmistakably composite *sūtra*s that grew over many decades, they are first attested in their present form in fifth-century China. It was also in China that the *Laṅkāvatāra* and *Saṅdhi-nirmocana* reached the pinnacle of their popularity, where they became paramount to the Yogācāra movement of the eighth and ninth centuries.

Thematically positioned at the other end of Mahāyāna creativity are the *Bhadra-kalpika* and *Suvarṇa-prabhāsottama*. The *Bhadra-kalpika* stands out for the wealth of mythological material brought together to embellish its biographical accounts of former *buddha*s. This legendary genre prevails also in several other Mahāyāna works, most notably the *Amitābha-vyūha, Kāraṇḍa-vyūha* and *Karuṇā-puṇḍarīka*. Consisting typically of picturesque accounts glorifying the powers, conduct and abodes of mythical *buddha*s and *bodhisattva*s, they are virtually devoid of philosophical thought, and serve to stir up sentiment in the devotee. Such mythological *sūtra*s became especially popular in the Far East where they gave rise to several Buddhist movements that were entirely based on faith and devotion (e.g., Pure Land Buddhism).

The composition of the *Suvarṇa-prabhāsottama* (fourth century CE) heralded the end of mainstream Mahāyāna. Although doctrinally still very much within the parameters of Mahāyāna thought, its inclusion of magic spells and ritual precepts clearly stepped beyond accepted convention. Enlaced with legends celebrating feats of *bodhisattvas* and goddesses in magico-ritualistic contexts, the *Suvarṇa-prabhāsottama* bears many traits foreshadowing the rise of tantric Buddhism.

VAJRAYĀNA *TANTRAS*

The scriptures of the Vajrayāna mark the closing phase in the canonical literature of Buddhism. Its output is extremely prolific and comprises several hundred works. The vast majority of *tantras* are preserved only in their Tibetan and Chinese translations. The earliest examples of tantric literature are short magic formulae, called *dhāraṇīs* or *vidyārājñīs*, that sprang up from around the third century CE. For the sake of propagation, they were regularly appended to well-known Mahāyāna *sūtras*. In some instances, *dhāraṇīs* became interpolated in specific *sūtras* which explained their use and praised their magic powers. The exact number of spells is difficult to assess, but just those that were handed down to us amount to several thousand.

From the fourth century onwards, *dhāraṇīs* rapidly gained momentum in Mahāyāna writings and developed into more elaborate treatises. Yet it was probably not before the end of the seventh century that the first comprehensive texts on tantric ritual and doctrine came into being. The most important works of this early period are the *Mahā-vairocana* and the *Vajroṣṇīṣa sūtras*. Following on these *sūtras*, there emerged a multitude of shorter works which set the foundation for the surge of interest in Vajrayāna in China, Korea and Japan.

According to Tibetan historians, the whole output of tantric literature falls into four categories, each describing specific aspects of tantric practice. First, there are *tantras* that lay down procedures at ceremonies and 'outer rituals' held in the worship of tantric deities. These are called *Kriyā-tantra* and make up the lowest, least esoteric, sets of texts. In the second category, the *Caryā-tantra* class, are those works that describe and characterize the conduct of more advanced tantric practitioners in 'outer ritual' and 'inner yoga'. The third category contains all those texts that set out to explain the working of esoteric and magical practices that spring from 'inner yoga'. As these are chiefly related to yogic trances and meditation, it is called the

Yoga-tantra class. The majority of *tantras* fall into this category. The fourth and highest category of *tantras*, the *Anuttara-yoga-tantra* class, constitutes the most esoteric group of *tantras*. Describing sexual symbolism in inner yogic practice, its texts are of the highest mystical order and strictly guarded by the initiated.

In order to attain authority and respectability, *tantras* were designed to share many formal features with their Mahāyāna predecessors. The protagonist in most *tantras* is a *buddha* who is also portrayed as the teaching's fountainhead. Only the sites in which *tantras* were preached differ from the places that are cited in the *sūtras*. They are no longer historic places in northern India, but became locations of mythical origin. In the *Anuttara-yoga-tantras*, the 'preaching site' is often the vagina (*bhaga*) of the Buddha's consort, symbolizing wisdom (*prajñā*).

Commentarial literature

The revelation of canonical writings was accompanied by a steady growth of commentarial literature. For the most part, commentaries refer to specific texts whose contents they explain on an individual basis. For the Śrāvakayāna, the only works preserved belong to the Theravāda and Sarvāstivāda. The most prolific commentator among the Theravāda was the fifth-century scholar Buddhaghosa. Besides writing important commentaries on the *Vinaya-*, *Sutta-*, and *Abhidhamma-piṭaka*, he composed several independent treatises on the Buddhist path. The most important of these is the *Visuddhi-magga*, which gives a systematic account of Buddhist meditation and its doctrinal foundations.

The commentaries of the Sarvāstivāda tradition are extant only in their Chinese translations. Unlike their Theravāda counterparts, they are not dominated by the genius of a single person, but were composed by various persons in the course of several centuries. The most noteworthy books are perhaps the *Mahā-vibhāṣā*, attributed to Vasumitra, and the Sarvāstivāda commentaries on *Abhidharma* issues, such as the *Abhidharma-kośa* by Vasubandhu.

Of the Mahāyāna *sūtras*, we possess a large body of commentarial literature that has been preserved in Tibetan and Chinese translations. The works are so numerous that they make up most of the second division of the Tibetan canon, the *bsTan-'gyur*. Sanskrit originals are extant in only a few cases. As with the early scripture, they fall into commentaries on specific *sūtras* and scholastic works of a more general nature. While the scope of the former is typically restricted to issues raised in the root texts, the latter set out to discuss Buddhist doctrine in a broader fashion.

Generally, one speaks of three major doctrinal currents in the exegetico-commentarial writings of the Mahāyāna. First, there are the treatises that were composed by the adherents of the Madhyamaka school of Buddhism. Its founder Nāgārjuna (second century CE) ranks also among the important writers of this school, and many works of great authority are attributed to him. His most influential work is doubtless the *Madhyamaka-śāstra*, better known as the *Madhyamaka-kārikā*, in which he postulates all the major tenets of Madhyamaka thinking. Besides this foundation-work, Nāgārjuna is credited with a large number of exegetical treatises. For the most part, however, these works are apocryphal. Other important texts belonging to the Madhyamaka school are Candrakīrti's commentary on the *Madhyamaka-śāstra*, the *Prasannapadā*, and Bhāvaviveka's *Prajñā-dīpa-mūla-madhyamaka-vṛtti*, which elaborate and interpret Nāgārjuna's original propositions.

Treatises by the Yogācāra school represent the second major current in Mahāyāna commentarial literature. The most prolific writers of the Yogācāra were the brothers Asaṅga and Vasubandhu. Converted from Sarvāstivāda and Mahīśāsaka thought to the Mahāyāna, they composed many of the most important treatises on Yogācāra philosophy. The school's scriptural backbone is formed by a body of texts known as the *Five Works of Maitreya*. Inspired by Maitreya (a celestial *bodhisattva* awaiting his time to return to earth as the next Buddha), but compiled and written down by Asaṅga, they comprise the *Mahāyāna-sūtrālaṃkāra, Ratna-gotra-vibhāga, Madhyānta-vibhāga, Abhisamayālaṃkāra* and *Dharma-dharmatā-vibhāga*. While the treatises of Asaṅga deal typically with a variety of subjects, the works attributed to his brother are more philosophic in nature. Vasubandhu's most important treatises are the *Trisvabhāva-nirdeśa* and the *Triṃśikā-* and *Viṃśatikā-vijñapti-mātratā-siddhi*, in which he refutes criticism on Yogācāra thought and presents the logic behind its own propositions. Comments on these texts by Dharmapāla and several other scholars have been combined in the *Vijñapti-mātratā-siddhi*, a work that has traditionally served as the chief source for Yogācāra study in East Asia.

The third current in Mahāyāna exegesis is represented by the writings of Diṅnāga, Dharmakīrti and Dharmapāla. In defence of Yogācāra thinking, Diṅnāga set out to systematize the foundation of the *Abhidharma* analysis into a sound logical framework. Proceeding from earlier *Abhidharma* criticism, he and Dharmapāla developed the epistemological ideas of the Yogācāra into a general critique of knowledge. Something of a foundation work to this school is Diṅnāga's introductory text on logic, the *Nyāya-mukha*. Other well-known treatises include the *Marma-pradīpa-vṛtti* and *Pramāṇa-samuccaya*. His work was continued by his disciples and successors, Asvabhāva and Dharmakīrti, who, always following basic Yogācāra propositions, set out to refine his theory and gradually transformed the Yogācāra into a logical tradition in its own right. These advances in epistemology culminated in the writings of Dharmakīrti, especially in his *Nyāya-bindu* (summing up Dharmakīrti's own views on logic) and *Pramāṇa-vārttika*. Profoundly influential and respected well beyond the Buddhist tradition, his system of logic won pan-Indian acclaim and was adopted by many epistemological schools.

Popular works

In addition to the spectrum of canonical writings and associated commentarial literature, Buddhist pietism produced a large corpus of 'popular' works. We saw that some of them, although apocryphal in origin but of great antiquity, found their way into canonical writings. Others were denied such status and were collected outside the canon proper.

The best known examples of this 'popular' genre are the *Dharmapada*s. In the Pāli, the canonical *Dhammapada* forms a collection of 423 stanzas drawn from a common stock of floating verse which prevailed in northern India since ancient times. Parallels to Jaina and Brahmanical works indicate that only a few of these verses are of Buddhist origin, but were probably adopted to broaden its popular base.[13] The number of different versions that are preserved of the *Dharmapada* genre attest the popularity of this type of non-sectarian literature. Expeditions in Central Asia brought to light a (longer) Sanskrit version, entitled *Udānavarga*, and an incomplete edition in Gāndhārī Prākrit. Although of different schools, all three have much in common and shared originally perhaps as many as 360 verses. The issues that are addressed in them are not specifically Buddhist, but reflect ancient Indian ideals of sanctity and ethics. Notwithstanding its generic origin and contents, the *Dharmapada* soon became one of the most celebrated of all Buddhist scriptures.

> If you aspire to honour, wealth, or after death
> A blissful life amongst the gods,
> Then ensure that you fulfil the maxims
> Of moral life.
>
> A discerning man lives a moral life
> When he realizes that it leads to four benefits.
> A sense of virtue gives him peace.
> His body is not overburdened.
>
> At night he sleeps a healthy sleep
> And when he wakes he arises with joy.
> A holy man endowed with insight,
> He thrives and prospers in the world.
>
> A man of wisdom who acts exemplarily,
> A man of morals who gives gifts,
> In this world and in the next too,
> He advances to happiness.
>
> His moral habits planted firm,
> His trance and wisdom excellent.
> Untiring, earnest,
> He gains release from suffering forever. (*Udānavarga*, vi, 1–3, 5, 8)

Its closest rival in popularity is perhaps the *jātaka* genre. Based on themes of Indian fables, *jātaka* stories purport to narrate the previous lives of Gautama Buddha before he gained enlightenment. Their chief task was to inspire faith and confidence in the Buddha. Embedded in folklore, which was adapted by the Buddhists to draw attention to their cause, the *jātaka* genre attained rapid popularity across India. They are regularly depicted in iconography at ancient Buddhist sites and occur in the scriptures of all schools. Verbatim parallels in Sanskrit literature and excerpts in the four *nikāya*s indicate that some *jātaka*s are of great antiquity. Beside the 547 stories that are included in the *Jātaka* book of the *Khuddaka-nikāya*, the Buddhist traditions of Southeast Asia preserve outside the canon a collection of 50 apocryphal *jātaka*s. Most of them run parallel to the motifs of the Pāli collection, but several have no Pāli equivalent and correspond to recensions of the northern Sanskrit tradition. Some of the northern *jātaka*s were compiled in separate collections, e.g., the *Jātaka-mālā* of Āryaśūra. Others found their way as illustrations of the Buddha's accomplishment into the *Vinaya* and Mahāyāna *sūtra*s. To whichever literature it was appended, the *jātaka* genre played at all times a prominent role in preparing the reception of Buddhist thought and proved an effectual vehicle to circulate and popularize its ideas.

Legends of the past lives of elders contemporary with the Buddha (*avadāna*s) exerted a similar fascination on the minds of ordinary people. In part, this appeal rested on the glorifying tone in which *avadāna*s describe the noble conduct of the elders. They inspire imitation of this conduct by showing that even the most minute wholesome act has the potentiality to prompt great results. In the Pāli Canon the *apadāna* (Pāli form of *avadāna*) texts are gathered in *Khuddaka-nikāya* as an independent collection of well over 500 stories. Although in character clearly related to the *jātaka* genre, *avadāna* legends differ since they do not refer to the Buddha and abound with mythological material of late origin.

The Sanskrit tradition broadened the concept of the *avadāna* to include, besides the *Avadāna* book of the *Kṣudrak-āgama*, a series of semi-historical works professing to retell the course of past – but factual – events. The earliest specimens of this type of literature, marking the beginning of Sanskrit extracanonical literature (second century CE), are the *Aśokāvadāna* and *Avadāna-śataka*. Other *avadāna*, such as the *Bodhisattvāvadāna-kapalatā* and the *Nandimitrāvadāna*, however, are of much later date. Research has shown that the claim to historicity, especially among the earlier *avadāna*s, may not be as preposterous as was previously held. In time and style, these early *avadāna*s stand between the original canonical writings and Mahāyāna literature. Citing whole passages from the early *sūtra*s, but rejecting stylistic practices imposed by Prākrit prototypes, *avadāna*s introduce whole series of new set phrases and formulae that occur otherwise only in the Mahāyāna. The combination of panegyric legends enlaced with canonical material assured the *avadāna* genre a secure place in Buddhist popular literature. Whenever told, it generated awe, admiration, faith and a sense of cultural identity in the audience, and flourished as a major source of Buddhist pietism.

Modes of transmission

The process of transmission of the Buddhist scriptures falls into two major phases. At first, for about 300 years after the Buddha's death, all texts were transmitted orally. During this period, the task of preserving the Buddhist canon was the responsibility of the *saṅgha*. Realizing that the number of texts remembered was too vast to be memorized by a single person, the monks followed the example set by the brahmins and divided the canon into more manageable collections (*nikāya*s).

Buddhaghosa reports that the grouping of scriptures into *nikāya*s was initiated at the council in Rājagṛha. Although the naming of individual *nikāya*s at Rājagṛha is probably an anachronism, it is quite conceivable that the collecting of discourses by length and contents began at that time – if not earlier. Once their contents had been determined, the collections were allotted to groups of monks for transmission to their pupils.

The desire for accurate preservation and the enormous size of the canon necessitated a carefully developed system of oral transmission. Already at an early age, monks in charge of *sutta*-conservation were subjected to a demanding training in memorization. Entrusted with the *Dhamma*, and well educated, the reciters (*bhāṇaka*s) gained a leading influence on scriptural matters and high standing in the community.

It is not known for how many centuries the *bhāṇaka* system was upheld. Buddhaghosa refers to it as if still practised in his time. Today, the practice of assigning groups of texts for oral preservation to *bhāṇaka*s has receded. The reason behind this discontinuation is obvious. The widespread practice of writing and the rising popularity of manuscripts rendered oral transmission through *bhāṇaka*s superfluous to the preservation of scripture.

According to Sinhalese chronicles, the writing down of the Pāli Canon started in the middle of the first century BCE. The reasons of war and famine leading up to that important change are plausible and probably genuine. Apparently, in Sri Lanka the number of monks had dropped so low that the *bhāṇaka* system approached collapse. Steps were therefore taken to compile the whole *Tipiṭaka* in writing.

The progressive use of writing increased public access to the scriptures. Although still kept in monasteries, they gradually eluded the control of the *saṅgha* and became available to everyone who showed sufficient perseverance to gain admission to the libraries. Once the exclusive ability to maintain the Buddha's sermons was taken away from the monks, a new phenomenon of immense reverberation emerged in Buddhism.

Thus far, the monastic community was able to control rigorously the contents of the canon. Prior to its admittance in the *Tipiṭaka*, every newly proposed text had to be approved by the *bhāṇaka*s. A work that failed to meet their criteria, whatever its claim to genuineness, was denied acceptance. This meant that nonconformist texts had little chance of survival, since there was no organization outside the *saṅgha* that could secure their transmission. The laity, however devoted, could not possibly achieve their preservation, as they lacked the training and organization needed for such a task.

This all changed with the introduction of writing. No longer was the chief requirement for a text's preservation conformity to the views of the establishment. Even the most obscure and neglected manuscript in a monastic library could be picked up and read, even translated, by a curious browser or visiting scholar. This gave a real chance of survival to every new text – irrespective of its doctrinal position – and weakened irrevocably the influence of orthodoxy.

By no coincidence, it is roughly from the first century BCE onwards that Buddhism experienced a large increase in its scriptures. With astonishing speed, numerous new works purporting (like the texts of early Buddhism) to disclose the word of the Buddha appeared. Referring to themselves as discourses of the 'great vehicle' (*mahā-yāna*), these new texts were of course the first exponents of Mahāyāna literature. In view of the fervent criticism they sometimes directed at the *arahat*s, and their dubious claim to authenticity, it is questionable whether they would have survived before the advent of writing.

Continuing revelation of scriptures

More than just allowing the rise of the Mahāyāna, the introduction of writing opened up the Buddhist canon to the possibility of 'continuing revelation'. It meant that from then onwards practically every text confident enough to claim to be *buddha-vacana*, or Buddha-word, could legitimately insist on canonicity. We saw that the first recorded assertions to this effect came from the Mahāyāna, beginning with its early *sūtra*s and persisting right through to the *tantra*s. Whether any such claim was ever made before the introduction of writing, we shall never know, as its scriptural basis was destined to be ephemeral. Of the texts which were written down, we know that they traced their origin often – though not invariably – to the historical Buddha, typically being seen as having been concealed in mythological realms, *stūpa*s or caves. Fear for their transmission at the hands of ill-prepared, philosophically immature Buddhists is the reason that is traditionally cited to explain their concealment. The transitional period between their claimed composition and eventual discovery frequently covered several centuries. The texts' re-emergence was generally 'held back' until people wise enough to understand their teachings correctly would prevail. Once brought to light, the texts were typically given a high profile which – bolstered by the mysterious circumstances of their discovery – helped their rapid dissemination. Judging by the immense literary output of the Mahāyāna, this new mechanism must have gained swift and widespread acceptance across India.

The boldest claim to canonicity, however, came from the Tibetan Buddhist tradition. While generally very conscientious in assessing scriptural authenticity – requesting a Sanskrit original as proof of genuineness – some Tibetans departed from this tested method and claimed canonicity for a series of 'revealed' works (*gter-ma*s; pron. *terma*) for which no Indian original could be produced. Analogously to their Indian predecessors, it was claimed that these texts had been deposited in secret places in former centuries to safeguard their transmission or to prevent untimely circulation. Recent research has shown that some of the earliest *gter-ma*s are indeed very ancient by Tibetan standards. However, their case was somewhat weakened by the great frequency with which *gter-ma*s were brought to light well into modern times. Leaving aside the question of their authenticity (an issue which, in substance, does not differ from the claims of the Mahāyāna), Tibetan *gter-ma*s are today the only surviving tradition of 'continuing revelation' in Buddhism.

Editions and scribes

The first reference to a written edition of the Buddhist canon goes back to the fourth century CE. It is found in the Sinhalese chronicles stating that the Theravāda Pāli Canon was recorded in writing during the first century BCE in Ceylon (Sri Lanka). This early edition is long lost. On the mainland the process of committing Buddhist scriptures to writing began in roughly the same period, although not with the scale and organization with which it was undertaken in Sri Lanka. Of these early Indian writings too, no specimen is known to have survived in its entirety. The dried palm leaves on which they were written – a resilient fibre which is long-lasting under favourable conditions, but susceptible to humidity, mildew and insects – failed to withstand the test of time and perished probably long ago.

The oldest Indian editions that survived to modern times go back to the sixth/seventh century CE. They belong to the Sanskrit tradition of northern India that flourished under the patronage of the Pāla dynasty in Bengal. In addition to these early witnesses, a sizable number of Sanskrit manuscripts were preserved in the monastic archives of Nepal. These manuscripts date mostly from the eighteenth and nineteenth centuries. The value of these copies is somewhat marred by the multitude of scribal errors that found their way into the manuscripts in the process of transmission.

Beyond India, expeditions to Central Asia uncovered manuscripts at famous ancient Buddhist sites. Written in Sanskrit or Prākrits, many of them go back to the fifth or sixth century CE. However, since most are extant only in fragments and still have not been deciphered, Central Asian manuscripts are seldom used as main readings, but are consulted chiefly as collateral material.

In China, manuscript editions are rare since printing was soon adopted for disseminating the Buddhist canon. Starting out with manuscripts on silk or paper, Chinese Buddhists drew early on advances in wood-carving, and in the tenth century commissioned the carving on to wooden blocks of the entire canon. With the availability of printed editions, manuscript copying was no longer required, since copies of the xylographic version could be circulated with ease throughout China. Once the idea of printing had gained acceptance among Chinese Buddhists, great prestige accrued to those who participated in the production. Vying for status and fame, Chinese craftsmen produced no less than fourteen blockprint editions in the course of one millennium.

Tibetan Buddhists followed in the footsteps of their Chinese counterparts. Initially, they too adopted the Indian model of text preservation. However, held back by Tibet's orientation towards Indian culture, scribes continued to copy out manuscripts well after the Chinese had introduced printing. Thus the monks of the Narthang monastery worked as late as the thirteenth century with hand-written manuscripts when they established the first Tibetan canon. Tellingly, the first printed edition of the Tibetan canon was not made in Tibet, but was carried out by the craftsmen of the Yuan court in Peking (Beijing). It consisted only of the *bKa'-'gyur*, but was soon supplemented by the *bsTan-'gyur* in ensuing blockprint editions of Tibetan origin. As with the Chinese canon, once the advantages of printing had become apparent, printed editions became the norm and prevailed to the present day as the standard format of the Tibetan canon.

These cultural differences in scriptural transmission rest, in part, on the professional status awarded to the people who held a key role in the process of preservation – the scribes. In India, scribes occupied a low position. Their involvement in the reproduction of texts was poorly valued and their education did not extend beyond the art of writing. Hence, Indian scribes were in plentiful supply and received little financial reward for their service.

In China, in contrast, writing was a skill reserved to the learned, since it involved, even for the most trivial text, exacting knowledge of complex character-formation. In view of these difficulties, copying of important Buddhist manuscripts was entrusted only to the most skilled calligraphers. The high professional standard of the copyist meant, of course, that far fewer scribal errors found their way into Chinese manuscripts. Emphasis on precision became imperative with the introduction of printing methods, since mistakes once carved in the block were difficult to correct. The use of printing from the tenth century onwards helped, therefore, to further contain the number of variant readings. Once the first printed edition was established, a model had been set for all subsequent editions. Such high standards in the field of copying imbue modern xylographs with great textual authority, since their readings are likely to be close to their ancient predecessors which recorded the original translation 2,000 years ago.

The same cannot be said of the scribal tradition in South and Southeast Asia, where the prestige remained with hand-written copies, and printing of the canon was never taken up. As a result, manuscripts frequently show inconsistent readings and copying mistakes introduced by poorly trained scribes.

Buddhist languages

The languages in which the editions of the Buddhist canon are preserved fall into two categories. First, there are the languages and dialects in which the texts circulated in India. These include local Prākrits such as Māgadhī, Pāli and the North-Western Prākrit as well as Sanskrit and its prakritized derivatives. Secondly, we have numerous languages of translation that preserved the canon outside India. The most important of these are Chinese and Tibetan.

The Buddha himself denied preference to any one language and adopted for his preaching the local dialects of the regions through which he travelled. Thus, it is incorrect to speak of an original language of Buddhism and observations about early Buddhist languages cannot but proceed on a text-to-text basis. However, since much of the preaching activity took place in the principality of old Magadha, it is probably true to say that the Buddha's discourses were based on an early variety of Old Māgadhī. Except for a few archaic root forms, no traces of Old Māgadhī have survived. After his demise, the sermons were gradually transposed into other dialects as part of the diffusion process.

A variation of Old Māgadhī is still preserved in the language of the Theravāda canon – Pāli. Originally from the region of Vidisa, it was employed by the missionaries who brought Buddhism to Sri Lanka to memorize the sermons, and it became accepted by the Sinhalese tradition as the 'language of the texts' (*pāli-bhāsā*). Although Pāli underwent morphologic and phonetic change in the course of several revisions, it is perhaps the closest approximation to the 'original' language of Buddhism.

With the beginning of the Christian Era, Prākrits became increasingly rivalled by the use of Sanskrit. Initially, Prākrit texts were interspersed with Sanskrit word-forms rather crudely. Achieving increasing sophistication as the *Dharma* was transmitted, this blend established itself and led to the peculiar hybrid that is found only in Buddhist writings. Modern scholars refer to this cross-breed as Buddhist Hybrid Sanskrit. In essence, Buddhist Hybrid Sanskrit is thus an amalgamation of languages, juxtaposing Sanskrit forms with Prākrit equivalents. Linguistic complexities suggest that its evolution is best credited to authors of considerable linguistic dexterity and not, as it was proposed, to poorly educated authors unable to write correct Sanskrit.

Yielding to the increasing popularization of Sanskrit, Prākrits and Buddhist Hybrid Sanskrit were gradually replaced by a more correct form of Sanskrit. This process began in the second century CE and made itself felt first in northern India, from where it travelled slowly into the south. In time, all the sects of the Indian mainland adopted Sanskrit as the vehicle for their scriptures. Texts that were conceived after this adjustment were of course directly composed in Sanskrit, but many of the earlier works needed to be transposed. Traces of this adaptation are preserved in the many composite works that include linguistic strands of Prākrits and Sanskrit proper.

Of the numerous languages of translation, Tibetan and Chinese are the most important, as they constitute the only languages into which the Indian texts were directly transmitted. Most other languages (with the exception of modern scholarly translations from the Sanskrit and Pāli) are secondary in the sense that they are based on either Tibetan or Chinese. This privileged position is reinforced by the towering volume of Tibetan and Chinese Buddhist writings, for no other culture has preserved nearly as many scriptures in its language. Above all, Tibetan translations stand out for their great accuracy and consistency, which were achieved by adapting the Tibetan language in translation specifically to Buddhist terminology. Hence, in Buddhist research Tibetan and Chinese rank on almost equal footing with the Indian languages.

In Buddhism, the concept of a sacred language is of little immediate applicability. For a language to become sacred, common perception requires unanimous acceptance by the adherents of that faith. Moreover, in most cases it will be the tongue in which the divine revealed itself to man. Neither of these conditions is met in Buddhism. We saw that the Buddha himself refused to give preference to any speech. His stance was widely adopted by his followers and there is indeed no single language that is read by all Buddhists. Nevertheless, undercurrents proposing allegiance to one language above others do exist. This is particularly true of Pāli, the language of the Theravāda canon. In the whole of Southeast Asia and Sri Lanka, Pāli is highly esteemed as the original language of Buddhism and given special status in the transmission of the canon. In the process of copying the canon, for instance, Southeast Asian scribes – yielding to the prestige of Pāli – will go to great lengths to preserve the phonology of Pāli in the regional script of their tradition.

In China, Japan and Korea, faith in the efficacy of sound is shown not to Pāli but to Sanskrit. There, in some circles, Buddhists chant routinely short *sūtra*s and magic formulae in the original idiom, convinced that reproduction of sound alone suffices to bring about salvation. Often ill-instructed in the wording of the chant, they trustingly place their fate in the hands of Sanskrit phonetics. If belief in the power of sound is anything to go by, Buddhism clearly has in Pāli and Sanskrit two tongues approaching the concept of a sacred language. However, as neither of them is accepted by all Buddhists they cannot be regarded unreservedly as such.

Utilization of scriptures

The areas in which sacred writings came to be used varied considerably in Buddhist history. During the first few centuries, the scriptural tradition of Buddhism must have been a very active one. All texts were probably regularly recited and intensely studied, as the mechanisms of oral transmission do not allow for a text to fall into oblivion. Because their preservation was entrusted to the *saṅgha*, it is reasonable to assume that much of these literary pursuits centred on monastic establishments. The growth in *Abhidharma* treatises suggests that the scholarly investigation of texts lasted well into the Christian Era. Lay access to the writings was granted to only a few selected texts, in line with the fact that the Buddha tended to give a limited range of his teachings to lay-people, other than those he judged to be ready to ordain.

With the introduction of writing, these restrictions could no longer be enforced. The speed with which this change began to show is not known. Chronologic discrepancies in the evolutionary process of the nascent Mahāyāna *sūtra*s and their manifestations in lay pietism indicate a delay of several centuries before the new ideas were transmitted to popular culture. We do not know the reason behind this delay. Judging by earlier practices, we may suspect a continuing monastic control on the textual tradition long after the introduction of writing.

The earliest traces of non-scholarly use of Buddhist scriptures go back to the second century BCE. It is found at Bhārhut and Sāñcī in the iconographic depictions of *jātaka* narratives. Engraved in the walls of temples and *stūpa*s, these illustrations received probably little scholarly attention but were designed to inspire piety in visitors and to disseminate the stories.

Another use of Buddhist writings is recorded in several early Mahāyāna *sūtras* which speak of a 'cult of the book'. Expedited by the increasing use of manuscripts and their role in sustaining Mahāyāna thinking, its texts became subject to cultic veneration at *stūpas*, where at first they were typically kept. The beginnings of this cult are only thinly documented. Besides a few references to this practice in the texts themselves, no corroborating evidence of its origins has been uncovered. According to reports by Chinese pilgrims, the concealing of scriptures in *stūpas* had become common practice by the fifth century CE. Recent finds of manuscript fragments underneath collapsed *stūpas* from that period confirm their accounts.

The foundations of scripture-worship go back to early Buddhism. The Buddha himself is reported to have endorsed the occasional use of protective texts (*parittas*) in order to forestall impending calamity. Once Buddhists had subscribed to the idea that a text possesses intrinsic magical powers, the ground was prepared for the cultic devotion of scripture prevalent in the Far East. An example of this cultic practice is found in a passage of Hsüan-tsang's biography, relating how Hsüan-tsang resorted to chanting his favourite text when confronted with danger on his travels. Among many Buddhists of China, Korea and Japan, this devotional attitude to scriptures is still widespread. Elaborate invocations in great numbers held in artistically furnished temples, and the recitation and copying of *sūtras*, assume to the present day an important place in the daily routines of Far Eastern Buddhists. The contents of the texts moved thereby gradually into the background, making way for magical and aesthetic dimensions. In some periods, many a recitation was enjoyed as a purely aesthetic activity, leading to competitions where beauty of melody and voice became the chief focus.

To the present day, for many East Asian Buddhists the most revered text is the *Saddharma-puṇḍarīka* (*Lotus Sūtra*). Numerous tales attest to the efficacy of faith in, reciting and copying of, and generally promulgating its contents – activities which are held to be sufficient for salvation. Turning early away from academic pursuits, its devotees place emphasis on devotional practices springing from the belief in the supreme power of the Buddha and its manifestations in scripture.

In Sri Lanka, belief in the intrinsic power of scripture is less pronounced. From its earliest days in the third century BCE, the

Theravāda *saṅgha* set scriptural learning among its main tasks. Moulded by the academic tradition of Indian scholasticism, the monks soon assumed the role of educators for the Sinhala people. Literacy was taught at village temples or monasteries and the materials used in teaching were invariably Buddhist. Responding to social requirements, Sinhalese monks thus from early on became scholars and teachers whose primary task consisted of studying the canon and its commentaries. Withdrawal from monastic learning in favour of seclusion or lay preaching was granted only after completion of a comprehensive course in canonical studies. Since it played an important role in general education and monastic training, the canon became quite naturally an object of learning and scholarly investigation.

This is true for all but a small portion of the canon, consisting of *sutta*s or verses used as protective spells (*paritta*s). Valued for their efficacy as charms or exorcisms for one's physical and material well-being, *paritta*s grew to be carefully studied by ceremonial specialists who also supervised their recitation at public services. Although *paritta* chanting is not documented before the tenth century, it is undoubtedly a very ancient custom. In order to accommodate the spiritual needs of a laity clamouring for magic and ritual, they came to be vigorously promoted in monastic studies, and today *paritta* training plays an important part in the education of practically every monk. However, as *paritta* studies are specifically aimed at lay needs, they never superseded monastic learning as the main purpose to which the canon was put.

In Tibetan Buddhism, depending on the sectarian contexts, the use to which sacred writings are put varies in kind and degree. In the dGe-lugs-pa order – the most academic of all schools – the study of Buddhist scriptures is a cornerstone in the monastic education and is regarded as a *sine qua non* for spiritual progress. Although the canonical texts are at all times available in superbly stocked libraries, it is relatively rare that a monk will study them. In practice, much of his reading material will consist of texts from the large corpus of highly esteemed commentarial writings. For the most part, these treatises rework material found in the *bKa'-'gyur*, which they reduce in size and cast into a more digestible format. The degree to which scriptures of any kind are studied depends, of course, also on the aspirations of the individual. Monks who show tenuous inclination to scholarly pursuits will meet with little exposure to sacred writings, while those who aspire to academic distinction are expected to undergo a long and demanding course of study.

Apart from scholarly contexts, virtually all monks encounter sacred scriptures at the numerous religious ceremonies that punctuate monastic life. At such occasions the texts are generally read aloud and relate directly to the purpose of the ceremony. They are invariably recited in Tibetan and their audience is expected to absorb their contents.

Belief in the intrinsic power of sound is less widespread in Tibet and restricted to the ritual context. There, it does play an important role and is regularly found. Typically, it is applied to short spells and formulae designed to secure magically the successful completion of the ritual. Encoded in cryptic language of little independent meaning, the spells are usually recited in their original idiom. Tapping a source of immense power, devotees attach great value to the correct intonation of individual syllables, since mistakes therein are feared to lead to great calamity. Spells of this kind are particularly frequent in tantric ritual where they assume a key role in the empowerment process. The exact purpose to which they are put varies greatly, ranging from the summoning of chief deities to the appeasing of local spiritual forces.

Finally, emulating their Indian predecessors, Tibetans will often deposit sacred scriptures on altars, holy places and, above all, in *stūpa*s commemorating events of religious importance. Representing the word of the Buddha, their presence is fundamental to the aura of holiness that surrounds these sites and turns them into places of worship and pilgrimage.

Apart from specifically commissioned *sūtra* recitation, scripture-worship is for the majority of the laity the only contact they will ever have with canonical writings. Constrained by a widespread unavailability of alternative instruction, the laity depend on monks for *sūtra* schooling, which is invariably channelled through monastic institutions. Like their ancient Indian predecessors, Tibetan lay Buddhists are mostly instructed in carefully drafted teaching-texts which touch only on points of immediate relevance to the lay path. Detailed study of canonical material – although theoretically open to all – is in practice left to the religious expert.

Notes

1 All references to the early Buddhist scriptures relate to the canon of the Theravāda tradition and are therefore given in Pāli. Sanskrit forms: *Tripiṭaka, Sūtra, Abhidharma*.
2 Sanskrit; Pāli Mahā-kassapa.
3 Sanskrit; Pāli Rājagaha.
4 Sanskrit; Pāli Vesālī.
5 In the Sanskrit tradition, the corresponding categories are called *Dīrghāgama, Madhyamāgama, Saṃyuktāgama, Ekottarāgama* and *Kṣudrakāgama*. These categories of texts represent the canon as it was known to the Sanskrit schools of northern India. Today, little of their canon is preserved in the original idiom. Most of it is found in translation in the Chinese *Tripiṭaka*. While the *āgama*s are fundamentally Sanskrit counterparts to the Pāli *nikāya*s, they exhibit several differences. First, the number of works included in the *āgama*s is greater than that in their Pāli correspondents. Secondly, the arrangement of the *āgama*s and their *sūtra*s does not always match that of the *nikāya*s. Thirdly, the texts themselves differ in contents and structure, depending on whether they appear in the *āgama*s or *nikāya*s. In most cases, the differences in contents are limited to the method of expression and arrangements of subjects. The doctrinal base itself is very uniform in both collections. The question whether these variants go back to deviations in the oral tradition or to deliberate modification based on written documents is, as yet, unresolved.
6 A Prākrit is an 'unrefined' language related to Sanskrit.
7 In the traditional order, the *Vinaya-piṭaka* comes before the *Sutta-* and *Abhidhamma-piṭaka*.
8 A lesser offence.
9 Sanskrit; Pāli Sāriputta.
10 Though not all the early schools developed their own *Abhidhamma*.
11 A term applied in early Buddhism only to *nirvāṇa*, as beyond arising or passing away in time.
12 Being one of the two key texts of the Hua-yen school. The other was *Mahā-parinirvāṇa Sūtra* (an entirely different text from the Pāli *Mahā-parinibbāna Sutta*), which emphasizes the idea of the *buddha*-nature.
13 To take the *Dhammapada* as 'apocryphal' is debatable. Some of its verses are found elsewhere in the Pāli Canon, ascribed to the Buddha; the Buddha may have agreed with and affirmed many of the floating verses he heard, as he did with the teachings of a number of his disciples as recorded in the *sutta*s; moreover, the format of the text is not such that it presents the verses as being composed by the Buddha, as such. (Ed.)

Further reading

Beal, S. (1882) *Buddhist Literature in China*. London: Trübner & Co.
Bechert, H. (ed.) (1980) *Die Sprache der ältesten buddhistischen Überlieferung (The Language of the Earliest Buddhist Tradition)*, AAWG. Göttingen: Van den Hoeck & Ruprecht.
Bechert, H. (ed.) (1985–87) *Zur Schulzugehörigkeit von Werken der Hīnayāna Literatur*, AAWG. Göttingen: Van den Hoeck & Ruprecht.
Conze, E. (1978) *Prajñāpāramitā Literature*. Tokyo: The Reiyukai Library.
Frauwallner, E. (1956) *The Earliest Vinaya and the Beginnings of Buddhist Literature*. Rome: Serie Orientale Roma, 8.
Law, B. C. (1933) *A History of Pāli Literature* (2 vols). London: Routledge and Kegan Paul.
Norman, K. R. (1983) *Pāli Literature*. Wiesbaden: Otto Harrassowitz.
Ruegg, D. S. (1981) *The Literature of the Madhyamaka School of Philosophy in India*. Wiesbaden: Otto Harrassowitz.
Stael-Holstein, Baron Anton von (ed.) (1926) *The Kāśyapaparivarta: A Mahāyāna Sūtra of the Ratnakūṭa Class*. Shanghai: Commercial Press.
Winternitz, M. (1933) *A History of Indian Literature*, vol. 2. Calcutta: Calcutta University Press.

2. Buddhist visions of the human predicament and its resolution

Peter Harvey

In a survey-book on world religions, Huston Smith[1] starts his chapter on Buddhism with the heading 'The man who woke up'. This aptly describes the nature of a *buddha*, meaning an 'Awakened One' or 'Enlightened One'. This term implies that most of us – including most Buddhists – are still spiritually asleep. But it also has the implication that all humans are capable of a similar kind of spiritual awakening from the 'slumber' which is our selective, biased and misconceived 'normal' state of consciousness.

The person who became known as 'the Buddha' was Siddhattha Gotama (*c.* 484–404 BCE). He lived in a period of much religious and philosophical debate concerning the nature of life and its problems. These were highlighted by a breakdown of the values of previously small-scale tribal republics, and the disease and suffering experienced in the expanding cities of the day.

The dominant religious influence then was exerted by the brahmins, priests of an early form of Hinduism known as Brahmanism. Many brahmins were still wedded to the mainly sacrificial form of their previous tradition, while others were influenced by the ideas expressed in the *Upsaniṣad*s. These related to *karma*, rebirth, and the contemplative quest to attain liberation from the round of rebirths by coming to know *ātman*: one's inner essence, or true Self. There were also those who rejected Brahmanism and sought new ways to find a basis of true and lasting happiness. Such renunciant ascetics or *samaṇa*s belonged to various groups. The

Jains espoused total non-violence and, through ascetic self-discipline and philosophical understanding, sought the liberation of the individual life-principle (*jīva*) from the round of rebirths. The Ājīvakas were fatalists who believed in the cycle of rebirths, but felt that one's form of rebirth was determined by an impersonal 'destiny' (*niyati*). This was in contrast to the belief of brahmins, Jains and Buddhists that one's rebirth was determined by the nature and quality of one's *karma*s, or actions. Of the remaining *samaṇa* groups, the Sceptics felt that humans could have no knowledge on such matters as *karma* and rebirth, and the Materialists had the view that one was totally annihilated at death. The times were thus ones in which the 'classical' Indian ideas of *karma* and rebirth had not yet been fully established, but were open to debate.

Gotama's entry into the religious scene of his day came after the renunciation of his previous life as the son of an elected aristocratic ruler. By the standards of his day, he had experienced a life of comfortable luxury. Yet this did not satisfy him: what for many people might be the goal of life was for him the starting point of his spiritual quest. In his twenties, after a sheltered upbringing, he came to realize that even he, in his comfortable existence, was not immune from ageing, sickness and death; so the 'vanities' of youth, health and life left him, and he therefore resolved to take up the life of a *samaṇa*, and join the quest for a timeless imperturbable state beyond change and suffering: *nirvāṇa*.

The problem of suffering later became the focus of Gotama's teaching, once he had found what he saw as its solution. Unlike most other religions, this solution did not involve God – only finite living beings and the overcoming of their weaknesses and limitations, by developing their potential and uprooting their negativities. From the perspective of his teaching, suffering became a stimulus for religious commitment and activity.

As a wandering *samaṇa*, Gotama spent six years trying some of the methods of religious training available in his day. He attained advanced meditative states through *yoga*, but felt that they did not go far enough; he then practised extreme asceticism, but found that such bodily mortification did not bring peace of mind and insight. He therefore set out to develop his own spiritual path. Sitting in meditation, he first established concentration on certain sensations associated with breathing. Then gradually his mind calmed – deeper and deeper, with greater concentration and inner stillness. At a certain point, his mind entered an altered state of consciousness known as the first *jhāna* (Sanskrit *dhyāna*) – a lucid trance in which he was unaware of his surroundings, but intensely aware of his object of concentration. There was thus an uplifting inner quietude and clarity of mind. This process of calming concentration was next taken further to the second, third, and then fourth *jhāna*: a state of profound clarity and stillness, from which even the previous intense joy and happiness had faded away. In such a state, the mind is seen to be a powerful and highly sensitive instrument of knowledge, freed of all the obscurations coming from its normal wandering agitations.

From this state, Gotama then went on to investigate certain aspects of reality, and develop the 'threefold knowledge'. The first was the confirmation, according to his own experience, of rebirth. Pushing his memory further and further back, he is said to have gradually remembered thousands of his past lives. The second 'knowledge' was his confirmation of the principle of *karma*. This was based on his psychic observation of beings dying and being reborn, in line with their past actions. The third 'knowledge' was the most crucial, and concerned his insight into the Four Holy or Ennobling Truths: the heart of his later teaching, focusing on suffering and on its transcending. In attaining this knowledge, he also experienced the goal of his quest, *nirvāṇa*, the ending of all suffering, rebirths and limitations. He was now an 'Awakened One' (Conze *et al.*, 1954, pp. 60–2).

The human predicament: the *karma*–rebirth perspective

Much of ordinary Buddhism is in some way related to the ideas of rebirth (*punabbhava*, literally 'rebecoming') and *karma*, for these provide the key framework within which life is understood. The present life is seen as the continuation of a countless series of lives, with no known beginning. The 'explanation' for any one of these rebirths lies in the cravings and energies left over in a being from previous lives, a process which will continue until all their craving-momentum is overcome, by the attainment of *nirvāṇa*. The cycle of rebirth is known as *saṃsāra*, literally 'wandering on' – a process which ambles on and on, indefinitely, with no inbuilt direction or purpose. According to Buddhism, this is the nature of the cosmos. Ultimately, it is an unsatisfactory situation, both in itself, and because of the many forms of suffering that rebirths entail, so that a key Buddhist goal is to transcend it. A lesser, and more easily attainable goal, though, is to act in such a way that one is reborn in the more pleasant realms of rebirth. For most Buddhists, this is their prime goal, along with helping others to do likewise, *nirvāṇa* being a more distant goal in a future life. Among Theravādins, a determined few do aim to attain *nirvāṇa* in *this* life. Moreover, the Mahāyāna has a threefold hierarchy of goals: a good rebirth, personal liberation (*nirvāṇa*), and, highest of all, working for the *nirvāṇa* of all beings, not just oneself, by becoming a *buddha*. The third of these is emphasized by the Mahāyāna, but is also a goal for some Theravādins.

KARMA

If, then, I am a Buddhist, what is seen as deciding the form of my next rebirth? A natural answer would be: 'why, my own actions, my *karmas*'. Broadly speaking, good actions are seen as leading to pleasant rebirths, and bad actions to unpleasant ones. This is not, however, seen as a case of 'rewards' and 'punishments'. A common analogy for *karma* is a seed, and the word for a result of *karma* is a 'fruit (*phala*) of *karma*'. Just as a seed naturally develops into a (plant and) fruit, so an action is seen as naturally leading to a certain kind of result. This all unfolds according to subtle laws of nature, not through the actions of gods or a God. What sets up this chain reaction is the volition behind an action, which is what *karma* is actually defined as being. That volition, with its good or bad motivation, leaves a psychic trace which will sooner or later bring about its results, both in terms of the form of rebirth, and in things which may happen to a person during the present, and future, lives. In this sense, a person is seen as the determiner of his or her own destiny – a destiny defined by the actions which he or she chooses to perform.

Intentional actions are seen as either wholesome/skilful (*kusala*; Sanskrit *kuśala*) or unwholesome/unskilful (*akusala*; Sanskrit *akuśala*), depending on the nature of the volition. If an action is intended to harm any being, or is motivated by greed, hatred or delusion, it is seen as unwholesome. If it is intended to benefit beings, or is motivated by generosity, kindness or wisdom, it is wholesome

(Brown and O'Brian, 1989, pp. 58, 85–6). The underlying basis of any unwholesome action is some form of delusion, or misperception of the nature of reality. Actions which are so based are seen as naturally leading to unpleasant results because, so to speak, they go against the grain of reality. Actions related to wisdom and seeing things 'as they really are' have the opposite effect.

Wholesome *karmas* are also said to have the quality of, or to generate, *puñña* (Sanskrit *puṇya*), a kind of 'auspicious purifying power'. The term *puñña* is usually, rather limply, translated as 'meritorious' (adjective) or 'merit' (noun). However, 'meritorious' implies deservingness, but what is referred to is something with a natural power of its own to produce happy results (cf. Cousins, 1996, p. 155); it does not depend on anyone to give out what is due to the 'deserving'. A *puñña* action is 'auspicious', 'fortunate' or 'fruitful', as it purifies the mind and thus leads to future good fortune. Indeed, through other Indo-European languages it may be related to the English words 'boon' and 'bounty' (cf. the Thai word for *puñña*: *bun*). As the noun *puñña* refers to the auspicious, uplifting, purifying power of good actions to produce future happy results, one might translate it as 'goodness-power', but this offers no convenient related adjective. A better translation would be '(an act of) karmic fruitfulness', with 'karmically fruitful' as the adjective. This makes a connection with the fact that actions (*karmas*) are often likened to 'seeds' and their results are known as 'fruits' (*phalas*) or 'ripenings'. While such *phalas* can be the results of either good or bad actions, and *puñña* relates only to good actions, the English word 'fruit' can also mean only edible, pleasant fruit such as apples, without referring to inedible, unpleasant ones. The link to 'fruitfulness' is also seen in the fact that the *saṅgha* is described as the best 'field of *puñña*', i.e. the best group of people to 'plant' a gift 'in' in terms of karmically beneficial results of the gift.

The opposite of *puñña* is *apuñña*, which one can accordingly see as meaning '(an act of) karmic unfruitfulness' or 'karmically unfruitful', i.e. producing no pleasant fruits, but only bitter ones. A synonym for *apuñña* is *pāpa*, which, while often translated as 'evil', really means that which is 'infertile, 'barren', 'harmful' (Cousins, 1996, p. 156) or 'ill-fortuned' (Cousins, 1996, p. 148). A good way of rendering these meanings would be to see *pāpa* as an adjective as meaning '(karmically) deadening', and as a noun as '(karmic) deadness', meaning that what is so described has a deadening effect on the psyche, making it more constricted and lifeless, rather than having an uplifting, fruitful effect.

The idea of *karma* helps to motivate both the avoiding of harming others, and also the performance of karmically fruitful actions, especially those involving generosity to Buddhist monks and nuns. The benefits of karmic fruitfulness can be shared with others. In the Theravāda school, the rationale for this is twofold. First, one can invite someone else to rejoice at one's own wholesome action, so that, by their rejoicing-at-goodness, they themselves generate karmic fruitfulness. Secondly, if a gift is offered on behalf of someone else, such as a dead relative, it is as if that person is himself or herself doing the auspicious deed. In this way, people can be drawn together in wholesome deeds and in sharing their good effect, and can benefit dead relatives. Mahāyānists speak, less guardedly, simply of a 'transfer' of karmic fruitfulness to others.

While belief in *karma* can sometimes be used as a cloak for fatalism, it is clear that it is a different kind of concept, and in practice, *karma* is not generally used in a fatalistic way. In Thailand and Myanmar (Burma), for example, good and bad fortune is seen as arising from a combination of past *karma* and present knowledge and effort. Admittedly, people are interested in indications, for example, as given by astrologers, of potential problems on the horizon, but their response to such warnings is not passive. Only when an unfortunate event has actually happened might they put it down to bad *karma* – and thus come to terms with, and then let go of, an unfortunate life event. Until it happens, they do what they can to avert it, using a variety of means including:

- normal secular effort involving, e.g., medicine or farming techniques;
- magical means, if these are believed in; and
- Buddhist means, such as doing good deeds, and chanting protective chants which draw on the beneficent power of the Buddha's words.

According to J. Ingersoll, this produces in rural Thai people an attitude which is 'Hopeful rather than optimistic, positive rather than dynamic, patient rather than assertive', such that they cope with life 'with quiet good humor'.[2] This is in line with a motto on the cover of the Thai-based *World Fellowship of Buddhists' Review*: 'We hope for the best, prepare for the worst, and do whatever is possible.' Nevertheless, some who make their living by unwholesome means, for example, fishermen, will say that it is their *karma* to be reborn into such a community. This is no real excuse, from a Buddhist point of view. Some circumstances one finds oneself in may be due to past *karma*, but one should use one's present freedom to choose so as to try to develop a way of life based on a wholesome livelihood. That said, if an unwholesome action is done because of poverty, it has a less bad effect than if done for mere greed or out of anger.

The *karma* doctrine, of course, has implications for how people with disabilities are thought of. A Buddhist would not tend to see disabilities, particularly those present from birth, as merely accidental – or as a 'gift' from God. They would be seen as the result of previous unwholesome action. This does not mean, though, that blaming disabled people for their plight, or guilt on their part, is appropriate. It is more that their plight is seen as an unfortunate natural result of having acted unwholesomely in the past. There is, however, no reason to look down on the disabled now – the past is the past, and the important thing is how we all act now: both the disabled person him/herself, and those who have dealings with him or her. We all have the same human potential, so should act with generosity and compassion in trying to develop this in ourselves and others. As regards guilt, this is not encouraged by Buddhism. It is good to regret a past bad action, but not to feel heavily 'guilty' about it, for this is a clouded, agitated state of mind not conducive to wholesome action. The important thing is to resolve to act better in the future.

GENDER

According to the *karma*–rebirth perspective, we have all been male and female, many times before (Harvey, 2000, pp. 353–410). Admittedly, gender has a tendency to stay the same from one life to the next, but it may change if a person has a strong aspiration that this be so, or if the working out of *karma* makes this appropriate. For example, in one text (Norman, 1971, pp. 41–4), an enlightened nun recalls some of her past lives, saying that, as a result of once being a male adulterer, some of her future lives were as females in unhappy marriages. In rebirth terms, a female form is seen as slightly less fortunate than a male one, but only because it tends to involve more forms of suffering. These include menstruation, pregnancy and childbirth, and the subordinate position of women in many societies (Woodward, 1927, pp. 162–3).

Both females and males are seen as having the same potential for attaining *nirvāṇa*, and it is this which persuaded the Buddha, after initial hesitation, to found an order of nuns (*bhikkhunī*s) as well as monks (*bhikkhu*s) (Conze *et al.*, 1954, pp. 23–6). His hesitation may have been due to its going against the existing view of the position of women in society, or concern about ribald accusations about the relationship of monks and nuns. In any case, he agreed on condition that nuns should follow certain extra rules. Along with the fact that marriage is not a religious obligation in Buddhism, the existence of the order of nuns has helped encourage, in Buddhist societies, a respect for the status of the unmarried woman as an independent agent in her own right. Within marriage, the leader of a household is usually a man, but it can be a woman, and Buddhist women, married and single, are often active in trade and commerce. In cultures influenced by the Confucian social ethic (China, Korea, Japan), though, the actual position of women in society has been clearly subordinate. As to the order of nuns, it survives in China, Korea, Vietnam and Japan but not, in its full original form, elsewhere. In Tibet, the full monastic form for women was never introduced, while in the Theravāda lands of Sri Lanka and Myanmar (Burma), it had died out by the thirteenth century. In all these countries, however, there are female renunciants, generally referred to as 'nuns', following a lesser number of monastic precepts than the full *bhikkhunī*s. At some time in the future, it is possible that the Tibetan and Theravāda *bhikkhunī* form could be revived via the Chinese ordination-line (a valid form requires ordination by *bhikkhunī*s whose tradition goes back unbrokenly to the Buddha).

Psychologically, men and women are seen as tending to have different characteristics, including characteristic strengths and weaknesses. In Tibetan Buddhist symbolism, for example, certain male holy beings represent compassionate 'skilful means' (appropriately adapted ways of helping and teaching people), while their female partners represent intuitive wisdom. Both qualities, though, need to be developed. Nevertheless, it is said that a female can be neither a *buddha* nor a *māra* (a tempter god similar to Satan) (Horner, 1959, p. 109). As gender is changeable from life to life, though, this is no long-term restriction on a person. Moreover, the Theravāda texts refer to many female *arahats*, or people who have experienced *nirvāṇa*, and the Mahāyāna includes female holy beings among those who are almost *buddhas* (i.e., advanced *bodhisattvas*).

HUMAN, ANIMAL AND OTHER REBIRTH REALMS

Rebirth can be as a human, but also as an animal: land animal, fish, bird or insect. Indeed, it would be said that we have all been animals in some of our past lives, and may well be born again in such forms, depending on the nature of our actions. This implies, of course, that humans and animals are not ultimately different in kind, but differ only in degree. The 'specialness' of humans is expressed, by Tibetan Buddhists, by talking of a 'precious human rebirth' (Harvey, 2000, p. 30), for a human life is a rare and precious opportunity for moral and spiritual development. This should be respected in others and made good use of in one's own case. It is at the human level that most good and bad *karma* is made, for *karma* is intentional, chosen action, and humans have most freedom to choose. To some extent, the higher animals can make some moral/spiritual progress, by choosing, within the limitations of their nature, to act in a less greedy, more giving, less aggressive and more loving way. In the main, though, animals are creatures of instinct and, according to Buddhism, live out the consequences of the previous bad *karma* which led to their state. In time, the backlog of past good *karma* will raise their state and lead back to a human rebirth.

Human beings may be superior to animals because of their spiritual potential, but they should show their superiority in good treatment of fellow sentient beings, not by exploiting them. The basis of Buddhist ethics is not to inflict on another what one would not like done to oneself (Woodward, 1930, pp. 308–11; Harvey, 2000, pp. 33–4). All beings, human or otherwise, are just like oneself in disliking pain and liking happiness, so 'Since the self of others is dear to each one, let him who loves himself not harm another' (Brown and O'Brian, 1989, p. 86). Moreover, it is said that whatever being one comes across will have been, in one or other of one's countless past lives, a close friend or relative (Rhys Davids, 1922, p. 128). As they were good to one then, so one should be good to them now. Thus the most important ethical precept, to 'abstain from injury to living beings', applies to the treatment of both humans and animals. The effect of this, in practice, varies (Harvey, 2000, pp. 157–66). Certainly a reluctance to kill any being is usual, though this reduces when one gets down to fishes and insects. Avoidance of all flesh foods has not been expected, except in China, Korea and pre-modern Japan. The crucial thing is no direct or instigated killing. Compassion for animals can lead to an old Tibetan lady removing slugs from the middle of the road and giving them some of her apple, or the buying and freeing of captured birds at certain festival times – but only after they have been caught for this purpose!

Less pleasant than an animal rebirth is that of frustrated ghostly beings (*peta*s), and hell beings (Brown and O'Brian, 1989, pp. 60–1, 132–3). The latter are seen as living in a state akin to a prolonged, pain-wracked nightmare, as a result of the suffering that they have inflicted on others. In time, though, their hellish rebirth passes; no form of rebirth is seen as eternal, and the only state which is eternal, or rather timeless, is *nirvāṇa*.

Along with human rebirth, the 26 forms of heavenly rebirths are seen as comprising the 'good' rebirths. The gods (*deva*s) of these heavens are said to live for nine million human years in the 'lowest' heaven, up to '84,000 eons' in the most subtle and refined one. Yet time is said to pass more quickly for them than for humans, and sooner or later they die and are reborn in some other realm. Thus such heavens are *this* side of salvation: they are not ultimate solutions to the problems of existence. Rebirth in them is simply the result of good actions and, as such, they are pleasant, calm and refined forms of existence, but they are still subject to limitations. Nevertheless, gods are less clearly confronted with the limitations of life than humans, human life being less pleasant. So humans are less likely to become complacent, and are thus more likely to be motivated to seek *nirvāṇa*, the 'deathless'.

GODS AND HOLY BEINGS

Despite the limitations of the gods, a traditional Buddhist may seek to interact with them in various ways (Gombrich, 1971, pp. 191–213). Only certain versions of Western-influenced Buddhism are completely non-theistic, or free of belief in, and recourse to, gods. Traditional Buddhism can be seen as 'trans-polytheistic':[3] accepting many gods, but looking beyond them for what is truly important.

Some of the divine realms are seen as so refined as to be beyond contact with humanity – except by deep meditation. Others, particularly the six lowest, are pleasant realms which are closer in nature to human existence. Buddhists may pray to the gods of these realms in order to bring about worldly benefit, such as good health or a good harvest. In some ways they are looked on in a similar way as politicians: powerful people that one can go to for assistance. They are all seen, though, as inferior in knowledge and influence to the Buddha, and many of the chants which seek their aid ask, in effect, that they give assistance in the name of the Buddha. Some of the gods are specifically said to be followers of the Buddha. Among these are Sakka (or Indra), chief of the pre-Buddhist Vedic gods, whom the Buddha is said to have converted, and one-time fierce Tibetan gods that are seen to have been tamed by the eighth-century Padmasaṃbhava, so as to become protectors of Buddhism. As Buddhism spread into different cultures, its cosmology had the space to encompass various indigenous gods, from nature deities upwards, provided these were not seen as supreme, eternal beings.

In Theravāda Buddhism, one of the ways of interacting with the gods is to share karmic fruitfulness with them, as they will die when their own supply wears out. In return for a share of the karmic fruitfulness made by humans, they will offer aid. In Sri Lanka, some Buddhists also take part in the Hindu-based cult of the god Kataragama, going into trances and making vows to the god. Some Theravādins also seek, by good deeds and aspirations, to be reborn in the heaven of the future *buddha*, Metteyya (Sanskrit Maitreya), or to be reborn on earth when he becomes the next *buddha*. Metteyya is the only future *buddha* referred to in early Buddhist texts but, later, Theravādins came to add others. For example, in Sri Lanka Viṣṇu, one of the major Hindu gods, is seen as one.

A being working for future Buddhahood is what is known as a *bodhisattva*, or 'being-for-enlightenment', and in Mahāyāna lands many of these are believed in (Harvey, 1990, pp. 130–3, 182–7; Williams, 1989, pp. 228–42). While the Mahāyāna encourages all to tread the path of the *bodhisattva*, those well advanced on this path are seen as existing at a heavenly level, as compassionate beings dedicated to the aid of those in need of help and inspiration. They are thus the focus of prayer and contemplation, and are requested to transfer some of their huge store of karmic fruitfulness to their devotees, for their worldly and spiritual uplift.

The Mahāyāna actually sees the historical Buddha as a manifestation on earth of a heavenly *buddha*, Śākyamuni, who had already been enlightened for countless ages (Harvey, 1990, pp. 125–8; Williams, 1989, pp. 167–84). Such a manifestation was to teach and inspire people in the Buddhist way. In the Theravāda view, Gotama did not become a *buddha* until his enlightenment experience at the age of 35. Prior to that, he had been working to develop the perfections of a *buddha* for many lives. At birth he was a (rather special) human, but from the time of his enlightenment he was no longer a 'human' but a *buddha*: an awakened being who, by perfecting his human nature, had transcended it (Conze *et al.*, 1954, pp. 104–5).

The human predicament: the unsatisfactoriness of life

The central 'discovery' of the Buddha's enlightenment experience, and the focus of his first sermon was the Four Ennobling Truths.[4] These deal with the most important aspects of the nature of the human condition – indeed the condition of all sentient beings – and how to transform this. They comprise the structural framework for all the more advanced teachings of the Buddha, intended for those who have prepared themselves by previous moral and spiritual development. Their form parallels the practice of doctors of the Buddha's day:

1 diagnose a disease

2 identify its cause

3 determine whether it is curable, and

4 outline a course of treatment to cure it.

The first Truth concerns the 'illness' of *dukkha* (Sanskrit *duḥkha*), the 'suffering' that we are all subject to. The second concerns the key cause of this: craving. The third affirms that by removing the cause of the 'illness', a cure is possible: from the cessation of craving, in the experience of *nirvāṇa*, suffering ceases. The fourth outlines the way to full health: the Ennobling Eightfold Path, or Middle Way.

In his first sermon, the Buddha formulated the first 'Truth' as follows:

> (i) Birth is *dukkha*, ageing is *dukkha*, sickness is *dukkha*, death is *dukkha*; (ii) sorrow, lamentation, pain, grief and despair are *dukkha*; (iii) association with what one dislikes is *dukkha*, separation from what one likes is *dukkha*, not to get what one wants is *dukkha*; (iv) in short, the five groups (as objects) of grasping (which make up a person) are *dukkha*. [numbers added]

Here the word *dukkha* refers to all those things which are unpleasant, imperfect, and which we would like to be otherwise. It is both 'suffering' and the general 'unsatisfactoriness' of life. The first Truth essentially points out that suffering is inherent in the very fabric of life.

The first features described as *dukkha* are basic biological aspects of being alive, each of which can be painful and traumatic. The *dukkha* of these is compounded by the rebirth perspective of Buddhism, for this involves repeated rebirth, re-ageing, re-sickness and re-death. The second set of features refer to physical or mental pain that arises from the vicissitudes of life. The third set of features points to the fact that we can never wholly succeed in keeping away things, people and situations that we dislike, in holding on to those we do like, or in getting what we want. The changing, unstable nature of life is such that we are led to experience dissatisfaction, loss and disappointment – in a word, frustration.

Is Buddhism 'pessimistic' in emphasizing the unpleasant aspects of life? A Buddhist's reply is that the transcending of suffering requires a fully realistic assessment of its pervasive presence in life. One must accept one is 'ill' if a cure is to be possible; ignoring the problem only makes it worse. The path to the end of suffering, moreover, is one in which the deep calm and joy of devotion and meditation play an important part. Buddhism, then, does not deny the existence of happiness in the world – it provides ways of increasing it – but it does emphasize that all forms of happiness (bar that of *nirvāṇa*) do not last. Sooner or later, they slip through one's fingers and leave an aftertaste of loss and longing – thus even happiness is to be seen as *dukkha*. This can be more clearly understood when one considers another classification of states of *dukkha*: *dukkha* as physical pain, *dukkha* due to change, and the *dukkha* of conditioned phenomena. When a happy feeling passes, it often leads to *dukkha* due to change, and, even while it is occurring, it is *dukkha* in the sense of being a limited, conditioned, imperfect state – one which is not truly satisfactory. This most subtle sense of *dukkha* is sometimes experienced in feelings of vague unease at the fragility and transitoriness of life.

The human make-up and human potential

A PERSON AS A CLUSTER OF IMPERMANENT, UNSATISFACTORY, NOT-SELF PROCESSES

When the first sermon summarizes its outline of *dukkha* by saying 'in short, the five groups (as objects) of grasping are *dukkha*', it is referring to *dukkha* in the subtlest sense. The five 'groups of grasping' (*upādāna-khandha*s) are the five factors which go to make up a 'person'. Buddhism holds that none of these is free from unsatisfactoriness. Each factor is a 'group' (*khandha*; Sanskrit *skandha*) of related states, and is an object of 'grasping' (*upādāna*) so as to be identified as 'me', 'I', 'myself'. The first is *rūpa*, 'material shape' or 'form': the material aspect of existence, whether in the outer world or in the body of a living being. The second factor is *vedanā*, or 'feeling', whether pleasant, unpleasant, or neutral. The third factor is *saññā* (Sanskrit *saṃjñā*), 'cognition', recognition and interpretation – including misinterpretation – of sensory or mental objects. It is *saññā* which classifies and labels them, for example as 'yellow', 'a man', or 'fear'. The fourth personality factor is the *saṅkhāra*s (Sanskrit *saṃskāra*s) or 'constructing activities'. These comprise a number of states which initiate action, or direct, mould and give shape to character. They include very active states such as determination, joy and hatred, and also more passive states such as sensory stimulation. While some are ethically neutral, many are ethically 'wholesome' or 'unwholesome'. The most characteristic 'constructing activity' is *cetanā*, 'will' or 'volition'. The fifth and final factor is *viññāṇa* (Sanskrit *vijñāna*), '(discriminative) consciousness'. This includes both the basic awareness of an object, and the discrimination of its basic aspects or parts, which are actually recognized by *saññā*. It is also known as *citta*, the central focus of personality, which can be seen as 'mind', 'heart' or 'thought'. This is essentially a 'mind-set' or 'mentality', some aspects of which alter from moment to moment, while others recur and are equivalent to a person's character. Its form at any moment is set up by the other mental *khandha*s, but in turn it goes on to determine their pattern of arising – in a process of constant interaction. In the Theravāda, the deepest aspect of 'consciousness' is seen as *bhavaṅga citta*: the latent ground-state of consciousness, which occurs uninterruptedly in dreamless sleep, but is rapidly flicked in and out of in normal consciousness (Collins, 1982, pp. 238–47). A similar, but more developed idea is also found in the Mahāyāna philosophy known as Yogācāra or Cittamātra, where there is reference to a kind of underlying unconscious mind, known as the 'storehouse consciousness' (*ālaya-vijñāna*). This stores the effect-potentials of past *karma*s, and then, through the ripening of these, moulds how a person perceives the 'world' (Harvey, 1990, pp. 107–9; Williams, 1989, pp. 90–3).

Much Buddhist practice is concerned with the purification, development and harmonious integration of the factors of personality, through the cultivation of devotion, virtue and meditation. In time, however, the fivefold analysis is used to enable a meditator gradually to transcend the naive perception – with respect to 'himself/herself' or 'another' – of a unitary 'person' or 'self'. In place of this, there is set up the contemplation of a person as a cluster of changing, conditioned physical and mental processes, or *dhamma*s, thus undermining grasping and attachment, which are key causes of suffering.

The fundamental 'three marks' of all conditioned phenomena are said to be that they are impermanent (*anicca*; Sanskrit *anitya*), *dukkha*, and not-Self (*anattā*; Sanskrit *anātma*). Buddhism emphasizes that change and impermanence are fundamental features of everything bar *nirvāṇa*. Mountains wear down, material goods wear out, and all beings die. The gross form of the body changes relatively slowly, but the matter which composes it is replaced as one eats, excretes, and sheds skin cells. As regards the mind, character patterns may be relatively persistent, but feelings, moods, ideas, etc. can be observed constantly to change. It is because things are impermanent that they are also *dukkha* – limited, and potentially painful and frustrating. Moreover, it is said, with respect to each of the five *khandha*s, that if it were truly Self, it would not 'tend to sickness', and it would be totally controllable at will, which it is not (Brown and O'Brian, 1989, p. 50). So, as each *khandha* is impermanent, *dukkha*, and of a nature to change, it is inappropriate to consider it as 'This is mine, this am I, this is my Self'. That is, it is not a permanent, self-secure, happy, independent Self or I.

In the Buddha's day, the spiritual quest was largely seen as the search for, identifying and liberating, a person's true Self (Sanskrit *ātman*; Pāli *atta*) or 'life principle' (*jīva*). Such an entity was postulated as a person's permanent inner nature – the source of true happiness and the autonomous 'inner controller' of action. The Buddha argued that anything subject to change, anything not autonomous and totally controllable by its own wishes, anything subject to the disharmony of suffering, could not be such a perfect true Self. Moreover, to take anything which was not such a Self as if it were one, is to lay the foundation for much suffering. This arises when what one fondly takes as one's permanent, essential Self changes in undesired ways.

The teaching on phenomena as not-Self is not only intended to undermine the Brahmanical or Jain concepts of self, but also much more commonly held conceptions and deep-rooted feelings of 'I'-ness. To feel that, however much one changes in life from childhood onwards, some essential part remains unchanged as the 'real me', is to have a belief in a permanent Self. To act as if only other people die and to ignore the inevitability of one's own death, is to act as if one had a permanent Self. To relate changing mental phenomena to a substantial self which 'owns' them – '*I* am worried ... happy ... angry' – is to have such a Self concept. To identify with one's body, ideas, actions, etc., is to take them as part of an 'I' or Self-entity.

The not-Self teaching can easily be misunderstood and misdescribed; so it is important to understand what it is saying. The Buddha accepted many conventional usages of the word 'self' (also *atta*), as in 'yourself' and 'myself'. These he saw as simply a convenient way of referring to a particular collection of mental and physical states. But he taught that, within such a conventional, empirical self, no permanent, substantial, independent, metaphysical Self could be found. The not-Self teaching does not deny that there is continuity of character in life, and to some extent from life to life, but persistent character traits are merely due to the repeated occurrence of certain *citta*s, or 'mind-sets'. The *citta* as a whole is sometimes talked of as an (empirical) 'self', but while such character traits may be long-lasting, they can and do change, and are thus impermanent – and so 'not-Self', insubstantial. A 'person' is a collection of rapidly changing and interacting mental and physical processes, with character-patterns recurring over some time. Only partial control can be exercised over these processes; so they often change in undesired ways, leading to suffering. Impermanent, they cannot be a permanent Self. Suffering, they cannot be an autonomous true 'I', which would contain nothing that was out of harmony with itself. While *nirvāṇa* is beyond impermanence and *dukkha*, it is still not-Self. Though it is unconditioned, it has nothing in it which could support the feeling of 'I'-ness, for this can only arise with respect to the conditioned *khandhas* and it is not even a truly valid feeling there (Collins, 1982, pp. 98–9).

The not-Self teaching is not, in itself, a denial of the existence of a permanent Self; it is primarily a practical teaching aimed at the overcoming of attachment. It urges that all phenomena that we identify with as 'Self' should be carefully observed and examined to see that they cannot be taken as such. In doing this, a person finally comes to see everything as not-Self, thereby destroying all attachment and attaining *nirvāṇa*. In this process, it is not necessary to 'deny' a Self; the idea simply withers away, as it is seen that no actual instance of such a thing can be found anywhere.

A common query put to Buddhists is: how can there be rebirth if no permanent Self is acknowledged? For Buddhism, though, after death a person is seen as neither annihilated nor continuing in the form of some permanent Self. The true situation is seen as a 'middle way' between these extremes, in the form of *paṭicca-samuppāda* (Sanskrit *pratītya-samutpāda*), 'conditioned arising' or 'dependent origination'. This teaching holds that everything – except for *nirvāṇa*, the unconditioned – arises according to appropriate conditions, and is part of a changing flow of processes. When a person dies, the energy of his or her craving-for-life, and the impetus of his or her past *karma*, causes the stream of consciousness to flow on and find a new life situation. In the case of a human rebirth, conception of a new being occurs in the womb when the appropriate physical conditions come together, along with an available stream-of-consciousness from a deceased being. A new human being then develops in the womb. When born, the individual will have a character and tendencies akin to, and produced by, that of the earlier person. That character will gradually change, though, through new life experiences and actions.

As death is the most important transition in life, it is seen as important to help a person have a 'good death'. Buddhists thus try to ensure that loved ones die recollecting good deeds, or mentally participating in ones done on their behalf. Monks may be asked to chant near them so that they die in a calm, uplifted frame of mind. In

Mahāyāna belief, there is a time-lapse between death and rebirth, and the Tibetans try to guide a 'person' through this period by reading the *Bardo Thotrol* (popularly known as the 'Tibetan Book of the Dead') to them (Conze, 1959, pp. 227–32). In the Theravāda, the orthodox view is that the moment of conception immediately follows the moment of death. Nevertheless, early Theravādin texts contain indications that the early Buddhists accepted a between-lives period, and popular Burmese belief refers to a 'butterfly spirit' leaving the body at death to await rebirth.[5] Belief in a between-lives existence can be seen to approximate to Western notions of the spirit leaving the body at death. However, a being in such a state is still seen as not-Self, being composed of a number of interacting processes of mind and subtle matter, which condition the following rebirth but no longer exist once it is attained. That is, such a 'spirit' is not unitary or immortal, but a bundle of processes driven on by craving for a new life.

THE 'BRIGHTLY SHINING MIND' AND THE '*BUDDHA*-NATURE'

Given the conditioned, limited nature of the processes comprising a human being, how is it that it is held possible to attain the unconditioned, *nirvāṇa*? One reason is that there is a potential for *nirvāṇa* in the depths of the mind. One early Theravādin text says: 'Monks, this mind (*citta*) is brightly shining, but it is defiled by defilements which arrive' (Brown and O'Brian, 1989, pp. 34–5, 71–2). The passage continues by saying that those who know this meditatively develop their minds: implying that they are aware of its potential, usually obscured by defilements such as sensual desire, ill-will and laziness. These arise through the interaction of the mind with the world of the senses – though a newborn baby already has latent defilements left over from previous lives (Horner, 1957, pp. 102–3). Many of these defilements have deep roots in the psyche, but the above passage implies that, at the deepest level of the mind, there is great purity and spiritual brightness. Indeed, the passage also refers to the great benefits of meditatively developing loving-kindness, implying that this is a quality already latent in the mind. Human nature may be stained, then, but not indelibly so. This amounts, in effect, to a doctrine of 'original sinlessness':[6] the inherent purity of human nature. The stains are real enough, but the process of removing them from the human make-up is like smelting the impurities out of gold-ore (Woodward, 1930, pp. 77–8), the qualities of the pure gold being there all along, waiting to be made available for use.

The potential for transformation, even in evil people, is symbolized in the story of Aṅgulimāla or 'Finger-garland', a robber-bandit who had the habit of cutting off the fingers of his victims. One day, the Buddha deliberately went out to meet him, as he had intuited that, with an appropriate nudge from himself, Aṅgulimāla could change his ways for the better. The bandit soon saw and chased him, but though the Buddha seemed to walk at only a slow pace, the running Aṅgulimāla was unable to catch him. On telling the Buddha to stand still, he received the reply that *he* should 'stand still' in the harming of living beings. The Buddha's charisma, psychic power of speedy walking, and his teaching led to a change of heart in Aṅgulimāla, who became his disciple. After ordination and assiduous meditation, he soon attained enlightenment (Horner, 1957, pp. 284–9). From a Buddhist point of view, though Adolf Hitler may still have a long period in a hell as a result of his actions, in some future rebirth he will be a human again, and, if he cultivates his seeds of perfection, may one day become enlightened too.

Theravādins see the 'brightly shining mind' as simply the *bhavaṅga* mind (see p. 78). In deep meditation, its purity comes to infuse more and more of the surface consciousness, bringing a clarity and calm which are an ideal basis for developing meditative insight. In the Mahāyāna, the 'brightly shining mind' came to be known as the *Tathāgata-garbha*, the 'embryo' (*garbha*) of the 'Thus-gone' (Buddha). In China, Korea and Japan, this was seen as the *buddha*-nature (see pp. 11–12, 22–3; Harvey, 1990, pp. 113–18; Williams, 1989, pp. 96–115; Conze *et al.*, 1954, pp. 181–4, 216–17; Brown, 1991). The Indian texts on the *buddha*-nature see it both as a potential to develop, and also as the full-blown perfection of buddhahood, already lying latent within. That is, it has an intrinsic purity which spiritual practice simply uncovers, an idea particularly stressed in the Ch'an (Chinese) or Zen (Japanese) tradition. As expressed by the famous thirteenth-century Zen master Dōgen, Buddhist practice is not in order to *become* a *buddha* – we already are – it is simply to manifest one's intrinsic *buddha*-nature, in more and more of one's life and being.

An alternative perspective, also found in Far Eastern Mahāyāna, is that of the devotional Pure Land schools. These emphasize that the world is now in such a period of moral and spiritual decline that human beings cannot save themselves by their own power. Instead, they must rely on the saving power of the heavenly Buddha Amitābha. Through deep faith in him, the devotee will, at death, be conducted by him to his Pure Land, where the conditions are ideal for attaining enlightenment (Williams, 1989, pp. 251–76; de Bary, 1972, pp. 197–207, 314–44; Conze, 1959, pp. 232–6). Shinran (1173–1263), the founder of the Japanese Jōdo-shin Shū, or 'True Pure Land School', was probably the most extreme of the Pure Land teachers in his condemnation of human nature. He regarded the *buddha*-nature as so deeply buried under the defilements of passion, depravity and ignorance that humans could be described simply as helpless sinners. Their only hope is complete faith in the saving grace of Amitābha, and avoidance of any vain and ungrateful thought that they could contribute to their own salvation.

The causes of suffering and evil

THE SECOND ENNOBLING TRUTH, ON THE ORIGIN OF SUFFERING

In the first sermon, the Buddha identified the cause of *dukkha* thus: 'It is this craving (*taṇhā*; Sanskrit *tṛṣṇā*), giving rise to rebirth, accompanied by delight and attachment, finding delight now here, now there ...'. *Taṇhā* literally means 'thirst', and clearly refers to demanding desires or drives which are ever on the look-out for gratification. These lead to suffering in a number of ways. First, they lead to the suffering of frustration, as their demands for lasting and wholly satisfying fulfilment are perpetually disappointed by a changing and unsatisfactory world. Secondly, they motivate people to perform actions whose karmic results lead on to further rebirths, with their attendant *dukkha*. Thirdly, they lead to quarrels, strife and conflict between individuals and groups.

The first sermon identifies three types of craving: for sensual pleasures, for existence, and for non-existence. The second type refers to the drive for self-protection, for ego-enhancement, and for eternal life after death as 'me'. The third is the drive to get rid of unpleasant situations, things and people. In a strong form, it may lead to the impulse for suicide – the rejection of one's whole present life situation. Such a craving, ironically, helps cause a further rebirth, whose problems will be as bad as, or worse than, the present ones. In order to overcome *dukkha*, the Buddhist path aims not only to limit the expression of craving, but ultimately to use calm and wisdom to uproot it completely from the psyche.

Two other important causes of *dukkha* are 'views' (*diṭṭhi*; Sanskrit *dṛṣṭi*) and 'conceit' (*māna*). The first refers to speculative viewpoints, theories or opinions, especially when they become dogmatic, narrowing a person's whole outlook on life. Such views are seen as hidden forms of self-assertion which lead to conflict with those of other opinions, be this in the form of verbal wrangling or ideological wars and bloody revolutions. Here, it is worth noting that Hitler, Stalin and the Khmer Rouge all had a theory of human nature to motivate and 'justify' their atrocities. The Buddha focused much critical attention on views concerning 'Self'. He felt that these all, in some way or another, located a substantial Self somewhere in the five *khandha*s, so as to lead to attachment.

Deeper than a Self-view, though, is a vague and non-specific feeling of 'I'-ness with respect to the *khandha*s. This is the 'I am' conceit: a deep-rooted self-assertion or egoism, which is concerned about how 'I' measure up to 'others'. So long as such Self or 'I am' ideas exist, one will suffer when what one identifies as 'me' changes or is threatened, and will act in 'self-ish' ways, causing suffering to others. Craving, conceit and views are themselves expressions of, or rooted in, spiritual ignorance – *avijjā* (Sanskrit *avidyā*). This is the persistent misperception of reality, which continually ignores or overlooks life's indications of the Four Ennobling Truths, and so mistakenly grasps at things as permanent, satisfying and Self. Thus classical Buddhism does not trace the root of human faults to wilfulness, a concept at the heart of the Christian concept of sin. Shinran's view, though, is similar to this.

MĀRA: THE EMBODIMENT OF EVIL AND DEATH

In its discussion of evil, Buddhism sometimes sees this as personified in the figure of Māra, 'Death', or the 'Evil One'. In the simplest sense, he is seen as one of the various gods, who uses the power derived from previous goodness so as to tempt people and keep them within the round of rebirth and re-death. Indeed, he is said to have tried to distract Gotama from his meditations leading to his enlightenment.

As with the Christian Satan, a 'fallen angel', he is seen as having had a good past, but uses his power to a perverted end. The sixth heaven, in which Māra dwells on the fringes, is the highest of the sense-desire realms, where most beings, including humans, live. All such beings perceive the world in a way largely coloured by the appearance of things as desirable or undesirable. The *brahmā* gods of the next set of heavens, the realm of pure form, perceive the world in a purer, more direct way. Māra thus exists at a transition point in the process of spiritual development.

Buddhism sees all the heavenly realms as parallel to certain meditative states. The meditative level corresponding to the beginnings of the pure form realm is the first *jhāna*, or meditative trance. It is attained once the spiritual hindrances of sense-desire, ill-will, laziness, agitation, and vacillation have been fully suspended. Māra, in effect, is seen as a being who could not quite make the transition to *jhāna*. Instead of developing power to transcend the realm of sense-desire, he went for power *over* it. This is always a possibility. Māra, in fact, is not the name for just one being, but for a kind of being. Like all gods, a *māra* will eventually die, but his position will be later taken over by another *māra*, another being who has fallen into the same trap, and who seeks to entrap others.

At a more philosophical level, *māra* is a term for all that is *dukkha*, all the limited, conditioned processes that make up the world and living beings. Here, it means 'subject to death'. Accordingly, in the Tibetan 'Wheel of Life', a common didactic painting, the various rebirth realms are depicted within a circle held by a demon representing *māra* – illustrating the fact that all rebirths end in death. Popular Buddhism does not refer to Māra much, though there is belief in nature deities who may be morally ambivalent, and in need of propitiation. For meditators, though, Māra may be a symbolic embodiment of death, and an actual embodiment of human weaknesses, tempting people to fall away from the path.

THE 'PROBLEM OF EVIL'

Over the centuries, Christians have offered many 'solutions' to the theistic 'problem of evil': how can an all-loving, all-powerful, all-knowing God allow evil and suffering in the world? Buddhism avoids this problem by not postulating such a God, and holds that, if a creator-God existed, he would be responsible for the world's suffering. It refers to 'Great Brahmā' as an all-loving god, but one who is limited in power and knowledge. Being mistaken in his belief that he created the world, he is in need of the Buddha's teachings. Suffering and evil, in the Buddhist view, are due to the spiritual ignorance of human beings, and the bad *karma* that they have performed in previous lives. This can even be used to explain the sufferings of animals.

In Mahāyāna Buddhism, though, a problem akin to the theistic problem of evil makes its appearance. The *Ratnagotra-vibhāga* sees the *tathāgata-garbha* (*buddha*-nature) as the basis for all mental activity, including 'unsystematic attention', which wrongly sees the conditioned world as permanent and substantial. This, in turn, is the basis for moral and spiritual defilements. The *Laṅkāvatāra Sūtra* explicitly says that the *tathāgata-garbha* 'holds within it the cause for both good and evil'. In the final analysis, though, *tathāgata-garbha* thought seeks to avoid the conclusion that genuine evil can come out of the pure *buddha*-nature. Thus the defilements are seen as insubstantial illusions produced by ignorance. Why this exists, though, is a mystery that only a *buddha* can fathom.

Buddhist goals

A good rebirth, and entry into a Pure Land, are Buddhist goals already discussed. What, though, of the ultimate goals of Buddhism: *nirvāṇa* and buddhahood? The Theravāda sees *nirvāṇa* as a transcendent state initially experienced in life, and then finally passed into at death. On attaining it, a person becomes an *arahat*, one who has had all possibility of attachment, hatred and delusion destroyed by the experience (Conze *et al.*, 1954, pp. 42–5; Katz, 1982). He or she thus has a radically transformed nature and is imbued with deep, unshakeable calm, profound insight, and warm loving-kindness, coming to fully embody the qualities of the *Dhamma*.

In postulating such a radical transformation of human nature, Buddhism has a very optimistic view of human possibilities, but it sees this as based on a realistic assessment of human weaknesses, their causes, and how to get rid of them. Attaining arahatship takes much dedicated, persistent effort, usually over many lives. But it is seen as a possibility open to all humans. Perhaps the most recent *arahat* in the Theravāda tradition was the Thai meditation master Acharn Mun, who died in 1949. The path can be begun at any time, and lesser benefits than arahatship, in the form of happier life-experiences, are to be found almost from its start. Prior to arahatship, the most crucial transition on the path is 'stream-entry' (Harvey, 1990, pp. 71–2). This occurs when, from sustained meditation, a person gains a first 'distant glimpse' of *nirvāṇa*. By thus attaining the '*Dhamma*-eye' and 'plunging into *Dhamma*', a person enters the 'stream' which will definitely lead to arahatship within seven lives at most. As for the *arahat*, there is no further possibility of rebirth, for all causes of it have been destroyed. When an *arahat* dies, final *nirvāṇa* is entered, and the state of the *arahat* becomes a profound mystery (Harvey, 1990, pp. 65–8). The Buddha did not accept that it could be said that the *arahat* beyond death either 'is', 'is not', 'both is and is not', or 'neither is nor is not'. All such notions mistakenly look for some Self-essence in the *arahat*, and wonder what happens to this after death. Nevertheless, it is clear that an *arahat* is seen neither as annihilated at death, nor as reborn (as some kind of individual being). Beyond that, perhaps all that can be said is that there is a transcendent, timeless state beyond all suffering.

Both the Theravāda and Mahāyāna traditions agree that an *arahat* has attained a somewhat lesser goal than a perfect *buddha*. In the Theravāda, the difference is, first, that a *buddha* is seen as having more extensive knowledge than an ordinary *arahat* (a *buddha* is also an *arahat*). A *buddha* is also seen as rediscovering the timeless *Dhamma* or Truth at a time in human history when it has been forgotten. Teaching it, he makes it possible for others to come to know and experience it, and so become *arahat*s. For the Theravādin, only a few beings need take the longer path, to perfect buddhahood – and some Theravādins have done this. It is best, though, that most seek to practise the *arahat*-path already made available by Gotama Buddha. In the Mahāyāna tradition, a *buddha* is seen as a glorious and omniscient heavenly being, who can live for countless eons before finally passing into final *nirvāṇa* (Harvey, 1990, pp. 125–33; Williams, 1989, pp. 167–84). He is also seen as compassionately sending down help to those in need of assistance and teaching: Gotama Buddha is seen as one such manifestation. Nevertheless, Mahāyānists emphasize that all have a duty, at some time, to tread the long path to perfect buddhahood, for the universe contains countless worlds, and there will always be a need for more *buddha*s to teach and help beings. Those who dedicate themselves to the path to buddhahood are said to be *bodhisattvas*, 'beings-for-enlightenment'. These are seen as more compassionate than *arahats*, for they are willing to spend longer in the round of rebirths, giving help to suffering beings. In stage six of their ten-stage path, they reach a level akin to that of the *arahats*, but rather than then transcending rebirth, they continue, in the form of heavenly saviour beings, until finally ripe for buddhahood. Yet prior to this, they still know *nirvāṇa*. In the Mahāyāna perspective, *nirvāṇa* is, in an ultimate sense, not different from the conditioned world of *saṃsāra*. This is because investigation of the make-up of the conditioned world reveals a mysterious 'emptiness', which cannot be differentiated from the 'emptiness' that is *nirvāṇa*, and also 'buddhaness' (*buddhatā*). Here, 'emptiness' is a term indicative of the lack of inherent nature or essence in anything, which means that the true nature of reality cannot be captured in human language and concepts (Harvey, 1990, pp. 95–104; Williams, 1989, pp. 55–76). The *bodhisattva*, then, is one who increasingly comes to know the nirvanic dimension of the world, and who aids other beings in maturing their *buddha*-nature.

Solutions to the human predicament

In the scheme of the Four Ennobling Truths, the solution to the problems of life, encapsulated in the word *dukkha*, is the practice of the Ennobling Eightfold Path. The Path has eight factors, each described as right or perfect (*sammā*; Sanskrit *samyak*):

1 right view or understanding;

2 right directed thought;

3 right speech;

4 right action;

5 right livelihood;

6 right effort;

7 right mindfulness;

8 right concentration or unification.

These factors are also grouped into three sections (Horner, 1954, pp. 362–3): 3–5 pertain to *sīla* (Sanskrit *śīla*), moral virtue; 6–8 pertain to *samādhi*, meditative cultivation of the heart/mind (*citta*); 1–2 pertain to *paññā* (Sanskrit *prajñā*), or wisdom. The eight factors exist at two basic levels, the ordinary, and the transcendent or noble, so that there is both an ordinary and an Ennobling Eightfold Path (Horner, 1959, pp. 113–21). Most Buddhists seek to practise the ordinary Path, which is perfected only in those who are approaching the lead-up to stream-entry. At stream-entry, a person fully enters the Ennobling Eightfold Path.

At the 'ordinary' level, the Path-factors are as follows. 'Right understanding' (*sammā-diṭṭhi*; Sanskrit *samyak dṛṣṭi*) relates mainly to such matters as *karma* and rebirth, making individuals take full responsibility for their actions. It also covers intellectual, and partial experiential, understanding of the Four Ennobling Truths. Right-directed thought concerns the emotions, with thought rightly channelled towards peaceful freedom from sensuality, and away from ill-will and cruelty to loving-kindness and compassion. Right speech is the well-established abstaining from lying, backbiting, harsh speech and empty gossip. Right action is abstaining from wrong bodily behaviour: onslaught on living beings, taking what is not given (theft and cheating), and wrong conduct with regard to sense-pleasures (adultery, etc.). Right livelihood is avoiding ways of making a living which cause suffering to others: those based on trickery and greed (Horner, 1959, p. 118), or on trade in weapons, living beings, meat, alcoholic drink, or poison. Right effort is directed at developing the mind in a wholesome way: avoiding and undermining states of mind which express attachment, hatred or delusion, and meditatively developing and stabilizing wholesome states of mind. Right mindfulness (*sati*; Sanskrit *smṛti*) is a crucial aspect of any Buddhist meditation, and is a state of keen awareness of mental and physical phenomena as they arise within and around one. Right concentration (*samādhi*) refers to various levels of deep calm known as *jhāna*s: states of inner collectedness arising from attention closely focused on a meditation object. At the 'noble' level, moral virtue becomes spontaneous, and right understanding is true wisdom – knowledge which penetrates into the nature of reality in flashes of profound insight, directly knowing the world as a constant flux of conditioned phenomena.

The order of the eight Path-factors is seen as that of a natural progression, though neither the ordinary nor the Ennobling Path is to be understood as a single progression from the first to the eighth factor. Once developed, the Path-factors mutually support each other to allow a gradual deepening of the way in which the Path is trodden. In terms of the division of the Path into virtue, meditation and wisdom (always given in this order), the Path can be seen to develop as follows. Influenced by good examples, the first commitment will be to develop virtue – a generous and self-controlled way of life for the benefit of self and others. To motivate this, there will be some degree of preliminary wisdom, in the form of some acquaintance with the Buddhist outlook and an aspiration to apply it, expressed as *saddhā* (Sanskrit *śraddhā*) – trustful confidence or faith. With virtue as the indispensable basis for further progress, some meditation may be attempted. With appropriate application, this will lead to the mind becoming calmer, stronger and clearer. This will allow experiential understanding of the *Dhamma* to develop, so that deeper wisdom arises. From this, virtue is strengthened, becoming a basis for further progress in meditation and wisdom. With each more refined development of the virtue–meditation–wisdom sequence, the Path spirals up to a higher level, until the crucial transition of stream-entry is reached. The Ennobling Path then spirals up to arahatship.

In the case of the Mahāyāna *bodhisattva*-path, the transition from its 'ordinary' version to its 'ennobling' version is the 'path of seeing', the first full experience of 'emptiness'. To be ready for the *bodhisattva*-path, a person must be prepared by prior spiritual training, and should then contemplate the plight of suffering beings, and the need for *buddha*s to help them. This prepares the mind for the experience of the arising of the 'thought of enlightenment' (*bodhi-citta*), the heartfelt aspiration to strive for buddhahood for the sake of others (Brown and O'Brian, 1989, pp. 152–68). The aspirant then takes various *bodhisattva*-vows to strengthen his or her resolve. In the Chinese tradition, these vows are part of the ordination ceremony for monks and nuns. The *bodhisattva* path consists, essentially, of the compassion-motivated development of six 'perfections' (*pāramitā*s): generosity, virtue, patience, vigour, meditation and wisdom (Harvey, 1990, pp. 121–4; Williams, 1989, pp. 204–14). Most of their content has parallels in the Theravāda tradition, but Mahāyānists see the underlying motivation as loftier. At the heavenly level, the *bodhisattva* fulfils four more perfections before final buddhahood is attained.

The above says little about devotion, but most Buddhist schools see this as a very useful preliminary and complement to other aspects of practice, as it develops a warm and pure heart and strengthens aspiration (see Chapter 4). Ultimately, though, it must itself be complemented by wisdom based on direct experience. The Mahāyāna provides a greater range of objects of devotion, in the form of the various heavenly *buddha*s and *bodhisattva*s; but Theravādins can equally develop great joy in their devotion to Gotama Buddha, both because of the teachings he gave to the world, and the goal that he embodied. In the Pure Land schools of Far Eastern Mahāyāna, devotion to Amitābha Buddha overshadows and sometimes replaces all other practices. This is expressed mainly through the medium of the oft-repeated chant *Nama Amida Butsu* (Japanese form), 'Hail to Amitābha Buddha!' Through this, a person can let go of 'self-power' – any attempt to improve or save oneself by one's own power – and open up to the saving 'other-power' of Amitābha. The Japanese Nichiren school also emphasizes devotion, though as a form of self-power. This is done by chanting *Na-mu myō-hō ren-ge-kyō*, which focuses on the truth-power embodied in the text known as the *Lotus Sūtra*.

For an ordinary Asian Buddhist, practice consists of some mixture of: generating karmic fruitfulness by supporting monks and contributing to Buddhist festivals and ceremonies; chanting in order to draw down the blessings of the Buddha's Truth, or of the heavenly *buddha*s and *bodhisattva*s; devotional/contemplative chanting; making offerings before *buddha* images; showing respect to and listening to the teachings and chanting of monks; keeping the ethical precepts; meditation on loving-kindness, or on a compassionate *bodhisattva*; and perhaps calming meditation on the breath. If commitment becomes stronger – or if family tradition urges it – a person may become a novice (prior to the age of twenty), or a monk or nun.

Monasticism was part of Buddhism from the very beginning, though originally the monks and nuns followed a wandering, rather than a settled life (Harvey, 1990, pp. 73–5, 217–43). Becoming a monk involves shaving the head – as a sign of the renunciation of vanity – taking a new name, wearing a monastic robe and, most important of all, committing oneself to over 200 monastic rules of training. These include ethical rules on such matters as non-violence and non-stealing, rules of self-discipline concerning complete sexual abstinence and fasting after noon, and rules aimed at producing calm and graceful behaviour. All are intended to aid the monk in becoming aware of, and gradually dealing with, the cravings, attachments and irritabilities that are part of human nature. This process is also aided by the chanting, study, work and meditation that are part of monastic life. Lay-people look to monks and nuns as inspiration, as teachers and advisers, and as focuses of religious giving, so as to do acts of karmic fruitfulness. They also go to them for the performance of a variety of rituals, such as the chanting of blessings, and, in Tibet, the performance of mystery plays. Monks may also act as educators, astrologers and, to some extent, doctors, to the laity. In Japan, however, Buddhism has become more lay-centred, particularly since a government decree in 1872 that all monks (but not nuns) could marry. Most now do so. Thus, the only real Buddhist monastics in Japan are now the nuns, and young men in training for becoming priests – essentially ritual specialists. Post-war Japan has also seen the development of a number of lay-led movements which are seeking to relate Buddhism in new ways to the needs and aspirations of an industrialized urban people.

In Theravāda countries, in Tibet, and to some extent in China, Korea and Vietnam, monasticism remains at the heart of Buddhism. It is the focus for the more intense Buddhist training, and the preserver, transmitter and re-invigorator of the tradition. It supports and inspires lay practice, and its members guide and serve the laity in a range of ways. Perhaps the most archetypal relationship between the laity and the *saṅgha*, or monastic community, is that of alms-giving. In this, the lay householder gives material support for a way of life based on renunciation and 'homelessness'. In 'return' the lay-person experiences the joy of giving to wholesome recipients, thus generating much auspicious, purifying karmic fruitfulness. This is seen as leading both to material benefits, such as good health and success, and to spiritual uplift. Of course, some monks take to monasticism as a lazy way of life, and some laity have a rather acquisitive attitude to accumulating karmic fruitfulness, but such is human nature!

Notes

1 Huston Smith (1958) *The Religions of Man*. New York: Harper Colophon, p. 80.

2 J. Ingersoll (1966) 'Fatalism in village Thailand', *Anthropological*

Quarterly, 39, p. 224.

3 N. Smart (1972) 'Problems of the application of Western terminology to Theravāda buddhism', *Religion*, Spring, p. 39.

4 The *Ariya-saccāni* or Noble-Truths are such because one who experiences their truth, at stream-entry, becomes a (spiritually) Noble person – thus they are best seen as 'Ennobling Truths'.

5 M. Spiro (1971) *Buddhism and Society*. London: George Allen and Unwin, pp. 85 and 249–53.

6 L. S. Cousins (1973) 'Buddhist Jhāna', *Religion*, 3, p. 117.

Further reading

Brown, B. E. (1991) *The Buddha-nature*. Delhi: Motilal Banarsidass.

Brown, K. and O'Brian, J. (eds) (1989) *The Essential Teachings of Buddhism*. London: Rider (translated extracts plus comments, all schools).

Collins, S. (1982) *Selfless Persons: Imagery and Thought in Theravāda Buddhism*. Cambridge: Cambridge University Press.

Conze, E. (1959) *Buddhist Scriptures*. Harmondsworth: Penguin (translations from all schools).

Conze, E., Horner, I. B., Snellgrove, D. and Waley, A. (1954) *Buddhist Texts Through the Ages*. New York: Harper and Row (translations from all schools).

Cousins, L. S. (1996) 'Good or skilful? *Kusala* in canon and commentary', *Journal of Buddhist Ethics* (free at: http://jbe.gold.ac.uk), 3, pp. 136–64.

de Bary, W. T. (1972) *The Buddhist Tradition in India, China and Japan*. New York: Vintage Books (translations from all schools; includes useful introductory essays).

de Silva, P. (1979) *An Introduction to Buddhist Psychology*. London: Macmillan.

Gombrich, R. (1971) *Precept and Practice: Traditional Buddhism in the Rural Highlands of Ceylon*. Oxford: Clarendon.

Harvey, P. (1990) *An Introduction to Buddhism: Teachings, History and Practices*. Cambridge: Cambridge University Press.

Harvey, P. (2000) *An Introduction to Buddhist Ethics: Foundations, Values and Issues*. Cambridge: Cambridge University Press.

Horner, I. B. (1954, 1957, 1959) *Middle Length Sayings*, vols 1–3. London: Pali Text Society (translations of *Majjhima Nikāya*, from Theravāda Pāli Canon).

Katz, N. (1982) *Buddhist Images of Human Perfection*. Delhi: Motilal Banarsidass.

Norman, K. R. (1971) *Elders' Verses*, vol. 2. London: Pali Text Society (translation of *Therīgāthā*, a collection of verses by enlightened nuns from

Theravāda Pāli Canon).
Rhys Davids, C. A. F. (1922) *Kindred Sayings*, vol. 2. London: Pali Text Society (translation from *Saṃyutta Nikāya*, from Theravāda Pāli Canon).
Suzuki, D. T. (1983) *An Introduction to Zen Buddhism* (3rd edn). London: Rider.
Williams, P. (1989) *Mahāyāna Buddhism: The Doctrinal Foundations*. London: Routledge and Kegan Paul.
Woodward, F. L. (1927, 1930) *Kindred Sayings*, vols 4, 5. London: Pali Text Society (translation from *Saṃyutta Nikāya*, from Theravāda Pāli Canon).

3. Portrayals of ultimate reality and of holy and divine beings

Peter Harvey

While Buddhism is not a religion focused on an all-powerful creator 'God', it does accept a range of beings and levels of reality which go beyond our everyday world, and these will be the subject of this chapter. In the Buddhist world-view, ultimate reality is generally not personalized, as a God, much less as a single God. It is seen in more impersonal terms as a state to be attained or realized: *nirvāṇa*. The personal dimension comes in when one looks at those who experience this reality: for Theravāda Buddhism, *arahat*s (saints) and earthly *buddha*s; for Mahāyāna Buddhism, Heavenly *buddha*s and advanced *bodhisattva*s, who are on the brink of buddhahood.

All schools of Buddhism also accept a range of gods: divine beings who have attained heavenly rebirths through their good deeds, but who will sooner or later die and be reborn (see pp. 73–4). *Buddha*s, arahats and *bodhisattva*s are said to be 'teachers of humans and gods', and even gods are said to revere the 'three treasures': the Buddha, the *Dhamma* and *Saṅgha*. Here, the *Dhamma* is the *buddha*s' teaching, the timeless truths they point to, the path of practice, and the states realized on the path, culminating in *nirvāṇa* itself. The *Saṅgha*, as a 'treasure' or 'refuge', are those who have fully or partially realized *nirvāṇa*, who are conventionally symbolized by the monastic community, also known as the *saṅgha*. Buddhism thus lacks a simple contrast between the 'human' and the 'divine'. There are humans, limited gods, and, further, holy beings who have fully or partially experienced that which is truly transcendent, *nirvāṇa*.

The gods

The gods (*devas*) are said to live in 26 heavens of a progressively refined and calm nature (Harvey, 1990a, pp. 34–7, 4–5; Conze, 1959, pp. 222–4). Those of the six lowest heavens gain their rebirth by generosity and moral virtue, and are not too distant from humans to be called on for help with such things as a good harvest, or to discipline troublesome nature spirits (Gombrich, 1971, pp. 191–213). The remaining heavens are all of a more subtle nature, and are only reachable by having attained a corresponding level of meditative calming. The life-span in the heavens is said to vary from 84,000 eons in the highest down to nine million years in the lowest. Yet time passes more quickly for the gods: in the lowest heaven, 50 human years pass in one divine 'day'. While many gods tend to be somewhat complacent about the need for further spiritual effort, some are wise. These include the helpful Sakka (or Indra; ruler of the early Hindu pantheon), who is said to have had a first glimpse of *nirvāṇa*, so as to become a 'Stream-enterer' (see p. 87). Also, the gods of the 'pure abodes' (heavens 18–22) are 'Non-returners', who almost became *arahats* as humans, but who will attain *nirvāṇa* in their present state. In the fourth, Tuṣita, heaven is Metteyya (Sanskrit Maitreya), who is a *bodhisattva* who will be the next *buddha*. Among the higher gods are also the Great Brahmās, said to have attained their level by deep meditation on loving-kindness, compassion, sympathetic joy and equanimity. Such glorious beings, though, have the unfortunate tendency to think themselves eternal creator Gods. The reason for this is explained in Walshe (1987, pp. 75–6, 213–15): periodically, the heaven of Great Brahmā, and lower realms, come to an end. After an eon, they re-appear, and a being is reborn, from a higher heaven, as a Great Brahmā again. In time, he becomes lonely and longs for the presence of others. Soon his wish is fulfilled, simply because other higher gods die and happen to be reborn, through their *karma*, as his ministers and retinue. Not remembering his previous life, Great Brahmā therefore thinks 'I am Brahmā, Great Brahmā . . . the Maker, the Creator . . . these other beings are my creation'. His godlings agree with this erroneous conclusion, and when some eventually die and are reborn as humans, they develop the power to remember their previous life, and consequently teach that Great Brahmā is the eternal creator of all beings! Buddhism sees no need for a creator of the world, as it postulates no ultimate beginning, and regards the world as sustained by natural laws. Moreover, if there were a creator, he would be seen as responsible for the world's sufferings. Yet a Great Brahmā's compassion is much valued, for such a being requests a *buddha* to teach after his enlightenment, when he wonders if anyone else could understand his profound discovery (Walshe, 1987, pp. 213–15).

Nirvāṇa in Theravāda Buddhism

Nirvāṇa fits within the Theravāda framework of belief as the third of the Four Ennobling Truths (see pp. 75–6): *dukkha* (suffering/unsatisfactoriness), craving as its cause, *nirvāṇa* as its cessation, through the ceasing of craving, and the Ennobling Eightfold Path, of morality, calming meditation and wisdom, as the way to the end of *dukkha*. *Dukkha* is equated with the five 'groups' (*khandhas*) of processes making up a person: material form, feeling, cognition, constructing activities and (discriminative) consciousness. *Nirvāṇa* is both a state realized during life, by one who thus becomes an *arahat*, and a state entered when such a person dies, never to be reborn (Conze *et al.*, 1954, pp. 96–7). *Nirvāṇa* literally means 'extinction', or 'quenching', being the word used for the 'extinction' of a fire. *Nirvāṇa* is the extinction of the 'fires' of attachment, hatred and delusion – the causes of *dukkha* – and of the processes of 'birth, ageing and death' – *dukkha* itself. *Nirvāṇa* during life is defined as the destruction of attachment, hatred and delusion, the 'defilements'. When individuals who have destroyed these die, they are totally beyond the remaining 'fires' of birth, ageing and death.

Nirvāṇa is seen as truly profound and mysterious (Harvey, 1990a, pp. 60–4; Conze, 1962, pp. 69–79; Brown and O'Brian, 1989, pp. 17–18, 62–4; Conze *et al.*, 1954, pp. 92–102; Conze, 1959, pp. 155–9). It is therefore not so much to be talked about as experienced; so more is said on how to attain it than the experience itself. Descriptions of *nirvāṇa* are not absent, but they tend to be negative, saying what *nirvāṇa* is *not*. This is to ensure it is not wrongly identified with any limited worldly phenomenon. One famous description is: 'Since, monks, there exists the unborn, unbecome, unmade, unconditioned (*asaṅkhata*), then there is apparent the leaving behind, here, of the born, become, made, conditioned' (*Udāna*, pp. 80–1; see Brown and O'Brian, 1989, pp. 63–4). This sees *nirvāṇa* as not subject to birth or, as said elsewhere, to dying; it is the Deathless which is beyond time and change. It is not the product of any process, is not constructed or conditioned by anything else: it can thus never fall apart or come to an end. Again:

> There exists, monks, that sphere where there is: (i) neither solidity, nor cohesion, not heat, nor motion; (ii) nor the sphere of infinite space, nor the sphere of infinite consciousness, nor the sphere of nothingness, nor the sphere of neither-perception-nor-non-perception; (iii) neither this world, nor a world beyond, nor both; (iv) nor sun-and-moon; (v) there, monks, I say there is no coming or going, nor maintenance, nor falling away, nor arising; (vi) that, surely, is without support (*patiṭṭhā*), it has no functioning, it has no object (*ārammaṇa*); (vii) just this is the end of *dukkha*. (*Udāna*, p. 80; numbers added. See Conze *et al.*, 1954, pp. 94–5)

That is, *nirvāṇa* is (i) totally beyond the four elements of matter, and (ii) beyond even the four 'formless' heavens, where only mental states occur. It is thus (iii) beyond *any* world, human, divine or whatever (for they all have their limitations). It is (iv) not any place in the cosmos, yet has its own intrinsic brilliance, outshining anything else. It is (v) beyond the processes involved in dying and being reborn. It is (vi) unsupported, as it exists without dependence on anything else; it is not something that 'functions', according to conditioning factors; and unlike all mental states, it does not have an object which it is aware of (and which would condition it). Finally (vii), it is the end of all *dukkha*: of all that is suffering, unsatisfactory, limited, imperfect. It is thus truly worthy of realization.

Among 'negative' characteristics of *nirvāṇa* are three emphasized in the developed Theravāda meditative tradition (Conze, 1962, pp. 59–71). In this, a meditator is said to perceive *nirvāṇa* as either the 'signless', the 'undirected' or as 'emptiness' (*suññatā*) (cf. p. 88). It is 'signless' in lacking any signs or indications that the mind can become attached to, being known in this way by those with strong insight into the ephemeral, limited nature of all conditioned processes. *Nirvāṇa* is 'undirected' or 'wishless' in that it is attained by the total 'letting go' which comes when all conditioned processes are seen as *dukkha*. *Nirvāṇa* is 'emptiness' in being void of any grounds for the delusion of a permanent, substantial Self, and because it cannot be conceptualized in any view which links it to 'I' or 'mine' or 'Self' (see p. 80). It is known in this respect by one with deep insight into everything as not-Self (*anattā*), 'empty' of Self (Brown and O'Brian, 1989, pp. 42–3, 50–1, 54, 77; Conze *et al.*, 1954, p. 91). Not only does Buddhism see ultimate reality as impersonal, then; even a human 'person' is seen as a collection of mutually conditioning mental and physical processes (*dhammas*) which are not a substantial Self, I or personal entity. As an overall collection, these changing states have no more than a relatively stable 'personality' or character-style.

Positive descriptions of *nirvāṇa* are generally of a poetic, suggestive nature. Thus it is said to be: the 'further shore' (beyond this 'shore' of life and its inherent suffering); the 'island amidst the flood' (a refuge from danger and suffering); the '(cool) cave of shelter' (a powerful image of peace and rest in the hot Indian climate); the marvellous. Certain positive descriptions give a less poetic indication of its nature. Thus it is 'peace, beyond the realm of reason, stable ... the sorrowless, stainless state ... the calming down of constructing activities, bliss' (see Brown and O'Brian, 1989, p. 64). It is truth and purity (Woodward, 1927, pp. 261–4). Some early canonical passages hint that it may be a radically transformed state of consciousness (*viññāṇa*). Such passages talk of *nirvāṇa* as a consciousness 'in which nothing can be made manifest' (Walshe, 1987, pp. 179–80), and of *nirvāṇa* being realized when consciousness, through non-attachment, is without any object (*ārammaṇa*) to act as its support (*patiṭṭhā*) (Woodward, 1925, pp. 45–6): which accords with item (vi) from *Udāna*, p. 80, above. Nevertheless, the developed Theravāda tradition does not take up this hint. While *nirvāṇa* is itself seen as objectless, an enlightened person's consciousness is seen to have it as its object. For the commentator Buddhaghosa's discussion of *nirvāṇa*, seeking to avoid both an over-negative or over-positive view, see Conze *et al.* (1954, pp. 100–2).

As *nirvāṇa* is beyond space and time, no place or time is 'nearer' or 'more distant' from it; but it exists as an ever-present possibility to be realized. Indeed, it is said that it is 'in' – i.e., to be realized in – the body (Brown and O'Brian, 1989, pp. 53–4). It is often thought that *nirvāṇa* during life is an ever-present state of the *arahat*, but it would seem that this cannot be so. As *nirvāṇa* is synonymous with the cessation of all *dukkha*, and *nirvāṇa* during life is not seen as inferior to *nirvāṇa* beyond death in any respect, it cannot be ever-present; for the *arahat* will sometimes have physical pain, and his normal mental processes are all changing and impermanent, hence *dukkha* (Conze *et al.*, 1954, pp. 66–7). *Nirvāṇa* during life must thus be a specific experience, in which the defilements are destroyed for ever, and in which there is a temporary stopping of all conditioned states. During life or beyond death, *nirvāṇa* is the unconditioned cessation of all unsatisfactory, conditioned phenomena. During life, it is where these phenomena stop, followed by their recurrence in the arising of normal experiences of the world; once attained, this stopping can be returned to. Beyond death (not 'after' it: *nirvāṇa* is beyond time), it is where they stop for good. Yet *nirvāṇa* is seen as existing whether or not anyone attains it. So one could perhaps say that the *arahat*'s experience of *nirvāṇa* during life is one of 'participating in' that unborn, unconditioned blissful reality.

As a proximate goal, *nirvāṇa* is the focus for a minority of Theravāda Buddhists. It has never been seen as *easy* to attain, and it is orthodox belief to say that people's true understanding and practice of the *Dhamma* has declined over the centuries since the Buddha's time. Most lay-people and many monks aim for a better rebirth next time, as a god or wealthy human, and aspire that, over many lives, they will become spiritually mature enough to make the effort to attain *nirvāṇa*. A common aspiration is that, in a future life, they will be in the presence of the next Buddha, Metteyya, and attain *nirvāṇa* under his guidance. A minority of middle-class lay-people now aspire for *nirvāṇa* within a few lifetimes. The minority of monks who are ascetic 'forest-dwellers' specializing in meditation also seek to attain arahatship or at least stream-entry (a first glimpse of *nirvāṇa*) in this life or soon after. For discussions of contemporary attitudes to the attainment of *nirvāṇa*, for Myanmar (Burma) see Spiro (1971, pp. 76–84); and for Sri Lanka see Gombrich (1971, pp. 16–17, 214–24, 290–2). Whether or not a person has *nirvāṇa* as a proximate goal, the 'contemplation of peace' – of the qualities of *nirvāṇa* – is recommended as a meditation leading to the arising of bliss, peace and self-confidence.

The Buddha and *arahat*s in Theravāda Buddhism

The person known to history as 'the Buddha' is generally known to Theravādins as Gotama Buddha. As a '*buddha*' he is one of the 'Awakened Ones' who arise over the ages. It is held that a 'hundred thousand eons ago', in a past life, he met and was inspired by a previous *buddha*, Dīpaṅkara (Conze *et al.*, 1954, pp. 82–4; Conze,

1959, pp. 20–4). He therefore resolved to strive for buddhahood, by becoming a *bodhisattva*. He knew that, while he could become an *arahat* under Dīpaṅkara, the path he had chosen would take many more lives to complete. It would, however, culminate in his becoming a perfect *buddha*, one who would bring benefit to countless beings by rediscovering and teaching the timeless truths of *Dhamma* in a period when they had been lost to human society. He then spent many lives as a human, animal and god, building up the moral and spiritual perfections necessary for buddhahood. Over the ages, he meets and is taught by a number of past *buddhas*. All these are said to go through a series of parallel events in their lives, for they are seen as fulfilling an eternal pattern of *Dhamma* that is of cosmic importance (Walshe, 1987, pp. 199–211). In descriptions of his life and character, Gotama is portrayed as a humane, tranquil, compassionate figure, who used his sharp, analytic intelligence and acute observation to guide those who sought the Beyond in which lies true happiness and an end to *dukkha* (Harvey, 1990a, pp. 14–31). His charismatic presence inspired many, and is even said to have drawn to him many divine beings. While modern Theravādins sometimes say that he was 'just a human', this is usually meant as an implicit contrast to Jesus, seen as the 'Son of God', or to the more divinized Mahāyāna view of the Buddha. It may also be due to a modern demythologizing. In the Theravāda Canon, Gotama was seen as *born* a human, though one with extraordinary abilities because of the perfections built up as a *bodhisattva*. Once he had attained enlightenment, though, he had gone beyond the deep-rooted unconscious traits that would make him a god or human; so he was neither of these, but a *buddha* (Conze *et al.*, 1954, pp. 104–5). In perfecting his human-ness, he had transcended it.

The Buddha is seen as having a mysterious nature closely linked to the *Dhamma*: 'Who, Vakkali, sees *Dhamma*, he sees me; who sees me, sees *Dhamma*' (Conze *et al.*, 1954, p. 103). He is one who 'has *Dhamma* as body' and who is '*Dhamma*-become' (Conze *et al.*, 1954, pp. 112–13). That is, he has fully exemplified the *Dhamma*-as-Path, in his personality or 'body', and has fully realized *nirvāṇa*, the supreme *Dhamma* (Brown and O'Brian, 1989, p. 63). The *arahat* is no different in these respects, for he is described as 'become the supreme' (*brahma-bhūta*) (Conze *et al.*, 1954, p. 42), a term equivalent to '*Dhamma*-become'. While Christians see Jesus as God-become-human, then, Buddhists see the Buddha (and *arahats*) as human-become-*Dhamma*. A *buddha* or *arahat* is 'deep, immeasurable, hard-to-fathom as is the great ocean' (Conze *et al.*, 1954, p. 106). Having 'become *Dhamma*', their enlightened nature can only really be fathomed by one who has 'seen' *Dhamma*, as *nirvāṇa*, with the '*Dhamma*-eye' of stream-entry.

The *arahat* is one who has been radically transformed by the complete destruction of attachment, hatred and delusion (Katz, 1982; Brown and O'Brian, 1989, p. 81; Conze *et al.*, 1954, pp. 42–5). His or her actions are pure and spontaneous: 'Calm is his mind, calm is his speech, calm is his behaviour who, rightly knowing, is wholly freed, perfectly peaceful and equipoised' (*Dhammapada*, v. 96). He 'keeps his cool' under all circumstances. While he may experience physical pain (as a result of past *karma*), no mental anguish at this can arise, for it is not identified with as 'mine' (Conze, 1959, pp. 159–62). Even the threat of death does not ruffle him, for he has transcended the idea of 'I', and so has nothing to feel threatened. The *arahat* has a strong mind, 'like a thunderbolt', in which flashes of insight arise, and he has fully developed the 'seven factors of enlightenment': mindful alertness, investigation of *Dhamma*, vigour, joy, tranquillity, concentration and equanimity. While he is one who has seen through the delusion of a permanent Self or I, lacking the 'I am' conceit, he nevertheless has an empirical self, or character, which is very well developed: he is 'one of developed self' (*bhāvit-atta*), not a 'small' person.

The Buddha is himself called an *arahat* – one who has fully experienced *nirvāṇa* – but he had a more extensive knowledge than other *arahat*s. For example, he could remember as far back into previous lives as he wanted, while other *arahat*s had limitations on such a power, or may not even have developed it. A *buddha* is seen as one who can come to know anything he pleases about the past and present, and can make many valid predictions about the future, such as how a person will be reborn. From his vast knowledge (Woodward, 1930, p. 370), he selects what is spiritually useful. Having rediscovered the Path, he skilfully makes it known to others, thus, enabling them to become *arahat*s (Brown and O'Brian, 1989, p. 82). Like him, they then become a *tathāgata*, a 'Thus-gone' or 'Truth-attained One'.

The Buddha was often asked about the destiny of a *tathāgata* after death: could it be said that he 'is', that he 'is not' (being annihilated), that he 'both is and is not', or that he 'neither is nor is not'? The

Buddha set aside these questions without answering them: they were 'undetermined' (Harvey, 1990a, pp. 65–8; Woodward, 1927, pp. 265–83). One reason for this was that he saw speculating on them as a time-wasting side-track from spiritual practice. Demanding answers to them was like a man, shot with a poisoned arrow, refusing to let a doctor cure him until he knew everything about who shot the arrow, and what the arrow was made of: such a man would soon die. The important thing was to get on with the task of overcoming *dukkha*. Moreover, the Buddha also saw that his questioners were really asking about what they conceived of as the fate of an (enlightened) substantial *Self* after death; as no such thing could be found during life, it was meaningless to discuss its state after death (Woodward, 1927, pp. 278–9).

Besides the above, what might the Buddha's silence on this issue mean? It is clearly unacceptable to say that a *tathāgata* is annihilated after death, for this is the view of the second undetermined question, which is seen as particularly pernicious: for only *dukkha* (the conditioned personality factors) ends at death (Woodward, 1925, pp. 93–6). Having destroyed all causes of rebirth, though, it cannot be said that a *tathāgata* 'is' after death, in a rebirth; nor that a *part* of him is reborn ('both is and is not'); nor that he is reborn in the very attenuated 'sphere of neither-perception-nor-non-perception' ('neither is nor is not'). Asking the four questions on a *tathāgata* is said to be like asking the meaningless question of which direction a quenched fire had gone in: east, west, south or north (Conze *et al.*, 1954, p. 106). Having said this, the Buddha stressed that a *tathāgata* (even in life) is 'deep, immeasurable, hard-to-fathom as is the great ocean'. While to a Western-educated person an extinct fire goes nowhere because it does not exist, the Buddha's audience in ancient India would generally have thought of it as going back into a non-manifested state as latent heat. The simile of the extinct fire thus suggests that the state of an enlightened person beyond death is one which is beyond normal comprehension, not that it is a state of nothingness: 'There exists no measuring of one who has gone out (like a flame). That by which he could be referred to no longer exists for him. When all phenomena are removed, then all ways of describing have also been removed' (Conze, 1962, pp. 77–9, cf. 113–14). Silence again. The only whisper in the silence is a hint that, beyond death, an enlightened person's consciousness may remain, in a radically transformed, 'unsupported' form (Conze *et al.*, 1954, p.

43); it would thus be objectless, unlimited, unconditioned, timeless: *nirvāṇa* (Harvey, 1995).

The Theravāda tradition emphasizes that the Buddha, since his death, is beyond contact with the world and cannot respond to prayer or worship. There is, though, a widely held belief in a kind of compassionate '*buddha*-force' which will remain in the world for as long as Buddhism is practised. This power-for-good can be drawn on through the Buddha's teaching (*Dhamma*) and even through the bodily relics which remained after his cremation. The chanting of certain texts known as *paritta*s is also seen as drawing down a protective power, both by releasing a truth-power inherent in the words of the Buddha, and by pleasing those gods who are Buddhist (Harvey, 1990a, pp. 180–2). At the popular level, Buddhists can also behave as if the Buddha is a being who actively responds to prayer. Richard Gombrich has described this situation by saying that while, *cognitively*, the Buddha is acknowledged as beyond worldly contact, *affectively*, at the level of feelings, he is often looked on as a living source of benefit (Gombrich, 1971, pp. 81–2, 122, 139–42).

The Mahāyāna perspective on *arahat*s and the Buddha

In the Mahāyāna, the final goal is not arahatship, but full, perfect buddhahood, a state of omniscience and compassion, which facilitates the liberation of countless beings. The teaching directed at the attainment of arahatship, the Four Ennobling Truths, is seen as simply a provisional teaching given by the Buddha to those not yet ready to understand the full teaching (Conze *et al.*, 1954, pp. 124–7). The *arahat* is seen as still having a subtle pride, and as lacking in compassion in his hope of escaping the round of rebirths, thus leaving unenlightened beings to fend for themselves. For the Mahāyāna, true *nirvāṇa* is only attained at buddhahood, and the way to this high goal is the path of the *bodhisattva*, which takes many, many lives of selfless striving. In the ten-stage path to buddhahood, *bodhisattva*s, at stage six, reach a level akin to that of the *arahat*s and could leave the round of rebirths if they wished. However, from compassion, they continue in the round of rebirths until they have sufficient spiritual perfections to attain full buddhahood (see further, pp. 109–10, 113–14).

According to the standards of arahatship preserved by the

Theravāda, the charge that the *arahat* is proud and selfish is absurd. By definition, he or she is one who has finally destroyed the 'I am' conceit, the root of all egoism and selfishness. He is also described as imbued with lovingkindness and as compassionately teaching others. The Theravāda still acknowledges that the long path to buddhahood, over many many lives, is the loftiest practice, as it aims at the salvation of countless beings. Nevertheless, while this *bodhisattva*-path has been and is practised by a few Theravādins (often lay-people), it is seen as a way for the heroic few only. Most have gratefully made use of Gotama Buddha's teachings so as to move towards arahatship.

In the Mahāyāna perspective, Gotama is referred to as Śākyamuni (Sage of the Śākyas) Buddha. Unlike in the Theravāda, he is not seen to have attained buddhahood in his life in the fifth century BCE. In the *Lotus Sūtra*, the Buddha explains that he became enlightened an unimaginable number of eons ago (Conze *et al.*, 1954, pp. 140–3; Williams, 1989, pp. 167–84). Since that time, over the ages, he has already appeared on earth in the form of past *buddha*s such as Dīpaṅkara (Brown and O'Brian, 1989, pp. 220–1). All such earthly *buddha*s teach those of lesser understanding that *buddha*s pass into final *nirvāṇa*, beyond contact with living beings, when they die. This is only a skilful means, however, to ensure that people do not become overly dependent on *buddha*s, but actually use the spiritual medicine that *buddha*s give. In fact, the heavenly Buddha (also known as Śākyamuni), who appeared in the form of earthly *buddha*s, will live on for twice the time that has passed since he became enlightened; only then will he pass into final *nirvāṇa*.

The historical Buddha is thus seen as a manifestation skilfully projected into earthly life by a long-enlightened transcendent being, who is still available to teach through visionary experiences (Conze *et al.*, 1954, pp. 139–40). At the popular level, the omniscient Śākyamuni Buddha is seen as an omnipresent, eternal being, watching over the world and supremely worthy of worship. While he is seen as enlightened for a hugely long length of time, however, the idea is still expressed that he became a *buddha* by practising the *bodhisattva*-path, starting out as an ordinary being. He is, then, neither a recently enlightened human who has passed into final *nirvāṇa*, nor an eternal monotheistic God-type figure. As a *buddha*, he does not exist forever, and is only 'eternal' in that he knows, and has become identical with, that which lies *beyond* time.

The Mahāyāna on *nirvāṇa*

The Mahāyāna perspective not only sees the Buddha in a different way, but also reassesses the relationship between *nirvāṇa* and the world (Eliade, 1987, vol. X, pp. 448–56). For early Buddhism and the Theravāda school, *nirvāṇa*, as the blissful unconditioned, is a clear contrast to the conditioned world in which we live: *saṃsāra*, the realm of rebirth and of constant change and suffering. Yet for the Mahāyāna, *nirvāṇa* and *saṃsāra*, when properly understood with insight and wisdom by the advanced *bodhisattva*, are seen as not different at all! The earliest expression of this perspective is found in the *Perfection of Wisdom (Prajñā-pāramitā) Sūtra*s (first century BCE and following) and in the philosophical school related to them, the Madhyamaka (founder Nāgārjuna, *c.* 150–250 CE) (see p. 47; Harvey, 1990a, pp. 95–104; Williams, 1989, pp. 37–76).

In the earlier literature known as the *Abhidharma*, personality had been analysed down into sets of interacting mental or physical processes known as *dharma*s (Pāli *dhamma*s). All of these were said to be 'empty' (*śūnya*) of a permanent, substantial Self. In the *Perfection of Wisdom* texts and the Madhyamaka school, the *dharma*s were said to be 'empty' in a further sense. As they could only be understood as part of an interacting web of *dharma*-processes, no *dharma* could exist or be anything on its own. All that a *dharma* 'is', is derivable from the other *dharma*s which condition it; but the same applies to them also. So a *dharma* has no 'nature' of its own, nothing 'belonging' to it apart from its relationship to other *dharma*s. *Dharma*s are thus said to be 'empty' of 'own-nature' (*svabhāva*), to lack any inherent nature of their own. They are thus said to share the mysterious quality of 'emptiness' (*śūnyatā*). This term points to the radical inter-relationship of *dharma*s, and thus to their relativity: they only exist in relationship to each other. More than this, the term points to the indescribable nature of reality. Language splits the world up into separate bits, and then tries to fit these back together to some extent by talking of various kinds of relationship between them. But on the *Perfection of Wisdom*/ Madhyamaka analysis, there really *are* no truly *separate* bits in the first place; so language will always distort to some extent. The term 'emptiness', though, can be used as a pointer to the fact that, in its true thusness or suchness (*tathatā*) – its as-it-is-ness or whatness – reality is not capable of being grasped in concepts. Yet this is precisely how *nirvāṇa* had always been seen: as an 'emptiness' that was beyond being grasped in positive concepts. Thus the unconditioned *nirvāṇa* cannot be differentiated from, is not different from, *saṃsāra*. As expressed in the brief text known as the '*Heart' Perfection of Wisdom Sūtra*, none of the five aspects of personality can be differentiated from nirvanic emptiness, for example: 'material form is emptiness, and the very emptiness is material form; emptiness does not differ from material form, material form does not differ from emptiness' (Conze *et al.*, 1954, pp. 152–3; Brown and O'Brian, 1989, pp. 200–2). In the inconceivable interacting field of emptiness, moreover, nothing stands out as a separate entity; so the *Heart Sūtra* continues by saying that 'in emptiness' there are none of the five aspects of personality, or even any of the Four Ennobling Truths, including *nirvāṇa*. All such provisional, limited concepts are transcended when the mind can truly let go, from insight into emptiness. And yet in doing so, true *nirvāṇa* is attained. As expressed in the *Diamond-cutter (Vajracchedikā) Perfection of Wisdom Sūtra*, to attain *nirvāṇa*:

> the *Bodhisattva*, the great being, should produce an unsupported (*apratiṣṭhita*) thought, i.e., a thought which is nowhere supported, a thought unsupported by sights, sounds, smells, tastes, touchables, or mind-objects. (Conze, 1968, pp. 47–8)

Such a *nirvāṇa* is seen as experienced by advanced *bodhisattva*s, of stage seven onwards, who remain in (the heavenly levels of) *saṃsāra* while knowing it is no different from *nirvāṇa*. The *nirvāṇa* they will reach at buddhahood is only superior to this in involving omniscience. The *nirvāṇa* experienced by advanced *bodhisattva*s is known as *apratiṣṭhita-nirvāṇa*: 'unsupported *nirvāṇa*', also translated as '*nirvāṇa* without standstill'. It is seen as a state in which the *bodhisattva*s are not resting content in *saṃsāra*, but nor have they abandoned it to rest content in *nirvāṇa*. Their minds can fluidly move between both. How these ideas might relate to earlier hints on *nirvāṇa* as a consciousness which is 'unsupported' (*apatiṭṭhita*: Pāli equivalent of Sanskrit *apratiṣṭhita*) is yet to be determined (see Harvey, 1995, pp. 214–26).

While the Madhyamaka was one of the major philosophical schools of Indian Mahāyāna, the other was the Yogācāra (Harvey, 1990a, pp. 104–13; Williams, 1989, pp. 77–95). This school produced a slightly different perspective on *nirvāṇa*. In its analysis, the world as we experience it is something which is purely mental. *If* there is anything beyond consciousness and mental states, we have no way of knowing: for these are all we ever experience. The content of a person's experience is said to be projected out of his or her deep unconsciousness, the *ālaya-vijñāna*, or 'storehouse consciousness' (Brown and O'Brian, 1989, pp. 106–7). This stores the traces left by one's previous *karma*/actions, which later mature to produce details of a world of apparent 'sights' and 'sounds' etc. The aim of Yogācāra meditations is to stop being taken in by these apparently 'external' objects, and to recognize them as mental projections. Further than that, the meditator should come to realize that the very idea of an inner 'subject' is itself linked to the contrasting idea of 'external' objects. When 'external' objects are transcended, so must a supposed 'inner' subject or Self be transcended. There is simply thought-only, with no 'inside' or 'outside' (Conze *et al.*, 1954, pp. 209–11; Brown and O'Brian, 1989, pp. 205–6). When this is fully realized, there is said to be 'reversal of the basis' (*āśraya-parāvṛtti*): that is, a revolution in the storehouse consciousness which is the 'basis' (*āśraya*) of the world as we know it. This 'reversal' or 'turning back' disrupts the normal flow of apparent objects, and lets the interpreting mind, the *manas*, turn round to know its basis. As is stated in a Yogācāra-related text, the *Laṅkāvatāra Sūtra, nirvāṇa* is, then, 'the storehouse consciousness which is realized inwardly, after a reversal has taken place' (Conze *et al.*, 1954, p. 207; Brown and O'Brian, 1989, pp. 203–4). Yet as *nirvāṇa* is beyond time, this cannot be an actual change, just a cessation of delusions, so, as in the Madhyamaka, 'there is no difference between *saṃsāra* and *nirvāṇa*' (Conze *et al.*, 1954, p. 207).

The *Laṅkāvatāra Sūtra* also contains elements of a strand of thought which became very influential in China and other parts of East Asia. This relates to the idea of the *tathāgata-garbha*, the 'embryo of the *tathāgata*', also known as the *buddha*-nature (see pp. 82–3; Harvey, 1990a, pp. 113–18; Williams, 1989, pp. 96–115; Brown and O'Brian, 1989, pp. 105–6; Conze *et al.*, 1954, pp. 181–4, 216–17). In the *Laṅkāvatāra Sūtra* (Suzuki, 1932, pp. 190–3) this is equated with the storehouse consciousness. The *tathāgata-garbha* is seen as an inner radiant purity which is the seed of enlightenment, though it is obscured by spiritual ignorance and other defilements. Indeed, without these obscurations, it is itself enlightenment: while being empty of all defilements, it is replete with the qualities of buddhahood. These, then, do not so much need to be developed, as uncovered, known and shown in one's actions. This approach is that favoured by the Ch'an (Chinese; Japanese Zen) school. Like most schools of Chinese and Japanese Buddhism, this talks little of *nirvāṇa*, with its Indian associations of escape-from-rebirth, and links with the 'discredited' *arahat* ideal. Rather, it focuses on 'awakening' (Chinese *wu*) or buddhahood. In the dominant, 'southern' strand of Ch'an/Zen, it is emphasized that one does not need to work at gradually purifying the mind of defilements, for these are empty, not ultimately real (Brown and O'Brian, 1989, p. 210). Rather, one should seek insight into one's pure, innate *buddha*-nature, and seek to express this in all one's actions. Thus Dōgen (1200–53), who introduced the Sōtō form of Zen into Japan, emphasized that sitting in meditation is not something done so as to become a *buddha*; one is already a *buddha*, and meditation is simply the best way to manifest this (Brown and O'Brian, 1989, pp. 265–7). Besides meditation, Ch'an/Zen has also seen enlightenment expressed in actions that are done with great awareness and compassion, and which combine the disciplined restraint of personal desires and spontaneous creativity, seen as an outpouring of the *buddha*-nature. The masters embodying these ideals have varied from fierce, unconventional, iconoclastic characters, to clowning 'fools', to saintly ascetic figures. All have emphasized: look within and find the *buddha*-nature.

Also influential in East Asian Buddhism, particularly in the Hua-yen school, is the outlook of the *Avataṃsaka Sūtra* (see pp. 42–3; Harvey, 1990a, pp. 118–20; Williams, 1989, pp. 116–38; Brown and O'Brian, 1989, pp. 207–8). This sees enlightenment as the omniscient vision of reality as the *Dharma*-realm: a vast, harmonious and wonderful array of phenomena which exist as an interpenetrating network of processes. In this, each particular reflects and is related to everything else in the cosmos, and the whole mystery of reality is present even in a grain of dust.

The Mahāyāna view of *bodhisattva*s and *buddha*s

The Mahāyāna is focused on the *bodhisattva*, whose task is to help beings compassionately while maturing his or her own wisdom (*prajñā*) (Harvey, 1990a, pp. 121–4; Williams, 1989, pp. 185–214; Conze *et al.*, 1954, pp. 127–35). From this, he knows that the beings helped are not ultimately different from himself, for 'self' and 'other' are equally empty of separate reality (Brown and O'Brian, 1989, pp. 158–60). He or she can also rub shoulders with wrong-doers, in an effort to 'reach' them, knowing that their bad characteristics are not inherent realities. Any potential pride at the good done is tempered by the reflection that his or her karmic fruitfulness is also 'empty'. A person may even do a deed leading to hell, if this is a necessary part of helping someone else and giving them a more wholesome outlook on life.

*Bodhisattva*s begin as ordinary human beings who have been stirred by the sufferings of all sentient beings to seek to become *buddha*s. With compassion as the driving force, they begin to practise the six 'perfections' of a *bodhisattva*: generosity, moral virtue, patience, vigour, meditation, and intuitive wisdom (Brown and O'Brian, 1989, pp. 168–86; Conze *et al.*, 1954, pp. 135–9). When insight reaches a deep level, they attain a first glimpse of emptiness, at the 'Path of Seeing'. This is the entry to the path of the Noble *(Ārya) Bodhisattva*. They then develop the perfections through the first six stages of the Noble *bodhisattva* path. On the sixth, they attain the true perfection of wisdom, and from the seventh to tenth stage, they are 'Great Beings': heavenly saviour-beings who aid beings in a variety of ways. They send manifestations into many worlds, so as to teach and help beings in appropriate ways; they also transfer karmic fruitfulness ('merit') from their vast store, so that beings who pray to them receive it as a free spiritual uplift of grace. Beyond the tenth stage, they finally attain buddhahood, in a heavenly realm of existence.

Buddhahood is understood according to the *Tri-kāya* or 'Three body' doctrine (Harvey, 1990a, pp. 125–8; Williams, 1989, pp. 167–84). This sees it as having three aspects: (1) the *nirmāṇa-kāya*, or 'Transformation-body', (2) the *sambhoga-kāya*, or 'Enjoyment-body', and (3) the *dharma-kāya*, or '*Dharma*-body'. The 'Transformation-body' refers to earthly *buddha*s, seen as teaching devices projected into the world to show people the path to buddhahood. The 'Enjoyment-body' is seen as a refulgent subtle body which is the product of the karmic fruitfulness of a *bodhisattva*'s training. It is adopted by a *buddha* for the 'enjoyment' of Noble *bodhisattva*s: in this form, the *buddha* teaches them through visionary experiences or, for the heavenly Great Beings, by a direct presence. The heavenly Buddha Śākyamuni is of the Enjoyment-body type, but there are many others, 'as numerous as there are grains of sand on the banks of the river Ganges', dwelling in various regions of the universe. Their form and wondrous powers vary slightly according to their past *bodhisattva*-vows and karmic fruitfulness. Each Enjoyment-body *buddha* is seen as presiding over his own 'Buddha Land' (*Buddha-kṣetra*), the world-system where he finally attained buddhahood in its Akaniṣṭha heaven. Many such Lands are said to be 'Pure Lands' (see p. 23), mystical universes created by the appropriate *buddha* using his immeasurable store of karmic fruitfulness. While these are described in paradisaical terms, they are primarily realms whose conditions are very conducive to attaining enlightenment. Pure Lands are outside the normal system of rebirth according to personal *karma*. To be reborn in one requires a transfer of some of the huge stock of karmic fruitfulness of a Land's presiding *buddha*, stimulated by devout prayer. Once faith has led to rebirth in a Pure Land, individuals can develop their wisdom and so become either an *arahat* or a Great Being *bodhisattva*. Besides the 'Pure' Buddha Lands, there are also 'impure' ones, normal world-systems like our own, Śākyamuni's realm.

The '*Dharma*-body' has two aspects, the first being the 'Knowledge-body' (*jñāna-kāya*), the inner nature shared by all *buddha*s: the omniscient knowledge, perfect wisdom, and spiritual qualities through which a *bodhisattva* becomes a *buddha*. It is regarded as having a very subtle, shining, limitless form from which speech can come, through the autonomous working of the *bodhisattva* vows. In this respect, the *Dharma*-body is given a semi-personalized aspect, making it somewhat akin to the concept of God in other religions. The *Dharma*-body is thus sometimes personified as the Buddha Vairocana, the 'Resplendent One' (Eliade, 1987, vol. XV, pp. 126–8; Brown and O'Brian, 1989, p. 240). In the tenth century, the process of personification was carried further, in the concept of the *Ādi*, or 'Primordial', ever-enlightened Buddha. The second aspect of the *Dharma*-body is the 'Self-existent-body' (*svabhāvika-kāya*). This is the ultimate nature of reality, thusness, emptiness: the non-nature which is the very nature of *dharma*s, their *dharma*-ness. It is what is known and realized on attaining buddhahood, it is *nirvāṇa*. Only for convenience of explanation are the Knowledge and Self-existent bodies described as different. In emptiness, there can be no differentiation between a *buddha*'s thusness and the thusness of all *dharma*s: buddha-ness is *dharma*-ness (Conze, 1973, pp. 193, 291).

On the ultimate level, only the *Dharma*-body exists; the other *buddha*-bodies are just provisional ways of talking about and apprehending it. They, Pure Lands, and Great Beings, then, are not truly real, any more than the book you are now reading or the eyes with which you read it (Brown and O'Brian, 1989, p. 258)! In emptiness, nothing stands out with separate reality. At the conventional level of truth, however, such *buddhas* etc. are just as real as anything else. Indeed, in popular Mahāyāna practice, the Enjoyment-body *buddhas* and Great Beings are treated as wholly real, and rebirth in their Pure Lands is ardently sought through faith. From the conventional perspective, such beings are those who have heroically striven to be close to, or attained to, buddhahood. From the ultimate perspective, they are the symbolic forms in which the 'minds' of empty 'beings' perceive the *Dharma*-body (Brown and O'Brian, 1989, pp. 283–4). *Buddhas* can know it directly, Noble *bodhisattvas* experience it as Enjoyment-bodies, while ordinary beings only know it when it appears as a Transformation-body. Those with great insight, though, can glimpse it in the thusness of any worldly object. To non-Buddhists such as Hindus, the *Dharma*-body appears in the form of the gods of their religion (Suzuki, 1932, pp. 165–6). Thus in Japan, the major *kami*, or deities of the indigenous Shintō religion, became identified with particular heavenly *buddhas* or Great Beings.

The Mahāyāna pantheon

Of the 'countless' heavenly *buddhas* and *bodhisattvas*, some of the named ones became focuses of devotion (Harvey, 1990a, pp. 129–33, 182–9; Williams, 1989, pp. 224–76). Besides Śākyamuni, important heavenly *buddhas* include Bhaiṣajya-guru, the 'Master of Healing', who offers cures for physical and spiritual ailments (Eliade, 1987, vol. II, pp. 128–30), and Amitābha, 'Infinite Radiance' (Eliade, 1987, vol. I, pp. 235–7; Brown and O'Brian, 1989, p. 219). The latter became of central importance in the Pure Land schools of East Asian Buddhism. The Larger *Sukhāvatī-vyūya* ('Array of the Happy Land') *Sūtra* tells how, as a *bodhisattva*, he had vowed that he would only become a *buddha* when his karmic fruitfulness was sufficient to produce the most excellent Pure Land possible. Its inhabitants would have the highest 'perfections', memory of previous lives, and the ability to see myriads of other Buddha Lands. They would immediately hear whatever teaching they wished, would have no idea of property, even with regard to their own bodies, and would have the same happiness of those in deep meditative trance. This Happy Land (Sukhāvatī) would be a paradise full of 'jewel-trees', which stimulate calm and contemplative states of mind, where everything would be as beings wished, in a realm free from temptation and defilement (Conze *et al.*, 1954, pp. 202–6; Conze, 1959, pp. 232–6). Most importantly, he vowed that he would appear before any dying being who aspired for enlightenment and devoutly called him to mind, so as to conduct him or her to his Pure Land (Brown and O'Brian, 1989, pp. 251–2). Entry to this is said to come from deep faith in Amitābha and the power of his gracious vows.

The notion of gaining rebirth in the Happy Land has long provided a hope to people struggling with existence, living less than perfect lives. If currently unable to behave like true *bodhisattva*s, the environment of the Happy Land will enable them to do so, and the immeasurably long life-span there will encompass the hugely long *bodhisattva*-path. Yet other perspectives on the Happy Land are also found. One idea which developed in the Japanese Jōdo school is that the Happy Land is everywhere: seeing it just needs an attitude transformed by faith. In the Japanese Jōdo-shin school, even one's faith is seen as coming from Amitābha; one must simply be open to his wondrous power: humans are seen as too sinful to attain salvation by their own power (Brown and O'Brian, 1989, pp. 254, 257). This school sees Amitābha as the embodiment of the *Dharma*-body, and even sees the Happy Land as the same as *nirvāṇa* (Brown and O'Brian, 1989, p. 258).

Maitreya, 'The Kindly One', is said to be a heavenly *bodhisattva* who, after attaining buddhahood, will send a Transformation-body to be the next *buddha* on earth (Eliade, 1987, vol. IX, pp. 136–41). In China, he is often portrayed in the form of one of his recognized manifestations, the tenth-century Pu-tai. This Ch'an monk was a jolly, pot-bellied, wandering teacher who carried presents for children in his cloth bag (*pu-tai*). In the West, images of him are often known as 'Laughing Buddhas'. Another important Great Being is Mañjuśrī, 'Sweet Glory', a helper of the heavenly Buddha Śākyamuni (Eliade, 1987, vol. IX, pp. 174–5). He is seen as the greatest embodiment of wisdom and has the special task of awakening spiritual knowledge. Accordingly, he is shown holding a copy of a *Perfection of Wisdom Sūtra*, and wielding a flaming sword, symbolic of the wisdom with which he cuts away delusion. He is seen as the patron of scholars and a protector of *Dharma*-preachers. Those who devoutly recite his name, and meditate on his teachings and images, are said to be protected by him, to have many good rebirths, and to see him in dreams and meditative visions, in which he inspires and teaches them.

By far the most popular of the Great Beings is Avalokiteśvara, who is said to aid Amitābha in his compassionate concern for the world. He is in fact seen as the very embodiment of compassion, the driving force of all *bodhisattva*s (Eliade, 1987, vol. II, pp. 11–14; Blofeld, 1977). His vows are such that he will not become a *buddha* till all beings are saved. As a *buddha*, he would have a limited, though huge, life-span, but as a *bodhisattva* he can remain in closer contact with suffering beings, helping them till the end of time. The name Avalokiteśvara means 'The Lord Who Looks Down (with compassion)'; in China he is called Kuan-yin, 'Cry Regarder', or Kuan-shih-yin, 'Regarder of the Cries of the World'. In all Mahāyāna lands, he is the focus of devout worship, contemplation, and prayers for help (Brown and O'Brian, 1989, p. 287; Conze *et al.*, 1954, pp. 194–6). He is seen to manifest himself as various compassionate beings: these may mysteriously disappear after they have appeared to help someone, or may live out a full life, or even a series of them, as in the case of the Dalai Lamas of Tibet. He even manifests himself in hells or as an animal. In one Chinese painting, he is shown appearing in the form of a bull, in order to convert a butcher from his wrong livelihood.

Like most other Great Beings, Avalokiteśvara is portrayed crowned and with royal garments, rather than the monastic robes of a *buddha* (Figure 3.1). This is to show that *bodhisattva*s are more in contact with the world than *buddha*s, and more actively engaged in helping beings. Avalokiteśvara holds a lotus bud, which symbolizes the pure beauty of his compassion, or the worldly minds of beings which he encourages in their efforts to 'bloom' into enlightenment. He is often shown with his hands cupped together around a 'wish-granting jewel', an emblem of his willingness to grant righteous wishes. Its clarity also symbolizes the natural purity, hidden by coverings of spiritual defilements, in the minds of beings. These defilements are suggested by the cupping hands, also said to be like a lotus bud. One of the many types of images of Avalokiteśvara shows him with 1,000 arms, each with an eye on its palm; this suggests his being ever on the look out for beings in distress, and his reaching out to help them.

Great Beings also include female forms, such as Prajñā-pāramitā, 'Perfection of Wisdom', symbolically seen as the 'mother of all *buddhas*', for buddhahood comes from wisdom (Conze *et al.*, 1954, pp. 47–9). In Tibet, the Green Tārā, or 'Saviouress', became the ever-popular patron-deity of the country. She is seen as grace-full, attractive and approachable, and as ever-ready to care tenderly for those in distress (Eliade, 1987, vol. XIV, pp. 337–9; Conze *et al.*, 1954, pp. 196–202). Her compassionate nature, in responding to those who call on her, is reflected in the story that she and the White Tārā were born from two tears of Avalokiteśvara when he saw the horrors of hell. In the Vajrayāna form of Buddhism in Tibet and Mongolia, male and female holy beings are often paired, as consorts. In such pairs, the female is known as the *Prajñā* or 'Wisdom' of her partner, and represents the wise, passive power which makes possible the active and energetic compassionate skilful means of the male. The pair is often represented, as *Yab*, 'Father', and *Yum*, 'Mother', in discreet sexual union. This form symbolizes the idea that, just as sexual union leads to great pleasure, so the union of skilful means and wisdom leads to the bliss of enlightenment (Eliade, 1987, vol. II, pp. 472–82).

The Buddhism of Tibet and Mongolia, and the Korean Milgyo and Japanese Shingon schools, are all Tantric or Mantra-yāna forms, making use of *mantras* (Eliade, 1987, vol. IX, pp. 176–7; Blofeld, 1978). These sacred words of power are mostly meaningless syllables or strings of syllables. When pronounced in the right way, with the right attitude of mind, the sound-arrangement of a *mantra* is seen as 'tuning in' the meditator-devotee's mind to a holy being he or she wishes to visualize. This may perhaps be compared to the way in which certain musical chords naturally tend to evoke reactions of sadness or joy in people. In the Yogacārin 'thought-only' perspective, the visualized being is seen not as 'external' to the devotee, but as a psychic force or level of consciousness latent within the person's own mind. A *mantra* is seen as acting like a psychic key which enables a person to visualize and communicate with a being/force whose *mantra* it is. Each holy being has its own *mantra*, which is seen to express its essence. For example, that of Tārā is *oṃ tāre, tuttāre ture svāha!* Each holy being also has a short 'seed' *mantra*: *trāṃ* in the case of the Buddha Ratnasaṃbhava. The most famous *mantra* is that of Avalokiteśvara: *oṃ maṇi padme hūṃ*. *Oṃ* and *hūṃ* are sacred sounds from the Hindu Veda, the first being seen as the basic sound of

Figure 3.1. A Tibetan painting showing some of the chief holy beings and symbols of Tibetan Buddhism. (Reproduced by kind permission of the Samye-Ling Tibetan Buddhist Centre, Scotland)

the universe. *Maṇi padme* literally means 'O jewelled-lotus lady'. In later exegesis, *maṇi* is seen as referring to the jewel that this *bodhisattva* holds, while *padme* refers to his symbol, the lotus. A complex set of symbolic explanations is also given to this *mantra*. For example, its six syllables are associated with the six perfections, or the six realms of rebirth. Figure 3.1 shows Avalokiteśvara with the syllables of his *mantra* emerging from him. Above him is Amitābha Buddha, his inspiration; to the right of the picture is Tārā, to the left is Padmasaṃbhava, the founder of Tibetan Buddhism. Below are two symbols: a *stūpa* and a *Dharma*-wheel.

In Vajrayāna Buddhism, the pantheon came to include beings portrayed in 'wrathful', as well as the more normal 'peaceful' forms (Harvey, 1990a, pp. 261–4; Blofeld, 1970, pp. 110–17). Male and female wrathful beings may be focused on by strong, unconventional people who are disgusted with the impermanent world and its dreary round of rebirths. The anger which the being shows is not that of a vengeful god, but, hate-free, it aims to open up the practitioner's heart by devastating his hesitations, doubts, confusions and ignorance. One such being is Yamāntaka, 'Conqueror of Death', the wrathful form of the Bodhisattva Mañjuśrī. He is depicted as free and unbridled, trampling on corpses, representing the 'I-am' conceit and its limiting, deadening influence. His head is that of a raging bull, on which is a crown of skulls, representing human faults.

These strongly symbolic forms are used as part of a system of meditative training in which a person's *guru* (Tibetan *lama*) selects a 'chosen deity' (Tibetan *yi-dam*) appropriate for the pupil to work with (Blofeld, 1970, pp. 174–82). A *yi-dam* is a particular holy being which is in harmony with the pupil's nature. By visualizing and meditatively identifying with it, a practitioner identifies with his own basic nature purged of faults. The *yi-dam* reveals aspects of his character which he persists in overlooking, for it visually represents them. Acting as a guide for his practice, the *yi-dam* enables the practitioner magically to transmute the energy of his characteristic fault into a parallel kind of wisdom, embodied by the *yi-dam*. The *yi-dams* may be 'peaceful' or 'wrathful', and are grouped into five 'families', each associated with a particular fault and with one of the main Vajrayāna *buddhas*. The first of these is the 'central' Buddha, seen as a personification of the *Dharma*-body: the ever-enlightened *Ādi* Buddha. As *Dharma*-body, he is seen as unifying and manifesting the other *buddhas*.

Buddha-images and symbols

In early Buddhist art, Gotama, even before his enlightenment, was only shown by symbols. This must have been due to the feeling that the profound nature of one nearing or attained to buddhahood could not be adequately represented by a human form. In Figure 3.2, he is portrayed by a throne surmounted by a *Dhamma*-wheel, symbolizing the *Dhamma* that the Buddha embodied. In ancient India, the wheel had associations with the eye (cf. the Buddha's wisdom 'eye') and the sun (cf. the Buddha as the 'light' of the world). A celestial wheel is said to have moved through the air when a compassionate Universal Emperor (*Cakkavatti*) peacefully spread his influence through the

Figure 3.2. An aniconic representation of the Buddha, from a carved relief from Nāgārjunakonda, third century CE. (Reproduced by kind permission of the UK Association for Buddhist Studies)

world. In parallel to this, the Buddha's inauguration of his influence in the world, the first sermon, is called 'The Setting in Motion of the *Dhamma*-wheel'. Just as the spokes of a wheel diverge from and are firmly rooted in the hub, so the various aspects of the *Dhamma*-as-teaching come from the Buddha. And just as the spokes converge on the hub, so the aspects of *Dhamma*-as-Path converge on *nirvāṇa*.

In time, the absence of the long-dead Buddha was keenly felt, and there arose a need for a representation of him in human form to act as a more personalized focus of devotion (Snellgrove, 1978). The development of Buddha-images, in the second century CE, was probably preceded by the practice of visualizing the Buddha's form. The period was also one in which a change in mood was affecting all Indian religions, leading to the portrayal of the founder of Jainism, and of major Hindu gods, as foci of *bhakti*, or warm 'loving devotion'. In Buddhism, this change had also contributed to the origin of the Mahāyāna. The craftsmen who made Buddha-images drew on the tradition that Gotama had been born with the 'thirty-two marks of a Great Man', which indicated that he would become either a *buddha* or a Universal Emperor. These bodily features are described as karmic results of specific spiritual perfections built up in past lives (Walshe, 1987, pp. 441–60). The most obvious one shown on images is Gotama's 'turbaned head', meaning that he had a head shaped like a royal turban, or that one with spiritual vision could see a royal turban on his head. In art, it came to be shown as a protuberance on the top of the head. The early texts see it as a result of previous moral and spiritual prominence; later texts see it as a kind of 'wisdom bump' to accommodate a *buddha*'s supreme wisdom. A feature of Buddha-images not among the 'characteristics' is the elongated ear-lobes. These signify Gotama's royal upbringing, when he wore heavy gold ear-rings, and thus his renunciation of the option of political greatness. They may also be seen as a common symbol for nobility of character, or indicative of the Buddha's 'divine ear', a meditation-based psychic ability. Such features were used in the portrayal of all *buddha*s: the earthly Gotama, past earthly *buddha*s, and heavenly Mahāyāna *buddha*s.

A good image, as in Figure 3.3, has life, vigour and grace, and its features suggest joy, compassion, wisdom, serenity and meditative concentration. Images remind a Buddhist of both the actions and the spiritual qualities of a holy being. Contemplation of an image helps to inspire, and also to stimulate the arising of similar qualities. On the consecration of such images and attitudes to them, see p. 132.

A key Buddhist symbolic monument, found at many temples, is the *stūpa* or pagoda. This is essentially a relic-container, but it also symbolizes the Buddha and his *nirvāṇa*-at-death. Relics placed in *stūpa*s are said to have been those of Gotama, *arahat*s, and even past *buddha*s. Having been part of the body of an enlightened being, they were considered to have been infused with something of the power-for-goodness of an enlightened mind, and to bring blessings to those who expressed devotion in their vicinity. Where funerary relics cannot be found, hair or possessions of holy beings, copies of bodily relics or possessions, or Buddhist texts have come to be used in their place.

A famous early *stūpa*, dating from the first century CE in its present

Figure 3.3. A nineteenth-century Burmese image of Gotama Buddha. His lowered hand, touching the earth, recollects his 'conquest of Māra', just prior to his enlightenment, when the earth is said to have shaken in response to his request for affirmation of his many lives of spiritual cultivation. It is a symbol of Gotama's conquest of the evil Māra, who is said to have then given up his attempt to prevent his attaining enlightenment. Other image forms show, for example, the Buddha with his hands together in his lap, in meditation, or at his chest, as if turning the 'wheel' of *Dhamma*, when teaching. (Reproduced by kind permission of Durham Oriental Museum)

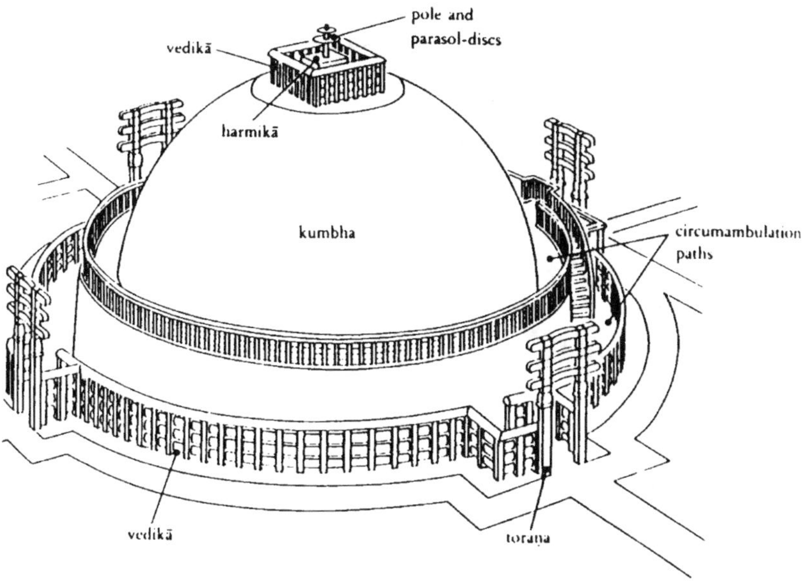

Figure 3.4. The Great *Stūpa* at Sāñcī. (Reproduced from Peter Harvey (1990) *An Introduction to Buddhism*. Cambridge: Cambridge University Press)

form, is at Sāñcī in central India (see Figure 3.4). The four gateways, or *toraṇas*, place the *stūpa* symbolically at a crossroads, as the Buddha had specified, perhaps to indicate the openness and universality of the *Dhamma*. The circular *vedikā*, or railing, marks off the site dedicated to the *stūpa*, and encloses the first of two paths for respectful circumambulation. The *stūpa* dome, referred to in early texts as the *kumbha*, or 'pot', is the outermost container of the relics. It is associated with an Indian symbol known as the 'vase of plenty', and symbolically acts as a reminder of an enlightened being as 'full' of uplifting *Dhamma*. On top of the Sāñcī *stūpa* is a pole and three discs, which represent ceremonial parasols. As parasols were used as insignia of royalty in India, their inclusion on *stūpas* can be seen as a way of symbolizing the spiritual sovereignty of the Buddha. The kingly connection probably derives from the ancient custom of rulers sitting under a sacred tree at the centre of a community to administer justice, with mobile parasols later replacing such shading trees. The parasol-structure on *stūpas* also seems to have symbolized the

Figure 3.5. A simplified *maṇḍala*, showing the five chief *buddhas* in symbolic form. (Reproduced from C. Trungpa (1976) *The Myth of Freedom*. Boston: Shambala Publications, p. 146)

Buddhist sacred tree, the *bodhi*-tree, under which the Buddha attained enlightenment. In later *stūpas*, the top part fused into a spire, and several platforms were often added under the dome to elevate it in an honorific way. It then became possible to see each layer of the structure as symbolizing a particular set of spiritual qualities, such as the 'four foundations of mindfulness', with the spire symbolizing the powers and knowledge of a *buddha*.

In Vajrayāna Buddhism, an important symbol is the *maṇḍala* or '(sacred) circle' (Eliade, 1987, vol. IX, pp. 155–8; Blofeld, 1970, pp. 102–9; Conze *et al.*, 1954, pp. 246–52) (see Figure 3.5). A *maṇḍala* may be temporarily constructed, for a particular rite, out of coloured sands or dough and fragrant powders, using a raised horizontal platform as a base. In a more permanent form, it may be painted on a hanging scroll. The *maṇḍala* symbolizes a related set of holy beings, represented by metal statues, painted images, symbols or seed-*mantra*s. The pattern of a *maṇḍala* is based on that of a circular *stūpa* with a square base. It can, in fact, be seen as a two-dimensional *stūpa*-temple, which contains the actual manifestations of the deities represented within it. The bands encircling the *maṇḍala* mark off its pure, sacred area from the profane area beyond, and also suggest the unfolding of spiritual vision gained by practitioners when they visualize themselves entering the *maṇḍala*. Having crossed the threshold, they then enter the central citadel, representing the temple of their own heart. Depending on the rite, the beings in the citadel will vary, though the five chief *buddha*s are most common. By being introduced to their *yi-dam*'s *maṇḍala*, practitioners can familiarize themselves with the deity's luminous Pure Land, with associated holy beings arrayed around the *yi-dam*. By vivid visualization of all this, meditators may master and integrate the psychic forces it represents, and achieve a wholeness in their life.

In contrast to this stylized form, Zen Buddhism often dispenses with either images or symbols, and seeks to hint at the Beyond by trying to capture the living thusness of a natural scene or event. It has thus inspired arts as various as landscape painting and the seventeen-syllable *haiku* poem form. A good example of the latter is:

> Under the water,
> On the rock resting,
> The fallen leaves.

Further reading

Blofeld, J. (1970) *The Tantric Mysticism of Tibet*. New York: Dutton.

Blofeld, J. (1977) *Compassion Yoga: Mystical Cult of Kuan Yin*. London: Unwin.

Blofeld, J. (1978) *Mantras: Sacred Words of Power*. London: Unwin.

Brown, K. and O'Brian, J. (eds) (1989) *The Essential Teachings of Buddhism*. London: Rider (translation extracts plus comments, all schools).

Conze, E. (1958) *Buddhist Wisdom Books – The Diamond Sutra, The Heart Sutra*. London: George Allen and Unwin.
Conze, E. (1959) *Buddhist Scriptures*. Harmondsworth: Penguin (translations from all schools).
Conze, E. (1962) *Buddhist Thought in India*. London: Allen & Unwin.
Conze, E. (1973) *The Perfection of Wisdom in Eight Thousand Lines*. Bolinas: Four Seasons (translations).
Conze, E., Horner, I. B., Snellgrove, D. and Waley, A. (eds) (1954) *Buddhist Texts Through the Ages*. New York: Philosophical Library (translations from all schools).
Eliade, M. (ed.) (1987) *The Encyclopedia of Religion* (16 vols). New York: Macmillan.
Gombrich, R. (1971) *Precept and Practice: Traditional Buddhism in the Rural Highlands of Ceylon*. Oxford: Clarendon.
Harvey, P. (1990a) *An Introduction to Buddhism: Teachings, History and Practices*. Cambridge: Cambridge University Press.
Harvey, P. (1990b) 'Venerated objects and symbols of early Buddhism' in K. Werner (ed.) *Symbols in Art and Religion: The Indian and Comparative Perspectives*. Richmond: Curzon Press, pp. 68–102.
Harvey, P. (1995) *The Selfless Mind: Personality, Consciousness and Nirvana in Early Buddhism*. Richmond: Curzon Press.
Katz, N. (1982) *Buddhist Images of Human Perfection*. Delhi: Motilal Banarsidass.
Snellgrove, D. L. (ed.) (1978) *The Image of the Buddha*. London: Serindia.
Spiro, M. E. (1971) *Buddhism and Society*. London: Allen & Unwin.
Suzuki, D. T. (1932) *The Lankavatara Sutra*. London: Routledge and Kegan Paul.
Walshe, M. (1987) *Thus Have I Heard*. London: Wisdom (translation of the *Dīgha Nikāya*).
Williams, P. (1989) *Mahāyāna Buddhism: The Doctrinal Foundations*. London: Routledge and Kegan Paul.
Woodward, F. L. (1925, 1927, 1930) *Kindred Sayings*, vols 2, 4, 5. London: Pali Text Society (translations from the *Saṃyutta Nikāya*).

4. Devotional practices

Peter Harvey

For most religions, the key type of practice is usually worship of the divine. This is not the case with Buddhism, for two reasons. First, Theravāda Buddhists hold that the nature of a *buddha* after his death cannot be specified, that he has passed beyond existence as a limited individual being (see pp. 102–4; Harvey, 1990, pp. 65–8). This being so, he cannot any longer be thought of as a 'person' who might respond to human actions (though he is seen as having left a store of power for others to draw on). It thus seems inappropriate to say that Theravādins 'worship' the Buddha. A more neutral description is to say that they show devotion to the Buddha and what he represents. Mahāyānists, though, can be said to 'worship' the heavenly *buddha*s and *bodhisattva*s.[1] Secondly, and more importantly, most classical Buddhist descriptions of the path to liberation are based on the triad of 'morality, meditation and wisdom', with meditation being the key practice (Harvey, 1990, ch. 11). Nevertheless, devotion plays a part here, as it can help purify the mind, and thus aid morality and meditation; in its more refined forms, it may also become a form of meditation.

While the Buddha was critical of *blind* faith, he did not deny a role for soundly based 'trustful confidence' (*saddhā*), for to test out his teachings, a person had to have at least some initial trust in them. The early texts envisage a process of listening, which arouses trustful confidence, leading to practice, and thus to partial confirmation of the teachings, and thus to deeper trustful confidence, and deeper practice, until the heart of the teachings is directly experienced. A person then becomes an *arahat*, a liberated saint who has replaced faith with knowledge. Faith/trustful confidence occurs as one item in the list of the 'five (spiritual) faculties': trustful confidence, energy, mindfulness, meditative concentration, and (reflective and intuitive) wisdom (Conze *et al.*, 1964, pp. 51–65, 185–6). Most Buddhist traditions agree that the faculty of faith should be balanced by, and balance, the faculty of wisdom: trusting, heart-based warmth and commitment must be in equipoise with the cool, analytical, meditative eye of insight. With the faculties strong and in balance, deeper insights can then be developed, which progressively remove the need for faith.

Nevertheless, in some of the schools of Eastern Buddhism (see p. 113) faith and worship came to play a completely central role. In China, Korea and Japan, very popular forms of Mahāyāna Buddhism are the Pure Land schools, which focus on faith in the salvific power of the heavenly *buddha* Amitābha (Japanese Amida) (Harvey, 1990, pp. 129–30, 152–3, 163–5). One Japanese Pure Land school, the Jōdo-shin, is indeed a religion of faith alone, in which one must rely totally on Amida's grace: even one's faith is seen to come from him! This is a religion of pure 'other-power', i.e., reliance on the power of another being. Alongside this school, though, is another Eastern form of Buddhism, Zen (Chinese Ch'an), which is seen as a way of 'self-power': attaining liberation by knowing and manifesting one's innate '*buddha*-nature'. Even here, though, devotional practices play their part, and one even needs faith in one's innate *buddha*-nature (Conze *et al.*, 1964, pp. 295–8)! Most forms of Mahāyāna Buddhism, in fact, are a mix of 'self-power' and 'other-power', combining an emphasis on the cultivation of one's own moral and spiritual qualities, with an emphasis on opening oneself up to the uplifting inspiration and assistance of the heavenly *buddha*s and *bodhisattva*s (Conze *et al.*, 1964, pp. 186–90). In Theravāda Buddhism, 'self-power' is more emphasized, but not exclusively: the Buddha advised his followers to have themselves as 'island' and 'refuge' (i.e., be mindfully self-composed and self-reliant), but also to have the *Dhamma* (path and teachings) as 'island' and 'refuge'. In this, the inspiring and guiding help of those more advanced on the path is also crucial (Brown and O'Brian, 1989, pp. 19–21).

Thus, while devotion is not the core of Buddhist practice (except in the Pure Land schools), it plays an important part in the life of most Buddhists. Even in Theravāda Buddhism, which often has a rather rational, unemotional image, a very deep faith in the Buddha, *Dhamma* and *Saṅgha* is common. Ideally, this is based on the fact that some part of the Buddha's path has been found to be uplifting, thus inspiring confidence in the rest. Many people, though, simply have *pasāda*: a calm and joyful faith inspired by the example of those who are well established on the path.

The refuges

The key expression of Buddhist devotion and commitment is 'taking the refuges'. The ancient formula for this, in its Pāli form, begins: *Buddhaṃ saraṇaṃ gacchāmi, Dhammaṃ saraṇaṃ gacchāmi, Saṅghaṃ saraṇaṃ gacchāmi*. This affirms that 'I go to the Buddha as refuge, I go to the *Dhamma* as refuge, I go to the *Saṅgha* as refuge'. Each affirmation is then repeated 'for the second time . . .' (*dutiyam pi* . . .) and 'for the third time . . .' (*tatiyam pi* . . .). The threefold repetition marks off the recitation from ordinary uses of speech, and ensures that the mind dwells on the meaning of each affirmation at least once. The notion of a 'refuge', here, is not that of a place to hide, but of something the thought of which purifies, uplifts and strengthens the heart. Orientation towards these three guides to a better way of living is experienced as a joyful haven of calm, a firm 'island amidst a flood', in contrast to the troubles of life. The 'refuges' remind the Buddhist of calm, wise, spiritual people and states of mind, and so help engender these states. Their value is denoted by the fact that they are also known as the *Ti-ratana*, or 'three jewels': spiritual treasures of supreme worth.

The meaning of each refuge varies somewhat between different traditions. The Theravāda understanding is expressed in a frequently used chant drawn from the Pāli Canon. On the Buddha, it affirms:

> Thus he is the Lord because he is an *arahat*, perfectly and completely enlightened, endowed with knowledge and (good) conduct, Well-gone [to *nirvāṇa*], knower of worlds, an incomparable charioteer for the training of persons, teacher of gods and humans, Buddha, Lord.

The 'Buddha' referred to here is primarily the historical Buddha, Gotama. He is regarded with reverence and gratitude as the rediscoverer and exemplifier of *Dhamma*, and the one who also showed others how to live by and experience it. As the benefits of living by *Dhamma* are experienced, this reverence and gratitude naturally develop greater depth. In Sri Lanka, one recently popularized liturgy states 'Thus infinite, possessing measureless qualities, unequalled, equal to the unequalled, god to the gods, to me the Lord, my own *Buddha* mother, my own *Buddha* father, the orb of dawn to the darkness of delusion . . .'. The Buddha refuge does not refer only to Gotama, but also to previous and future *buddha*s, and to the principle of enlightenment as supremely worthy of attainment. In this respect, the first refuge can also be taken as a pointer to the faculty of wisdom developing within the practitioner.

The Pāli chant on *Dhamma* is:

> Well-expounded by the Lord is *Dhamma*, visible here and now, timeless, inviting investigation, leading onward [to the stages of sanctity and finally *nirvāṇa*], to be experienced within by the wise.

This emphasizes *Dhamma* as immediately accessible to all, and as of progressively greater benefit. As refuge, *Dhamma* is explained as the Ennobling Eightfold Path. More generally, it refers to: (a) *pariyatti*, or the body of teachings, (b) *paṭipatti*, or the 'practice' of the way, and (c) *paṭivedha*, or 'realization' of the stages of sanctity – in the highest sense, *nirvāṇa* itself. *Dhamma*, then, is to be heard/read and understood, practised, and realized. It can also mean the 'law-orderliness' inherent in nature, phenomena always occurring according to the principle of Conditioned Arising, from appropriate conditions.

The Pāli chant on the *Saṅgha*, or spiritual Community, is:

> Of good conduct is the Community of the disciples of the Lord; of upright conduct . . .; of wise conduct . . .; of proper conduct . . .; that is to say, the four pairs of persons, the eight kinds of individuals; this Community . . . is worthy of gifts, hospitality, offerings, and reverential salutation, an incomparable field of karmic fruitfulness for the world.

Here, the 'four pairs of persons, the eight kinds of individuals' are the *arahat* and three lesser grades of saints (the Non-returner, Once-returner and Stream-enterer[2]), and those established on the paths to these spiritual 'fruits' (Harvey, 1990, pp. 64–5, 71–2), that is, all who have attained *nirvāṇa*, glimpsed it, or are on the brink of glimpsing it. This is the precious *ariya-Saṅgha*, the Community of 'Noble' persons, who may be found within the monastic *saṅgha*, its symbolic representative, or among spiritually advanced lay-people or even gods. Being of exemplary conduct, its members are worthy of gifts and respect; the monastic *saṅgha* seeks to emulate them in this. The concept of a 'field of karmic fruitfulness' is that, just as a seed planted in better ground yields better fruit, so a gift given to a more virtuous person generates more karmic fruitfulness (*puñña* or 'merit'; see pp. 68–9). This idea is partly based on the fact that, if one gives to someone of suspect character, one may regret the act somewhat; whereas in giving to a virtuous or holy person, one puts all one's heart into the act and can rejoice at it. Giving also sets up a bond of association. The Noble *Saṅgha* therefore benefits the world with the opportunity for generating abundant auspicious, purifying, karmic fruitfulness.

In the Mahāyāna, the 'Three body' (*Trikāya*) doctrine (see pp. 110–12) views buddhahood at three levels: earthly 'Transformation-body' *buddha*s, heavenly Enjoyment-body *buddha*s who manifest these on earth, and the *Dharma*-body, which is the mysterious inner nature of all *buddha*s and, indeed, of all reality (Harvey, 1990, pp. 125–8). Thus for a Mahāyānist, the Buddha refuge refers not only to Gotama and other Transformation-body *buddha*s, but also, and more importantly, to the Enjoyment-body *buddha*s (Brown and O'Brian, 1989, pp. 111–12, 134–7; Conze *et al.*, 1964, pp. 139–40, 190–4). In the Pure Land schools, emphasis is primarily or exclusively on Amitābha. In Ch'an/Zen, the emphasis is on the historical Buddha as a heroic, stirring example, but more particularly on the idea of the *buddha*-nature within: 'take refuge in the three treasures in your own natures. The Buddha is enlightenment, the *Dharma* is truth, the *Saṅgha* is purity ... take refuge in the Buddha within yourselves ... If you do not rely upon your own natures, there is nothing else on which to rely' (Yampolsky, 1967, sec. 23). Transformation-body *buddha*s are also figuratively seen as good and wise thoughts within one's mind, and refuge is taken in 'the future perfect Enjoyment-body in my own physical body' (Yampolsky, 1967, sec. 20). In the Mahāyāna, the *Dharma* refuge, in its highest sense, refers to the *Dharma*-body, ultimate reality (Brown and O'Brian, 1989, pp. 283–4, 137–8). Noble *bodhisattva*s are included in the *Saṅgha* refuge, and taking refuge in them is allied to taking vows, often repeated on a daily basis, to become like them.

In the Vajrayāna of Northern Buddhism (see p. 12), extra refuges are taken. Prior to the three usual ones, a person takes refuge in his *lama* or *guru* (Blofeld, 1970, pp. 133–5, 153; Brown and O'Brian,

1989, pp. 133–4, 111–17). He or she is seen as the source of the deepening knowledge of the other refuges, and regarded as an embodiment of their virtues. After the usual refuges, individuals may then take refuge in their *yi-dam*, a holy being which is their tutelary deity. An adept preparing for training in meditative visualizations must also complete preliminary practices of a devotional and purificatory nature. Five or six such practices are generally given, each of which must be done a hundred thousand times. One is the 'grand prostration', which is done while holding wooden blocks, to prevent the hands being blistered by repeatedly sliding along the floor (on a special wooden board) to the fully prostrate position. As this is done, the devotee may say: 'I, so-and-so, on behalf of all sentient beings and freely offering my body, speech and mind, bow to the earth in adoration of the Guru and the Three Precious Ones' (Blofeld, 1970, p. 151). Accompanying this affirmation is the visualization of a 'refuge tree': a concourse of holy beings whose radiant light suffuses the devotee. After a period of struggle and pain, the practice is said to induce great joy. It also conduces to a balance of self-power and other-power: relying on oneself and on the power of holy beings.

Focuses and locations of devotional acts

Devotion to *buddhas* and *bodhisattvas* is focused or channelled by the use of various artefacts such as images. At home, it can be expressed before a home shrine, which may be as simple as a high shelf and a picture in a quiet corner. In temples, there will always be some kind of shrine-room or image-hall, where large images are housed: in Theravāda temples, these are of Gotama Buddha, sometimes flanked by his two chief *arahat* disciples; in Mahāyāna ones, there is often a group of three heavenly *buddhas*, or a *buddha* and two *bodhisattvas*, perhaps with images of sixteen or eighteen chief *arahat* disciples along the walls of the hall. There will always be accommodation for monks and/or nuns, or, as in Japan, married clerics. Thus temples are in fact temple-monasteries, Theravāda ones often being known by the Pāli term for a monastery, *vihāra*. There is frequently a *stūpa* (relic-mound) of some kind (see p. 119), including the multi-roofed form, known in the West as a pagoda, which evolved in China (Harvey, 1990, pp. 78–9). Most *stūpas* are such that one cannot enter them, except for the East Asian multi-roofed form.

They can be anything from a metre high, with some large ones being the major feature of a temple. The famous Shwe-dāgon *Stūpa* in Rangoon, capital of Myanmar (Burma), is 112 metres tall. It is said to contain some hairs of Gotama, and belongings of three previous *buddhas*. Because of the sanctity of these, it has been encased in gold plates and gold leaf, and topped by an orb studded in diamonds. Temples may also have: a meeting/preaching hall; a separate meditation hall, as in Zen temples; a *bodhi*-tree (the type of tree under which the Buddha attained enlightenment, or *bodhi*), as at many Theravāda temples; a library and administrative buildings, and finally shrines for one or more gods or nature spirits. Most temples are free-standing, but throughout the Buddhist world there are also natural and specially excavated caves, whose cool, calm, rather awesome interiors have been used as temples.

Devotional artefacts may be paid for by a community or an individual. In either case, the community can share in the embellishment: in Southeast Asia, images are often gradually gilded with individual squares of gold-leaf. As giving is an act of karmic fruitfulness, which can be shared, artefacts may be specially donated, perhaps for the benefit of a new-born child, someone who has recently died, success in a business venture, or an end to a war. In 1961 the government of Myanmar (Burma) organized the making of 60,000 temporary sand *stūpas* to avert a world calamity predicted by astrologers throughout Asia. The motive of doing karmically fruitful actions means that temples often have more images than are 'needed', and new *stūpas* may be built beside crumbling old ones. This is because there is generally more joy in starting something new than in repairing it. Greater joy leaves a stronger wholesome 'imprint' on the mind, and so is seen as producing better-quality karmic fruits. In Myanmar, '*Stūpa* Builder' is a title of respect, and 'karmic fruitfulness' *stūpas* are so popular that several can be seen in any landscape.

Attitudes to images

Images always function as reminders of the spiritual qualities of holy beings, if in no other way. When a Theravādin, for example, expresses devotion before an image of Gotama Buddha, he is reminded of his struggle for enlightenment, his virtues, his teachings, and the ideal represented by him. He joyfully recollects the Buddha, developing a warm heart and a pure mind. The spiritual qualities expressed by the form of a good image also help to stimulate the arising of such qualities in one who contemplates it.

In Northern and Eastern Buddhism, except perhaps in Ch'an/Zen, images function as more than reminders. Especially in Vajrayāna schools, they are seen as infused with the spirit and power of the being they represent. Moreover, as image and being 'meet', in both being ultimately 'thought-only' or emptiness (as everything is, in Mahāyāna philosophy), the image comes to be seen as an actual form of the being. For this, it must have the traditional form and symbolism and be consecrated. This is done by chanting prayers and *mantra*s over it; by placing in it scriptures or relics, and even internal organs of clay, and by completing and wetting the eyes. This associates it with holy sounds and objects, giving it a power-for-good, and animates it, the wet eyes suggesting the response of a living gaze.

Even in Southern Buddhism, a temple image seems to act as more than a reminder, for it is generally thought that it must be consecrated before it can function as a focus for devotion (Gombrich, 1971, pp. 101, 138–40). Consecration involves the placing of relics in the image, and a monk reciting some Pāli verses over it. In Sri Lanka, these verses are the ones said to have been spoken by the Buddha immediately after his enlightenment. This harmonizes with the fact that the eyes are often completed at around 5 am, the time at which Gotama became fully enlightened. These two aspects seem to suggest that the consecrated image is seen as a representative of, rather than just a representation of, the Buddha. Other aspects of consecration reinforce this idea. In Sri Lanka, the lay craftsmen completing the eyes act as if this were connecting the image to a source of power which, like electricity, is dangerous if handled carelessly. They ritually prepare themselves for hours, and then only look at the eyes in a mirror while painting them in; till it is completed, their direct gaze is considered harmful. Some Westernized monks deny that there is any need to consecrate images.

In Southern Buddhism there is a widely held belief in a kind of '*buddha*-force' which will remain in the world for as long as Buddhism is practised. Indeed, a booklet produced by a Thai temple in London says of the Buddha: 'Although now his physical form no longer exists, his spiritual form, that is his benevolence and great compassion remains in the world.' This attitude is reflected in the way that Southern Buddhists regard relics and *bodhi*-trees as having a protective power-for-good. The '*buddha*-force', which many believe in, is particularly associated with images, especially ones used in devotion for centuries, suggesting that these are seen as having been thus 'charged up' with the Buddha's power. Less educated Southern Buddhists sometimes go so far as to regard the Buddha as still alive as an individual, and as somehow present in consecrated images of himself (Gombrich, 1971, pp. 103–43).

Bowing, offerings and chanting

Most Buddhist devotional acts are not congregational in essence, though they are frequently occasions for coming together in a shared activity and experience. In the home, they are often carried out in the morning and/or evening. Temple-visits can be at any time, though they are most common at festivals, or on special 'observance days' (four per lunar month). On visiting a temple, a person performs acts which amount to showing devotion to the 'three refuges'. The Buddha is represented by image, *stūpa* and *bodhi*-tree; the *Dhamma* is represented by a sermon, or informal teachings which the monks may give, and the *Saṅgha* is represented by the monks. Devotion at home or temple is expressed by *pūjā*: 'reverencing' or 'honouring', which involves bowing, making offerings, and chanting.

In Buddhist cultures, people bow on many occasions. Children bow to parents and teachers; adults bow to monks, nuns, *lama*s and the elderly; and monks bow to those ordained for longer than themselves. Such lowering of the head acknowledges someone else as having more experience of life or of spiritual practice, and develops respect and humility. It is natural, then, to bow before sacred objects which point towards the highest reality, and also to locate a *buddha*-image on the highest 'seat' in a room (Khantipalo, 1974, pp. 12–17). Within a shrine-room or the compound surrounding a *stūpa* or *bodhi*-tree, humility is also shown by not wearing shoes, for in ancient times, wearing shoes was a sign of wealth and status.

Bowing before sacred objects is generally done three times, so as to show respect to the 'three refuges'. A person stands or kneels with palms joined in a gesture known as *namaskāra*. They are held at the chest and forehead or, in Northern Buddhism, at the head, lips and chest, symbolizing respect offered by mind, speech and body. From a kneeling position, a person then places the elbows, hands and head on the ground. In Northern Buddhism, a fuller form known as a 'grand prostration' involves lying full-length on the ground (Brown and O'Brian, 1989, pp. 122–3). Devotion is also shown by circumambulation of *stūpa*s, *bodhi*-trees and temples, which in Northern Buddhism may be done by repeated prostrations (Ekvall, 1964, ch. 8). Clockwise circumambulation respectfully keeps one's right side facing the revered object, and indicates that the object ideally symbolizes what lies at the centre of one's life and aspiration. In Eastern Buddhism, another important practice is repeated bowing before an image in a spirit of repentance.

Offerings are usually accompanied by appropriate chanted verses. Together, these aim to arouse joyful and devout contemplation of the qualities of a holy being, and aspiration for spiritual progress. Such acts consequently generate karmic fruitfulness (Gombrich, 1971, pp. 114–27; Khantipalo, 1974, pp. 8–12). The most common offerings are flowers. One Theravāda set of flower-offering verses say, in Pāli:

> This mass of flowers, fresh-hued, odorous and choice,
> I offer at the blessed lotus-like feet of the Lord of sages.
> With diverse flowers, the Buddha/*Dhamma*/*Saṅgha* I revere;
> And through this karmic fruitfulness may there be release.
> Just as this flower fades, so my body goes towards destruction.

These combine joyous reverence, aspiration, and reflection on the impermanence of human life. A Zen flower-offering verse aspires that the 'flowers of the mind' should 'bloom in the springtime of enlightenment'.

The pleasant odour of smouldering incense-sticks frequently greets a person entering a Buddhist temple. A Pāli incense-offering verse refers to the Buddha as 'He of fragrant body and fragrant face, fragrant with infinite virtues'. This reflects the idea that the Buddha had an 'odour of sanctity', a certain 'air' about him suggestive of his glorious character and virtues. Incense both reminds a person of this and also creates a sense of delight, which can then be focused on the Buddha. Another common offering is the light of small lamps or candles, a reminder of *buddha*s as 'enlightened' or 'awakened' beings who give light to the world through their teachings. A Theravāda offering verse thus describes the Buddha as 'the lamp of the three worlds, dispeller of darkness'.

In Northern Buddhism (Ekvall, 1964, ch. 6), butter-lamps of finely wrought silver often burn perpetually before images. It is also common for seven kinds of offerings to be set before an image. Water 'for the face' and 'for the feet' symbolizes hospitality, while flowers, incense, lamps, perfume and food represent the five senses, ideally expressing devotees' dedication of their whole being to spiritual development. The offerings are placed in seven bowls, or water and grain in these are visualized as being the offerings. Devotees also use *mudrās*, ritual gestures representing offerings such as flowers, a lamp, or the whole world, all of this being co-ordinated with complex *mantras* (Beyer, 1978, pp. 143–226). They may additionally offer a white cotton or silk 'scarf of felicity' (Tibetan *kha-btags*; pron. *kuttha*) to an image. These are normally used as a friendship-offering to put a relationship on a good footing. Here they are used to form a bond of friendship with a holy being.

In all schools of Buddhism, chanting is very common as a vehicle for devotion or other ceremonial acts and, indeed, is the most common form of meditation – i.e., practice to generate certain mind-states – in most traditions. Its use derives from early Buddhism, when Indian society made little use of writing, and a learned person was 'much-heard' rather than 'well-read'. Chanting aided accurate memory of the Buddha's teachings, as it has a rhythm which encourages the mind to flow on from word to word, and lacks melody, which might demand that the sound of some words be distorted. It is also a public medium, so that errors of memory could be known and corrected. After the teachings were written down, it was still thought better that they be well memorized, and chanting had also become part of devotional life.

Buddhist chanting is neither singing nor a monotonous dirge. While being deep-toned and slightly solemn, it holds the interest with its small variations of pitch and rhythm. It is particularly impressive when a group of monks chant, for they may use different keys, all blending into a harmonious whole. The chants are usually in ancient languages, such as Pāli or old Tibetan, thus giving them an added air of sanctity. This, plus their sound-quality and accompanying thoughts, generates a mixture of uplifting joy, often felt as a glow of warmth in the chest, and contemplative calm. Such states tend to arise even in those listening to a chant, if they do so with a relaxed but attentive mind. Thus monks and nuns can transmit something of the tranquillity of their way of life when chanting for the laity. Many monks know the full meaning of the chants, as they know the relevant language to some extent, and can explain them to the laity. Vernacular chants also exist.

In all traditions, the most common chants are short verbal formulae, which may be strung together or repeated to form longer continuous chants. A very common Southern Buddhist chant, honouring Gotama Buddha, is *Namo tassa bhagavato, arahato, sammā-sambuddhassa*, 'Honour to the Lord, *arahat*, perfectly and completely Enlightened One!' This is repeated three times, and is usually followed by the chanted avowal of commitment to the 'three refuges' and the five moral precepts.

In all traditions, rosaries can be used to count off repeated chants. In Southern Buddhism, a *mantra* may be used such as *du sa ni ma; sa ni ma du; ni ma du sa; ma du sa ni*. This is based on the initial letters of the words for the Four Ennobling Truths: *dukkha* (suffering), *samudaya* (origin of it), *nirodha* (cessation of it), *magga* (path to its cessation). It concentrates the mind, keeps it alert, and opens it to understanding. A devotional rosary-chant used in Southern Buddhism is *Buddha, Dhamma, Saṅgha*.

Protective chanting

In all schools of Buddhism, chanting, or listening to it, is often used as a form of protection. In Southern Buddhism, chanted passages called *paritta*s or 'safety-runes' are used (Harvey, 1993). Most are excerpts from the Pāli scriptures, the most common one being that on the qualities of the three refuges, as translated above. Other popular ones include: the *Karaṇīya-metta Sutta*, which radiates feelings of loving-kindness to all living beings (Brown and O'Brian, 1989, pp. 88–9); the *Maṅgala Sutta*, which describes such 'blessings' as a good education, generosity, hearing the *Dhamma*, and attaining *nirvāṇa* (Brown and O'Brian, 1989, pp. 87–8); and the *Ratana Sutta*, which calls down the protection of the gods and praises the 'three jewels' (Nanamoli, 1960, pp. 4–6). While most *paritta*s are used as a general protection, some are used against particular dangers, such as one against death from snake-bite, said in the *sutta*s to have been given by the Buddha specifically as a '*paritta*' (*Khandha paritta*). *Paritta*s are used, for example, for warding off wild animals, human attackers or ghosts, exorcizing people, curing illnesses, and averting dangers from accidents or natural disasters. They are also used to gain a good harvest, to help pass an examination, to bless a new building, or simply as an act of karmic fruitfulness. There are limits to their power, though. They are said to work only for a virtuous person with confidence in the 'three refuges', and cannot, for example, cure a person of an illness if it is due to his past *karma* (Horner, 1969, vol. I, pp. 211–17). Within these limits, the working of *paritta*s is seen as involving a number of factors.

First, to chant or listen to a *paritta* is soothing and leads to self-confidence and a calm, pure mind, through both its sound-quality and its meaning. As the mind is in a healthier state, this may cure psychosomatic illnesses, or make a person more alert and better at avoiding the dangers of life. Secondly, chanting a *paritta*, especially one which expresses loving-kindness to all beings, is thought to calm down a hostile person, animal or ghost, making them more well-disposed towards the chanter and listeners. Thirdly, as well as making new karmic fruitfulness, *paritta*-chanting is thought to stimulate past karmic fruitfulness into bringing some of its good results immediately. Fourthly, chanting or listening to a *paritta* is thought to please those gods who are devotees of the Buddha, so that they offer what protection and assistance it is in their power to give. Finally, the spiritual power of the Buddha, the 'greatly compassionate protector' (*Mahā-jayamaṅgala Gāthā paritta*), and of the truth he expressed, seems to be seen as continuing in his words, with its beneficial influence being liberated when these are devoutly chanted. This partly relates to the concept, found in the early texts, of an 'asseveration of truth'. By affirming some genuine virtue of oneself or someone else, or publicly admitting an embarrassing fault, a wonder-working power-for-good is liberated, to the benefit of oneself and others. Accordingly, a *Ratana Sutta* refrain, 'by this truth, may there be well-being!', is repeated after various excellences of the 'three jewels' have been enumerated.

While an ordinary lay-person or specialist chanter can activate the power of the Buddha's words by chanting, it is more efficacious for monks to do so. This is because they try to live fully the way of life taught by the Buddha. When members of the monastic *saṅgha* chant the *Dhamma*, as taught by the Buddha, there is a powerful combination, of benefit to listening lay-people. To symbolize the protective power passing from the monks, they hold a cord while chanting a *paritta*. This is also tied to a *buddha*-image, suggesting that the image is being impregnated with the *paritta*'s power, or, equally, that it is discharging some of its previously accumulated power to add to that of the *paritta*. Afterwards, pieces of the '*paritta*-cord' are tied to the lay-people's wrists as a reminder of, and a 'store' of, the *paritta*'s protective power. When the cord is tied on, a Pāli verse is uttered which means 'By the majesty of the power attained by all *buddhas*, solitary *buddhas* and *arahats*, I tie on a complete protection'.

In Eastern and Northern traditions, including Ch'an/Zen, chanted formulae used in a similar way to *parittas* are *dhāraṇīs*, utterances 'preserving' Buddhism and its followers (Kato *et al.*, 1975, pp. 328–32). These are strings of Sanskrit words and syllables, originating as mnemonic formulae summarizing a *sūtra* or teaching, which may be unintelligible without explanation. The Southern *du, sa, ni, ma* ... rosary chant quoted above is akin to these. Likewise, in Northern Buddhism, the use of *mantras* is common, both in devotion and meditation.

Devotion to Avalokiteśvara

Devotion to Avalokiteśvara pervades Eastern and Northern Buddhism (see pp. 114 and 115–16). A text much used in liturgies is the verse section of the *Avalokiteśvara Sūtra*, an extract from the *Lotus Sūtra* (Kato *et al.*, 1975, pp. 319–27; Conze *et al.*, 1964, pp. 194–6). Expressing profound devotion, this speaks of:

> True regard, serene regard, far-reaching wise regard, regard of pity, compassionate regard, ever longed for, ever longed for! Pure and serene in radiance, wisdom's sun destroying darkness. ... Law of pity, thunder quivering, compassion wondrous as a great cloud, pouring spiritual rain like nectar, quenching the flames of distress!

Statues and paintings of Avalokiteśvara are found in abundance, depicting him in around 130 different ways, each aiming to express some aspect of his nature. In China, as Kuan-yin, 'he' gradually came to be portrayed as female. This may have been because the Chinese saw his compassion as a female quality; it may also have been partly due to the female reference in his *mantra* (see below). Moreover, from the fifth century, some of 'his' popular incarnations were female, and 'he' may also have merged with a pre-Buddhist goddess thought to care for mariners. Kuan-yin thus became an all-compassionate 'mother-goddess', the most popular deity in all of China, being portrayed as a graceful, lotus-holding figure in a white robe. An artistic form common in Tibet and Japan shows Avalokiteśvara with 'a thousand' arms (fewer, for practical reasons, in statues) and eleven heads. Seven hands hold various emblems, while the rest represent his boundless skilful means (ability to help in the most appropriate way). Each makes a *mudrā* or 'gesture', denoting 'be fearless', and on its palm is an eye, representing his ever-watchful nature, ready to rush to the aid of beings. His eleven heads are explained by a story that, on seeing so many beings suffering in the hells, his horror and tears caused him momentarily to despair of fulfilling his vow to save all beings. His head then split into ten pieces, as he had said it would if he ever abandoned his resolve. Amitābha Buddha then brought him back to life to renew his vow. Making each of the head-fragments into a new head, he assembled them on Avalokiteśvara's shoulders, and surmounted them with a replica of his own head, symbolizing that he would continue to inspire the *bodhisattva* in his work. With eleven heads, Avalokiteśvara was now even better equipped to look for beings in need! From Avalokiteśvara's tears, moreover, two forms of Tārā, the 'Saviouress' *bodhisattva*, had been born: themselves the focus of much devotion in Tibet (Conze *et al.*, 1954, pp. 196–202).

The *Avalokiteśvara Sūtra* says that Avalokiteśvara will instantly respond to those who 'with all their mind call upon his name'. 'By virtue of the power of that *bodhisattva*'s majesty', they will be unburnt by a fire; saved at sea in a storm; the hearts of murdering foes will turn to kindness; as prisoners, guilty or innocent, they will be set free from their chains; merchants will be freed from the dangers of robbers; threatening wild beasts will flee; success will be attained in a court of law or battle; and a woman will have a virtuous child, of the sex of her choice. Devotees will also be freed from attachment, hatred and delusion by 'keeping in mind and remembering' Avalokiteśvara. Much of this is comparable to the power attributed to *paritta*-chanting. The wondrous help of Avalokiteśvara is understood both as a literal intervention in the world, perhaps through the aid of a mysterious stranger, or a vision guiding someone through mists on a dangerous mountain, and as coming from the power of a devotee's faith. In the *Śūraṅgama Sūtra*, it is said that Avalokiteśvara aids beings by awakening them to their compassionate *buddha*-nature, and in accordance with this, any act of great kindness may be seen as the 'help' of Avalokiteśvara.

Ch'an/Zen, for which 'To be compassionate is Kuan-yin' (Yampolsky, 1967, sec. 35), generally understands his/her aid in purely internal, spiritual terms: for a 'storm' is anger, 'fire' is desire, 'chains' are simply those of fear, a sense of oppression comes from lack of patience, and animals only threaten one who has ill-will. Accordingly, Ch'an/Zen devotion to Kuan-yin is thought of primarily in terms of 'developing the heart of Kuan-yin': growing the seed of great compassion so that one becomes ever-ready to help others.

In Northern Buddhism, the *mantra Oṃ maṇi padme hūṃ* is very popular in invoking the help of Avalokiteśvara and in developing compassion (Ekvall, 1964, pp. 115–23). *Oṃ* and *hūṃ* are ancient Indian sacred sounds, the first being seen as the basic sound of the universe. *Maṇi padme* literally means 'O jewelled-lotus lady', but in developed exegesis, *maṇi* is seen as referring to the jewel that this *bodhisattva* holds, while *padme* refers to the lotus as his symbol. The jewel symbolizes both his willingness to grant righteous wishes, and the pure clarity in the depths of the minds of beings. The lotus symbolizes both the pure beauty of Avalokiteśvara's compassion, and the worldly minds of beings which he encourages to 'bloom' into enlightenment. Accompanied by the click of rosaries, the *'Maṇi' mantra* is frequently heard on the lips of all who have any degree of devotion to Buddhism. It may be uttered as a person goes about his or her business, either under the breath or as an audible rhythmic murmur called 'purring' by the Tibetans. The Tibetans also activate the power of this *mantra*, and generate karmic fruitfulness, by use of the '*Maṇi* religion wheel', known in the West as a 'prayer wheel'. The formula is carved or painted on the outside of a short cylinder, and is written many times on a tightly rolled piece of paper inside. Each revolution of the cylinder is held to be equivalent to the repetition of all the formulae written on and in it, an idea related to that of the Buddha's first sermon as the 'setting in motion of the *Dhamma*-wheel'. '*Maṇi* religion wheels' are of various types. Hand-held ones have cylinders about seven centimetres long, mounted on handles about twelve centimetres long; a small weight attached to the cylinder on a chain enables it to be spun on a spindle fixed in the handle. Wheels around 25 centimetres high are also fixed in rows along the sides of *stūpa*s or monasteries, so that people can turn them as they circumambulate these. The largest wheels, found at the entrance to temples, may be four metres high and two metres in diameter, and contain thousands of *Maṇi* formulae, along with scriptures and images. There are also wheels driven by streams or chimney smoke. The *Maṇi mantra* is also carved on stones deposited on hill-top cairns, on rock-faces by the side of paths, on long walls specially built at the approaches to towns, and is printed on 'prayer flags'. Karmic fruitfulness accrues to those who pay for any of these or produce them, to all who glance at them, thinking of Avalokiteśvara and his compassion, and even to insects who come into contact with them.

Devotion to Amitābha

Devotion to Amitābha Buddha (see pp. 112–13) is found within most schools of the Mahāyāna, but is the essence of the Pure Land schools (Conze *et al.*, 1954, pp. 202–6; Brown and O'Brian, 1989, pp. 99–100, 218–19, 251–8). Here, practice centres on the 'Buddha invocation' (Chinese *nien-fo*, Japanese *nembutsu*): repetition of *Nan-mo A-mit'o Fo* (Chinese) or *Nama Amida Butsu* (Japanese), translations of the Sanskrit *Namo Amitābhāya Buddhāya*, meaning 'Hail to Amitābha Buddha' (Pallis, 1980, pp. 84–101). In China, recitation is done in tune with the steady and natural breath, and may be repeated many times a day, as the practitioner never knows when he has done it the minimum necessary 'ten times' with 'unwavering concentration'. A by-product of concentration, focused on Amitābha and the enlightenment attainable in Sukhāvatī, his Pure Land, is that the mind is purified of distracting passions. The *nembutsu* also has a certain *mantra*-like quality, in that it is seen as opening up a channel between a holy being and a devotee: in this case, the channel of grace. Furthermore, when the practice is done wholeheartedly, it becomes spontaneous, and can be seen as reciting itself in a mental space in which the ego has temporarily dissolved. Through association with *nembutsu*-practice, a person's rosary often comes to be a revered object; touching it may immediately start the recitation revolving in the mind, and bring on the associated mental states.

In China, Shan-tao (613–681) came to emphasize the invocation as the 'primary' Pure Land practice. 'Secondary' ones included: chanting the Pure Land *sūtras*; visualization of Amitābha and his Pure Land; worship of various *buddhas*; singing hymns of praise to Amitābha;

resolving to be reborn in his land; and developing generosity and compassion by helping the needy, and through vegetarianism. In Japan, the Jōdo-shin school came to put single-minded emphasis on Amitābha Buddha, and on the *nembutsu* as including all other practices, though the secondary practices could be done as expressions of gratitude for salvation. The sole aim of the *nembutsu* is to facilitate the awakening of faith; the moment when this truly occurs is seen as a transcendental, atemporal experience in which the devotee is at one with Amitābha in the form of the numinous *nembutsu*. After faith has arisen, any recitation is done solely as an expression of gratitude, often shown by merely wearing a rosary wrapped around the hand. This is also a reminder that 'sinful humans' are but a bundle of passions compared to Amitābha. Devotees express joyful adoration of Amitābha, and liken him to father and mother, so that he is commonly called *Oyasama*, 'The Parent'.

Amitābha is often depicted seated in meditation, with the meeting of his index fingers and thumbs indicating that devotees should give up 'self-power' and rely on 'other-power' for salvation. One famous gilded wooden statue of him is in the Phoenix Hall, near Kyoto, Japan. Made in 1053 CE, it became the model for many later Japanese images of Amitābha. It shows him as a noble, gentle and compassionate being whose light and graceful form seems to float on its lotus-base above a small lake, as if in a vision. In the halo of the image are figures which represent beings newly born in Sukhāvatī, the 'Happy Land', which is depicted in paintings and statues on the walls of the image-hall. The aim of the whole is to re-create Sukhāvatī on earth, so as to stimulate an uplifting spiritual experience and deepen the aspiration to be reborn, by Amitābha's power, in this Pure Land. Indeed, much Mahāyāna art has been inspired by visionary experiences and has helped to inspire further experiences of a similar kind.

Devotion to Bhaiṣajya-guru

Devotion to the heavenly Buddha Bhaiṣajya-guru, the 'Master of Healing', is important in both Northern and Eastern Buddhism (Birnbaum, 1979). In Chinese temples, image-halls most commonly have images of him and Amitābha flanking one of Śākyamuni (the Mahāyāna term for the historical Buddha, and the heavenly *buddha* who manifested him on earth). He generally holds a bowl said to be made of lapis lazuli, an intensely blue gemstone thought to have healing properties. His body is also said to be like lapis lazuli, and to blaze with light. In one Chinese healing rite, a person keeps eight vows for seven days, makes offerings to monks, worships Bhaiṣajyaguru, recites his *sūtra* 79 times, makes seven images of him, and then contemplates his image so that it comes alive with his spiritual force and healing energy. Tuning into this, the devotee then mentally merges with him.

Devotion to the *Lotus Sūtra*

Within the Japanese Nichiren school, the symbolically rich title of the '*Lotus Sūtra* of the True *Dharma*', *Myōhō-renge-kyō*, is a revered focus of devotion. This is known as the *daimoku*, and is seen to represent ultimate reality in its intrinsic purity. Prefaced by *Namu*, 'honour to', it forms the seven-syllable invocatory formula *Na-mu myō-hō ren-ge-kyō*, whose repetition, accompanied by drums, is the central practice. Chanting this with sincere faith in the power of the truths of the *sūtra* is held to purify the mind, protect and benefit the chanter, lead to the moral uplift of the individual and society, develop the *bodhisattva* perfections, and activate the *buddha*-nature within. The title is also written or carved on a scroll or plaque known as the *gohonzon*, or 'chief object of worship'. Down the centre of this is the invocation in bold Japanese characters; above, left and right, are the names of Prabhūtaratna Buddha, a past *buddha* who re-manifests himself in an incident in the *Lotus Sūtra*, and Śākyamuni; at its sides are the names of the 'four great kings', guardian deities who live in the lowest heaven described in ancient Buddhist cosmology; in the remaining space are names of various holy beings mentioned in the *sūtra* – including the *bodhisattva* that Nichiren said he was an incarnation of – and of certain Shintō deities. The *gohonzon* is seen as representing the final truth, as revealed in the *sūtra*, emphasizing Śākyamuni Buddha as all-pervading reality and universal power. The *gohonzon* is thus the primary focus of worship and object of contemplation, prominently displayed in Nichiren temples between images of Śākyamuni and Prabhūtaratna. The sub-sect known as the Nichiren Shō-shū, however, has an image of the founder of the Nichiren school, Nichiren (1222–82), in a central position. A secondary Nichiren practice is to chant the sections of the *Lotus Sūtra* on skilful means and the 'eternal' life-span of Śākyamuni. In the twentieth century, a number of 'New Religions' have arisen in Japan, several based on Nichiren Buddhism. The best known is the Sōka-gakkai, once the lay arm of Nichiren Shō-shū, which is a very successful movement which actively seeks converts overseas.

Pilgrimage

Pilgrimage is a fairly common practice in Buddhism, and may be done for a variety of reasons: to bring alive events from the life of holy beings and so strengthen spiritual aspirations; to perform karmically fruitful actions; to be suffused by the power-for-good of relics and *bodhi*-trees; to receive protection from deities at the sites; or to fulfil a vow that pilgrimage would be made if aid was received from a certain *bodhisattva*. The most ancient sites are those of the Buddha's birth, first sermon, enlightenment and passing into final *nirvāṇa* at death. The Buddha said these should be visited with thoughts of reverence, such that anyone dying on the journey would be reborn in a heaven (see p. 300). The most important is Bodh-gayā, whose focus is an ancient *bodhi*-tree directly descended from the one under which Gotama attained enlightenment. Its sagging boughs are reverently propped up, prayer flags flutter from its branches, and pilgrims treasure any leaves which fall from it.

As Buddhism spread beyond India, new focuses of pilgrimage developed. For details, see Chapter 10 below.

Festivals

Buddhists enjoy and appreciate festivals as times for re-affirming devotion and commitment, performing karmically fruitful actions for the benefit of the individual and community, strengthening community ties and values, and merry-making (Brown, 1986, chs 3, 4 and 8). The Southern, Northern and Eastern traditions each have their major festivals, and there are also national variations on these, as well as local festivals on, for example, the anniversary of the founding of a temple. Some festivals which Buddhists celebrate are not Buddhist as such, but pertain to the agricultural cycle, national deities, or traditions such as Confucianism.

In Southern Buddhism, most major festivals occur at the time of a full moon (Spiro, 1971, pp. 219–31; Terwiel, 1979, pp. 223–37). As in Northern Buddhism, the lunar cycle also marks off the sabbath-like *uposatha*s, or 'observance days', at the full moon, new moon and, less importantly, two half-moon days. Except at times of major festivals, observance days are attended only by the more devout, who spend a day and night at their local monastery. The monks are solemnly offered food, commitment to certain ethical precepts is made, the monks chant for the laity, and sometimes a sermon is given; these features also occur at all Southern Buddhist festivals. The rest of the time is spent in expressing devotion, reading, talking to the monks, and perhaps in some meditation.

In the lands of Southern Buddhism, the festival year starts at the traditional New Years, celebrated at various times, for up to four days, in mid-April. On the first day, houses are thoroughly cleaned of the dirt of the old year. Water, sometimes scented, is ceremonially poured over *buddha*-images and the hands of monks and elderly relatives, as a mark of respect. In Southeast Asia, this is frequently followed by a good-humoured period when the laity throw water at all and sundry. On the second day, in Thailand, Cambodia and Laos, sand *stūpa*s are built in temple-compounds or on river banks. When the new year starts on the next day, the sand is spread out to form a new compound floor, or is washed away by the river. Its dispersal is seen as symbolically 'cleansing' a person of the past year's bad deeds, represented by the grains of sand. Reflecting on past misdeeds, people thus re-dedicate themselves to Buddhist values. Accordingly, the New Year is also a time for aiding living beings by releasing caged birds and rescuing fish from drying-up ponds and streams. Accompanying festivities may include boat races, kite fights, music, traditional dancing and plays.

At the full moon of the lunar month of Vesākha, usually in May, comes *Vesākha Pūjā*, celebrating the Buddha's birth, enlightenment and final *nirvāṇa* at death. In Sri Lanka, this is the most important festival, when houses are decorated with garlands and paper lanterns, and driveways and temple-courtyards are illuminated. People wander between pavement pantomimes and pavilions displaying paintings of the Buddha's life, with food being given out from roadside alms-stalls. In Myanmar (Burma), *bodhi*-trees are watered with scented water, while in Thailand, Cambodia and Laos, the monks lead the laity in a three-fold circumambulation of a temple, *stūpa* or *buddha*-

image. The sermon which follows, on the Buddha's life, sometimes lasts all night.

In Sri Lanka, the next full-moon day marks the *Poson* festival, celebrating the spreading of Buddhism to the island by Mahinda. Paintings of him are paraded through the streets to the sound of drumming, and pilgrimages are made to Anuradhapura and nearby Mihintale, where he met and converted the king.

The next full moon marks *Āsālha Pūjā*, celebrating the Buddha's renunciation and first sermon, and marking the start of the three-month period of *Vassa* (the 'Rains'). During this, monks stay at their home monasteries, except for short absences, for concentration on study and meditation, and many young men in Southeast Asia take temporary ordination. The laity also deepen their religious commitment. They tend to avoid festivities, especially secular ones such as marriages, and more people than usual observe *uposatha*s at their local monasteries. Most ordinations take place in the time leading up to *Āsālha Pūjā*, with their karmic fruitfulness seen as contributing to the timely start of the rains.

At the full moon marking the end of *Vassa*, the monks hold the ceremony of *Pavāraṇā*. When they chant and meditate, wax drips into a bowl of water from a burning candle, and it is thought that something of the monks' karmic fruitfulness, built up during *Vassa*, suffuses and sacralizes the water. This is then sprinkled on the laity as a blessing. In Southeast Asia, especially Myanmar (Burma), the following day is the *Tāvatiṃsa* festival, celebrating the time when the Buddha, after spending *Vassa* in the heaven 'Of the Thirty-three (gods)' teaching his mother, descended to earth. As the 'light' of the world was then accessible again, this is a festival of lights, which illuminate houses, monasteries and *stūpa*s and may be floated on rivers in small leaf-boats. A special food-offering is also made to a procession of monks, headed by a layman holding a *buddha*-image and alms-bowl, symbolizing the returning Buddha.

The following month is the season for *Kaṭhina* celebrations, at which new robes, useful goods and money are given to the monasteries. The focal act is the donation of patches of cloth which the monks dye and make into a special robe, during the same day, commemorating the robes made from sewn-together rags in early Buddhism. These highly auspicious ceremonies, held at most local *vihāra*s, complete the annual round of the more important festivals in Southern Buddhism.

Other than in Nepal, several festivals in Northern Buddhism more or less coincide with corresponding Southern ones: the celebration of the enlightenment and final *nirvāṇa* of the Buddha (his birth being celebrated eight days earlier), the first sermon and the descent from a heaven (here seen as the *Tuṣita* heaven). The different schools also have festivals relating to their founders, with the death of Tsong-kha-pa (in November) being of general importance; monasteries also have festivals relating to their specific tutelary deity. An important and characteristic festival centres on the Tibetan New Year, in February. In the preceding two weeks, monks dressed in masks and brightly coloured robes perform impressive ritual dances before a large lay audience. Accompanied by booming alpine horns, drums, shrilling oboes and clashing cymbals, they act out a series of solemn but impressive movements, lasting several hours. These are seen as driving away evil powers, while other rituals seek to help beings to progress towards enlightenment. From the fourth to the twenty-fifth day of the first month, monks perform the ceremonies of *sMon lam* (Tibetan; pron. *Monlam*), the 'Great Vow', centred on a five-day celebration of the Buddha's 'marvel of the pairs' at Śrāvasti (which is said to have involved the Buddha levitating and issuing fire and water from his body). As an event in which rival teachers were confounded, this became an appropriate symbol for the overcoming of evil forces, and of Buddhism's past victory over Bon, the pre-Buddhist religion of Tibet. On the thirteenth day, dances portray Tibetan Buddhism's fierce protector-deities in their struggle against demons and spiritual ignorance. These are represented by a small human effigy which is ritually killed, symbolizing victory over evil and the securing of a safe and prosperous new year. To raise people's energy levels for the new year, horse races and archery competitions are held around this period.

In the lands of Eastern Buddhism, the annual round of festivals has fewer Buddhist elements, and more from Confucianism, Shintō and folk traditions. In Communist China, festivals are now largely secularized and politicized, though they continue much as before in Taiwan and Hong Kong and among expatriate Chinese. Among the Chinese, who determine festivals by a lunar calendar, the birth of the Buddha is celebrated in May, as in Korea, while in Japan it is celebrated on 8 April. The principal rite recalls the story that the new-born Śākyamuni stood and was bathed by water sent down by gods: small standing images of the child are placed in bowls, and scented water or tea is ladled over them. For Chinese Buddhists, the festival is also a popular time for the release of living beings into the water or air. In Korea, it is a time for illuminating temples with paper lanterns. In Japan the festival is known as *Hana matsuri*, the 'Flower Festival', and retains elements of a pre-Buddhist festival involving the gathering of wild mountain flowers so as to bring home deities to protect the rice-fields. The Buddhist connection is that Śākyamuni was born in a flower-laden grove, so that the infant-Buddha images are housed in floral shrines.

The other important Chinese Buddhist festivals are those of the 'birth', 'enlightenment' and 'death' of Kuan-yin, and especially *Ullambana*, which is also celebrated by non-Buddhists. This 'Festival of Hungry Ghosts', in August/September, is when ancestors reborn as ghosts are said to wander in the human world, as a potential source of danger. At the full moon, which ends the three-months 'Summer Retreat', monks transfer karmic fruitfulness, put out food and chant *sūtra*s for them, so as to help them to a better rebirth. The laity sponsor the rites and participate by burning large paper boats which will help 'ferry across' hungry ghosts to a better world, thus showing filial regard for ancestors. A favourite story told at this time is that of Mu-lien (Pāli Moggallāna), a key *arahat* disciple of the Buddha, who discovered that his mother was reborn as a hungry ghost or in a hell (there are two versions of the story). On the advice of the Buddha, he then helped her attain a better rebirth by transferring karmic fruitfulness to her. In Japan, *Ullambana* became *O-bon*, the 'Feast for the Dead', celebrated from 13 to 15 July. Graves are washed and tended, and an altar is set up in or near the home for offerings of fresh herbs and flowers. A fire and candles are lit to welcome ancestral spirits to partake of the offerings and a Buddhist priest is invited to chant a *sūtra* in each home in his parish.

It can thus be seen that Buddhism has a full and rich spectrum of devotional life. It may have a greater range of objects of devotion than some religions, and may contain traditions which warn against an excess of devotion, yet devotion runs deep within its blood, in ways paralleling many other religions. Devotion is a good way to open the heart to calm and the development of liberating wisdom. For the Pure Land tradition, complete faith and devotion are *themselves* the gateway to liberation.

Notes

1 Beings-for-enlightenment, dedicated to attaining buddhahood.

2 The Stream-enterer (see p. 87), through insight that gains a distant glimpse of *nirvāṇa*, cannot be reborn at less than a human level and will become an *arahat* within seven lives at most. The Once-returner further weakens various spiritual fetters so that his or her future rebirths will include only one more at the level of humans or the lower gods. The Non-returner is one whose insight is almost enough to become an *arahat* in his or her present life, but not quite. The Non-returner is thus reborn in one of several 'pure abodes' – heavenly rebirths where only Non-returners are found. There their insight matures until they become long-lived *arahat* gods.

Further reading

Beyer, S. (1978) *The Cult of Tārā: Magic and Ritual in Tibet.* London: University of California Press, pp. 1–226.

Birnbaum, R. (1979) *The Healing Buddha.* London: Rider (Chinese texts and rituals).

Blofeld, J. (1970) *The Tantric Mysticism of Tibet.* New York: Dutton.

Brown, A. (ed.) (1986) *Festivals in World Religions.* London: Longman.

Brown, K. and O'Brian, J. (eds) (1989) *The Essential Teachings of Buddhism.* London: Rider (translations and comments from all schools).

Conze, E., Horner, I. B., Snellgrove, D. and Waley, A. (eds) (1954) *Buddhist Texts Through the Ages.* New York: Philosophical Library (translations from all schools).

Ekvall, R. B. (1964) *Religious Observances in Tibet.* London: University of Chicago Press.

Gombrich, R. (1971) *Precept and Practice: Traditional Buddhism in the Rural Highlands of Ceylon.* Oxford: Clarendon Press.

Harvey, P. (1990) *An Introduction to Buddhism: Teachings, History and Practices.* Cambridge: Cambridge University Press.

Harvey, P. (1993) 'The dynamics of paritta chanting in Southern Buddhism' in K. Werner (ed.) *Love Divine: Studies in Bhakti and Devotional Mysticism.* London: Curzon Press.

Horner, I. B. (1969) *Milinda's Questions.* London: Luzac (a Theravādin text).

Kato, B., Tamura, Y. and Miyasaka, K. (trans.) (1975) *The Threefold Lotus Sutra.* New York: Weatherhill (a Mahāyāna text).

Khantipalo, Bhikkhu (1974) *Lay Buddhist Practice* (*Wheel*, 206/207).

Kandy, Sri Lanka: Buddhist Publication Society.
Nanamoli, Bhikkhu (1960) *Minor Readings and Illustrators.* London: Pali Text Society (a Theravādin text and commentary).
Pallis, M. (1980) *A Buddhist Spectrum.* London: Allen & Unwin.
Spiro, M. E. (1971) *Buddhism and Society: A Great Tradition and Its Burmese Vicissitudes.* London: Allen & Unwin.
Tay, N. (1976–77) 'Kuan-yin: the cult of half Asia', *History of Religions*, 16, pp. 147–77.
Terwiel, B. J. (1979) *Monks and Magic: An Analysis of Religious Ceremonies in Thailand.* London: Curzon Press.
Yampolsky, P. B. (1967) *The Platform Sutra of the Sixth Patriarch.* New York: Columbia University Press (a Ch'an/Zen text).

5. Rites of passage

Christopher Lamb

Buddhism, as a universal religion, seems remarkably deficient in rites of passage as marking in a sacred way the stages of life. There is nothing comparable with circumcision in Judaism or christening in Christianity by which a child is recognized as a member of the community, no ceremony specifically marking the passage into adulthood, no universal ceremony of marriage. Sociologically speaking, Buddhism seems to regard marking these stages of life as a matter for secular arrangement and local custom.

Buddhism is unique among world religions in its radical denial of the existence of the self as an ontological category. Everywhere it insists on the impermanence of compounded things. Attachment to the idea of a substantial self is the primordial ignorance that holds one in bondage to *saṃsāra*, the round of rebirths. This is why Buddhist rites of passage conduct one away from the world. Victor Turner has observed this tendency in *The Ritual Process*:[1]

> Nowhere has [the] institutionalisation of liminality been more clearly marked and defined than in the monastic and mendicant states in the great world religions.

Buddhist rites and ceremonies

Among the fetters to spiritual liberation that Buddhism outlines is that of *śīla-vrata-parāmarśa* (Sanskrit; Pāli *sīla-bbata-parāmasā*), which has sometimes been translated as 'grasping at rites and rituals'. This wrongly gives the impression that Buddhism is doctrinally averse to rituals. The term actually means 'grasping at precepts and vows' and refers to the belief that if one keeps to certain moral norms (even Buddhist ones), or keeps certain vows, this alone will be sufficient to attain liberation. It is also a critique of any tendency to do things in a fixed and rigid way. For Buddhism, rituals can be of value if they help arouse wholesome states of mind, such as calm, joy or compassion, and can play a role in spiritual development as a complement to other practices.

From the beginning Buddhism, in common with other groups of religious renouncers, did not accept the Brahmanical *varṇāśrama-dharma*-classification of the duties of life into four stages for at least males of the top three of four divinely-ordained social classes. Brahmanism regarded the householder-stage as an essential duty to be undertaken, but Buddhism saw this as a hindrance and treated marriage as a social contract, with no parallel to the Hindu *saṃskāra* or the Christian sacrament. Though most married Buddhists are monogamous, fraternal polyandry and even sororal polygyny have been practised in the Tibetan ethnic area (Dargyay, 1982). Certain rituals survive from folk-religion, and rites of protection are performed by monks, even though they have more to do with a happy continuance in the round of rebirth than liberation from it (see pp. 66–7). In places, old animistic and shamanistic beliefs and practices have been adapted to the Buddhist Path to lead people's minds to faith; elsewhere, in Sri Lanka for instance, Western values have had their effect.

The threefold refuge

The threefold 'going for refuge' (see p. 127), known in Sanskrit as *Tri-śaraṇa-gamana* and in Pāli as *Ti-saraṇa-gamana*, is a ceremony used by all Buddhists, monks and laity alike, regardless of the tradition they belong to. Commonly, it is a rite of veneration of the Three Jewels, *Tri-ratna* (Pāli *Ti-ratana*) – the Buddha, the *Dharma* and the *Saṅgha*.

The first reference to such a ceremony is ancient indeed; it occurs in the *Vinaya* (Code of Discipline) in the Pāli Canon. Soon after the Buddha's enlightenment two merchants bringing rice cakes and lumps of honey approached him and then took refuge 'in the Blessed One and in the *Dhamma*'.

> Thus these came to be the first lay-disciples (*upāsaka*s) in the world by using the two-word formula. (Horner, 1951, p. 6)

As yet, the Buddha had no followers among the renouncers; so there was no *saṅgha* or community of monks until he preached his first sermon at Sārnāth. From this point the Three Jewels became the central focus of reverence in Buddhism. The first lay disciples to use the threefold formula in its present form took refuge shortly afterwards (Horner, 1951, p. 24).

Nowadays laymen and women seeking to become *upāsaka*s (male) or *upāsikā*s (female) vow to observe Five Precepts after recitation of the refuge formula. On full- and new-moon days they also observe Eight Precepts, taken after going for refuge. Going for refuge is also done before the *pravrajyā* (Pāli *pabbajjā*) and *upasaṃpad* (Pāli *upasampadā*) ceremonies of monastic ordination, and before *bodhisattva* vows are taken. In tantric ceremonies a fourth refuge in the *guru* prefaces the other three.

A. Van Gennep in *The Rites of Passage*[2] mentions how in Bengal an outcast becomes a Muslim to escape the hierarchy of caste. In recent times a clear example of refuge as a rite of separation is the case of the Untouchables (now called Dalits) of Pune, many thousands of whom were led by Dr Ambedkar, himself a member of the so-called Scheduled Castes, to adopt Buddhism in order to escape from low status and low self-esteem inflicted by caste Hinduism. In 1950 he headed a mass conversion of his people into Buddhism by the act of refuge.

Taking refuge in the Three Jewels is what defines a Buddhist but not everyone taking it necessarily means the same thing by each of the Jewels (see pp. 127–30). The Tibetan scholar Sakya Pandita in the twelfth century differentiated between the mundane and transcendent ways of taking refuge. The mundane refuge is simply for personal advancement and welfare in present and future lives, taken by ordinary people. Whether it is taken in an inferior object, such as a god, mountain or a tree, or even in the Three Jewels, such a motivation will not bring release from *saṃsāra*. On the other hand, the transcendent way may be either common, such as the *śrāvaka*s' way (see p. 10), which is to attain personal liberation, or unique, such as the *bodhisattva*s' way, which is to attain the omniscience of buddhahood to help other beings. H. Saddhatissa (1967) gives a modern Theravādin interpretation.

Method of taking refuge

The formula of refuge in Pāli is usually prefaced by a short acclamation: *namo tassa bhagavato, arahato, sammā-sambuddhassa*, 'Praise to the Blessed One, the *Arahat*, the Perfectly Enlightened One', repeated three times. The refuges proper then follow:

buddhaṃ saraṇaṃ gacchāmi
dhammaṃ saraṇaṃ gacchāmi
saṅghaṃ saraṇaṃ gacchāmi
dutiyam pi buddhaṃ saraṇaṃ gacchāmi ...
tatiyam pi buddhaṃ saraṇaṃ gacchāmi ...

I go to the Buddha for refuge
I go to the *Dhamma* for refuge
I go to the *Saṅgha* for refuge
A second time I go to the Buddha for refuge ...
A third time I go to the Buddha for refuge ...

Persons taking refuge may make an offering of flowers, fruit and incense. In Thailand and other countries where they grow in abundance, it is usual to offer lotus buds. Throughout Asia the lotus, growing in muddy pools but raising its leaves and flowers above the surface of the water, symbolizes the spiritual potential of humans, rooted in the world but able to transcend it. Flowers with thorns, like roses, are not considered auspicious.

Having removed their shoes, the individuals come before the monk, *lama* or shrine and make three obeisances or prostrations. In the Theravādin tradition they stand with their palms joined, or they kneel down and sit back on their heels. Then they raise their joined palms to their chests and bow forward to touch their foreheads on the ground. In the Tibetan tradition prostration is altogether more energetic. The joined hands are moved up from the chest to the lips, to the forehead. Prostration is done from the standing position each time and may be made in one of two ways. The first way is to raise the joined hands to the head and then fall to the knees and bow to the ground. The full prostration is performed from the standing position as before, but on sinking to the knees the whole body slides forward till it is flat on the ground. The palms are then brought together at the crown of the head and raised into the prayer position. In 1985 I myself saw dozens of people performing this devotion to the Three

Jewels hundreds of times over before the main doors of the Jo-khang temple in Lhasa. Pilgrims often measure their own length in prostrations along the route surrounding the sacred place. Atīśa (1983, pp. 24–39) gives a ritual of Sevenfold Worship of the Three Jewels.

The fourfold refuge

Strictly speaking, the notion of the *guru* (Tibetan *bLa-ma*, pron. *lama*) belongs to the Vajrayāna, the Diamond Vehicle, a development of the Mahāyāna, practised in Tibet and parts of China and Japan. Its religious texts are the *tantra*s (Wayman, 1973); it uses *mantra*s (utterances that protect the mind), *maṇḍala*s (sacred cosmograms), ritual implements, vestments and special rituals. Teachings are given only after the disciple has received empowerment or initiation from the *guru*. The ritual complexity, richness of symbolic meaning and esoteric content make tantric initiation rites quite different from monastic ordination.

The fourfold refuge sometimes introduces purely Mahāyāna practices. The present Dalai Lama composed a *sādhana* or liturgy entitled *A Mahāyāna Method of Accomplishment: The Sādhana of the Inseparability of the Spiritual Master and Avalokiteshvara* when he was nineteen years of age. It was first printed in Tibet in 1954. Its opening lines appear also in the Tantric Ritual-Feast Offering to one's *guru* by the First Panchen Lama:

Namo Gurubhyaḥ	In the Spiritual Masters I take refuge
Namo Buddhāya	In the Awakened Ones I take refuge
Namo Dharmāya	In the Truth I take refuge
Namaḥ Saṅghāya	In the Spiritual Beings I take refuge.

There follows the refuge in the more familiar threefold form, with generating *bodhicitta*, the aspiration for enlightenment (Atīśa, 1983, pp. 42–63), in which the *bodhisattva* dedicates himself to working for others.

In the Supreme Awakened One, his truth and the spiritual community
I take refuge until becoming enlightened
By the merit from practising giving and other perfections,
May I accomplish Full Awakening for the benefit of all. (Three times)

Monastic ordination

It was not ruled out for a lay-person to achieve liberation as a householder, but the early texts make it clear that once this was achieved, the new *arahat* had no alternative but to take ordination into the *saṅgha*. Clearly, early Buddhism regarded the monastic calling as the royal road to liberation, though it needed the laity for support.

Monastic ordination is not a sacrament, but it confers a legal status which has validity in so far as it conforms with the prescriptions of the *Vinaya* and is performed by persons suitably qualified in a duly constituted quorum. In a 'central country', where there are all four classes of disciple – monk (Sanskrit *bhikṣu*, Pāli *bhikkhu*), nun (Sanskrit *bhikṣuṇī*; Pāli *bhikkhunī*), layman (*upāsaka*), laywoman (*upāsikā*) – ten monks make a quorum. For *bhikṣunī* ordinations ten nuns plus ten monks are required (except in the Mūlasarvāstivādin *Vinaya*, followed in Tibet, where ten monks and ten nuns plus one preceptress and one instructress are needed). In a 'distant country' just five of each would suffice.

The pattern of monastic ordination is more or less the same throughout Buddhism. Within the Buddha's lifetime it developed through several stages into the form we recognize today. At first the ceremony of becoming a fully ordained monk was conferred by the Buddha himself with the minimum of ceremonial. The *Vinaya* (Horner, 1951, pp. 18–19) tells how the first five ascetics became followers after his first sermon. They requested the *pravrajyā* (Pāli *pabbajjā*) and the *upasaṃpad* (Pāli *upasampadā*) ordinations from the Buddha. He responded with the words:

> 'Come monks', the Lord said, well taught is *Dhamma*, fare the Brahma-faring [holy life] for making an utter end of ill.

Later he allowed monks themselves to confer ordinations:

> First, having made him have his hair and beard cut off, having made him put on yellow robes, having made him arrange an upper robe over one shoulder, having made him honour the monks' feet, having made him sit down on his haunches, having made him salute with joined palms, he should be told: 'Speak thus, "I go to the awakened one for refuge, I go to the *Dhamma* for refuge, I go to the Order for refuge . . .".' (Horner, 1951, p. 30)

Eventually the two stages of ordination were separated. A person may receive the lower ordination as a *śrāmaṇera* (Pāli *sāmaṇera*) or novice from eight years of age. He remains under a preceptor until the higher ordination to *bhikṣu* at the age of twenty (from conception).

The Pāli rite of ordination is conducted as follows.[3]

THE *PABBAJJĀ*: LOWER ORDINATION

The candidate is presented by his preceptor, dressed as a layman but with the yellow[4] monk's robe over his arm. After making obeisance to the assembled *bhikkhu*s he asks three times to be admitted as a *sāmaṇera* in order to destroy all sorrow, in order to attain *nirvāṇa*. Then he offers the robes, using the same formula. The president of the assembly takes the robes and ties the yellow band around the candidate's neck while reciting the meditation on the perishable nature of the human body. The candidate then withdraws to change into the monk's robe, meanwhile reciting a commitment to wear the robe in humility, for use and not for show. He then returns to his preceptor's side before the assembly and says:

> Grant me leave to speak. I make obeisance to my lord. Lord, forgive me all my faults. Let the merit that I have gained be shared by my lord. It is good, it is good. I share in it. Grant me leave to speak. Graciously give me, lord, the three refuges and the precepts.

He kneels and repeats the request. The preceptor leads the 'going for refuge' formula, repeated, sentence by sentence, by the candidate, and then the Ten Precepts:

> I undertake the rule of training to avoid taking life.
> I undertake the rule of training to avoid taking what is not given.
> I undertake the rule of training to avoid non-celibacy.
> I undertake the rule of training to avoid false speech.
> I undertake the rule of training to avoid the use of intoxicants.
> I undertake the rule of training to avoid eating at the wrong hour [after noon].
> I undertake the rule of training to avoid dancing and worldly amusements.
> I undertake the rule of training to avoid adorning myself with garlands and scents.

> I undertake the rule of training to avoid the use of high [comfortable] beds.
>
> I undertake the rule of training to avoid accepting money.

The candidate then rises, makes obeisance and repeats the request that the 'merit' should be shared by his preceptor. In return he asks to share in his preceptor's 'merit'.

THE *UPASAMPADĀ*: HIGHER ORDINATION

If the candidate is to go on to be ordained a *bhikkhu* at the same ceremony will have had the next part follows immediately. If he is already a *sāmaṇera* he will have had to receive the *pabbajjā* ordination again before the *upasampadā* is given at the same ceremony.

Returning with his preceptor, he makes obeisance and presents an offering to the president.

> Permit me to speak. Lord, graciously grant me your sanction and support.

He kneels and requests three times more:

> Lord, be my superior.

The president says:

> It is well,

and the candidate responds:

> I am content. From this day forth my lord is my charge. I am charge to my lord. (Repeated three times)

The candidate rises and, after making obeisance, returns alone to the foot of the assembly where the alms bowl is strapped to his back. His preceptor then goes down to him and leads him back by the hand. A monk from the assembly stands and places himself beside the candidate on the other side from the preceptor. The two then with the permission of the assembly question the candidate as to his fitness:

Your name is N——?
It is so, my lord.
Your preceptor is the venerable N——?
It is so, my lord.
Praise be to the Blessed One, the *Arahat*, the supremely enlightened Buddha.

They then enquire whether the candidate has an alms bowl and robes. He then retires backwards to the foot of the assembly where he is examined concerning his fitness (i.e., freedom from certain impediments such as diseases, that he is a human male, not required for military service, not a debtor, has parental permission, is of the full age of twenty years, and so on). When satisfactory answers have been given the preceptors request the president for permission to tell the candidate to approach. He comes forward to stand between the preceptors, makes obeisance and kneels, to say:

> Monks, I ask the assembly for ordination; Monks, have compassion on me and raise me up. (Repeated three times)

The preceptors examine the candidate again concerning his freedom from impediments. This is the examination in the midst of the assembly. One of the preceptors reports that the candidate desires ordination under the venerable ——, is free from impediments, has alms bowl and robe intact. He then says:

> The candidate asks the assembly for ordination under his preceptor the venerable N——. The assembly gives ordination under his preceptor the venerable N——. If anyone approves the ordination of the candidate under the venerable N——, let him remain silent; if any objects, let him speak. (Repeated three times)

The preceptors make obeisance and say:

> The candidate has received ordination as a *bhikkhu* under his preceptor the venerable N——. The assembly approves the resolution: therefore it keeps silence. So I understand your wish.

After each candidate has been ordained in turn, the group of newly ordained *bhikkhu*s is instructed in keeping the full 227 rules of the Theravādin *Vinaya*.

In parts of China the practice of moxibustion (lighting of cones of herbs on the skin for curative purposes) was combined with the ordination rites of monks. In such a case, five cones were placed on the head of the ordinand, perhaps for their therapeutic value but also as a metaphor of the curative nature of the Noble Truths as diagnosis, aetiology, prognosis and medicament.

The training of a Zen Buddhist monk (Suzuki, 1934, pp. 3–13) opens with a period of harsh austerity spent on the threshold of the community (the liminal stage) that tests his will to persevere to the utmost before he is given admittance. The aspirant must present himself at the door with a certificate saying he is a regularly ordained disciple (the preliminal stage) of a Zen priest, who will have tonsured him and provided his *kesa* and *koromo* (priestly robes), a razor, a set of bowls, some money for his burial in case of unexpected death; all these objects are carried in a papier-mâché box suspended from his neck by a sash.

Dressed in cotton leggings and wearing a broad bamboo hat and straw sandals, the novice presents himself at the porch of the monastery. He is firmly refused entry on some pretext such as that the meditation hall is full. He meets further refusal and is left alone. He must persevere by remaining crouched over his baggage. Sometimes he is physically ejected beyond the gate. There he sits in meditation until nightfall. He may be invited inside, but not to sleep. Instead, he is shown into a room where he must sit facing the wall in meditation. When morning comes he must gather his bags and return to the porch to crouch over them. This period of *niwa-dzume* (occupying the entrance court) might last three days. After this he is allowed to come inside and pass another three days isolated in a room, spending all day in meditation. Finally, he is advised that he is to be admitted into the meditation hall. He puts on his *kesa* (robe) and is ushered in by a monk to pay homage to the image of Mañjuśrī. He spreads his *zagu* (meditation cloth) and prostrates three times. His admission is announced and a tea ceremony follows. A few days later he is introduced to the master. At the threshold he spreads his *zagu* on it, makes three bows and offers incense. A tea ceremony follows. At the evening *sanzen* he will gather with the other monks before the master in the Rinzai sect of Zen, and receive his *kōan*. Thus his life as a monk begins (incorporation stage).

The establishment of the order of nuns

Mahā-Prajāpatī (Sanskrit; Pāli Mahā-Pajāpatī), the Buddha's aunt and stepmother, succeeded after much perseverance to get herself and her companions ordained as nuns (*bhikṣuṇīs*) (Harvey, 2000, pp. 383–91). However, they are said to have been required to keep the Eight Strict Rules (*garu-dhammā*) in addition to all the other precepts kept by fully ordained monks. These are as follows:

1 A nun even of 100 years' standing shall salute a monk and rise up even if he is only newly ordained.

2 A nun shall not spend the rainy season retreat in a place where there is no monk.

3 Twice monthly the nuns shall ask for the time of the *uposatha* ceremonies (when the disciplinary code is recited and fully ordained members undertake thorough self-examination) from the monks and the time when a monk will come to preach.

4 The final ceremony of the rainy season retreat is to be held by the nuns before both the monks' and the nuns' *saṅgha*s.

5 Certain offences are to be declared before both *saṅgha*s.

6 A probationer (Sanskrit *śikṣamāṇā*; Pāli *sikkhamānā*) after training in the six rules[5] for two years shall ask for ordination from both *saṅgha*s.

7 A nun is forbidden to rebuke or abuse a monk on any pretext.

8 Nuns are forbidden to admonish monks but it is not forbidden for monks to admonish nuns. (Horner, 1952, pp. 354–5)

The *bhikṣuṇī* lineage was transmitted from India to Sri Lanka by Saṅghamittā, the daughter of the emperor Asoka who reigned about 268–239 BCE. In 429 CE and 433 CE two groups of Sri Lankan *bhikṣuṇīs* went to China. The *bhikṣuṇī* lineage died out in Sri Lanka probably in the late tenth century (Gombrich and Obeyesekere, 1988, p. 274). Apart from any natural difficulties for women leading the homeless life, what other factors may have caused it to die out? The ordination of a nun required a double ceremony; first she was to be ordained by the *bhikṣuṇī-saṅgha* and then by the *bhikṣu-saṅgha*. There were some countries in the Buddhist world where the full ordination of nuns was never introduced. In Tibet women were ordained as *śrāmaṇerikā*s (novices) but the order of *bhikṣuṇī*s was never introduced. It is more surprising that *bhikṣuṇī*s were never introduced into Thailand, though the lineage existed in Burma (Myanmar) during the Pagan period from the eleventh century until the Mongol invasions in the thirteenth.

In modern times there have been moves, largely led by Westerners, to reintroduce the order into the Theravāda and to introduce it for the first time into the Tibetan tradition from the Chinese *bhikṣuṇī* order that follows the Dharmaguptaka *Vinaya* to this day. Since the Chinese nuns got their lineage from Sri Lanka originally, there is a strong argument for reintroduction, even though the modern Chinese nuns are Mahāyānists. What matters is that the *prātimokṣa* (Pāli *pāṭimokkha*) rules of *Vinaya* should have been correctly kept and transmitted according to the tradition laid down in the *Vinaya*. In Tibet, male and female novices wear the same robes as *bhikṣu*s, that is maroon with a yellow ceremonial outer robe, but in Southeast Asia women are not commonly seen in the yellow robe. There they more usually wear white or brown. They are regarded as lay by the Thai state (see Harvey, 2000, pp. 395–400).

Tantric initiation or empowerment: *abhiṣeka*

Before practising on the third vehicle, the Vajrayāna, it is necessary to receive a permission or empowerment (*abhiṣeka*, Tibetan *dbang-bksur*) from a master who has received his own empowerment in a direct line purporting to go back to the Buddha himself. Initiates in all classes of *tantra* become *bodhisattva*s, if they are not already so, by taking the *bodhisattva* vows (Atīśa, 1983, pp. 88–109). In the Yoga and the Highest Yoga classes, extra tantric vows are taken besides vows specific to one of the five *buddha*-families that the initiate is to join when he or she enters the *maṇḍala* (see pp. 122–3).

The stages preliminary to initiation include the request of the disciples to the *guru*, the rituals for preparing the site of the ceremony, preparations for the construction of the *maṇḍala*, analysis of the *guru*'s dreams to ensure that the conditions are propitious, actual construction of the *maṇḍala*, and veiling the *maṇḍala*. At this point a tantric dance may be performed. At the next stage the initiates request initiation, take the *bodhisattva* and tantric vows and receive a blessing of their body, speech and mind with consecrated water. Each receives from the *guru* two sheaves of kusha grass and a red protection string with instruction to sleep in the same posture as the Buddha at death (i.e., on the right side). Dreams reported to the *guru* next day are analysed and the *guru* stands to make a prophecy as a *buddha*, that the initiates will one day achieve enlightenment. It is a prophecy from which no one can be excluded, for the Mahāyāna foresees a time when all beings will eventually be liberated.

The initiates wear blindfolds of red cloth. They cast a flower into the *maṇḍala*; the place where it falls establishes the *buddha*-family to which they belong. They receive a tantric name and then remove the blindfold to view the *maṇḍala*. Alex Wayman (1973, p. 62) explains that the actual procedures are often different from what is read about them in some accounts. For example, the blindfold is not worn over the eyes but around the forehead. The petal of the *champa* flower (which had earlier been thrown into the *maṇḍala*) is not worn 'as a garland' but pasted in the middle of the forehead after the 'blindfold' has been removed. The blindfold is not so much to conceal the *maṇḍala* from the uninitiated as to symbolize the former blindness of primordial ignorance and the opening of the third wisdom-eye.

The Highest Yoga *tantra*s generally have four initiations or consecrations: the Vase or Jar, the Secret, the Wisdom-gnosis and the Word or 'Fourth'. The Vase consecration gives permission to practise the Generation stage and the three later consecrations apply to the Completion stage.[6] Only a brief outline of Generation stage consecrations can be attempted here.[7]

The Jar consecration

This consecration is normally sub-divided into water, crown, *vajra* (sceptre), bell and name initiations for the Yoga and Highest Yoga *tantra*s. Each of the consecrations corresponds to one of the five Wisdoms: e.g., water to the Mirror-like Wisdom of Akṣobhya Buddha, crown to the Wisdom of Sameness of Ratnasaṃbhava, *vajra* to the Discriminating Wisdom of Amitābha, bell to the All-accomplishing Wisdom of Amoghasiddhi, name to the Wisdom of the pure Absolute of Vairocana.

The royal associations of these consecrations cannot be missed: water brought from all the sacred rivers of India was used for royal anointings in ancient times. The crown refers not only to a royal diadem but to the *uṣṇīṣa*, the bump on the head of a *buddha* (see p. 280). This betokens wisdom and is one of the 32 marks of a *mahāpuruṣa*, a person destined to be either a fully enlightened *buddha* (*samyak-saṃbuddha*) or a universal monarch (*cakravartin*). The *vajra* is the diamond-hard indestructible truth; it is also the thunderbolt of Indra, a royal sceptre. The bell initiation is additionally known as the Sovereign or the Royal consecration.

Asceticism as a route to consecration as a *buddha*

Extreme asceticism is practised by the monks of Mount Hiei in Japan who undertake to complete certain marathon pilgrimages around the holy mountain. If they succeed they are revered as living *buddha*s, but if they fail they must commit ritual suicide. Generally suicide is disapproved of in Buddhism, though in the *Jātaka* tales, stories of the former lives of the Buddha, there are several accounts of the *bodhisattva* laying down his life out of compassion for other beings. Ritual self-immolation, as practised by monks during the Vietnam war, will be discussed below (p. 175).

Popular Buddhism: accommodations for the 'stages of life'

As a result of its refusal to concern itself directly with the stages of worldly life, Buddhism has left the lay Buddhist somewhat unprovided for. However, Buddhism has usually been tolerant towards pre-Buddhist indigenous religions. They have sometimes been left to provide those rites that Buddhism does not provide, as, for example, in Japan, where people generally marry by Shintō rites but have a Buddhist funeral. One of the clearest examples of Buddhism adapting its own institutions to meet a gap in the provision of rites of passage may be seen in countries of Southeast Asia, such as Thailand, Myanmar (Burma), Laos and Cambodia. Here laymen often spend brief periods of their lives as either novices or full monks. The first time a boy takes the robe the ceremony is performed with great splendour. His family dresses him in royal robes and a golden crown. As Gotama Buddha himself gave up rank and possessions to take up the homeless life, so the boy puts off his finery, has his head shaved and is dressed in the yellow robe. He receives the lower ordination and must keep the Ten Precepts for a week or two. The ceremony marks a stage in the child's development when be becomes capable of spiritual and moral discernment. From another point of view the ordination shows that, however tender in years or however old the candidate is, the spiritual ideal is the same for all, with no special duties for each stage of life. As Buddhism saw birth-based class as unimportant, every Buddhist child may wear royal robes, in order to discard them for the yellow robe, which itself bestows a status higher than royalty. Temporary ordination for adults is often prior to marriage, with time as a monk seen to mature a young man, or in old age, to help prepare for the next life.

Mary Shepherd Slusser, in her cultural study of the Kathmandu valley of Nepal,[8] has observed a form of Vajrayāna Buddhism that is practised alongside Hinduism. For historical and social reasons the celibate monkhood died out but it was never entirely forgotten. It has given rise to a strange phenomenon in the Newar community – two dynasties of married 'monks'. Children of the Buddhist priestly *Vajrācārya* caste, whose ancestors were probably tantric *yogin*s, possibly with brahmin connections, and the *Śākya-bhikṣu*s, who claim to belong to the same clan as (Gotama) Buddha himself, and whose ancestors were once monks, receive the rite of tonsure. This rite has become a kind of *saṃskāra*[9] by which they become 'monks'; in the case of the *Vajrācārya*s, priests also. The ceremony must be performed in the same *vihāra* in which it was done for the boy's ancestors. Nowadays the rites are performed on groups of candidates, who might be mere babes in arms, boys or youths. They present themselves, fasting, for a ritual bath and head shaving. Then they are given the yellow robe, staff and begging bowl. They remain as monks for four days and then return to the *vihāra* to renounce the robe formally.

A *Vajrācārya* boy receives further investitures of the *yogin*'s *vajra* and bell. If he does not complete this rite he forfeits his status as a priest not only for himself but for his descendants as well. Thereafter they would have only *bhikṣu* status.

Buddhist marriage

Usually Buddhism has not regarded the institution of marriage as sacred in any way (see Harvey, 2000, pp. 101–3, 404–8). However, in Sri Lanka the influence of colonial and missionary activities brought about a change in the traditional practice of Buddhist marriage as part of a larger reaction that Gombrich and Obeyesekere (1988, pp. 255–73) have called Protestant Buddhism. Up to this period both polygyny and polyandry were sometimes practised in Sinhala villages, and divorce was easy to obtain. In a typical marriage that took place at the beginning of the nineteenth century, the bridegroom came with his relations to the bride's parents' house. A white cloth was spread out over a plank and fresh rice was scattered on it. The bride's maternal uncle then placed the bride and groom on the plank. The bridegroom gave the bride gifts of a gold chain, a cloth and a jacket, followed by an exchange of rings. To the bride's mother he gave a white cloth. Then the uncle tied the couple's thumbs together. A plate was held under their joined thumbs and some milk poured over the knot. Sometimes the couple's little fingers were joined instead of their thumbs, and in some places the groom put the chain around the bride's neck. There was no religious officiant, nor were religious texts recited. In fact, the presence of a monk, who was dedicated to celibacy and so seen as asexual, would have been inauspicious for the fertility of the union. The giving of gifts and the wedding banquet were to mark the bringing together of two kin-groups. Only one element in the marriage ritual seems to have been common: the giving of the white cloth by the groom to his new mother-in-law. A white cloth is also given by the relatives of the deceased to the monks who officiate at a funeral. In both cases the cloth symbolically absorbs pollution. The white cloth is worn by the bride on her wedding night and this cloth absorbs the pollution of sexual intercourse.

The ceremony of the plank (*pōruva*) has now become universal in the marriage ceremony. The *pōruva* is a flat board used in preparing the seed-bed of paddy fields; sprinkling it with rice grains in the context of the marriage ceremonial symbolizes the fertility of the union. Nowadays it is decorated to resemble a throne, certainly in urban upper-class weddings, and though the term *pōruva* is still used, its fertility associations seem to have been forgotten. The royal associations are reinforced by the sumptuous wedding clothes of the bride and groom.

White is a colour used to absorb impurity; it is both the colour of mourning and the colour of chastity, worn by those who have taken the Eight or Ten Precepts, and so is associated with sterility. It seems odd, therefore, that Buddhist brides should have increasingly taken to wearing white, but in order to sacramentalize marriage within the context of Buddhism, certain features of the Christian rite have provided the model. Little girls dressed as bridesmaids chant a medieval Pāli *paritta* text, the *Jayamaṅgala Gāthā*, following the *pōruva* ceremony. The text has nineteen four-line stanzas, each one celebrating a victory of the Buddha. The irony of this is probably missed by the wedding guests who would only recognize the words *jaya* (victory) and *maṅgala* (auspiciousness). Gombrich and Obeyesekere relish the irony that the theme of the text is the triumph of ascetic renunciation over sex and procreation, sung by pre-pubescent girls dressed in sterile white!

By the mid-1970s, not only had monks made occasional appearances at weddings, but some had even solemnized them in temples. After the *pōruva* ceremony the monks chant *pirit*. The Sinhala word *pirit* (Pāli *paritta*), originally meaning 'safety-rune', denotes a group of texts which are recited in a ritual to bring blessings or avert misfortune (see pp. 136–8). A thread is held by the monks reciting *pirit* and passed around to contain all the people present, any of whom may also hold the thread. A bottle of water is placed under the table holding the texts during the recitation. Everyone is sprinkled with the water after the end of the recitation. Gombrich (1971, pp. 201–9), in addition to describing it fully, considers some of the doctrinal anomalies in the practice.

The most recent development is the introduction of a special wedding celebrant who operates rather like a brahmin priest. In one such case, Gombrich and Obeyesekere (1988, p. 269) observed 'the Buddhicization of the previously secular ceremony'; a brief outline of their complete description is all that can be given here. The celebrant opens with a formal request of permission to perform the marriage from the Buddha, *Dhamma* and *Saṅgha*, and also from the gods, parents and congregation. Prior to the *pōruva* ceremony, the celebrant utters an exposition of the 'original' Buddhist marriage between the then Prince Siddhārtha (the future Buddha) and Yaśodharā, in the presence of all the great gods. The god Īśvara provided a *pirit* thread and tied the fingers of the couple. The god Brahmā poured water over their hands and by this they were brought to liberation. The celebrant then sings the last stanzas of the *pirit*. The *pōruva* ceremony now follows. The groom, after asking permission from the authorities listed before, places a ring on the bride's fourth finger of her left hand. The other ceremonies of the necklace and the white cloth follow. It is the father of the bride (not her maternal uncle, as used to be done in the villages) who ties the couple's fingers while the celebrant gives a blessing:

> By the influence of all the glorious Buddhas, Pacceka [solitary] Buddhas, and *Arahat*s I secure your protection in every way.

The father pours *pirit* water over their hands and the bridesmaids sing the *Jayamaṅgala Gāthā*. The couple give food to each other and give a betel leaf to relations and guests. When the couple descend from the *pōruva*, a coconut is smashed before them to banish the evil eye, mouth and thoughts, and to obtain the blessing of Gaṇeśa and the Earth Goddess. They light a lamp for the Buddha and go to sign the marriage register.

In the Himalayan regions, among the ethnic Tibetans, marriages are sometimes played out as a kind of symbolic 'kidnapping'. The poorer party is kidnapped by the richer. This usually means the man's family does the kidnapping, but not invariably. The one who is abducted, woman (or man), sobs while she (or he) is being led to the groom's (or bride's) house. In former times marriages were arranged by the parents within classes, but since the invasion of Tibet social stratification has become less rigid. At various stages of arrangement and engagement white silk scarves are presented by the man's family to the woman's. She is also presented with a striped apron which forms part of a married woman's dress, and a marriage contract is drawn up in duplicate.

On the wedding morning the groom sends a representative on horseback with a retinue, carrying the headgear, coloured arrows decorated with mirrors, and jade ornaments, to the bride for her wedding attire. Before they arrive she makes a grain offering and drinks *chang* (barley beer). The groom's representative enters her house, fixes the arrows to her back to show that she has now changed over to the groom's family and places the jade ornament on her head to indicate that she has charge of the groom's spirit. If one is available, the bride rides back on a mare in foal. As she leaves, one of her family on the roof of the house, holding an arrow and a leg of mutton, repeatedly cries out after them 'Do not take away our family's good fortune'. The bridal party is met by members of her new family offering refreshments at three points on the route.

At the bridegroom's house the bride dismounts on to a mat made of bags of barley and wheat covered in brocaded silk. A swastika[10] is formed out of sprinkled barley grains on top of the mat. As the bride crosses into her husband's household, an auspicious omen might be read and blessings given. Tadeusz Skorupski (1986) has translated such a rite, an example of the accommodation of Buddhist ceremony mixed with animistic ritual to the secular rite of marriage:

1 The elimination of evil *'dre*s who precede the bride: this is effected by the powers of the Buddhist religion:

> By the truth of the noble lamas of Buddhist religion,
> The truth of the Buddha, his Doctrine and Community [i.e., the Three Jewels]
> The truth of the secret *mantra*s, *vidhyā*s, *dharaṇī*s and *mudrā*s,
> The truth of the Absolute Sphere, pure and free of cause and effect,
> In particular by the truth of the Peaceful and Wrathful Deities
> Who have assumed manifestations as Mañjuśrī,
> The truth of the noble and holy Religion-Protectors,
> Those of the highest and worldly ranks.
> And by the blessing of the Great Truth.

2 The purification of the bride: because the household deities are liable to be polluted by the new bride, she must be purified by pouring water in front of a mirror in which an image of a deity is reflected on to the bride. Her purity will now be the same as that of the deity.

3 The spreading of the carpet: the preface to the spreading of the carpet which promotes the bride's life-force, power and good luck refers to the legend by which the two Buddhist wives, one Chinese and one Nepali, of the king Songtsen Gampo (Srong-btsan-sgam-po) landed in central Tibet on a magic carpet.

4 The presentation of the three white things: milk, curds and butter to give long life.

5 The bestowal of the new name.

6 The presentation to the house deities: holding a garlanded arrow which has a complex symbolism, the officiant presents the bride to the house deities and asks that 'the body, speech and mind of this noble maiden be protected, defended and blessed' by many deities of all kinds, including the four *tantra*s and the benign host

of peaceful and wrathful deities, for example, Vajravārāhī, the White Tārā, five classes of *ḍākinī*s, and more.

7 The rite of summoning good fortune.

8 The final prayer invokes on the bride the blessing of 'victorious lamas and their spiritual sons', 'hermits who follow the truth', and the Three Jewels. It asks that the 'celestial constellations ... be auspicious', 'the Buddhas display ... miraculous powers' and 'the *Arhat*s annihilate misery'.

The ceremonies of death

In an early account in the Pāli Canon the *Mahā-parinibbāna Sutta* tells that just before his death the Buddha gave instructions to the monk Ānanda on how his funeral rites were to be conducted according to elaborate rites for the cremation of a universal monarch (*cakravartin*). A *stūpa* was to be raised over the relics at a crossroads. However, the monks were to hand over the funeral arrangements to the laity.

> Do not worry yourselves about the funeral arrangements, Ānanda. You should strive for the highest goal, devote yourselves to the highest goal, and dwell with your minds tirelessly, zealously devoted to the highest goal. There are wise Khattiyas, Brahmins and householders who are devoted to the Tathāgata: they will take care of the funeral. (Walshe, 1987, p. 264)

Though we do not know how soon after the Buddha's own funeral monks began the custom, in modern Sri Lanka Theravādin monks take part in funerals. The presence of monks at funerals is not to pray for the deceased but to aid the bereaved and transfer 'merit' to the dead person (see Harvey, 1990, pp. 43–4; 2000, pp. 65–6). A funeral is a reminder of mortality and impermanence and it is quite appropriate that monks should take the opportunity to preach *buddha-dharma* out of compassion for the bereaved. Monks are formally given food a week after the death, three months later and then on the anniversary at a commemorative ceremony. One of the chief ways by which the laity gain 'merit' (for an auspicious rebirth, ideally, from which to reach *nirvāṇa*) is by offering food to monks, either at the daily almsround or by inviting monks for meals. In the case of the dead, the 'merit' gained by the relatives is thought to be transferable to the dead person (see p. 69; Gombrich, 1971, pp. 232–40).

At the funeral itself a white cloth is laid on the coffin. A monk leads the taking of refuge in the Three Jewels and the Five Precepts. Then he says three times, repeated by all present:

> I give this corpse-clothing to the *Saṅgha* of monks.

The monks spread the cloth over the coffin and chant a stanza spoken first at the death of the Buddha:

> Impermanent are compounded things, prone to rise and fall,
> Having risen, they're destroyed, their passing truest bliss.
> (Walshe, 1987, p. 271)

The monks pick up the white cloth which has symbolically absorbed the 'pollution' of the corpse;[11] they are immune from it. It also symbolizes, quite separately, an optional ascetic practice whereby monks could make their robes from cloths discarded on dust-heaps or in cremation grounds. The outer robe of a monk today is still made up of pieces of cloth stitched together, even if they have been cut from the same bolt of new cloth. Though this is supposed to destroy the 'value' of the cloth and any ensuing hubris a monk might have in wearing it, the patchwork finish is also a reminder of the way the earliest renouncers came by their robes.

Following removal of the cloth, water is poured from a jug into a bowl until it overflows (or a coconut is split to spill its milk) while the monks chant the following verses:

> As the full water-bearing [rivers] fill the ocean,
> so indeed does what is given here benefit the dead (*preta*).
>
> As water rained on a height reaches the low land,
> so indeed does what is given here benefit the dead (*preta*).

A sermon is preached and the monks usually depart, leaving the relatives to conclude the actual burial or cremation, possibly to conform with the precedents of the Buddha's funeral.

Normally the feast (*dānē*[12]) for the dead person is rigorously observed on the seventh day after death. The one three months later, and the anniversary, while not being obligatory, are commonly observed. Sometimes monks give *dānē* for their parents or predecessors. The donor gives food to the monk, who recites a Pāli verse and dedicates the 'merit'.

The invitation to the *dānē* for the seventh day is given to the *saṅgha* rather than to an individual monk. Usually a minimum of five is expected, though poor people may invite fewer and rich people more. A sermon is preached on the evening before and the monks are invited to eat in the donor's home. On this occasion only the relatives and closest friends attend. The three-month *dānē* is a semi-public affair to which all who knew the deceased are invited. It usually starts with *pirit*. The food is offered with the Pāli formula, repeated three times:

> I give this alms-food to the community of monks.

A little food is put outside for the *preta*s (hungry ghosts – along with animals and hell-beings, making up the three woeful destinies one can be reborn to). This tradition of feeding the *preta*s is found throughout Buddhism; food is put out for *preta*s during the tantric liturgical feast-offering to the *guru (bLa-ma chos-pa)*.

After food the monks may be offered small gifts; then a bowl and a jug of water are set before them. The donor pours water into the dish until it overflows, as was done at the funeral. When the chant and water-pouring are over the people say *Sā* (Pāli *sādhu*, 'it is good'). A short sermon on impermanence is given and then the donor transfers the 'merit' of the actions to the dead by means of a formula recited in Pāli that means:

> May this be for my relatives. May my relatives be happy.

In Tibet funeral rites are unusually varied; corpses may be disposed of by 'sky' burial, water burial, earth burial, cremation or by being placed in a *stūpa*, according to the status of the dead person. Prior to the burial, whatever form it is to take, a period of preparation must be undertaken to help the dead person come to terms with his or her new state. The body, covered by a white cloth, is laid out and the ceremony of reading the *Bar-do Thos-grol* into the ear of the dead person for a period of three to five days is undertaken by monks. This text guides the newly departed through the celebrated *bar-do* state, made famous by Evans-Wentz's publication of a translation of the *Tibetan Book of the Dead* (1985). In the Tibetan and some Far Eastern traditions, but not in the Theravāda – though Ven. Rahula connects the seventh-day *dānē* with it (Gombrich, 1971, p. 232) – there is a belief in an intermediate state between death and rebirth lasting between seven and 49 days. The ceremony of reading may be begun before death if the person is mortally ill. Relatives and friends come to pay their respects and bring gifts for the grieving family and a ceremonial white silk scarf for the deceased. All ornaments of the house are put away, the family do not wash their faces or comb their hair during the period of mourning. No person touches the corpse, in order to allow the *bar-do* body to separate itself from the material body. This might be helped by a *'pho-bo*, an officiant who attempts to extract the consciousness principle. He commands the consciousness to give up its attachment to its now defunct body, its living relatives and goods. He draws out a few hairs above the 'Aperture of Brahmā' at the line of the sagittal suture on the top of the skull to aid the departure of consciousness.

Next the body is stripped, the knees are drawn up to the chest and bound in the embryonic posture. Then the body is wrapped in a woollen blanket. Disposal of the body takes place when it is certain that separation of body and consciousness have taken place. Until that time the mourners are fed and a portion of food and drink is offered to the deceased spirit. After the funeral proper has been carried out an effigy of the dead person is placed in the room and offered food for the full 49 days of the *bar-do*; the number of days is said to correspond to the period during which the Buddha reflected on and explored his experience of awakening.

During the funeral rites and reading of the *Bar-do Thos-grol*, other monks in relays chant a text to help the deceased reach the Western Paradise of Amitābha (Sukhāvatī). The corpse is carried to the door of the house and placed on the back of the undertaker to be taken to the place of burial. The procession is led by a *lama*, who holds one end of the white scarf which has been tied to the body.

The commonest form of funeral for ordinary folk, sky burial, may have been influenced by the Zoroastrian practice of exposing the dead in Towers of Silence. The body is taken up to a high outcrop of rock and a fire of cypress wood lit. *Tsam-pa* (roasted barley flour) is sprinkled on and the smoke signals to the sacred vultures to assemble. The flesh is cut from the corpse in pieces and heaped on one side; then the bones are crushed and mixed with *tsam-pa*. This is fed to the vultures before the flesh so that every part of the body is consumed. It is regarded as a very bad omen if the vultures do not complete their task or are scared off. The Chinese authorities have now stopped tourists in Lhasa disturbing the sacred birds from their meal with flashlight photography.

Water burial is used for beggars, destitutes and the widowed; earth burial is for robbers, murderers and those who die of leprosy and smallpox; cremation is for the nobility and higher-ranking monks. Possibly the first time cremation in the Tibetan manner was done in the West was for Lama Yeshe, a Geshe in exile who inaugurated the Foundation for the Preservation of the Mahāyāna Tradition (FPMT). The ceremony was conducted in 1984 near Boulder Creek in California, using the Yamāntaka fire *pūjā*. The body was placed in the *stūpa* with the knees drawn up and tied with white scarves. The arms were crossed and a *vajra* and bell were placed in the hands. Upon the head was placed a black *bodhisattva*'s hat adorned with a crystal rosary. A red cloth was placed over the face. The *stūpa*, made of bricks covered in mud and whitewash, was built up round the body. Wood was stacked around and oil poured over it. There were four holes around the base and two more for receiving offerings on the upper part. The fire had to be kindled by someone who had not received the Lama's teachings.

The highest kind of burial, inurnment in a *stūpa*, is reserved for the highest lamas, such as the Dalai and Tashi Lamas. The corpse is mummified with salt and spices, covered in a cement-like substance, covered in gold and the face-part painted. There are funeral halls holding the mummies of former Dalai and Tashi Lamas in the Potala palace, Lhasa, and in the Tashilhunpo monastery at Shigatse.

Mummification may seem an incongruous practice in face of the Buddhist insistence on the transience of the person. Corpses in cremation grounds may be used for meditation on impermanence, but they are unstable and have to be disposed of quite quickly; indeed, the fact that they do decompose is the very point of the contemplation. Skeletons and even stillborn babies in formalin may occasionally be seen in wats in Thailand, but their purpose is undoubtedly different from the veneration of mummies that seems to have emerged as such an important feature of Ch'an/Zen. Here the point of this contemplation is the body of a *buddha*. In his critique of the ritualization of death in Ch'an/Zen, Bernard Faure (1991, p. 134) argues that the production of *śarīra* (crystalline fragments left from cremation) and 'flesh-body' (mummy) can both be classified as 'secondary burial', the goal of which was to obtain an incorruptible body. As in the West, relics, though they could be handled, 'belonged not to the transitory world but to eternity'. 'Self-mummification' is a very slow fast to death, bringing about a virtual desiccation; this and self-immolation probably attempt the same goal through different funerary practices.

Ritual suicide

The *Lotus Sūtra*, written in India in the first century CE, may have inspired the practice of ritual self-immolation, though only in the Far East. Walpola Rahula[13] says:

> The monk who prepared himself for self-cremation gradually reduced his intake of cereals and partook of incense, perfume and oil. After a period he became emaciated and his body was, therefore, more combustible. It was then both a lamp-offering and an incense-offering.
>
> ... A niche large enough for a person to sit cross-legged was prepared in the middle of the pyre. The hero-monk entered the niche, sat cross-legged, set fire to the pyre himself, and with palms folded in salutation to the Buddha recited a sacred text (such as the *Amitābha-sūtra*) calmly and serenely until he died.

The first recorded case of self-mummification was a monk of Dunhuang who died in 385 CE after a seven-year fast (Faure, 1991, p. 158). At first such 'relics' were abandoned in mountain caves but at the beginning of the T'ang period (618–907), when Chih-i the founder of the T'ien-t'ai school died, his mummy was enshrined in a memorial hall. Incorruptibility came to be seen as the result of impregnation by morality, concentration and wisdom, tokens that the hero would be reborn in Amitābha Buddha's Pure Land.

Funerary rituals in Ch'an/Zen

The shift in Ch'an/Zen from being a 'self-power' philosophy of life to funerary ritualism, reliant on 'other-power' of Amitābhism, seems to have dated from the fourteenth century. Faure says of the early Ch'an ideology of death:

> Reinforcing the no-self theory of early Buddhism, the Mahāyāna doctrine, as exemplified by the *Heart Sūtra*, further blunted the scandal of death by denying its ontological reality; in emptiness (*śūnyatā*) there is neither birth nor death, neither coming nor going. Accordingly temporality and finitude were ultimately negated as karmic delusions. (Faure, 1991, p. 180)

The first effect of this was to lead to the theoretical rejection of funeral rites; one patriarch, Fa-ch'ih (637–702) of the Niu-t'ou school, ordered his corpse to be left to wild animals so that they would absorb his virtue and produce the thought of enlightenment (*bodhicitta*). But eventually, as a 'skilful means' (*upāya*), or a synthesis with the old ancestor worship, funerary rituals became firmly rooted.

The ritual preliminaries of the death of a Ch'an master from early times began with the prediction of the precise time of death, closely modelled on the Buddha's own *parinirvāṇa* (Faure, 1991, p. 184). On New Year's Eve one covers the ears with both hands and knocks the skull for the number of months and days in the coming year. When the point is reached where there is no sound, that is the day of one's death.

The Ch'an master's next task was to compose his 'death verse' (*gāthā*). Very rarely he refused to comply; or he expressed reservations:

> Life's as we
> Find it – death too.
> A parting poem?
> Why insist? (Daie-Soko (1089–1163))

The death of a master became a public event and so it was necessary that he should meet his end reclining on his right side like the Buddha or seated in the lotus posture of *samādhi*.

Funerals of monks who had reached enlightenment were different from those of ordinary monks. These last eventually became the model for lay-people in Japan. A master's funeral had nine rites: placing the body in a coffin; transferring the coffin to the lecture hall; closing the coffin; placing a portrait of the master on the shrine; the wake; removal to the cremation ground; offering a tea libation; offering a hot water libation; lighting the pyre. The rites at all stages were accompanied by tea offerings, chanting of *dhāraṇīs* and *sūtras*, dedication of 'merit' and burning of incense.

For those who are not yet enlightened, certain extra rites are performed to help them achieve liberation. The most important innovation for lay people is their *post mortem* tonsuring and ordination as monks or nuns as part of their preparation for deliverance. If possible this is done before death. Then the lineage chart is transmitted, incorporating the dead into the lineage of the Buddha's family. A sermon is preached on impermanence and the coffin is taken on a circumambulation of the cremation ground, weaving in and out of four gates set at the four points of the compass. The gates symbolize the Four Sights[14] seen by the young Siddhārtha as he left the city of Kapilavastu through its four gates. The circumambulation also symbolizes the processional route the Buddha's funeral procession took through Kuśinagara. Lastly, the circuitous route is supposed to lose the mind of the deceased so it will not try to find its way back.

Finally, the post-liminal rite of reincorporation involves ten to fifteen days of tea and hot water offerings to the relics, depositing them in a reliquary and 'closing the grave' to prevent the dead spirit returning.

The ritualist/antiritualist dilemma of the Ch'an/Zen funeral is expressed in a verse inscribed on banners at the sides of the cremation site:

> Due to delusion, the three worlds are completed;
> Due to awakening, the ten directions are empty.
> From the outset, there is neither east nor west;
> Where could there be a north and a south? (Faure, 1991, p. 194)

Zen deals with death by embracing its defilement and transmuting it to purity through its own version of the Buddhist alchemy; as the thirteenth-century Zen master Dōgen says:[15]

> Simply understand that birth and death is itself *nirvāṇa*, there is nothing to reject as birth and death, nothing to seek as *nirvāṇa*.

Notes

1 V. Turner (1969) *The Ritual Process*. London: Routledge and Kegan Paul, p. 107.
2 A. van Gennep (1960) *The Rites of Passage*. London: Routledge and Kegan Paul, p. 103.
3 J. F. Dickson (1875) 'The *Upasampadā-Kammavācā* being the Buddhist manual of the form and manner of ordering of priests and deacons. The Pāli text, with a translation and notes', *Journal of the Royal Asiatic Society of Great Britain and Ireland*, New Series (London), VII, Article I, pp. 1–16. See also Wijayaratna (1990), pp. 117–21.
4 The colour of the monk's robe varies between yellow, orange and orangy-brown in Theravāda lands, russet-red in Tibet, usually grey in China and Korea, and generally black in Japan. In the latter Mahāyāna lands, additional robes of the original yellow/orange may be used in rituals and ceremonies.
5 The first six of the novices' precepts. These had to be followed even by adult candidates for becoming nuns, who did not have to first become novices. There is no similar category for men.
6 The Generation stage concerns the building up of the visualization of a holy being and the Completion stage concerns the drawing on divine energies based on this. For brief details see Harvey (1990), pp. 266–7.
7 For a close account of these, see Gyatso and Hopkins (1985), pp. 257–353. For a discussion of the further consecrations of the Completion stage the reader should consult D. L. Snellgrove (1987) *Indo-Tibetan Buddhism*. London: Serindia Publications, pp. 243–77; D. Cozort (1986) *Highest Yoga Tantra*. Ithaca, NY: Snow Lion Publications, pp. 65–133, where he compares the Completion stages of the *Kālacakra* and the *Guhyasamāja tantra*s; or G. H. Mullin (1985) *Selected Works of the Dalai Lama I, Bridging the Sūtras and the Tantras* (2nd edn). Ithaca, NY: Snow Lion Publications, pp. 149–86; this contains the First Dalai Lama's commentary on both stages of the *Kālacakra tantra*, with its emphasis on the Completion stage.
8 Mary Shepherd Slusser (1982) *Nepal Maṇḍala* (2 vols). Princeton, NJ: Princeton University Press, pp. 294–8.
9 Hindu term for a life-cycle ritual.
10 An Indian symbol of good luck, which long pre-dates the 'swastika' perversely used by Hitler.
11 The Hindu idea of ritual pollution finds no place in Buddhist doctrine, but traces of it are occasionally found in Buddhist practice.
12 Pāli and Sanskrit *dāna*, which is also a term for 'giving' or 'generosity'.
13 Walpola Rahula (1978) *Zen and the Taming of the Bull*. London: Gordon Fraser, p. 113.

14 A sick person, an old person, a corpse and a calm renunciant.
15 *Shōbōgenzō: Zen Essays by Dōgen*, trans. Thomas Cleary (1986). Honolulu: University of Hawaii Press, p. 122.

Further reading

Akira, H. (trans. P. Groner) (1990) *A History of Indian Buddhism from Śākyamuni to Early Mahāyāna*. Honolulu: University of Hawaii Press.

Atīśa, trans. Richard Sherburne SJ (1983) *A Lamp for the Path and Commentary*. London: Allen & Unwin.

Bechert, H. and Gombrich, R. (1984) *The World of Buddhism: Buddhist Monks and Nuns in Society and Culture*. London: Thames and Hudson.

Dargyay, Eva (1982) *Tibetan Village Communities*. Warminster: Aris & Phillips.

Evans-Wentz, W. Y. (1985) *Tibetan Book of the Dead* (3rd edn). Oxford: Oxford University Press.

Faure, Bernard (1991) *The Rhetoric of Immediacy: A Cultural Critique of Chan/Zen Buddhism*. Princeton, NJ: Princeton University Press.

Gombrich, Richard F. (1971) *Precept and Practice: Traditional Buddhism in the Rural Highlands of Ceylon*. Oxford: Clarendon Press.

Gombrich, Richard F. and Obeyesekere, Ganath (1988) *Buddhism Transformed: Religious Change in Sri Lanka*. Princeton, NJ: Princeton University Press.

Gyatso, Tenzin (the Dalai Lama) and Hopkins, Jeffrey (1985) *The Kālachakra Tantra: Rite of Initiation for the Generation Stage*. London: Wisdom Publications.

Harvey, P. (1990) *An Introduction to Buddhism: Teachings, History and Practices*. Cambridge: Cambridge University Press.

Harvey, P. (2000) *An Introduction to Buddhist Ethics: Foundations, Values and Issues*. Cambridge: Cambridge University Press.

Horner, I. B. (1951) *The Book of the Discipline (Vinaya-piṭaka) Volume 4 (Mahāvagga)*. London: Luzac.

Horner, I. B. (1952) *The Book of the Discipline (Vinaya-piṭaka) Volume 5 (Cullavagga)*. London: Luzac.

Saddhatissa, H. (1967) *Buddhist Ethics* (2nd edn). London: Rider.

Skorupski, Tadeusz (1986) 'A Tibetan marriage ritual', *The Journal of Asian and African Studies*, 31, pp. 76–95.

Suzuki, Daisettz T. (n.d.) *The Training of the Zen Buddhist Monk*. New York: Globe Press Books (facsimile of 1934 edn, Kyoto: The Eastern Buddhist Society).

Walshe, M. (1987) *Thus Have I Heard: The Long Discourses of the Buddha*. London: Wisdom Publications.

Wayman, Alex (1973) *The Buddhist Tantras: Light on Indo-Tibetan Esotericism*. New York: Samuel Weiser.
Wijayaratna, M. (1990) *Buddhist Monastic Life – According to the Texts of the Theravāda Tradition*. Cambridge: Cambridge University Press.

6. Making moral decisions

Stewart McFarlane

An initial impression of Buddhist teaching and practice would suggest that for the Buddhist, moral decision-making is not problematic. The detailed training rules of conduct and deportment (*pāṭimokkha*) for the monks and the five precepts (*pañca-sīla*) for lay-people are apparently straightforward behavioural, moral and ritual guidelines. All that appears to be required of the Buddhist is to follow these guidelines as best they can, with little need for moral reflection and analysis. In reality the situation is more complicated for practising Buddhists and for observers seeking to understand the moral dimensions of the tradition.

The fundamental distinction between monk and lay-person is only one of a whole range of levels of spiritual and moral attainment that are acknowledged in Buddhism. Not only are the behavioural requirements varied according to the level of practice reached, but the understanding of the moral and psychological theory will differ according to the spiritual level of the individual. Ordinary lay-people and untrained monks do not generally understand the detailed psychological theory underlying the notion of *karma*, the notion of the correlation between intentions, actions and their consequences in the life or future lives of the individual. Still less are they expected to have achieved an experiential understanding of the workings of *karma* in action. Such experience is only available to advanced-level meditators who are systematically pursuing the Buddhist path (*magga*) to liberation (*nirvāṇa*), the cessation of suffering or supreme awakening (*saṃbodhi*). However for the advanced levels of practice and for adepts (*asekha*) who are expected to teach and direct others, such levels of meditational experience and understanding are necessary.

Another factor which makes Buddhist moral reflection more problematic is the fact that the time-scale and cosmology on which Buddhist moral processes take place are very different from Western assumptions about the nature of human life and the functioning of the universe. The historical Buddha, Gotama, and the legendary material about him illustrate these differences very clearly. Buddhists understand the Buddha's final lifetime as one dedicated to his primary role as a teacher and exemplar of *Dhamma* (Sanskrit *Dharma*). *Dhamma* is the truth or teaching which provides the way to the cessation of suffering which is *nirvāṇa* or Supreme Awakening. *Dhamma* is such an important concept that it comes to take on the meaning of truth or reality itself, because it is the means by which the liberated state is achieved. In the Buddhist understanding, Gotama's career began thousands of years before his final lifetime, when as an ordinary human being he expressed the wish to be awakened, and a previous *buddha*, Dīpaṅkara, observing his virtue, spiritual worth and aspiration, predicted that he would later be a *buddha* (Conze, 1959, pp. 19–24). The progress of the *bodhisattva* or *buddha*-to-be is partly recorded in the legendary but very important material of the *Jātaka* stories (see pp. 49–50), which describe numerous incidents over a whole series of lives in which the *buddha*-to-be demonstrates his virtue and refines his understanding as preparation for his final life as the fully awakened Buddha; his full knowledge and understanding of the nature of that process, largely a matter of an experiential understanding of *karma*, is not attained until immediately prior to his awakening (Robinson and Johnson, 1977, pp. 38–9). The *Jātaka* stories themselves are important sources for examples of Buddhist ethics in action, albeit in an exaggerated 'mythic' framework. The notion of successive lives of the Buddha, and the progressive spiritual development and moral refinement he undergoes, provides an ideal model for the process of refinement and progression which Buddhism tries to institute for all beings.

Realistically, of course, it is just as possible for beings to decline morally and spiritually through successive lives. This kind of time-scale and the underlying moral theory associated with it explains why the Buddhist view of human nature and the cosmos is both developmental and hierarchical. Beings living at the same time are clearly at different stages of moral and spiritual development. Therefore, different types of teaching and guidance are going to be appropriate to different beings. Traditionally Buddhist teaching is not a generalized activity, but is carried out with regard to specific individuals and groups at certain levels of attainment. Texts were only available after the traditional method of teaching was established, and for many centuries 'texts' were memorized and transmitted within the monastic order (*saṅgha*), and were not generally available (see pp. 51–2). The developmental and hierarchical nature of Buddhist assumptions about the universe means that considerable flexibility is applied in the practical teaching offered by Buddhist authorities. Even straightforward teachings on moral matters can be modified, sometimes intensified, sometimes relaxed in the course of teaching and transmission. Examples of this will appear throughout this chapter. This process has also happened historically, as Buddhism has been transmitted to diverse cultural and religious environments. The examples of meat-eating and Buddhist attitudes to violence will be considered later.

We return now to the developmental and hierarchical nature of the Buddhist understanding of the universe and of the human place in it. A sophisticated vocabulary of technical terms is adopted in Buddhist texts, which reflect this type of understanding. Some examples and their meanings are: (1) *lokuttara* (supermundane); *lokiya* (worldly); (2) *asekha* (adept); *sekha* (learner); *puthujjana* (ordinary man); (3) *paramattha-sacca/paramārtha-satya* (ultimate truth); *sammuti-sacca/samvṛti-satya* (conventional truth).

The way moral decisions are reached will depend on what level of understanding is being expressed and addressed. Another distinction now frequently employed by Western scholars was that developed by M. Spiro. It is not an indigenous classification, although it does closely relate to the types of distinction and classifications used above. Spiro classifies Theravāda Buddhism into three different types.

1 Nibbanic Buddhism relates to the teachings, practices and concerns of the 'spiritual élite' within the *saṅgha* (monastic community), who are directing their practice to the attaining of liberation (*nibbāna/nirvāṇa*).

2 Kammatic Buddhism (relating to *kamma/karma*) is concerned with the performance of wholesome actions, and through them the attaining of a desirable rebirth, either as a god, or as a wealthy and powerful man, or as a monk who will then be in a position to follow the path to liberation more fully. Spiro sees the

nd concerns of the majority of Theravāda Buddhists ng in this type of Buddhism.

ıddhism (i.e., Buddhism which supplies the means and threats are 'turned away' and resisted) is with using the 'magical' or 'meritorious' power of *Buddha-Dhamma* and its representatives to protect people from natural and supernatural calamities. It includes using Buddhist ritual chanting (*paritta*) to protect against such things as demons or droughts, and in exorcism and healing procedures (see p. 136).

Spiro acknowledges the extent to which the activities and concerns within these categories can interact and overlap. He clearly does not present them as self-contained systems or as completely rigid categories (Spiro, 1971, p. 12). Despite some criticisms of Spiro's terminology and classifications, which often turn out to be criticisms of an over-rigid use of them, his analysis has considerable value in understanding the complexity of Buddhist ethical, social and soteriological thinking.

The structure of Buddhist ethical teaching

Given that Buddhism traditionally operates with hierarchical and developmental notions of spiritual understanding and moral attainment, it follows that beings at different levels of understanding will be given teachings and methods which are appropriate to their level of understanding. This means that general statements about the nature of Buddhist teachings must be treated with caution, as the level of teaching and the kind of group or individual to which it is directed needs to be considered. This applies to questions about moral decision-making in Buddhism, as it does to other issues of *Buddha-Dhamma*. One clear example of the hierarchical and developmental nature of Buddhist teachings, which is of special importance for Buddhist ethical teachings, is the *Dhamma* formula, or summary of the structure of Buddhist teaching which occurs over twenty times in the Pāli Canon (the basic authoritative texts of Southern or Theravāda Buddhism). A significant part of the content outlined in this formula is concerned with applying an understanding of *karma* (*kamma*) to the practical implications of ethics, cosmology and spiritual attainment. The structure of the formula is as follows:

1. Step-by-step discourse: a) first part: giving (dāna), precepts (sīla) and the heavens [i.e., the different levels of refined existence, which correspond to levels of refinement in consciousness and moral practice]: b) second part: the defects of sensuality and positive gain in freedom from it.

2. The particular teaching: the Four Noble Truths, suffering, its arising, its cessation and the path to its cessation. (Cousins in Hinnells, 1985, p. 300)

The detailed content which provides the specific message within this formula was adapted according to the circumstances in which it was delivered. In some texts it occurs in little more than the summary provided above. In others it is expanded with detailed explanation and examples. As Lance Cousins points out, the texts often describe the Buddha delivering this teaching, followed by the hearer of the teaching gaining a direct perception and heightened understanding of *Dhamma*. The Pāli term for this perception and sudden understanding is *Dhamma-cakkhu* (*Dhamma* eye or spiritual vision); it marks the person's entry on to the supermundane (*lokuttara*) path (see p. 87), and so their serious commencement of higher practice and attainment. One dramatic example of this attainment taking place suddenly, and to an unlikely candidate, is the case of Aṅgulimāla (see p. 82). He was a murderer and bandit, who pursued the Buddha one day with the intention of killing him. The Buddha used his psychic mastery to outpace the running Aṅgulimāla, without appearing to move quickly at all. The Buddha gave the perplexed Aṅgulimāla a very brief *Dhamma* talk on harmlessness, and the would-be assassin attained the *Dhamma-cakkhu*, threw away his weapons and became a monk. Shortly after this he attained liberation as an *arahat*.[1]

It is important to notice that the 'step-by-step discourse' is predominantly directed towards ethical concerns and teachings. It could therefore be said to relate to 'kammatic' (pp. 183–4) concerns. Within this teaching there is a subtle shift from the external features of moral conduct in the first part to more psychological aspects of ethical teaching in the second part. These two parts of the step-by-step discourse provide a platform of moral behaviour and mental stability, so that the follower is ready to achieve a fuller understanding of the particular teaching of the Four Noble Truths. These are obviously soteriological in orientation, and constitute what Spiro has classified as 'Nibbanic Buddhism'. The difference in content between the two types of teaching should not blind us to their conceptual and functional inter-relatedness.

The first part of the step-by-step discourse begins with giving (*dāna*). This is understood as a formal religious act rather than a generalized act of charity. It is directed specifically to a monk or spiritually-developed person. Its ethical and religious significance is often ignored in doctrinally orientated Western accounts of Buddhism. Originally, *dāna* was taught as a non-violent replacement for the Brahmanical sacrifice. It has the effect of purifying and transforming the mind of the giver:

> The inner intention of the giver is reflected in the care, attention and joy with which the giving is performed. The higher the state of mind the more powerful the action (*kamma*). Important too is the state of mind of the recipient, made infectious as it were by the special nature of the act of giving. Either of these is sufficient to make the act effective. The two together are even more powerful. (Cousins in Hinnells, 1985, p. 301)

The emphasis on the intention and attitude underlying the act is characteristic of Buddhist ethical teaching and practice. The popular understanding of the 'merit' (*puñña*) which results from the practice of *dāna* (see pp. 68–9) is an important feature of lay Buddhist practice in all Buddhist countries (see Gombrich, 1988, pp. 124–7). For those aspiring to systematic practice and attainment on the Path, *dāna* helps the preliminary settling of the mind, and reduces selfishness, and provides a natural preparation for undertaking the Precepts (*sīla*). For the laity there are normally five precepts. Again the formal undertaking of the precepts, which usually follows the 'going for refuge' to Buddha, *Dhamma* and *Saṅgha*, constitutes a religious act which brings about benefits and 'merits'. The refuges and precepts are therefore chanted at the outset of most formal Buddhist activities. The wording of the precepts is significant; it translates as follows: I undertake the training rule of refraining from:

1 destroying life;

2 taking what is not given;

3 wrong behaviour in regard to sense pleasure;

4 untrue speech;

5 causes of intoxication.

The precepts are formulated not as imperatives or commandments, but as training rules voluntarily undertaken to facilitate practice.[2] For the laity there are no externally imposed sanctions for transgression of the precepts. According to Buddhist action theory (i.e., *karma*), unwholesome acts will result in unpleasant tendencies and results. Spiro observed in Myanmar (Burma) that the main motivation for complying with the precepts was fear for the 'karmic' consequences of non-compliance, rather than the positive 'meritorious' benefits of compliance (Spiro, 1971, p. 99). Behaviourally, one could argue that this amounts to the same result, but Spiro is rightly concerned with the psychological or motivational factors behind moral behaviour.

In his study he lists the set of conventional Burmese beliefs about the specific consequences of failure to comply with specific precepts. They are as follows: for adultery, the man will be reborn with a small penis, the woman will be reborn as a prostitute. For adultery with a married woman, the consequence is hell. For killing, the consequence is usually an interminable period in one of the hells, the length of duration depending partly upon the moral, spiritual and 'biological' status of the victim, and sometimes on their relationship to the killer. Killing a monk or one's parents is clearly among the gravest of offences. Killing other people or animals is certainly serious but the time in hell will be shorter. For less grave cases of killing, a short human life rather than hell may be the result. Killing mammals is graver in its consequences than killing reptiles; killing invertebrates is the least grave. Stealing will result in an impoverished future life; the consequences of white lies can be removed by 'meritorious' acts. As Spiro points out, there are many variations in the detailed 'karmic' correlations which ordinary Burmese people maintain (Spiro, 1971, pp. 98–102).

Spiro observed that among the Buddhists of Myanmar positive acts such as giving (*dāna*), the support of monks or building *stūpa*s, or the purchase and release of animals intended for slaughter, are considered more effective methods of acquiring 'merit' rather than simple compliance with the precepts (Spiro, 1971, pp 103–13). Similar findings have been observed among Thai Buddhists.[3] Unfortunately Spiro tends to interpret such beliefs only in rather mechanistic terms, and formally separates considerations of 'merit' accumulation from considerations of morality. This procedure seems to be informed by Western assumptions about the nature of moral worth, and ignores the extent to which positive accumulation and avoidance of unwholesome acts form a complementary process; and one makes little sense without reference to the other. As Lance Cousins points out, the cultivation of giving (*dāna*) and moral conduct (*sīla*) will themselves refine consciousness to such a level that rebirth in one of the lower heavens is likely even if further practice and entry on the Path are not developed (Cousins in Hinnells, 1985, p. 304).

It should be emphasized that there is nothing improper or un-Buddhist about limiting one's aims to this level of attainment. Many of the ways in which Buddhist practices and institutions actually function represent a very subtle fusing of 'popular' concerns for the accumulation of 'merit' and a beneficial rebirth, with 'élite' monastic concerns over the dissemination of *Buddha-Dhamma*, and the continuation of lay support.

One perfect illustration of this fusion of concerns and interests is the traditional phenomenon of temporary monkhood, which is still widely practised in Myanmar and Thailand. In it young boys or men are temporarily admitted to monasteries as novices or as monks. The age of the boys is generally eleven, and the period of this temporary monk status is traditionally three months, but there are wide variations (Spiro, 1971, p. 247). The temporary ordination procedure serves a number of functions. From the 'kammatic' and popular point of view, it achieves considerable 'merit' for the boy and his sponsor (usually his family). In ritual or 'apotropaic' terms the actual ordination ceremony generates considerable magical and protective power for the boy and his sponsors.

From an institutional point of view, the monastery is gaining revenue for the service and, even more important, it is establishing a clear link between that individual and the *saṅgha* which will influence his attitude to Buddha, *Dhamma* and *Saṅgha* for the rest of his life. He will in adult life expect to be a donor or supporter of monks if his resources allow. In a small number of cases the boy or man decides that he finds the life of a monk rewarding or worthwhile, or possibly less harsh than the life of work and hardship in the world, and decides to remain as a monk. In other words, the ordination can be an important means of recruitment to the *saṅgha*. Finally, from a dhammic point of view, he is being exposed, albeit in a diluted form, to the discipline of monastic life and the value of restraint. Spiro

(1971, p. 105) tends to minimize this dimension of the procedure, but it should not be ignored.

In Buddhist societies both past and present, 'Nibbanic Buddhism', or the systematic following of the Path (*magga*), with the overt intention of rapidly gaining liberation and the spiritual status of being an *arahat* (Sanskrit *arhat*, 'worthy one') is the concern of a minority of monks within the *saṅgha*. The majority of devout Buddhists, including most monks, are concerned with what Spiro describes as the 'proximate salvation' offered by 'Kammatic Buddhism'. The concepts relating to and derived from the 'radical salvation' sought in 'Nibbanic Buddhism' are of course highly important. They have an indirect influence on all forms of Buddhist practice and belief. But the temporary salvation offered by improving one's status and destination in the next life through the accumulation of 'merit' (*puñña*) is the more common concern of the majority of devout Buddhists.

The second part of the step-by-step discourse moves on to address the dangers of attachment to sensory experience. These dangers include the distortion of mental clarity, partiality, selfishness, craving, grasping, violence, dishonesty, theft. The most direct and positive antidote to many of these states is the cultivation in meditation of the four *brahma-vihāras*, or sublime states, of loving-kindness (*mettā*), compassion (*karuṇā*), sympathetic joy (*muditā*) and equanimity (*upekkhā*). It has been convincingly demonstrated that these states are meditational achievements and are concerned with attitudes, rather than with practice or providing the direct motivation to social or ethical action.[4] Aronson distinguishes these states from the more general socially motivating qualities of 'simple compassion' (*karūṇa*) and 'sympathy' (*anukampā*) which are available to all Buddhists whether they are proceeding to an advanced level of practice on the Path, or ordinary householders. He points out that it was this primary motive of sympathy which caused the Buddha to arise and teach in the first place. The sublime states cultivated in meditation will produce a refining of consciousness to such a level that rebirth in a less corporeal realm of existence will be possible. Alternatively meditators may choose to follow the path to a higher level of attainment, cultivate their meditational practice and so move on to the level referred to in the 'particular teaching', which is concerned with an understanding of the Four Noble Truths and the advanced levels of meditation practice (see Cousins in Hinnells, 1985, pp. 305–9).

The importance of *karma*

It is clear that underpinning and pervading the whole of the Buddhist teaching on the Path, at both ordinary (*lokiya*) and supermundane (*lokuttara*) levels, is the notion of *karma*. Because a general knowledge of Buddhist teaching about *karma* is now quite common in the East and West, it is easy to underestimate the impact of the Buddha's innovative reworking of a traditional Brahmanic concept. This impact is dramatically described in early texts dealing with the Buddha's final stages of attainment and his enlightenment. In these accounts, the fourth higher knowledge (*abhiññā*) gained by the Buddha is of his own previous lives, and how his wholesome actions give rise to beneficial consequences. This is followed by the fifth higher knowledge, which is the ability to observe the previous lives of other living beings, giving a vivid and direct understanding of the nature of their actions and the attendant consequences (*karma-vipāka*). The sixth superknowledge consists in the knowledge of the destruction of the influxes (*āsava*), unwholesome tendencies and mental states, followed by the Buddha's direct experience of the nature of the human condition as suffering or imperfection, its cause, its cessation and the Path to its cessation, i.e. the Four Noble Truths.

The Buddha's important contribution to the theory and concept of *karma* has been to give an ethical and psychological orientation to the Brahmanic notion of *karma*, which referred to effective ritual action. The emphasis in Buddhism is on the determining or volitional intention behind the action, and it is this which produces the seeds and tendencies which affect or determine future states and conditions. In the Buddhist context, the meaning of *karma* has shifted from ritual act to volitional act or intention (see p. 67). 'It is choice or intention that I call *karma* – mental work – for having chosen, a man acts by body, speech and mind.'[5] This is reflected in the traditional Buddhist emphasis on the need for controlling and understanding the mind if moral practice and spiritual training are to be cultivated to their higher levels.

The emphasis on the psychology of intentions in traditional Buddhist ethical teaching and spiritual practice should not lead to the undermining of physical behaviour and actual consequences. It would be incorrect to say that the intention or will to perform an unwholesome act, which was not actually carried out, would produce the same effect as the actual performance of such an act. The subtlety of levels of intention and the relationship between intention and behaviour are acknowledged. For example, the casual thought 'I wish X were dead' is certainly unwholesome, and will produce some unfortunate result. But the results would be much more serious in the case of someone who wishes X dead and makes detailed plans for murder. The results would be even more grave in the case of someone who raises the initial thought, plans and then actually carries out the murder. The degree of intention or volitional energies (Sanskrit *saṃskāra*; Pāli *saṅkara*) involved in the final scenario is clearly greater than those involved in the first two.

It is clear that the notion of *karma* permeates all levels of Buddhist teaching and practice. A generalized 'knowledge of the ownership of deeds' greatly facilitates cultivation of giving and moral conduct. It is also clear that a full understanding of the detailed operation of *karma* and its implications is available only at the highest levels of attainment and practice. It is interesting to note that it is only at this level of practice and attainment, when intentional acts producing harmful consequences are no longer performed, that a full understanding of the nature of that action and results is achieved (Robinson and Johnson, 1977, pp. 38–9). This does not mean that beings at this advanced level no longer act. The teaching career and activities of the Buddha and the *arahat*s (worthy/enlightened ones) disproves this. It simply means that their acts are of such a quality that they no longer generate fresh tendencies and consequences in performing them.

Given the causal processes involved in the operation of *karma* at the lower or provisional levels, and given the more subtle processes operating at the higher level, we can perhaps describe the Buddhist ethical and spiritual path as a form of spiritually rarified utilitarianism. What counts as 'good' in Buddhism is understood in terms of liberation or overcoming suffering. The subtle pleasurable nature of meditative states (e.g. the *brahma-vihāra* and *jhāna* states and resultant heavenly realms) is often overlooked. *Nirvāṇa* itself is frequently characterized as supremely blissful, peace, etc. The incentive value of the pleasurable aspects of the path is employed at both popular and higher levels. Here again, the thinking underlying such uses is distinctly consequentialist.[6]

The moral rules of the *saṅgha*

The issue of the training rules or precepts (Sanskrit *prātimokṣa*; Pāli *pāṭimokkha*) of the monastic order (*saṅgha*) is one of supreme importance in understanding the functioning of Buddhist ethical thought. The training precepts and rules constitute the core of the *Vinaya-piṭaka* (Discipline Collection) section of the Buddhist Canon. They are a list of offences recited regularly at the confession ceremony known as *uposatha*, which occurs on the days of the new moon and the full moon. The early form of this ceremony involved the acknowledgement of any transgression before the whole community (*saṅgha*). Gombrich notes that the developed procedure involves the acknowledgement of offences in pairs, followed by the communal recitation by all the monks present (Gombrich, 1988, p. 109).

It nevertheless remains true that the formal and public dimensions of this ritual are central to the maintenance of the *saṅgha*. It is important to note that a monk's digressions from the rule can be officially acknowledged only if they are confessed voluntarily by the monk himself. Many offences are concerned with details of deportment and decorum, and the simple acknowledgement of them incurs no further consequences. Gombrich (p. 108) notes that 75 of the 227 offences in the *pāṭimokkha* code of the Theravāda tradition are of this nature. Only four types of offence result in permanent exclusion from the *saṅgha*. These are: killing a person, engaging in sexual intercourse, theft, and the false claiming of higher knowledge and powers. Lesser offences may result in temporary exclusion. Gombrich has rightly indicated the importance of the fortnightly acknowledgement of offences and communal recitation of the *pāṭimokkha* in Buddhist history (Gombrich, 1988, pp. 106–14).

It is clear that it is the sharing of a common *pāṭimokkha* which is crucial in determining an ordination tradition, and it is the common *pāṭimokkha* and ordination tradition which is what defines and determines a sect or monastic fraternity (*nikāya*). Although to an outsider the differences between the *pāṭimokkha* of the different sects seem to be inconsequential, it is the preserving of the integrity of these lists of offences in detail which gives the sect its continuity and ensures that lineage's identity. As Gombrich observes, the formation and definition of a sect (*nikāya*) in traditional Buddhism is much more a question of observance and corporate ritual identity than primarily a matter of doctrinal agreement (Gombrich, 1988, pp. 110–14).

The *saṅgha*, ethics and society

For the issue of Buddhist morals and society, what is of equal importance is how the personal practice of the individual monk interweaves with the communal and institutional dimensions of the *saṅgha*. Gombrich (p. 72) has described early Buddhism and the Theravāda tradition as representing a form of religious individualism (i.e., relying only upon one's own resources and efforts to realize a goal). Early Buddhist texts describe the Buddha identifying the Path by his own example and providing the means for beings to find liberation. It is up to self-reliant individuals to employ these means and follow the Path through their own efforts. Buddhist traditions have been virtually unanimous throughout Buddhist history that the most effective and reliable way of following the Path is within the community of the *saṅgha*. This necessarily involves engaging with the social dimensions of the *saṅgha*, which is best seen as a communal institution with a soteriological orientation, in Gombrich's words, 'an association of self reliant individuals' (p. 89). This dual nature of the *saṅgha* and its effective embracing of individual spiritual concerns and communal institutional concerns has given rise to considerable discussion by Western scholars and commentators. It has often been at the heart of some of the more obvious conflicting characterizations of Buddhism in scholarly accounts. One dimension of the *saṅgha* has often been emphasized at the expense of the other.

One example of a difference in emphasis in modern scholarship, which relates to the above issues, is to be found in the differences between T. O. Ling and R. F. Gombrich. Ling sees early Buddhism as a psycho-social philosophy which incorporates 'a theory of existence consisting of a diagnosis (of the human malaise) and the prescription for a cure'.[7] He rightly takes the teaching of not-Self as central to Buddhism, but interprets it specifically as a teaching designed to overcome the 'disease of individualism'. He sees the communal life of the *saṅgha* as providing the context and environment where individualism can be most effectively broken down. On the issue of the relationship between *saṅgha* and lay society, Ling maintains that the Buddha consciously modelled the *saṅgha*'s constitution and organization on the methods of government of the tribal republics of north India, and that these principles were ideally seen as a model for government for society in general. His case for the latter largely rests on his interpretation of the 'conditions of welfare' passage in the

Mahā-parinibbāna Sutta. In this text, King Ajāttasattu of Magadha plans to invade the neighbouring states of the Vajjian Confederacy. The king asks the Buddha about the likely outcome. The Buddha replies that, providing the Vajjians continue to hold their regular public meetings, take decisions in concord, and honour their established traditions and institutions, then they will survive and prosper. Shortly after, he says that providing the Buddhist *saṅgha* operates along the same lines, and upholds its own rules and institutions, then it too will survive and prosper. Ling is suggesting that in this text, the Vajjians are regarded as democratic, and that their system of government is presented as a worthy model, for the *saṅgha* and for society as a whole (Ling, 1981, pp. 144–52; McFarlane in Pauling, 1986, pp. 98–9; Walshe, 1987, pp. 231–4).

Ling's emphasis here is upon the observance of collective decision-making, as well as a moral orientation, and it is these which are seen as the signs of a strong tradition, state or institution. Ling concedes that, in practice, the early *saṅgha* had to come to terms with the contemporary reality of increasingly powerful centralized and expansionist monarchies in north India. It would appear that the characterization of early Buddhism offered by Gombrich reflects a radically different perspective. He sees Buddhism as an early form of religious individualism with a theory of effective individual action which appealed to an increasingly important mercantile class (Gombrich, 1988, pp. 72–81).

Despite the apparent differences between Ling and Gombrich in their characterizations of early Indian Buddhism, it is possible to reconcile significant aspects of their positions. One could argue that a soteriological religion of self-help and individual responsibility, with its ethic of 'merit' at a popular level, and spiritual endeavour at the élite level (Gombrich), would be forced to confront the psychologically and spiritually damaging implications of its own individualism. Taking this process further, efforts of an individual and inherently 'self-authenticating' kind must be made in order to overcome or uproot the excesses of individualism arising from a misperception of the nature of the 'individual'. One can, of course, interpret this as an impossible and paradoxical vicious circle; or one can assume the Mahāyāna Buddhist perspective of skilful means and see it as using a thorn to take out a thorn.

Mahāyāna ethics

The ethical and social teaching of Mahāyāna Buddhism will now be considered in more detail. Although not exclusive to the Mahāyāna traditions, it was among these that the concept of the *bodhisattva* was refined and developed into an ethical and spiritual practice and ideal in its own right (*bodhisattva* means literally 'being of awakening'). It is impossible to treat Mahāyāna Buddhism as a single unified entity, but the *bodhisattva* as the embodiment and exemplar of supreme wisdom (*mahā-prajñā*) and supreme compassion (*mahā-karuṇā*) does provide the nearest thing to a core concept for all the diverse traditions and practices of the Mahāyāna. Many of the familiar virtues and meditational states exemplified in traditional Buddhism reappear in the qualities and practices of the *bodhisattva*, known as the perfections (*pāramitā*). These are: giving (*dāna*), moral conduct (*śīla*), patience (*kṣānti*), energy (*vīrya*), absorptive meditation (*dhyāna*), and wisdom (*prajñā*). Some later texts add skilful means (*upāya-kauśalya*), resolution (*praṇidhāna*), strength (*bala*), and knowledge (*jñāna*).

A feature evident in this combination of perfections (and in many Mahāyāna texts) is the tendency to universalize or generalize central concepts and values. In this way, ideas and norms which for earlier traditional forms of Buddhism would have been restricted to the spiritual élite within the *saṅgha* are extended or made available to the laity as well. Frank Reynolds and Robert Company have noted this tendency and have identified the concept of the *bodhisattva* as 'an ideal that combined the social virtues of a righteous householder with the ascetic ideals of a meditating monk, bridging what was perceived by its proponents as a gap between monastic and popular Buddhism' (Reynolds and Company, 1985, p. 501).

One feature of this universalizing process is the replacing of the supposedly narrow and 'self-regarding' goal of *nirvāṇa* as achieved by the *arahat* or accomplished *śrāvaka* (see p. 10) with the universal goal of supreme enlightenment (*saṃbodhi*) for all beings, as exemplified by the *buddha*s and *bodhisattva*s. In theory, the *bodhisattva* Path is open to all whether monk or lay-person, man or woman. In practice, its higher stages are more likely to be achieved within the context of the *saṅgha*. Further evidence for the process of universalizing or generalizing at the level of values and norms can be found in texts which take ethical requirements previously confined to the *saṅgha* and teach them as norms for the laity. For example, the Chinese Mahāyāna version of the *Brahmajāla Sūtra* requires both monks and lay people to abstain from violence and involvement with military affairs. In the Pāli version such requirements are directed only at members of the *saṅgha*.[8] Similarly, showing compassion to animals, which is encouraged in early Buddhism (Horner, 1967, *passim*), becomes requirements in the Mahāyāna; hence instructions for *bodhisattvas* to avoid meat are to be found in the Mahāyāna *Brahmajāla Sūtra*.

This process is also evident in doctrinal matters. One of the great heroes of the Mahāyāna is the *bodhisattva* Vimalakīrti, a wealthy householder with a family and many concubines, who teaches the senior monks and whose wisdom and skill equal that of Mañjuśrī.[9] A number of other Mahāyāna texts give prominence to advanced lay teachers of *Dharma* (see Williams, 1989, pp. 21, 125, 129, 154). I agree with Williams (1989, pp. 22–6) that it would be incorrect to conclude from such texts that the Mahāyāna represents a product of innovations developed by lay Buddhists. With the exception of the modern Japanese lay Buddhist movements such as the Sōka-gakkai, the *saṅgha* has always remained at the centre of Mahāyāna religious life and doctrinal development. It is almost certain that these spiritually egalitarian *sūtras* were inspired and transmitted by monks.

There are philosophical or doctrinal reasons behind the Mahāyāna tendency to universalize across the *saṅgha*/householder distinction. One of the fundamental insights of the Mahāyāna is the non-differentiation of the round of craving, grasping, suffering, rebirth (*saṃsāra*) and the cessation of suffering in the liberated state (*nirvāṇa*), because all states and appearances are manifestations of the same underlying *buddha*-nature (Japanese *bussho*), which is empty of self (*śunyatā*). The non-differentiation of *saṃsāra* and *nirvāṇa* was articulated by Nāgārjuna (see p. 47), and developed in relation to Mahāyāna thought and practice in the 'Perfection of Wisdom' literature and all later Mahāyāna systems. Such an undifferentiated insight tends to facilitate a kind of spiritual egalitarianism which sees no ultimate distinction between monk and householder, ordinary being and *buddha*. However, Mahāyāna texts and teachers accept that it is at the level of delusion and differentiation that beings need to be taught and guided. So the methods and teachings must be carefully moderated and adapted to the level of understanding appropriate to such beings. The crucial importance of teaching at the conventional level of truth should not be underestimated. In articulating the distinction between ultimate truth (*paramārtha-satya*) and conventional/provisional truth (*saṃvṛti-satya*), Nāgārjuna makes it clear that it is only by recourse to the conventional that the ultimate can be attained (trans. in Williams, 1989, p. 69).

One aspect of the skilful means (*upāya-kauśalya*) of *buddha*s and *bodhisattva*s is their ability to know which expressions of conventional truth to employ in order to bring beings to the Path to liberation most effectively. The Mahāyāna identification of levels of truth means there is no real tension between the spiritual egalitarianism expressed in some Mahāyāna texts and the more traditional Buddhist acknowledgement of a spiritual and moral hierarchy.

The problem for commentators is that different levels of truth and different means (*upāya*) interweave in the same passages and texts. This is perfectly illustrated in the context of Mahāyāna ethics, psychology and soteriology, in the account of Mañjuśrī's 'attempt' to kill the Buddha, in a text extant in the Chinese *Mahā-ratnakūṭa* collection. The whole incident is a skilful means devised by the Buddha in order to rid 500 *bodhisattva*s of the spiritually debilitating knowledge of their heinous offences in past lives. The Buddha causes Mañjuśrī to attack him with a sword, then instructs Mañjuśrī that the real way to kill him is to see the Buddha (or any being) as possessing self or person. In reality, the Buddha, all beings and all *dharma*s are empty of self. To see them otherwise is actually to 'kill' them. In as much as they are ultimately without self, form or person, then killing them is an impossibility. On realizing the emptiness of all *dharma*s, the 500 *bodhisattva*s abandon their remorse over past crimes and continue their practice. One of the interesting features of this account is that in creating this skilful means the Buddha ensures that all the novice *bodhisattva*s of lesser understanding simply do not see the incident or hear the resulting discussion on emptiness and *karma*. This clearly demonstrates the principle of accommodation to different levels of ability and understanding which is central to the concept of skilful means.

It is clear from a wide range of Mahāyāna texts and teachings that the compassion and skilfulness of *buddha*s and *bodhisattva*s may permit or even require them to set aside traditional moral or doctrinal norms. The *Lotus Sūtra (Saddharma-puṇḍarika Sūtra/Myōhō renge kyō)*, which exerted such an influence in Far Eastern Buddhist teaching and practice, contains many such cases. For example, in chapter 8 the Buddha declares that *bodhisattva*s may appear to adopt deluded and heretical views in order to gain the confidence of beings and lead them to liberation.[10] The most famous case of skilful means occurs in a parable in the third chapter of the *Lotus Sūtra*, where the deception of a father (the Buddha), in promising toys which he does not have to his sons, is justified because the promise tempts them out of a burning house (*saṃsāra*).

The underlying principles of skilful means are apparent in early Buddhist texts, even though the technical vocabulary and detailed theory are lacking. One striking example is where the Buddha shows the lovesick monk Nanda the beauty of the nymphs in a heavenly realm to break his attachment to his new wife, and so causes Nanda to renew his efforts in meditation, in order to be reborn there. In fact, Nanda progresses to become an *arahat*, and forgets all about his desires for either human or heavenly maidens (Pye, 1978, p. 122).

Texts dealing with skilful means, non-duality, emptiness and other central Mahāyāna concepts frequently resort to extreme rhetorical exaggerations to make their point. There is a clear intention to shock conventional Buddhist hearers or readers out of their prosaic assumptions. These considerations are evident when *bodhisattva*s are described changing their sex at will,[11] or when the Buddha, in a previous life, breaks a vow of celibacy and lives with a woman for twelve years to prevent her death (Chang, 1983, p. 433). In another life he kills a bandit with a spear to save 500 traders, who are really *bodhisattva*s, and in doing so saves the man from the consequences of his intended actions.

It is clear from the circumstances of these and similar accounts, and from the high spiritual status of the performers of these deeds, that they are not intended to be employed as blanket justifications of moral transgressions in ordinary situations, outside the context of spiritual training and practice (McFarlane in Pauling, 1986, vol. 1, pp. 101–2). In scholarly treatises associated with the great Buddhist philosopher Asaṅga (fourth or fifth century CE), there is evidence of attempts to formulate a dharmically and karmically coherent rationale for such transgressions. In these discussions and in the challenging examples used, there seems to be a willingness to test to the limit the demands of compassion and skilful means. Asaṅga's most challenging statement on these matters occurs in his *Bodhi-sattva-bhūmi* treatise:

> There are certain offences of nature which the *bodhisattva* may practise through his skilful means, whereby he commits no fault and indeed produces much merit. For instance, when the *bodhisattva* sees a thief or bandit ready to kill many hundred beings, even great beings such as *śrāvakas*, *pratyekabuddhas*, or *bodhisattvas*. Seeing this, he refines his thought and reflects: 'If I kill this being I will be reborn in a hell, but I am willing to suffer it. This being may later act in such a way as to avoid hell.' Resolving in this way, the *bodhisattva*, with kind thoughts towards the being, one with him in his heart, with compassionate regard to his future and abhorring his act, kills him. He is free from fault and produces much merit.
>
> So, too, is the *bodhisattva* when there are kings or great ministers who are excessively cruel and have no compassion for beings, intent on causing pain to others. Since he has the power, he makes them fall from command of the kingdom, where they cause so much demerit; his heart is compassionate, he intends their welfare and happiness. If there are thieves and bandits who take the property of others, or property of the *saṅgha* or a *stūpa*, making it their own to enjoy, the *bodhisattva* takes it from them, reflecting 'Let not this property be a disadvantage and misfortune to them for a long time'. So he takes it and returns it to the *saṅgha* or to the *stūpa*. By this means, the *bodhisattva*, though taking what is not given, does not have a bad rebirth, indeed much merit is produced. (Asaṅga, *Bodhisattvabhūmi*, Wogira (ed.), 1930, pp. 165–7)[12]

Such examples and arguments are certainly open to casuistic exploitation, though the explicit use of the concept of skilful means to justify or rationalize known cases of moral transgressions is actually quite rare. However, it would be misleading to suggest that they never occurred. One notable example is the celebrated assassination of the Tibetan king gLang-dar-ma by the monk dPal-gyi rdo-rje, in 842 CE. The king was violently persecuting the *saṅgha* and the monk acted to save the *Dharma*, and save the king from perpetuating his own wicked acts and their consequences (Williams, 1989, p. 190). It is significant that even though the Mahāyāna ethic of skilful means theoretically justified the act, the offending monk admitted his offence and excluded himself from ordination ceremonies. In another supposedly historical incident, which is typical of the kind of rhetorical extremes already mentioned, the great Mādhyamika teacher Āryadeva invokes the notions of emptiness and non-duality, and the illusoriness of the victim and perpetrator of murder. He does this not to justify an act of killing on his part, but rather when he has just been fatally stabbed by an assassin, to whom he proceeds to teach the above *Dharma*, and whom he provides with the means of his escape (Khantipalo, 1964, pp. 174–5).

Vajrayāna ethics

Like other major developments in Buddhist teachings and methods, the Vajrayāna (Adamantine Vehicle) (see p. 12) represents both a continuity with the Buddhism from which it emerged as well as a creative departure from it. The antecedents of the Vajrayāna are basically twofold:

1 The radical emptiness teaching of the 'perfection of wisdom' (*Prajñā-pāramitā*) and Mādhyamika texts, which asserts the non-differentiation of *saṃsāra* and *nirvāṇa* (p. 196), and the ultimate 'sameness' of all *dharmas*, and so encourages dispassion and detachment with regard to *dharmas*.

2 A strongly devotional or affective type of Buddhist practice, which was familiar with the magical potency of Buddhist ritual. This could be classified using Spiro's category of 'apotropaic'. It should be acknowledged that even the 'Perfection of Wisdom' texts and their related practices are not devoid of this magical dimension of Buddhist practice (Conze, 1959, pp. 96–100, 118–25).

The aim of practice in Vajrayāna is to focus the mental, volitional and physical energies of the initiate, and refine them through meditational, mantric and ritual means, eventually transforming them to a point where their qualities are the same as those of the body of a *buddha*. In other words, it is to use the ordinary qualities of the body, speech and mind, and transform them into the extraordinary qualities of the *Dharma*-body (true body of all *buddhas*).

Some more radical Vajrayāna treatises or *tantras* (*tantras* are ritual texts attributed to the Buddha, which offer access to spiritual mastery and power) seem to start where Asaṅga and the extreme cases in the *sūtras* cited above left off. Some appear to insist uncompromisingly on the initiate's demonstration of the non-differentiation between *saṃsāra* and *nirvāṇa*, or between pure and impure. Actions such as the following are all recommended, in the appropriate circumstances: killing (usually restricted to killing beings about to commit actions which would take them straight to hell), lying (usually recommended in the interest of *upāya-kauśalya*), stealing (usually to prevent those who crave possessions from themselves stealing), adultery (usually to provide human rebirths for the recently deceased who are in danger of descending into a hell), wine drinking (usually to sever attachments and overcome discrimination between fellow initiates and worldlings), consorting with low-caste women (usually explained as a means of overcoming attachment to the 'pure' and aversion to the 'impure', i.e. a practical demonstration of sameness and non-discrimination).

Although Vajrayāna Buddhism developed in India from as early as the fifth and sixth centuries CE, the bulk of the commentarial literature on the *tantras* (see pp. 12, 45–6, 162–3) is preserved in Tibetan texts, although some *tantras* are preserved in Sanskrit. These texts and their commentaries continue to perplex many Western scholars, who are generally approaching the texts in isolation from the meditational and ritual practices associated with them, as well as from the rich oral tradition which supports their practice.

Two excellent recent studies of the ways of interpreting complex Vajrayāna texts are those of Michael M. Broido and Robert A. F. Thurman (both in Lopez, 1988, pp. 71–118, 119–48). Broido points out that there are clearly intended multiple levels of explanation apparent in these texts. He demonstrates how the fundamental distinction between a *neyārtha* (provisional or exoteric) level of explanation and a *nithartha* (final or esoteric) level is explicitly applied to one such text (Broido in Lopez, 1988, pp. 72–82). The *neyārtha* explanation follows very much that outlined above. But the *nithartha* explanation treats the language of killing, lying, stealing, adultery, etc. as a detailed code for a variety of specific meditational, physiological and mantric procedures, largely concerned with the generation of internal heat through sound (*mantra*), and the retention and redirection of semen. A very general relationship between mental/behavioural control and mental/physiological control could perhaps be argued for in attempting to relate the two levels of explanation here, but it would be difficult to sustain with any real conviction. What is clear is that tantric texts and their commentarial material cannot simply be taken at face value.

Overview

The diversity, complexity and flexibility of moral practice and moral reponse to be found in Buddhist traditions make generalization about the nature of Buddhist moral decision-making extremely difficult. The apparent simplicity of the precepts for lay people and the training rules for monks serves as a guide for the ordinary follower, and alleviates the need for detailed reflection on the nature of moral or karmic processes. The implicit message for the ordinary Buddhist is to follow the moral guidelines provided by *Dharma*, and, even in the absence of a full understanding of the detailed operations of *karma*, a happy future life will be achieved. Even underlying this implicit message is a pragmatism which is typical of all Buddhist thinking. The soteriological and pragmatic orientation of higher levels of Buddhist practice (Nibbanic Buddhism) means that considerable flexibility is apparent at the level of practice. Hence for the advanced *bodhisattva* in the higher levels of Mahāyāna practice and teaching, breaking the formal precepts may be expedientially necessary. In such cases, of course, the overriding consideration remains a moral one, in that the *bodhisattva* only acts in such a way in the interests of great compassion (*mahā-karuṇā*). He uses desperate measures and skilful means only in particular and exceptional circumstances; and does so only in the interest of benefitting or teaching deluded beings. The underlying motivation remains both moral and soteriological.

The Vajrayāna tradition, despite its strange, coded language and apparently bizarre practices, operates on the same underlying assumptions as the Mahāyāna tradition from which it emerged. The aim of literal transformation into the form and attributes of an enlightened *buddha* also entails an engagement with the fundamental qualities of supreme wisdom (*mahā-prajñā*) and supreme compassion (*mahā-karuṇā*). It should also be emphasized that the extreme measures sanctioned by Asaṅga and other Mahāyāna authorities, and the sometimes bizarre-sounding rites of the Vajrayāna tradition, were generally envisaged as being practised by monks, who were normally following the discipline and restraint of the training rules of the *saṅgha*, and who were always under the direct supervision of an experienced teacher. In such a context, transgressions, even in the context of skilful means for the sake of others, were seen as the exception and not the rule.

Notes

1 I. B. Horner (trans.) (1975) *Middle Length Sayings*, vol. 2. London: Pali Text Society, pp. 284–92.
2 See J. Bowker (1983) *Worlds of Faith*. London: BBC Ariel Books, p. 132.
3 S. J. Tambiah (1968) 'The ideology of merit and the social correlates of Buddhism in a Thai village' in E. R. Leach (ed.) *Dialectic in Practical Religion*. Cambridge: Cambridge University Press, pp. 69–70.
4 See H. B. Aronson, *Love and Sympathy in Theravāda Buddhism*. Delhi: Motilal Banarsidass, ch. 5, and 'Motivations to social action in Theravāda Buddhism' in A. K. Narain (ed.) *Studies in History of Buddhism*. Delhi: B. R. Publishing Corporation, pp. 1–12 (both 1980).
5 *Aṅguttara Nikāya*, III.415, quoted in M. Carrithers (1983) *The Buddha*. Oxford: Oxford University Press, p. 67.
6 Though the consequences are not seen as accidentally related to their causes: the path to *nirvāṇa* – the end of attachment, hatred and delusion – is one of working to undermine attachment, hatred and delusion. Keown (1992) in fact argues that the best parallel to Buddhist ethics is Aristotelian virtue ethics, not utilitarianism. (Ed.)
7 T. O. Ling (1973) *The Buddha*. London: Temple Smith, p. 120.
8 T. W. Rhys Davids and C. A. F. Rhys Davids (1969) *Dialogues of the Buddha*, Part 1 (*Dīgha Nikāya*). London: Pali Text Society, pp. 4, 6, 13; see also Walshe (1987), pp. 68, 69, 70–1.
9 E. Lamotte, trans. S. Boin (1976) *The Teaching of Vimalakirti*. London: Pali Text Society, ch. 8.
10 L. Hurvitz (1976) *Scripture of the Lotus Blossom of the Fine Dharma*. New York: Columbia University Press, p. 160.
11 D. Y. Paul (1985) *Women in Buddhism*. London: University of California Press, ch. 5.
12 With thanks to my colleague David Smith for the help with the translation of the Sanskrit text.

Further reading

Asaṅga (1930) *Bodhisattvabhūmi*, ed. U. Wogira. Tokyo: [n.p.]. A translation of part of this is Tatz, M. (1986) *Asaṅga's Chapter on Ethics*. Lewiston, NY: Edwin Mellen Press.

Chang, Garma C. C. (ed.) (1983) *A Treasury of Mahāyāna Sutras*. University Park: Pennsylvania State University Press.

Collins, S. (1982) *Selfless Persons*. Cambridge: Cambridge University Press.

Conze, E. (1959) *Buddhist Scriptures*. London: Penguin.
Cousins, L. S. (1985) 'Buddhism' in J. R. Hinnells (ed.) *A Handbook of Living Religions*. London: Penguin.
Gombrich, R. F. (1988) *Theravāda Buddhism*. London: Routledge and Kegan Paul.
Harvey, P. (2000) *An Introduction to Buddhist Ethics: Foundations, Values and Issues*. Cambridge: Cambridge University Press.
Horner, I. B. (1967) *Early Buddhism and the Taking of Life*, The Wheel publication no. 104. Kandy, Sri Lanka: Buddhist Publication Society.
Keown, P. (1992) *The Nature of Buddhist Ethics*. London: Macmillan.
Khantipalo, P. (1964) *Tolerance: A Study from Buddhist Sources*. London: Rider.
Ling, T. O. (ed.) (1981) *The Buddha's Philosophy of Man*. London: Dent.
Lopez, D. S. (ed.) (1988) *Buddhist Hermeneutics*. Honolulu: University of Hawaii.
McFarlane, S. (1986) 'Buddhism' in L. Pauling (ed.) *World Encyclopedia of Peace*, vol. 1. Oxford: Pergamon, pp. 97–103.
Pye, M. (1978) *Skilful Means*. London: Duckworth.
Reynolds, F. E. and Company, R. (1985) 'Buddhist ethics' in M. Eliade (ed.) *The Encyclopedia of Religion*, vol. 2. New York: Macmillan, pp. 498–504.
Robinson, R. H. and Johnson, W. L. (1977) *The Buddhist Religion*. Belmont, CA: Dickenson.
Spiro, M. E. (1971) *Buddhism and Society*. London: Allen & Unwin.
Walshe, M. (1987) *Thus Have I Heard: The Long Discourses of the Buddha*. London: Wisdom.
Williams, P. (1989) *Mahāyāna Buddhism*. London: Routledge.

7. Women in Buddhism

Rita M. Gross

Modern commentators on the participation of women in Buddhism are likely to focus on two broad generalizations. The first observation is that the core teachings of this 2,500-year-old tradition are gender-free and gender-neutral, perhaps to a greater extent than is the case with any other major religious tradition. Contemporary Buddhist teachers themselves often respond to questions about the role of women in Buddhism by stating that the Buddha's teachings apply, without exception, to all sentient beings and that no relevant distinctions can be made between women and men regarding their ability to become enlightened and realize Buddhism's deepest insights into reality. But this has not meant that women and men have been accorded the same status or expected to accomplish the same things throughout most of Buddhist history. Buddhism emerged in a culture that was quite male-dominated and in which there were strong gender roles. Throughout its history Buddhism has accommodated itself more to these patriarchal norms than it has stood against them, though in every period of Buddhist history there are records of highly accomplished women and of great teachers who argued against cultural perceptions of female inferiority (cf. pp. 70–2). When asked to comment on this historical and institutional slighting of women throughout Buddhist history, many contemporary Buddhist teachers attribute it to 'cultural factors', thus agreeing with the conclusion that such disempowerment of women does not accord well with basic Buddhist teachings. However, to date, little has been done within Buddhism to correct these 'cultural factors' that have been so detrimental to women.

In this chapter, I shall focus on those aspects of Buddhism, both institutional and doctrinal, that most easily enable us to discern women's participation in Buddhism and Buddhist attitudes towards women. After a brief outline of Buddhist teachings, I shall discuss issues pertaining to women in each of the three major phases of Buddhist intellectual-spiritual development: early Indian Buddhism, Mahāyāna Buddhism, and Tantric or Vajrayāna Buddhism. Then I shall rapidly survey the development of Buddhism outside India, with reference to women's roles in those developments. In conclusion, I shall discuss the situation of women in the contemporary Buddhist world, surveying new developments, both theoretical and practical, that redefine women's presence in Buddhism.

Survey of major Buddhist teachings

Buddhism is a non-theistic religion. Its central teachings point out to its adherents the cause of and the cure for human suffering, locating both within human attitudes towards life. Buddhism is not concerned about the existence of a supreme being, because a supreme being would be unable to relieve human suffering, as it is defined by Buddhists. A supreme being cannot cause humans to give up the attitudes that produce human misery. Only human beings are capable of that feat.

According to Buddhism, the cause of misery is located in negative habitual patterns common to all unenlightened beings. Succinctly put, human beings suffer because, while still unenlightened, all beings strive with all their energy for unattainable goals. Disliking boredom and discontent, they strive for perfect complete bliss; disliking uncertainty, they strive for complete security; and disliking death and finitude, they strive for perfect complete permanence in personal immortality. According to Buddhism, these desires are completely impossible to attain under any conditions; therefore, striving to attain them is counterproductive, and serves only to deepen the pain of inevitable failure. That is the bad news, traditionally communicated by Buddhism's first and second Noble Truths – the truth that conventional existence is pervaded with suffering, and the truth that the cause of such suffering is desire rooted in ignorance.

The good news, according to Buddhism, is that human beings do not have to remain in such useless and counterproductive, desire-ridden states of being; they can lay down the burden and experience the calm and tranquillity of enlightenment. This is the third truth, the truth of the cessation of suffering. The best news of all is that there is a simple and workable path that can be used to good effect by everyone who wants to diminish the burden of excessive desire and compulsion. Called the Noble Eightfold Path, it is commonly summarized as consisting of three main disciplines: morality, meditation and wisdom.

Buddhism can seem like an extremely complex religion, especially when one first begins to study it. But all the doctrinal developments found in its many schools and denominations, and all the manifold philosophical texts and meditation manuals it has produced, could well be considered commentary on the four Noble Truths, discovered by Siddhārtha Gautama, the Buddha of our historical epoch, during his enlightenment experience, and outlined above.

Buddhism can also seem to be an excessively difficult religion to comprehend at the beginning of one's studies. This difficulty may well be due to Buddhism's great simplicity. The four Noble Truths are extremely simple and basic, but psychological and spiritual truths that are simple in their profundity are often glossed over, resisted, or made unduly complex in conventional thinking. Initially, most people do not want to hear that the solution to human misery lies in giving up unattainable desires, rather than in attaining what one desires, whether by one's own efforts or as the gift of a supreme being.

Women and early Indian Buddhism

Two stories, both very well known in Buddhist literature, set the tone for discerning attitudes towards women during Buddhism's first several hundred years. The first story recounts how the future Buddha, having resolved that he would abandon the householder life to become a world-renouncer in order to seek enlightenment, silently and secretly gazed upon his sleeping wife and new-born baby, but did not awaken them to bid them farewell. The second story occurs about five years after the Buddha's enlightenment experience, when women loyal to the new religion first gained formal permission to adopt the world-renouncer's lifestyle favoured by the Buddha. His aunt and foster-mother Mahā-Prajāpatī, who had raised him from early infancy, came with 500 women followers to ask the Buddha for admission to the monastic order, already well established for men (see pp. 161–2; also Harvey, 2000, pp. 383–91). They were refused the first time they asked, but they persisted and asked again at a later date. At that time, the Buddha's personal attendant Ānanda took up their cause. He asked the Buddha if women could achieve the same spiritual states as could men. The Buddha replied that they could, whereupon Ānanda suggested that, since women could benefit spiritually from living the homeless life, they should be allowed to renounce the world. The Buddha agreed, contingent upon the condition that the women world-renouncers accept eight special rules, the effect of which was to make the nuns' order dependent upon and subservient to the monks' order. The eight special rules were accepted and the nuns' order began.

Both these stories are set in the context of the belief that world-renunciation is essential to the successful pursuit of the religious life. That is why the future Buddha felt compelled to abandon his wife and child, and why it was so essential for women to found a nuns' order parallel to the monks' order. If the nuns' order had not been established, early Buddhism would have been an extremely disadvantageous religion for women, since they would not have been able to participate in its fundamental institution and, consequently, would have been greatly hampered in their ability to attain its highest goals. Though Buddhism has also devised various methods for lay or householder participation in the religious life throughout its history, reliance on a monastic core has been both the strength and the weakness of Buddhism in its various cultural manifestations. Therefore, it is important to understand what this lifestyle involved and why it was valued so highly.

Siddhārtha Gautama, the Buddha, did not originate the world-renouncer lifestyle; he was merely adopting a value widespread in the India of his day while adding various refinements to it. The lifestyle involved renouncing the securities of conventional life along with its major tasks of economic production and biological reproduction. Without significant possessions, without consort, without significant ties to parents or children, and often without a permanent dwelling, the world-renouncer's life was dedicated full-time to the pursuit of spiritual insight, meditative calm and awareness, and detachment. Such achievements brought freedom from the curse of rebirth into the endless rounds of cyclic existence that was believed to be the lot of those who remained fettered to their desires and compulsions. The householder's life, by contrast, was burdened with cares and responsibilities; deep insight into reality, calm awareness and detachment were thought to be almost impossible to attain while involved in economic or reproductive pursuits.

These assessments of the relative value of householder or monastic life-styles did not turn on a body–spirit dichotomy and did not regard sexuality or the body as evil and degraded, as did similar Western forms of monasticism. Rather, the problem that had to be overcome was attachment, clinging or desire. One lifestyle bred those enslaving attitudes; the other fostered freedom from them. Thus, when Siddhārtha Gautama abandoned his wife, it was not because of her evil or sexual nature, but because of his own attachment to her. Other monks, whose attitudes are recorded in early Buddhist texts, could not so readily locate their problems in their own attachments, but blamed women for their sexual desires. Because of these stories and statements, some scholars have regarded early Buddhism as misogynist in its views of women, but I believe that such views do not represent the norm in early Indian Buddhism. Attachment itself, rather than that to which one is attached, was recognized as the fundamental obstacle by the tradition as a whole.

The other major story raises much more serious questions about the treatment of women in early Indian Buddhism. Why did the Buddha resist the women who wished to renounce the world, as men had already done? Why didn't the Buddha himself encourage women, as well as men, to leave the householder lifestyle behind? Why did he hedge the nuns' order in with the eight special rules?[1] And why did he predict that the 'true *Dharma*' would last only 500 years, instead of 1,000 years, as a consequence of the women's ordination? None of these questions is easy to answer and they probably cannot be answered with certainty. That these events were included as part of the Buddhist record demonstrates that, from its beginnings, Buddhism was male-dominated or patriarchal, even though it was not misogynistic.

Though various explanations for these attitudes and practices have been put forward, I believe the simplest and most adequate explanation recognizes that the Buddha, though enlightened regarding certain deep spiritual truths, was not entirely free of the social conditioning of his times. I do not believe that enlightenment entails a timelessly perfect social conscience or universal scientific and historical knowledge. Therefore, it did not occur to the Buddha to encourage women to be equal to men in their unconventionality and counter-cultural activities. Nor did he immediately welcome the idea of a parallel women's order. Good guesses as to why he did not welcome the women renunciants include the fear of hostility from householders if their wives and daughters suddenly had an option to renounce their domestic roles, and fear of gossip regarding the interactions of nuns and monks.[2] And it is very clear from another story that, even after he had accepted the idea of a women's order, he could not fathom any other principle than a male-dominant gender hierarchy by which to regulate the interactions of the two orders. The first of the eight special rules decreed that even the most senior nun must defer to the most recently ordained monk. The founder of the nuns' order is said once to have asked the Buddha for a special boon – that monks and nuns greet each other by seniority, without regard for gender. The Buddha is said to have replied that even in poorly run sects, the men never deferred to the women and that such behaviour would be unthinkable for his order.

Women in early Indian Buddhism were, however, far more able to participate fully in their tradition as nuns who had to observe the eight special rules than they could have if the nuns' order had not been founded at all. Thus, though the modern tendency may be to criticize the Buddha for his unequal treatment of women, it is probably far more accurate, in the historical context, to recognize how radical it was to provide women with an alternative to domesticity. Furthermore, the eight special rules in no way inhibit women's spiritual development, since women practise a religious life identical with that practised by men.

According to the records of early Indian Buddhism, women used their option well. Many women, in varying domestic situations – married, widowed, abandoned, suffering from the death of children, leaving their children behind, with grown children – renounced their domestic lives. Many attained the tradition's goal of freedom, peace and release from cyclic existence. Many are celebrated as having become highly accomplished at various achievements valued by the tradition. Their stories and poems are recorded in the *Therīgāthā*, one of the most remarkable and under-recognized texts in world religious literature (Rhys Davids and Norman, 1989). In these poems, women sing of their joy in liberation, of their former sorrow and attachment, and their freedom from the constraints of gender stereotypes. Though not nearly so frequently mentioned by historians of Buddhism as is the story of the Buddha's reluctance to initiate the nuns' order, these stories of the great female exemplars of the early tradition deserve to become a prominent part of the record regarding women and Buddhism. If they were better known, scholars and students of Buddhism could form a more balanced and complete picture of the role of women in early Indian Buddhism.

In the long run, however, the nuns' order did not fare as well as did the monks' order, in India or elsewhere in the Buddhist world. The nuns' order may have existed in India for about 1,500 years, until the final days of Buddhism there, but its fortunes eventually declined from the glory of its earlier years. There were fewer nuns; they appear to have been poorly supported by the laity and they were poorly educated. There is no indication that they were involved in the great monastic universities, such as Nālandā university, that were so famous in the late period of Indian Buddhism.

It is difficult to isolate a single cause for this decline, but several interrelated factors probably explain why the order declined in India and was not carried with other aspects of Buddhism to some Asian Buddhist countries. Probably the single biggest difficulty faced by the nuns was the patriarchal definition of women's place as the domestic and reproductive sphere. This cultural norm at first limited even the Buddha's vision regarding the nuns' order. Throughout Asian patriarchal cultures, people simply could more easily envision men taking up the homeless life than they could imagine women taking up the same lifestyle. In such cultures, they could also more easily give men the prestige and the economic support accorded to those who do renounce the conventional lifestyle in favour of spiritual development. The eight special rules also seem to have played a part in this decline (Falk, 1989, p. 159). Because nuns were forbidden by the eight special rules to instruct monks, nun scholar-teachers could not build the basis of prestige that their male counterparts could, even if they were well educated, which became more difficult for them over the centuries. Lay donors preferred to contribute to famous rather than obscure monastics, which meant that the nuns were last on the list and became poorer and less well educated. Furthermore, such a community was unattractive to more capable recruits. And so a downward spiral developed, which, once in place, was difficult to reverse.

Women in Mahāyāna Buddhism

By 500 years after the beginnings of Buddhism, a new movement in Buddhism, the Mahāyāna, had developed and was being practised along with the older schools. Mahāyāna Buddhism is famous for its philosophical teachings concerning emptiness, which can be briefly defined as the claim that lack of a permanent essence or lack of independent existence is the central trait of all phenomena. Mahāyāna Buddhism is equally famous for its elaboration of the *bodhisattva* ideal. The *bodhisattva* vows to achieve 'complete perfect enlightenment' for the sake of all beings, over the course of many lifetimes, rather than to rest content, achieving only her own freedom from cyclic existence. Though monasticism continued to be popular, at least theoretically, Mahāyāna Buddhism also came to elevate the lay, householder lifestyle to a much higher status. No longer was it assumed that only monks and nuns stood any chance of achieving enlightenment, and Mahāyāna texts are full of tales of householders, both women and men, who are highly advanced.

In principle, these Mahāyāna innovations have great implications for women's participation in Buddhism. Unfortunately, in terms of historical records, little is available and there is little indication that women's roles in Buddhist life and institutions were different in any significant way from what they had been in older forms of Buddhism. But the literature of Mahāyāna Buddhism includes a wide variety of opinions about women and their potential for spiritual achievement. From this literature, it is evident that, even if there was not a women's movement in Mahāyāna Buddhism, the intellectual foundations for such a movement were being laid.

Some famous and important Mahāyāna scriptures reinforce the view, already articulated in early Indian Buddhism, that female rebirth is an unfortunate condition. This view is easily misunderstood in a cultural context, such as that of the West, in which belief in rebirth is not assumed and in which many religious symbols encode a view that women are evil and inferior. On the contrary, the emphasis of the Mahāyāna texts that do speak of the misfortune of female rebirth is that, since women (under patriarchal conditions) suffer many liabilities that men do not suffer, their greater suffering must be a result of their more negative *karma*, or inherited moral balance sheet from previous lives. In the future, however, this misfortune can and will be overcome. Therefore, for example, the all-compassionate

Buddha Amitābha graciously arranges that in his Pure Land there will be no unfortunate rebirths, including no female rebirths, and that women, in their current lives, can assure themselves of rebirth into the Pure Land as easily as can men. To a modern Western feminist, the evaluation that female rebirth is unfortunate sounds very negative, but it is important to realize that the Buddhist who holds this belief and the feminist agree on an important issue. They agree that women's lives in patriarchal societies are painful and filled with suffering. What they disagree about is that the feminist would eliminate patriarchy, rather than female rebirth. But that option probably seemed impossible to most people in the societies in which such texts were written.

Other Mahāyāna texts concern themselves with the question of how much spiritual depth a person might develop while manifesting in a female rebirth. Most of them consciously refute the claim that only in a future male rebirth could a female really attain deep insight. Instead, they demonstrate that *now*, in her female body, a particular person has attained the highest levels of wisdom and insight. Many texts include narratives in which the highest truths and most complex philosophical arguments of Mahāyāna thought are articulated, with complete ease and competence, by a woman, often a young girl, to an astounded audience of male elders, who cannot believe what they are hearing. Thus the Mahāyānist demonstrates that religious attainment is not restricted to a monastic élite, that even those most disadvantaged under the prevailing system can experience and express the indwelling enlightenment common to all beings, according to Mahāyāna analysis.

In these Mahāyāna texts, a range of levels of acceptance of such accomplished and competent women is found. In many texts, the conservative male elders remained adamantly unconvinced until the woman or girl performs an instantaneous sex change into a male. In one famous story the woman, instead, briefly changes her adversary into a woman. In some widely used and important texts, the teacher is a mature woman who expounds Buddhist teachings with great clarity and skill to an audience which accepts her without challenge to her womanhood as incongruent with her accomplishments.

In the first motif to be analysed, the girl or woman accomplishes a sexual transformation to confirm her demonstration of her advanced understanding of the Buddhist teachings and her status as an advanced *bodhisattva*. Stories of this genre occur in many Mahāyāna texts, indicating that the ideas behind it were widespread among Mahāyānists. In the story, the female uses both logic and magic to demonstrate her advanced understanding. It is important to see the place of each clearly; otherwise it would be easy to draw the conclusion that, in the long run, all highly competent and advanced beings must be or become males.

We may use the famous story of the Nāga Princess in the *Lotus Sūtra* as a good example of this genre. The eight-year-old Nāga Princess is praised by Mañjuśrī, the *bodhisattva* of wisdom, as 'superior in knowledge and understanding'. Another *bodhisattva* objects to his judgement, stating that because of the amount of time it takes to attain the *bodhisattva* way, such a young girl would not have been able to acquire so much wisdom. Suddenly the Nāga Princess appears and proclaims that she will teach the *Dharma* which liberates from suffering. Śāriputra, exemplar of older, more conservative forms of Buddhism, objects that she cannot accomplish that goal because a female cannot attain the 'five stations' (prominent positions in the cosmos, including that of being a *buddha or* a *māra* (evil tempter deity)). To demonstrate to him that she will attain buddhahood anyway, she gives a jewel to the Buddha, which he accepts. She asks Śāriputra to confirm that the Buddha accepted the jewel quickly, not slowly. Then she declares that she will attain 'the unexcelled perfect way and achieve supreme enlightenment even more quickly than that'. In that instant, her 'female organ disappeared and the male organ became visible'. She appeared instantly as a *bodhisattva* and then immediately thereafter as a *buddha* with the 32 marks of an enlightened being teaching the *Dharma* (Paul, 1979, pp. 187–90).

The point of her becoming male, by means of her magical powers, is not that males are more worthy, but that only such a demonstration would convince the thick-headed (and male chauvinist) Śāriputra.[3] The knowledge possessed by a *bodhisattva* or a *buddha* was hers already; they were not added on with the penis she grew when she changed her empty form from female to male. But her knowledge and logic had been overlooked by those who fixated on her empty female form as if it had intrinsic essential traits that defined her. She must demonstrate more concretely an important implication of the Mahāyāna teachings about emptiness – gender, like every other phenomenon, has no fixed essence and so does not limit those who bear its illusory outward signs.

Another famous Mahāyāna story again involves Śāriputra. In the

Vimalakīrti-nirdeśa Sūtra, he is discussing Buddhist philosophy with a mature female called simply 'the goddess', who has been meditating and studying for twelve years. He is extremely impressed with her understanding and asks her (apparently not remembering the act of the Nāga Princess) why she doesn't change her female sex. Her reply is classic: 'I have been here twelve years and have looked for the innate characteristics of the female sex and haven't been able to find them. How can I change them?' She compares her femaleness to the femaleness of a magically created illusion of a woman, which Śāriputra agrees could not be changed since it possesses no innate determinative characteristics of its own. Her femaleness, she says, no more has innate characteristics than does the femaleness of the illusion. Then she changes Śāriputra into a likeness of herself and herself into a likeness of Śāriputra and asks Śāriputra, who has been changed into a female form, 'Why don't you change your female sex?' Śāriputra is quite confused and the goddess lectures to him that if he could be changed into a female form, then all women could also change, which is why the Buddha said 'all are not really men or women'. After changing him back into his original male form, she asks him where the innate female traits were now. His reply demonstrates that he has acquired a much deeper understanding of emptiness. 'The female form and innate characteristics neither exist nor do not exist' (Paul, 1979, p. 230).

The final Mahāyāna text to be discussed presents an example of a great female Buddhist teacher who simply, and with great authority, teaches advanced Buddhist doctrine. She is the heroine of the *Śrīmālādevī Sūtra*, a laywoman and queen of her people. Her parents perceived her extraordinary abilities as a child and brought a teacher to her. She immediately received a prediction that she would attain buddhahood. But, unlike many other stories involving the prediction that a woman would eventually attain buddhahood, no sex change is predicted or hinted at in her story. She does not, for example, receive as part of her prediction a male name that she will bear when she becomes a *buddha*. After completing her studies, she preaches 'eloquently with the "lion's roar" of a Buddha' (Paul, 1979, pp. 292–301). No one challenges her in any way, nor is her female gender even discussed. At the end of the *sūtra*, everyone in her realm converts to Mahāyāna Buddhism, beginning with the women, who are followed by her husband, and then, finally, by the rest of the men.

In her study of this *sūtra*, Diana Paul has argued that implicitly

Queen Śrīmālā is a *buddha* in female form, since she receives a prediction that she will achieve full and complete buddhahood in the future, and in her present incarnation she preaches with the eloquence and effect of a *buddha*. That is the meaning of her epithet, 'one who has the lion's roar'. Thus her story takes us far beyond the most conservative Mahāyāna viewpoint in which the compassionate Amitābha creates a Pure Land where the misfortune of female rebirth will not be known.

Women in Vajrayāna Buddhism

The third major phase of Buddhist spiritual-intellectual development is called the Vajrayāna, or Tantric Buddhism. Building upon early Indian Buddhism and the Mahāyāna as essential foundations which must first be mastered, Vajrayāna Buddhism mainly involves elaborate and esoteric meditation practices that are believed to speed up enormously the progress of a *bodhisattva* towards complete perfect enlightenment. The emergence of this form of Buddhism is difficult to date with certainty, but by the sixth century CE it was well established in parts of India. Somewhat later, it was well known at the great monastic universities of late Indian Buddhism. Eventually this form of Buddhism was carried to Tibet, where it became the dominant form of Buddhism and has flourished until the present. Today, it is mainly represented in Tibetan refugee communities and by great Tibetan *lamas*, who are teaching around the world.

Though the situation of the majority of ordinary Buddhist women probably did not change significantly under Vajrayāna influence, theoretical concepts about femininity and women did change significantly. These changes correlated with changes in views about sexuality and the emotions. Rather than being dangerous territory that was best avoided, sexuality and the emotions are regarded as an extremely provocative working basis for enlightenment, *provided that they are experienced with mindfulness and detachment rather than with absent-minded lust.* Thus, a whole new symbolic, meditative and ritual universe was developed to train Buddhists in a mindful, detached and liberating approach to sexuality and the emotions, whether they were experienced in actual rituals or internally through visualizations.

Vajrayāna Buddhism is concerned with the vivid, but relative, phenomena that arise out of emptiness, with 'suchness' or 'thusness' (*tathatā*), as it is technically known in Buddhist thought. Relative phenomena, seen with clear or purified perceptions, are focuses for experiencing ultimate reality, which is to say that phenomena are symbols of ultimate reality. Among phenomenal symbols, none more clearly express the Vajrayāna view of reality than sexuality, than the dynamic and dyadic unity of a couple in sexual embrace. In the Vajrayāna view, unity and harmony are the underlying reality not always evident in ordinary experience. This unity, however, is not static or monolithic; it is colourful, playful and multiform. The varied elements in phenomenal reality retain their distinctiveness within their unity. No symbol better expresses this complex, subtle insight, which is almost inexpressible in words, than the symbol of a couple, multiple yet unified, consisting of distinctive elements, yet one entity. Therefore, this symbol became perhaps the central image in Vajrayāna Buddhism, painted, sculpted, visualized, sometimes physically acted out, not as an endorsement of lust but as a method of experiencing reality and enlightenment.

In this symbolism, masculine and feminine principles each clearly and consistently stand for basic elements in the dyadic unity. Most of the important aspects of the phenomenal and spiritual universes are seen as aspects of either masculine or feminine principles and are paired with each other. Thus, the feminine principle is seen in the openness of vowels, the vividness of red, the constancy and brilliance of the sun, the all-pervasive basicness of space or emptiness, the sharp clarity of wisdom, and the left side of the body, among others. The masculine principle, in unifying contrast, is seen as the specificity of consonants, the foundational quality of white, the reflective illuminating power of the moon, the definiteness and specificity of forms that arise in space, the accommodating, out-reaching quality of compassion, and the right side of the body. The two principles are also symbolized by the ritual implements that the meditator holds in the left and the right hands – the bell in the left, feminine, hand, and the *vajra*, or ritual weapon and sceptre, in the right, masculine hand. When the left and right hands, holding the bell and the *vajra*, are crossed in the ritual gesture (*mudrā*) of embracing, the feminine and masculine principles are united. When the hands form independent gestures, in correlation with each other, the masculine and feminine principles co-operate in constructing the world and seeking enlightenment.

These symbolic associations are also personified in the mythological universe of Vajrayāna Buddhism. A vast pantheon of *yi-dams*, perhaps best translated as 'non-theistic' deities, and understood as 'myth-mirrors' or as 'personifications of enlightenment', is known and available to the Vajrayāna meditator, who, when properly initiated, meditates on herself as one of the *yi-dams* or as the dyadic unity of a male with a female *yi-dam*. Because enlightenment is personified and because the initiated meditator can identify with these personifications, the body, whether female or male, is spiritually acknowledged and valorized. This valorization extends to specifically female or male biology, a phenomenon rare in the great world religions.

Among human beings, however, the enlightened meditator is not bound by or limited to the traits that correspond to his or her physiological sex. Women do not exemplify only the feminine principle, nor men the masculine. In so far as they might be so limited in earlier stages of spiritual development, this is seen as a problem rather than a requirement or an ideal. Therefore, male and female initiates are given identical meditational exercises, in which both identify themselves with both masculine and feminine principles in order to develop their inherent enlightenment.

This high evaluation of the feminine principle, combined with the practice of training women and men in the same spiritual disciplines, might lead one to expect the status of women to be high under Vajrayāna Buddhism. One might expect that options previously closed to women would be opened and that women would take a more equal role in the religious community. But the social situation for women under Vajrayāna Buddhism does not correspond completely to the symbolisms outlined above. In some ways, social norms did change to reflect the increased appreciation of women and femininity, but in other ways, long-standing patriarchal social realities were too deeply entrenched for such changes to occur.

The importance and high regard given to feminine symbolism does seem to have had a direct impact on certain standards and norms central to Vajrayāna Buddhism. In addition to the vows of refuge in the Three Jewels (Buddha, *Dharma* and *Saṅgha*), taken to affirm basic Buddhist affiliation, and vows of aspiration to be a *bodhisattva*, taken to affirm one's Mahāyāna affiliation, Tantric practitioners have additional obligations to uphold and downfalls to avoid. Among these obligations, which become downfalls if they are not fulfilled, is the fourteenth:

> If one disparages women, who are of the nature of wisdom, that is the fourteenth root downfall. That is to say, women are the symbol of wisdom and *śūnyatā*, showing both. It is therefore a root downfall to dispraise women in every possible way, saying that women are without spiritual merit and made of unclean things, not considering their good qualities. (Willis, 1973, p. 103)

This obligation, which is the normative social and religious view regarding women, nevertheless contrasts sharply with many popular attitudes. Widely held popular belief still regards female rebirth as 'low' and unfortunate, compared with male rebirth. This attitude is so pervasive that the Tibetan word for woman literally translates as 'born low', a connotation that is fully known to all users of the language (Aziz, 1989, p. 79). These attitudes result in a socially created sense of inferiority that begins with reactions to the birth of a girl and lasts throughout a woman's life. Even women who take up a lifestyle involving serious spiritual discipline often retain such attitudes about being female (Tsomo, 1989, p. 123).

Given these various attitudes towards women and femininity, it is not surprising that the institutions of Vajrayāna Buddhism do not either completely support or suppress women's spiritual inclinations. Women who wished to become nuns did not fare well under Vajrayāna Buddhism, despite the fact that their male counterparts were honoured, both in India and Tibet. By the time Vajrayāna Buddhism emerged in India, the nuns' order was already in serious decline. Apparently, full ordination for nuns was never transmitted to Tibet along with the rest of Vajrayāna Buddhism, though the novice ordination was. Throughout the history of Tibetan Vajrayāna Buddhism, many women have taken vows and lived all their lives as novice nuns. Though in some ways, such as dress and behaviour, they are very much like fully ordained nuns, they were never as well supported or educated as their male counterparts, nor did their renunciation bring them the prestige and value that it brought to the monks.

Vajrayāna Buddhism did, however, bring a new role to women. Many of the most famous and highly regarded practitioners of Vajrayāna Buddhism did not observe monastic vows, though they were completely dedicated to a life of spiritual discipline, but did not live as conventional householders either. Known either as *siddha*s (accomplished ones) or as *yogi*s and *yoginī*s, these seekers often lived highly unconventional lives on the fringes of society and achieved deep levels of realization. Frequently, part of their *sādhana*, or the spiritual exercises assigned to them by their religious teachers, included actions contrary to older Buddhist requirements for spiritual discipline. For many of them, spiritual discipline included living with a consort who was a partner on the path toward enlightenment.

Women did become *siddha*s. Because the literature focuses more on the male practitioners, we often read about the nameless consort of a male *siddha*. This lack could give us the impression that the consorts were mere enablers or ritual implements used by the male *siddha* in his spiritual practice. But that impression is probably incorrect, because the literature about the *siddha*s often includes the comment that both partners attained high states of realization. In a much smaller sample of the stories, the main character is a female *siddha*, and the focus is on her struggles and her accomplishments. Though such women are much rarer and even more unusual than their male counterparts, those who did manage to break away from conventional life and to achieve deep levels of spiritual insight, are valued equally with the male *siddha*s. Every *siddha* struggles greatly against conventional expectations, since they keep the norms of neither monastics nor householders, but the women seem to have faced even greater obstacles than did the men in being able to pursue their unusual spiritual vocation. Negotiating their way out of conventional marriage was much more difficult for them than it was for male *siddha*s, just as men could more easily abandon their wives to become monks during the period of early Indian Buddhism than women could abandon their husbands to become nuns. Once on the path of a *siddha*, however, the women experienced no greater difficulties than did the men, thus bearing out the conclusion, already reached by Mahāyāna Buddhists, that 'the *Dharma* is neither male nor female'.

The most famous of these female *siddha*s, perhaps the single most famous woman in Buddhist history, was Yeshe Tsogyel, an eighth-century Tibetan woman so important to the transmission of Buddhism to Tibet that she is still included by some schools of Tibetan Buddhism among the revered lineage holders of the *Dharma*, standing between the historical Buddha and the present lineage holders. Her story, part of the biographical literature that functions to inspire present-day meditators to great effort in their spiritual discipline, recounts how, despite many obstacles, she attained buddhahood in a single lifetime, thus refuting frequent claims in older Buddhist literature that such a feat was impossible for a woman. Though her story is filled with exemplary incidents, we can learn a lot about the situation of women overall in Buddhism by quoting in full her own assessment of how women are treated and her teacher's assessment of their potential – two passages found almost back to back in her biography. She describes what happens to her:

> I am a woman – I have little power to resist danger.
> Because of my inferior birth, everyone attacks me.
> If I go as a beggar, dogs attack me.
> If I have wealth and food, bandits attack me.
> If I do a great deal, the locals attack me.
> If I do nothing, the gossips attack me.
> If anything goes wrong, they all attack me.
> Whatever I do, I have no chance for happiness.
> Because I am a woman, it is hard to follow the *Dharma*.
> It is hard even to stay alive. (Tarthang Tulku, p. 105)

From her own perspective, she sees all the additional obstacles put upon her by a culture hostile to accomplished women. But her teacher, who as a male is less aware of how debilitating such obstacles can be, focuses on her outstanding qualities, which he claims as the potential of all women:

> Wonderful *yoginī*, practitioner of the secret teachings!
> The basis for realizing great enlightenment is a human body.
> Male or female – there is no great difference.
> But if she develops the mind bent on enlightenment,
> The woman's body is better. (Tarthang Tulku, p. 102)

A summary of traditional Buddhist attitudes towards women

Vajrayāna Buddhism represents the last major new intellectual development in Indian Buddhism. As Buddhism spread beyond India into the rest of Asia, new developments occurred, but none of them constitutes a whole new phase of Buddhist thought, as does the passage from early Indian Buddhism to Mahāyāna Buddhism and then to Vajrayāna Buddhism. Furthermore, no great elaborations or additions to the attitudes towards women or institutional innovations regarding their participation in Buddhism occurred in these non-Indian movements. Therefore, before surveying what happened to Buddhism outside India and what is happening currently regarding women's issues in Buddhism, it is useful to summarize briefly the history surveyed above.

Three generalizations, also important to understanding the role of women in Buddhism altogether, provide such an overview. First, in every period of Buddhist history, there are at least two views about women, neither of which ever fully wins out. Some texts record fairly negative views of women, even some outright misogyny, though it is important to remember that misogyny is different from patriarchy or male dominance. The negative views of women often see them as more materialistic, emotional and sexual than men, less able to renounce desire, and generally less capable of making significant progress on the Buddhist path. Not uncommonly, their best hope was thought to be rebirth as a male, whether offered out of pity and compassion, given the difficulties of women's lives, or recommended out of scorn for women's limited abilities. But, in every period, others stated and argued that women were not inherently deficient or inferior to men in their ability to achieve the calm and insight required to attain Buddhism's highest goals. This opinion is attributed even to the historical Buddha, despite his apparent reluctance to found the nuns' order, and some rather nasty comments about women also attributed to him.

The second major generalization is that in the broad sweep of Buddhist history, from early Indian Buddhism to Mahāyāna to Vajrayāna, the bias against women becomes less acceptable. The more important texts, stories and teachers argue that 'the *Dharma* is neither male nor female', and that to denigrate women 'who are the symbol of wisdom and Śūnyatā, showing both' is a serious root downfall.

Thirdly, on the whole, Buddhist attitudes towards women throughout history are not overwhelmingly misogynistic, if misogyny is narrowly defined, and not confused with male dominance. This judgement is especially clear when Buddhism is compared with other major world religions. However, androcentrism and male dominance are almost unrelieved throughout Buddhist history (Sponberg, 1992). Most of the inadequacies regarding Buddhist treatment of women that would be pointed out by many contemporary Buddhists sympathetic to feminism stem from Buddhism's traditional androcentrism and male dominance.

Women in Buddhism outside India

Buddhism is among the minority of major religions that have spread successfully beyond their homeland into cultures very different from the one that gave them birth. Such religions always focus on a message that is relatively culture-free and universal in its implications; furthermore, they do not emphasize a detailed, and therefore culture-bound, code for daily living. Thus the same factors that make Buddhism relatively gender-free, at least in its abstract teachings, also worked in favour of Buddhism's success as a portable religion. However, the cultures into which Buddhism spread were just as male-dominated as the Indian culture from which Buddhism came. Therefore, its institutionalized practices favouring monks and men in general were not challenged or modified during its wanderings throughout Asia. However, as Buddhism, in fulfilling ancient but enigmatic prophecies it has retained for centuries, comes to the West, it is encountering, for the first time, the challenge to mesh its gender-free vision with more egalitarian-feminist praxis.

In India, Buddhism was always largely carried and maintained by its monastic core, and the monastic lifestyle was usually regarded as the ideal method for practising Buddhism, even among Mahāyānists. This monastic core, usually consisting of monks rather than nuns, was also critical in the spread of Buddhism to other Asian countries. For the most part, Buddhism did not spread primarily in conjunction with colonialism or military conquest. Instead, wandering monks, often travelling with trading caravans, spread the religion, which was adopted slowly by an élite and then from the top down in the receiving society. In addition, once Buddhism became established to any degree in a society, inhabitants of that country frequently went on arduous pilgrimages to the lands from which Buddhism had come, in an attempt to gain deeper understanding of their newly adopted religion. Monks were also well suited to these reverse missions. All these factors together meant that monasticism also dominated Buddhism in its non-Indian developments. In fact, monasticism was so highly valued that some would claim that Buddhism is not genuinely established in a country until it can boast a flourishing monastic community. Because of the continued emphasis on monasticism, a survey of women's involvement in Buddhism outside India yields little information on Buddhist laywomen throughout the centuries in the Asian Buddhist countries.

Unfortunately, even more than had been the case in India, the monastic community, with a few notable and important exceptions, favoured monks over nuns. For a variety of reasons, many Asian Buddhist countries do not have a nuns' order. To be fully ordained, according to the ancient and nearly universal Buddhist regulations for monastics, a nun must be ordained by a group of five monks and five nuns (ten of each within the original Buddhist heartland in India; cf. pp. 161–2). Without the initial group of five nuns, a broken lineage could never be restored nor proper ordination procedures begun. Because of the greater difficulties and diminished support often experienced by the nuns, that initial group of nuns required to begin an ordination lineage was often difficult to assemble. Sometimes, not enough nuns could travel to a newly established outpost of Buddhism. Sometimes, after the lineage was destroyed, its re-establishment was opposed. Under such circumstances, women who wish to live as renunciants must resort to makeshift approximations of ordination, often without much support from their culture. They may live and dress as nuns, but they are regarded as novices or laywomen by the Buddhist establishment. As such, they do not receive the economic support, education or respect that would be due to them as nuns. Nevertheless, in all Buddhist countries where monks are found, some form of nuns' community is also found, with the exception of Mongolia (Tsomo, 1988, p. 103).[4] Under such conditions, it is noteworthy that some version of nunship does exist in most Asian Buddhist countries.

Theravādin Buddhism, directly descended from the ancient Indian Buddhism characteristic of the first period of Buddhist intellectual and spiritual development, has become the dominant form of Buddhism in Sri Lanka and Southeast Asia. Most of the values of ancient Indian Buddhism, including its very strong emphasis on monastics as the ideal Buddhist practitioners, and its views about women, have been faithfully transmitted to these areas. Though the nuns' ordination lineage was transferred to some Theravādin Buddhist countries, it has since been lost in all of them. Under current conditions, it would be relatively easy to re-introduce the ordination lineage from China, but many Theravādin authorities – though not all – are quite unsympathetic to this development.

Sri Lanka was the first country outside the borders of modern India to become Buddhist. Usually the initial conversion is credited to the son and the daughter of the Indian emperor Asoka, who founded, respectively, the Sri Lankan monks' and the nuns' orders in the third century BCE. The nuns' order existed until the tenth century CE and is usually credited as the source of the ordination lineages still preserved by Chinese nuns. In the eleventh century, the monastic institutions were severely damaged, if not destroyed, by South Indian invaders. When efforts were made, successfully, to re-introduce monks' ordination lineages from other Theravādin Buddhist countries, there were, apparently, no attempts to re-introduce the nuns' ordination lineages as well. Until the twentieth century, it does not seem that Sri Lankan women had any formally organized and recognized renunciant community. During this century, women have begun to take up the nuns' lifestyle but, without the formality of full ordination, they lack prestige and support from their Sri Lankan compatriots – though moves towards full ordination are being explored.

The current situation of nuns in Myanmar (Burma) and Thailand, the other major Theravādin countries, is similar (Harvey, 2000, pp. 395–8). Women live the nuns' lifestyle and dress distinctively, but they do not receive formal vows and are not legally or religiously treated as nuns by either their governments or the religious establishments in their countries. Often, though their discipline is strict, they are poorly supported and poorly educated. A woman who takes up the life of such a nun does not receive the praise and respect that her male counterpart would receive. There is evidence that the nuns existed in Myanmar as late as the eleventh to the thirteenth centuries CE, but most commentators conclude that the nuns' ordination never reached Thailand (Tsomo, 1988, p. 105).

In Mahāyāna Buddhist countries, the situation varies considerably (Harvey, 2000, pp. 393–5, 399–400). The East Asian culture area received Buddhism through China and all the East Asian forms of Buddhism retain some Chinese imprint. The nuns' order has been rather strong in China for many centuries and ordination lineages have been preserved there, which has affected other East Asian forms of Buddhism to some extent. Between 429 and 433 CE, when Buddhism was becoming a dominant influence in China, nuns from Sri Lanka travelled to China to provide the quorum of five nuns required for ordination as a full-fledged nun (Tsomo, 1988, p. 106; Conze *et al.*, 1954, pp. 291–5). Since then, these lineages have been preserved in China, Taiwan and in many overseas Chinese communities, as well as in Korea and Vietnam. Today, in many non-mainland Chinese Buddhist communities and in some Korean communities, nuns outnumber monks, are almost completely independent to run their own affairs, and include many young, well-educated women, a situation not found elsewhere in the Buddhist world.

Historically, there are also a number of strong and noteworthy figures. A Chinese text, the *Pi-ch'iu-ni-chuan* (Tsai, 1994), contains biographies of 65 Chinese nuns who lived between 317 and 516 CE. They were a 'highly literate, active, influential group of women' (Schuster, 1985, p. 98). At least one Chinese Ch'an (Zen) Buddhist nun is recorded in Ch'an records as an important teacher and a highly realized being (Levering, 1982). Buddhist laywomen of the imperial court also gained considerable power at some points in Chinese history. Probably the most successful and important was Empress Wu (625–705 CE), who, though maligned by later Chinese historians, ruled China successfully and well, using Buddhist ideas to justify her rule and her policies (Paul, 1989).

In Japan, the prestige of the monastic community has broken down more than anywhere else in the Buddhist world, so that today, though Buddhism is thoroughly intertwined into Japanese culture, celibate monks or nuns ordained according to ancient Indian norms used elsewhere in the Buddhist world are almost non-existent. At one time, monks were ordained according to the Indian texts and rules, but the full quorum of five nuns required to confer the nuns' ordination was never successfully assembled in Japan. However, early in the ninth century, under the influence of one of Japan's greatest Buddhist teachers, the idea that receiving the *bodhisattva* precepts was equivalent to receiving the monastic precepts was introduced. Over the centuries, particularly as Japan began to allow and affirm a married Buddhist priesthood, this form of ordination took precedence over the form of monastic ordination used elsewhere in the Buddhist world. All nuns are ordained in this 'non-monastic' fashion, though they live a lifestyle much closer to the ancient Indian norms for monks and nuns than do their male counterparts. Unlike most male 'monks', they do not marry or drink alcohol. Sometimes they serve as temple priests, though, unlike their male counterparts, they would not marry if they are to be considered nuns. Currently, there is also a growing number of married female priests or priests' wives who have taken on many of the duties and privileges of priesthood. However, becoming a nun is not currently a popular option in Japan.

Vajrayāna Buddhism came to Tibet directly from India, beginning in the seventh century. By the mid-eighth century, monastic ordination had begun, but again, the quorum of five nuns required to initiate the nuns' ordination lineage was never assembled in Tibet. From the beginning, however, many Tibetan women have taken novice ordination, worn monastic robes, and lived a monastic lifestyle. Though they are not as well supported economically, and generally not as well educated as their male counterparts, and do not have the same level of prestige as do monks, they are regarded as monastics, not laywomen, by their culture. Some of them come to be very highly regarded for their discipline and spiritual attainments. Because Vajrayāna Buddhism is the major form of Buddhism in Tibet, the *siddha* or *yoginī* ideal prevails alongside the monastic ideal. Throughout the centuries, many dedicated and determined Tibetan women have not taken vows as novice nuns, but have lived as wandering *yoginī*s or as strict retreatants instead. If anything, the women who have chosen this path are even more respected and renowned than are the nuns. The most famous and important of them are Yeshe Tsogyel (Gross, 1989) (see pp. 220–1) and Machig Labdron, but many others are known (Allione, 1984). Today, Tibetan Buddhism survives most strongly in exile communities in India and among a rapidly growing number of Western converts. The exile communities are often poor; even when they are not, support for women religious seekers is not high on the list of favoured projects, despite the honour accorded theoretically to women and to the feminine principle.

The latest development in the long history of Buddhism is its transmission to the West, begun early in this century but growing exponentially during and after the 1960s. At present, all major forms of Buddhism are represented in Western countries, especially in North America and Europe. Buddhism is coming to the West, not only with Asian immigrants who maintain Buddhism as part of their ethnic tradition, but also as the religion of choice of an articulate, dedicated and idealistic minority of Europeans and Americans of European descent. These European Buddhists are well educated, both in Western and in Buddhist learning, and often are extremely dedicated to their new religion. Some of them become monks and nuns, but, thus far, the majority of them remain lay-people. Because of their dedication to Buddhist learning and meditation practice, they may well be in the forefront of a new style of Buddhism, which would not be so characterized by the dichotomy between monks and laypeople.

Of utmost importance for the future of Buddhism is the fact that many of the most dedicated and able European Buddhists are women who are not content with the role traditionally allotted to women in Asian male-dominated forms of Buddhism. They study Buddhist doctrine and practise Buddhist meditation equally with their male counterparts and expect to take leadership roles in emerging Western Buddhism. In the endless debates and comments about similarities and differences between Asian and Western forms of Buddhism, it has been noted, cogently, that the single biggest difference is the presence of numerous women in meditation halls and classrooms, studying and practising with men. As these women gain greater understanding of Buddhism and greater self-confidence, major new developments in Buddhism are likely, as Sandy Boucher has indicated by the title of her book *Turning the Wheel: American Women Creating the New Buddhism* (Boucher, 1993).

Current issues involving women and Buddhism

The major contemporary issues concerning women and Buddhism are also important issues for the future of Buddhism as a whole. They turn on the age-old problem in Buddhism of the relationship between the monastic and the lay communities, and on the need for both of them to be renewed and modernized.

The issues and the needs regarding women and the monastic community are relatively simple and straightforward, which does not mean that they will be easily resolved within the Buddhist world. Many voices call for the re-introduction of the nuns' ordination into those forms of Buddhism in which it has been lost. Given modern means of transport and the existence of fully ordained nuns in some parts of the Buddhist world, the solution would seem to be straightforward. A quorum of five nuns could ordain a group of women (at least five, preferably more) who meet the criteria for ordination and wish to be ordained, but cannot in their own form of Buddhism because the lineage has died out there. Once a quorum of nuns exists in Theravādin or Tibetan communities, it could again become self-maintaining. Unfortunately, some powerful Buddhist monks are quite opposed to this possibility, especially in Theravādin countries. They claim that ordination of Theravādin Buddhists by representatives from lineages currently existing only in Mahāyāna Buddhism would be unacceptable from a Theravādin point of view. It can easily be countered that the differences between Theravādin and Mahāyāna Buddhism are doctrinal, not behavioural, and that, in fact, there are no significant differences between Theravādins and Mahāyānists regarding monastic discipline. Others worry that perhaps, at some point in history, the Chinese nuns' ordination lineages were improperly maintained, which would invalidate the ordinations they confer. However, similar fears about the validity of male ordination lineages are seldom, if ever, voiced. In the Tibetan monastic community, there are some fears and hesitations regarding these Chinese ordination lineages, but important authorities, such as the Dalai Lama, have voiced their general support of the movement to institute full ordination for nuns in Tibetan Buddhism (Tsomo, 1988, pp. 268–9).

Deeper problems concerning attitudes towards women would still remain, however. Throughout Buddhist history, and in most parts of the contemporary Buddhist world, nuns simply are not as well supported or as well respected as are monks. As a result, they are often poor, which inhibits their efforts to develop themselves through study and practice. They often have only minimal opportunities for Buddhist education and often experience great difficulty in taking on the more advanced meditations that are so important in many schools of Buddhism. Because their attainments are low, a downward spiral is maintained. They are less attractive recipients of support than their more accomplished male counterparts, and so the cycle continues, as it seems to have spun itself out time after time in Buddhist history.

Receiving full nuns' ordination would probably alleviate some of these problems, since Chinese and Korean nuns do seem to be better educated and better supported than Tibetan or Theravādin women who practise either as novices or as 'lay nuns' (Tsomo, 1988, pp. 103–6). However, even fully ordained nuns must deal with certain liabilities *vis-à-vis* the monks, especially their inability to develop fully as teachers, given the confines of the eight special rules. The eight special rules are themselves rooted in and reflective of the androcentric consciousness and male-dominant world-view that were characteristic of ancient India. Really solving, in any definitive way, the problems facing Buddhist women is unlikely so long as Buddhism remains androcentric in its outlook and male-dominant in its praxis.

To reform the androcentrism and male dominance of classical

Buddhism is an immense task. If it can be accomplished at all, many of the reforms are likely to come from lay Buddhists, and from Western Buddhists, especially from the women who simply would not adopt Buddhism if they were required to conform to conventional male-dominant Buddhist practices in order to be Buddhists.

A potentially extremely significant development in Buddhism is the emergence of groups of Buddhist lay-people who, nevertheless, define themselves as serious Buddhist practitioners striving for the same goals that are often thought of as goals attainable only by monastics – some deep level of personal transformation through the realization of insight and tranquillity. The means pursued to attain these goals are also the classic monastic methods – study of Buddhist teachings and the practice of meditation. In their lifestyle, these lay meditators usually combine elements of the householder lifestyle with elements of the monastic lifestyle. Meditation centres, for the first time in Buddhist history, can include childcare facilities. People with families periodically withdraw from economic and domestic responsibilities for intensive study and practice. When they return to their economic and domestic responsibilities, they seek to infuse their ordinary activities with meditative awareness cultivated during their retreats. In short, the dichotomy between serious, detached monastic Buddhists and hopelessly attached, desire-driven Buddhist householders is being broken down. This development is even more significant for women than it is for men, because precisely those 'lay' activities that traditionally are women's sphere – sexuality, family and reproduction – are the most destructive aspects of worldly life, according to traditional Buddhism.

Lay Buddhism is significant for women also because it is much easier and more attractive for most women to become involved in serious lay Buddhism than in monastic Buddhism. And many, many women are becoming so involved in all forms of Buddhism, especially among Westerners. Most of them are still undergoing traditional Buddhist training, but eventually, whether authorized by their communities or by their own inner transformation, they will begin, indeed already have begun, to lead their communities and to teach. The emergence of a large and strong core of women teachers who are well educated, well practised, articulate and not male-identified, will be one of the most significant events ever in the intellectual and spiritual development of Buddhism. Because of androcentrism, male dominance, and the eight special rules, it has never before happened.

Previously, those women who did excel at Buddhist practice and understanding rarely taught; those few who did teach did not seek to overcome the traditional androcentrism and male dominance of Buddhism, probably because the historical causes and conditions favouring such a transformation were not yet in place.

It is possible to envision Buddhism after patriarchy (Gross, 1991b; 1994), a Buddhism no longer driven by subtle or obvious preference for men and their interests. As is the case with most major world religions, post-patriarchal transformation in Buddhism is likely to include two basic developments. In the first development, the resources of Buddhism will be utilized to call for a prophetic reform of Buddhist institutions that brings Buddhist praxis in line with Buddhist vision. It can easily be argued (Gross, 1991a) that the normative teachings of Buddhism are remarkably free of gender bias favouring either women or men, that the fundamental teachings of Buddhism apply, without exception, to all human beings, without reference to gender, race or class. It can be shown with equal ease that Buddhism, in its institutional forms, both monastic and lay, has never lived up to its own vision, or even come close to living up to its own vision. But, it would be argued, given the intolerable contradiction between view and practice, the practice of male dominance, rather than the view of gender neutrality, should be given up. To begin that task, Buddhists would need to introduce nuns' ordination everywhere in the Buddhist world, upgrade the status and well-being of nuns, and take laywomen seriously as Buddhist practitioners. These steps are already occurring, at least to some extent, and are being discussed by all Buddhists.

Post-patriarchal Buddhism, however, also involves a deeper question, the same question brought up in most major religions by the post-patriarchal revolution. Once the male-dominant institutions are reformed, will everything else stay as it has always been? Or will some of the rules of the game change with the input of women's culture? Women's spirituality and feminist psychology are now well-developed resources that can hardly be ignored by anyone seeking to understand and experience personal and social transformation. Those resources suggest that post-patriarchal Buddhism will need to emphasize connection, community and communication in ways that will go beyond what has previously been the norm for Buddhism, though they will not contradict those norms. In this subtle but profound revalorization of Buddhism, alienation between people and between humans and our environment may well come to be viewed as problematic for spiritual well-being, in the same way that attachment has always been viewed as a major obstacle for spiritual well-being by Buddhists. Balancing out the fear of attachment with an equal fear of alienation may well bring Buddhists to a deeper understanding of a Middle Way that is equally relevant to women and men.

Notes

1 The historicity of the eight rules being given at the very start of the nuns' order is challenged by Ute Hüsken (2000) 'The legend of the establishment of the Buddhist order of nuns in the Theravāda Vinaya-Piṭaka', *Journal of the Pali Text Society*, XXVI, pp. 43–70.

2 This, in fact, allows us to read the Buddha's initial refusal to ordain women not as a 'reluctance' but as a 'hesitation': that he was happy for it to occur but wanted to ensure that it was done in a way which did not jar too much with existing social attitudes, so as to undermine support of the *saṅgha* as a whole. In the early texts, in fact, it is held that the Buddha was destined to have nun disciples (Walshe, 1987, p. 454), knew soon after his enlightenment that he would ordain nuns (Walshe, 1987, pp. 250–1), and the holy life instituted by him would have been incomplete if he had not instituted an order of nuns (Horner, 1957, pp. 169–71). The *Buddha-vaṃsa*, a relatively late text of the Pāli Canon, also gives the names of the two chief nun disciples of 24 past *buddha*s (e.g. ch. 24, verse 214), reflecting the view that *buddha*s always institute an order of nuns. (Ed.)

3 While represented in this way in some Mahāyāna texts, in the Pāli *sutta*s Sāriputta (Pāli form of Sanskrit Śāriputra) is one of the Buddha's two chief disciples, famed for his wisdom. (Ed.)

4 Fully ordained nuns (Sanskrit *bhikṣuṇī*s, Pāli *bhikkhunī*s) still exist in China, Taiwan, Korea, Vietnam and amongst Chinese communities elsewhere in Asia. In Tibet, nuns follow the ten precepts of female novices. In Theravāda lands, some of which once had full *bhikkhunī*s, lay 'nuns' follow eight or ten precepts, but are not counted as novices. In Japan nuns likewise do not follow the rules of full nuns, though neither do their male counterparts now follow the Indian monastic code for monks. (Ed.)

Further reading

Allione, T. (1984) *Women of Wisdom*. London: Routledge and Kegan Paul.

Aziz, B. (1989) 'Moving toward a sociology of Tibet' in Willis (1989), pp. 76–95.

Bartholomeusz, T. (1994) *Women Under the Bo Tree: Buddhist Nuns in Sri Lanka*. Cambridge: Cambridge University Press.

Blackstone, K. R. (1998) *Women in the Footsteps of the Buddha: Struggle for Liberation in the Therīgāthā*. London: Curzon Press.

Boucher, S. (1993) *Turning the Wheel: American Women Creating the New Buddhism* (updated and expanded edition of original 1988 edn). Boston: Beacon Press.

Cabezón, J. I. (ed.) (1992) *Buddhism, Sexuality and Gender*. Albany: State University of New York Press.

Conze, E., Horner, I. B., Snellgrove, D. and Waley, A. (1954) *Buddhist Texts Through the Ages*. New York: Harper and Row, pp. 291–5.

Dewaraja, L. S. (1981) *The Position of Women in Buddhism*, Wheel pamphlet no. 280. Kandy, Sri Lanka: Buddhist Publication Society.

Falk, N. (1989) 'The case of the vanishing nuns: the fruits of ambivalence in ancient Indian Buddhism' in N. Falk and R. Gross (eds) *Unspoken Worlds: Women's Religious Lives*. Belmont, CA: Wadsworth, pp. 207–24.

Gross, R. (1989) 'Yeshe Tsogyel: enlightened consort, great teacher, female role model' in Willis (1989), pp. 11–32.

Gross, R. (1991a) 'The Dharma is neither male nor female: Buddhism on gender and liberation' in H. Grob, H. Gordon and R. Hassan (eds) *Women's and Men's Liberation: Testimonies of Spirit*. New York: Greenwood Press, pp. 105–27.

Gross, R. (1991b) 'Buddhism after patriarchy' in P. Cooey, W. Eakin and J. McDaniel (eds) *After Patriarchy: Feminist Reconstructions of the World's Religions*. Maryknoll, NY: Orbis, pp. 65–86.

Gross, R. M. (1994) *Buddhism After Patriarchy: A Feminist History, Analysis, and Reconstruction of Buddhism*. Albany: State University of New York Press.

Harvey, P. (2000) *An Introduction to Buddhist Ethics: Foundations, Values and Issues*. Cambridge: Cambridge University Press.

Havnevik, H. (1991) *Tibetan Nuns Now: History, Cultural Norms and Social Reality*. Oslo: Norwegian University Press.

Horner, I. B. (1930) *Women Under Primitive Buddhism: Laywomen and Almswomen*. New York: E. P. Dutton.

Horner, I. B. (1957) *Middle Length Sayings (Majjhima Nikāya)*, vol. 2. London: Pali Text Society.

Kabilsingh, C. (1991) *Thai Women in Buddhism*. Berkeley, CA: Parallax Press.

Kawanami, H. (1990) 'The religious standing of Burmese nuns (*Thelá-shin*): ten precepts and religious honorifics', *Journal of the International Association of Buddhist Studies*, 13(1), pp. 17–39.

Levering, M. (1982) 'The Dragon Girl and the Abbess of Mo-Shan: gender and status in Ch'an Buddhist tradition', *Journal of the International Association of Buddhist Studies*, 5(1), pp. 19–35.

Levering, M. L. (1992) 'Lin-chi Rinzai Ch'an and gender: the rhetoric of equality and the rhetoric of heroism' in Cabezón, pp. 137–56.

Murcott, S. (1991) *The First Buddhist Women: Translations and Commentary on the Therigatha*. Berkeley, CA: Parallax Press.

Paul, D. (1979) *Women in Buddhism: Images of the Feminine in Mahayana Tradition*. Berkeley, CA: Asian Humanities Press, pp. 191–206.

Paul, D. (1989) 'Empress Wu and the historians: a tyrant and saint of classical China' in N. Falk and R. Gross (eds) *Unspoken Worlds: Women's Religious Lives*. Belmont, CA: Wadsworth.

Rhys Davids, C. A. F. and Norman, K. R. (1989) *Poems of Early Buddhist Nuns*. Oxford: Pali Text Society.

Schuster, N. (1985) 'Striking a balance: women and images of women in early Chinese Buddhism' in Y. Haddad and E. Findly (eds) *Women, Religion and Social Change*. Albany: State University of New York Press, pp. 87–111.

Schuster, N. (1987) 'Buddhism' in A. Sharma (ed.) *Women in World Religions*. Albany: State University of New York Press, pp. 105–34.

Sponberg, A. (1992) 'Attitudes towards women and the feminine in Early Buddhism' in Cabezón, pp. 3–36.

Tarthang Tulku (trans.) (1983) *Mother of Knowledge: The Enlightenment of Yeshe Tsogyel*. Berkeley, CA: Dharma Publishing Co.

Tsai, K. A. (trans.) (1994) *Lives of the Nuns: Biographies of Chinese Buddhist Nuns from the Fourth to Sixth Centuries*. Honolulu: University of Hawaii Press (translation of *Pi-ch'iu-ni-chuan*).

Tsomo, K. L. (1988) *Sakyadhita: Daughters of the Buddha*. Ithaca, NY: Snow Lion.

Tsomo, K. L. (1989) 'Tibetan nuns and nunneries' in Willis (1989), pp. 118–34.

Tsomo, K. L. (1995) *Buddhism Through American Women's Eyes*. New York: Snow Lion.

Walshe, M. (1987) *Thus Have I Heard: The Long Discourses of the Buddha*. London: Wisdom Publications.

Willis, J. (1973) *The Diamond Light: An Introduction to Tibetan Buddhist Meditations*. New York: Simon & Schuster.

Willis, J. (ed.) (1989) *Feminine Ground: Essays on Women and Tibet*. Ithaca, NY: Snow Lion.

8. Attitudes to nature

Ian Harris

Ecological thinking came to the fore in the late twentieth century. If this view is accepted, then one will be hard pressed to discover more than the odd resonance of environmentalism in the literature of the ancient world.[1] This fact is recognized by many influential representatives of the ecological movement today. Thus, Eugene C. Hargrove (1989), in his examination of the thought of ancient Greece, concludes that it was impossible for Greek philosophy to think ecologically. The metaphysical assumptions underpinning much of the thought current at that time were clearly at variance with those operating today; therefore a concern for the natural world is highly problematic in the Greek context.

It may seem rather strange to begin a discussion on the attitude of Buddhism to the environment by reference to Greek thought, but there is method in my madness. In an influential and, in terms of recent interest in environmental ethics, early piece of work, John Passmore (1980) concludes that Western philosophy is incompatible with a concern for nature. Passmore is particularly scornful of the negative role played by Christianity. For him the doctrine of human dominion over nature, found in the writings of Augustine, Aquinas, Calvin, etc., has done much to alienate the modern industrialized world from its natural environment. More recent commentators on the impact of Christianity on environmental ethics have shown that Passmore tends to overstate his case. Robin Attfield (1983) is a good case in point. While it is true that some remarkably negative statements on our relations with nature are to be found in the writings of major theologians, another more positive tradition of stewardship and care for the environment runs side by side with the negative throughout most of the history of Christianity. This attitude is exemplified in the traditions of Francis of Assisi, and in the works of some Orthodox theologians. Christianity, then, appears to contain an essentially negative official attitude to the environment, underpinned by an influential but minority position far more favourable to an environmentalist ethic. Some writers, most notably Lynn White Jnr (1967), have claimed that Eastern religions, and Buddhism in particular, are more explicitly positive in their concern for the natural world. I find this attitude difficult to square with any actually occurring Buddhist tradition and shall argue that the Christian situation is more or less precisely mirrored in Buddhism.

Buddhism and the natural world

In its earliest phases Buddhism was essentially a world-denying religion. Existence was conceived of as having the characteristics of suffering (*dukkha*), impermanence (*anicca*) and insubstantiality (*anattā*) (see pp. 78–80) and thus the goal of the monk (i.e. *nirvāṇa*) was thought of as outside this world, though attained by understanding its nature. In other words, the best thing that one could do was to let go of the world – and hence escape from it. The essence of this way of thinking is contained in the Buddha's celebrated first sermon in which he outlines the Four Noble Truths. In this sermon we hear of the inherent unsatisfactoriness of conditioned things (i.e., the idea that all causally produced entities are impermanent and, as such, fail to confer happiness), and of the path which leads away from the suffering associated with the world. It is not surprising, given this rather sombre vision, that the early Buddhist texts fail, in any systematic way, to develop a coherent world picture. Beyond the occasional snippet of information, the Pāli Canon of Theravāda Buddhism, the earliest collection of Buddhist scriptures available, is notable in its relative lack of cosmological lore. It shows only very occasional interest in cosmic and relative human origins (cf. Walshe, 1987, pp. 409–14). This is probably connected to the character of early Buddhism, which denies the existence of a divine creator, though Buddhists have always accepted the existence of a plurality of gods who have the capacity to bring about real effects in the human realm. The recognition and appeasement of these divine beings is enormously important in the lives of rural lay Buddhists today, but, having said this, it is clear that Buddhism is unique in the religions of the world for its disinclination to offer a prominent theory of creation. It is difficult to know precisely why, but this situation was not allowed to continue in the Buddhist tradition down to the present day.

Approximately 1,000 years after the death of the Buddha a number of prominent Buddhist commentators appeared on the scene, and they seemed to recognize the need for a more fully worked-out cosmology than that present in the canon itself. Perhaps this shift in position was felt to be necessary in order to get into effective dialogue with, and demonstrate superiority over, members of other religious traditions, most notably the Hindus. Certainly at this stage in their history the Hindus had a fairly complex and elegant world picture, which possessed the advantage that it could be used to predict certain simple natural phenomena, such as the distinction between night and day. One assumes that their Buddhist opponents may have felt at a bit of a disadvantage. In time, then, the Hindu world picture was adopted by the rival religious tradition and revised to bring it into line with fundamental Buddhist axioms. The two most prominent Buddhists in this connection are Vasubandhu, a fourth-century writer from northern India, and Buddhaghosa, a very exceptional commentator on the Pāli Canon, who lived approximately a century after Vasubandhu. This being the case, the relatively late *Abhidharma-kośa* of Vasubandhu, and the *Visuddhimagga* of Buddhaghosa, provide us with the most comprehensive descriptions of the world as seen from a Buddhist point of view. They are remarkably consistent with each other and I shall draw on both for the following description.

TIME AND MEANING

In line with Hindu thought as well as various scattered references in the early Buddhist texts, Buddhists hold that the world is periodically brought into being and, at a later stage, many millions of years in the future, it is destroyed. This process has no beginning and no end. In this sense, the Indian religions differ from Judaism, Christianity and Islam. Unlike the latter traditions, which hold an essentially linear idea of history based on a definite starting point and an equally definite conclusion to the world process, Indian thought prefers to deal in enormously long cycles of history, one following the other for all eternity. In other words, the physical world persists for a lengthy period, is dissolved, and at some stage in the future is again brought forth out of a more subtle realm until it meets the same fate, and so on, and on. Now this fact alone provides us with a useful means by which we may contrast the Buddhist understanding of existence with that more familiar to us from the Christian tradition, in which creation is brought into being by a benign and purposeful creator.

The purpose or meaning of the Buddhist world order is more difficult to establish. For one thing it does not come into being as the result of the activities of a Supreme Being. In the second place, there is no indication that it is moving towards any condition of fulfilment. It simply runs on, from one cycle to another, *ad infinitum*. Rather than being a purposeful process leading inevitably to an unknown but meaningful conclusion, the Buddhist vision of the world is more pessimistic. The world is endless, meaningless and purposeless.[2] This does not mean that the Buddhist must be seized by despair, for after all the Buddha has taught the means to escape from conditioned existence. As such, the Buddha's teaching (*Dhamma*) is regarded as a very remarkable thing, the greatest of all gifts. Nevertheless, the world is viewed, particularly in the earliest phase of Buddhism, as a vicious circle (*saṃsāra*). Knowledge that this is so leads to the inevitable desire to find the means of escape from such an unsatisfactory state. Since desires for worldly things are considered to bind us even more strongly to existence and increase our suffering, Buddhism extols the virtues of the world-renouncer. For Buddhism, the renouncer *par excellence* is the monk (*bhikkhu*). Membership of the monastic community (*saṅgha*) is considered to be the most effective means of hastening one's spiritual liberation.

The traditions preserved in the Pāli Canon give the strong impression that during the Buddha's lifetime a considerable number of persons experienced liberation. On the attainment of enlightenment (*nirvāṇa*), a person is referred to as an *arahat*. Study of the relevant early texts seems to suggest that arahatship could be brought about in two basic ways. For some individuals, presumably already far advanced on the path as a result of their own efforts, merely hearing the word of the Buddha was sufficient. However, the majority of *arahat*s were required to put the teachings they received from the Buddha into practice for some finite period in order to achieve *nirvāṇa*. In effect, the methods recommended in the teachings fairly rapidly brought the practitioner to a state in which all demanding desires were uprooted. Now it seems as though the death of the Buddha brought these spectacular and sudden transformations in spiritual status pretty much to an end.

As time went on, the time required for a monk to achieve liberation increased. The canon tells us that the Buddha predicted such a state of affairs. He taught that, from the time of his death, the teachings (*Dhamma*) would go slowly and inexorably into decline until the stage was reached when they would disappear altogether. Perhaps the increased time that a monk appears to have needed in order to attain his goal was a function of this decline in the *Dhamma*. Another explanation is simply that the fervour of the early period, in which the founder was still present and ministering to his disciples, was replaced by a more relaxed attitude to the possibility of liberation. Whatever the explanation, a new attitude towards the world and the beings it contains began to develop. The spiritual path began to take on a more gradual character. The possibility of sudden enlightenment began to seem less realistic. As a result, the likelihood of a monastic career spanning a good many lives (perhaps many millions of lives) became the norm. In this way the career of the monk began to share some of the characteristics of the lay path, which had been seen as an enormously lengthy process from the earliest period of Buddhist history. Not surprisingly, the radical other-worldliness of the early period is pushed out of the foreground in the thinking of the *saṅgha*, and a slightly more positive vision of the world begins to form. It should be noted that the Buddhist laity probably always regarded the natural world in a more concerned manner than the largely urban members of the *saṅgha*. It is a pity that we do not possess any substantial account of their views on the subject, though this is not surprising, given the fact that learning and literacy were almost entirely the preserve of the monks. Nevertheless, as the tradition develops and becomes more realistic, even the outlook of its community of renouncers starts to see the natural world in a new light.

COSMOLOGY

The description of the world contained in the writings of Vasubandhu and Buddhaghosa has come down to the Buddhists of the present day virtually unchanged (see Gethin, 1998, pp. 112–32). In this respect

Buddhism differs from Christianity. In the Christian tradition a radical redrawing of the cosmos was occasioned by the crisis caused by the rise of science in the early modern period. The findings of Galileo and Copernicus, despite initial condemnation by the church, were ultimately to win the day. However, the essentially alien nature of Western scientific thinking has had a marginal impact on the traditional systems of thought of Asia, perhaps because, at least in part, the status of myth and story has been higher in the East than in the West (cf. Bowker, 1990). Nevertheless, recent evidence suggests that in some regions of the Buddhist world, most notably in Thailand and Sri Lanka, the situation is changing, and Buddhist doctrine is, in educated circles, coming to align itself with the findings of science.

For traditional Buddhism the world in which we live is a golden disk floating on a mighty cosmic ocean. This ocean is in turn supported by a circle of wind which itself rests on space. In one of the few cosmological fragments of the Pāli Canon (Walshe, 1987, pp. 247–8), the Buddha explains that earthquakes may be caused by turbulence in the circle of wind which causes a similar effect in the ocean. This is communicated to the golden earth which then shakes. Many contemporary Buddhists, particularly in Sri Lanka, regard this as a surprisingly modern view of the origin of earthquakes, but when read in context, we discover that this is only one special category of earthquake discussed in the text. By far the most prominent of the explanations given for these apparently natural occurrences is based on non-naturalistic principles. Most of the causes of earthquakes discussed are particular activities of a *buddha*. Decisive moments in the life of one destined to obtain enlightenment, such as his birth, renouncing of home, moment of enlightenment, death, etc., are said to be accompanied by earthquakes.

An enormous mountain, Mount Meru, some 84,000 *yojana*s high (one *yojana* = about nine miles) is said to be situated at the centre of our golden earth. It is surrounded by seven concentric rings of mountains, each one half the height of the former as one moves outwards to the perimeter of the disc. All of the mountains are golden. At the extreme rim of the disc is a circle of iron mountains. Between the last range of golden mountains and circles of iron (Sanskrit *cakravāla*; Pāli *cakkavāḷa*) we find an ocean. Four island continents are located at the four cardinal points within this ocean. Humans live on the most southerly of the islands, which, because of the nature of its vegetation, is called the Rose-apple land (Sanskrit

Jambudvīpa; Pāli *Jambudīpa*). We are said to share this land with the animals and the hungry ghosts (Sanskrit *preta*s; Pāli *peta*s). Animals also flourish in the ocean surrounding our continent. On terraces cut into the slopes of Mount Meru live the gods (*deva*s), their status in the divine hierarchy determined by their position on the mountain. At the summit is the palace of Indra, the chief deity in Vedic times, known to Buddhists as Sakka. Other gods with more subtle bodies are held to exist in realms above the summit. At a distance as far below the earth as Indra's palace is above it, we find the abodes of the denizens of hell. There are a range of hellish existences, each one characterized by a different form of suffering for its inhabitants. In the Buddhist cosmos, then, five distinct kinds of being are to be found: humans, animals, ghosts, gods and denizens of hell (see pp. 72–4). Some texts add a sixth group, the demi-gods (*asura*s), who spend their time locked in conflict with the gods themselves.

These six discrete destinies (*gati*s) are interrelated. As beings eternally process around the circle of birth and deaths (*saṃsāra*) they are destined to spend innumerable lives in each of the *gati*s. As a consequence, we are intimately related to a very wide range of beings. A horse in the field may, for instance, have been our brother in a previous existence. This state of affairs clearly leads to a strong feeling of solidarity and fellow feeling with all beings. We are all in the same boat together. We are all circulating through various forms of suffering (even the divine destinies involve suffering, though on a more subtle level than we experience as humans), and are all, in our own way, capable of obtaining eventual release.

THE CONDITIONED WORLD OF CHANGE

A visually striking representation of the six destinies is found in the Buddhist wheel of life (Sanskrit *bhava-cakra*; Pāli *bhava-cakka*). These complex and symbolic works of art are found particularly in the Tibetan tradition, and consist of a six-spoked wheel in which the gaps between the spokes contain scenes depicting the life-styles of beings in each of the six *gati*s. At the hub of the wheel one generally finds three animals in a circle attempting to devour the tail of the creature in front. These are the pig, the cockerel and the snake, which respectively represent greed, hatred and delusion, the three aspects of ignorance (Sanskrit *avidyā*; Pāli *avijjā*), which is the destructive principle at the root of all forms of rebirth. The message of this image is straightforward. No perfection is possible by rebirth within the realm of conditioned things.[3] Everything, no matter how attractive it appears on the surface, is marked by suffering (*dukkha*), impermanence (*anicca*) and insubstantiality (*anattā*). Without going into enormous detail, it might be worth examining one further feature of the wheel of life (*bhava-cakra*). The outer rim of the wheel contains a series of twelve images which, when put together, depict the progress of beings from one life to another. The strength of the series is that it explains the inevitability of the causal process at work in the world. Our deluded desires are shown to bind us ever more closely to the world, with the consequence that on death the force of our desire impels us on into a new life. This life, even if it reaches its natural span, must inevitably close with old age, sickness and death. Yet still our demanding desires force us ever onward into fresh forms of existence. The principle of causation which imparts the sense of inevitability to things was the fundamental discovery of the Buddha on attaining enlightenment (see p. 80). It is referred to as dependent origination (*pratītya-samutpāda*) and the series of twelve images on the rim of the wheel represent an attempt to give this principle visual form.

Some recent scholars have claimed that the Sanskrit word *pratītya-samutpāda* (Pāli *paṭicca-samuppāda*) is the nearest equivalent in Buddhist sources to our term 'nature'. They go on to argue that since this is so, it is self-evidently the case that Buddhism, from its inception, has had a concern for nature. We now need to examine this view in more depth. The doctrine of dependent origination highlights the Buddhist notion that all apparently substantial entities within the world are in fact wrongly perceived. We live under the illusion that terms such as 'I', self, mountain, tree, etc., denote permanent and stable things. The doctrine teaches that this is not so. What appears to be permanent is, in fact, in a state of perpetual flux. The Theravādin position is that the ordinary objects of consciousness may actually be resolved into a stream of momentary and mutually conditioning entities called *dhammas* (Pāli; Sanskrit *dharmas*). Someone skilled in meditation may observe the rise and fall of these *dhammas*. For them the illusion of permanence and substantiality is undermined at a more fundamental level by the flux of radical change. The world is like a raging torrent which never remains the same from one moment to the next. Now, modern environmentalist thinking makes much of the interdependence of things in the natural world, and it is certainly true that the doctrine of *pratītya-samutpāda* is in tune with a world-view which accepts complex, interdependent relationships. However, there is a problem associated with making a comparison between Buddhism and environmentalist thinking which the scholars mentioned above fail to acknowledge. The Buddhist analysis of things, be they animate or inanimate, is far more radical than that adopted by Western ecology.

Let us take the example of an endangered species such as the black rhino. For the environmentalist the potential demise of these noble creatures is a matter of sadness and concern. To counteract this possibility, measures will be taken to protect the species by mitigating the destructive forces at work in the rhino's habitat, be they human-made or essentially independent of humanity. In this sense, environmentalism represents a 'fight against pollution and resource depletion'. A Buddhist is unlikely to view things in this way. I am not suggesting for one moment that Buddhists would rejoice at the extinction of the black rhino – very far from it – but, as we have previously noted, change, dissolution, suffering and death are the hallmarks of all conditioned things (cf. Harvey, 2000, pp. 183–4). At the deepest level, what we take to be a rhino is nothing more than a complex series of momentary *dhamma*s which have come together in a certain pattern. To the eye of ignorance this patterning appears as a bulky African quadruped. Looked at from a different perspective, the rise and fall of things, whether they be mountains or animals, is part of the inexorable process Buddhists call *saṃsāra*. In a sense, contemplation of this fact brings home to us our own lack of substance and permanence. It may have a positive impact on the development of the spiritual life. The recognition of this deep impermanence may prompt us to investigate the teachings of the Buddha and opt to follow the Buddhist path which leads to *nirvāṇa*.

If we take stock of the argument to this point, it becomes clear that Buddhism does not provide the kind of doctrinal foundation from which environmental concerns can be easily developed in the way that some other religions, notably the Semitic religions of Judaism, Christianity and Islam, do. In these traditions the natural world is the creation of a loving and Supreme Being. The natural world, since it is part of the created order, must have a distinct purpose in the divine scheme of things, and it can be coherently argued that humans must get their relations with this order right for the final purpose of existence to be realized. As we have already noted, Buddhism repudiates that kind of theism and the theistic response to the world. Purpose and meaning as such are missing from the equation, but we should be on our guard against misinterpreting the Buddhist outlook on the world. Far from being cold-hearted or nihilistic, Buddhism places great stress on loving-kindness and compassion to all beings. After all, we are all in the same boat. Let us now examine this strand of the tradition in more detail.

Non-injury in the Buddhist tradition

The principle of non-injury is one of the characteristic features of many ancient Indian religious traditions (see p. 7). There is some evidence to suggest that the avoidance of harming living things predates the arrival of the Aryans in the subcontinent some 4,500 years ago. The religion of the Aryans, preserved as it is in the Vedic writings, is an essentially sacrificial religion and, as such, was dependent from time to time on the sacrifice of animals. In contrast, we find no evidence of such practices in the classical system of Yoga or in the religion of the Jainas. The same may be said for Buddhism. It is noteworthy that these three traditions were essentially traditions of renunciants. Since renunciation is not easily reconciled with the martial and life-affirming world-view of the Aryans, there may be some substance to the view that both renunciation and the practice of non-injury were indigenous Indian modes of behaviour. Certainly non-injury (*ahiṃsā*) is stressed quite frequently in the early texts of Buddhism.

The frequency of occurrence of this doctrine is at least partly explained by Buddhist adherence to the idea of rebirth. As we have already noted, our very large number of previous lives means that we have already established intimate relations with virtually the whole of the animal kingdom (see p. 72). We are in some, unconscious, sense part of an enormous family of fellow sufferers. To contribute to the further suffering of any individual member of this family would be a parallel offence, at a lesser level, to harming one's present mother or father. Anthropologists and psychoanalysts tell us that offences of this kind are treated with particular opprobrium in the majority of cultures.[4] However, in the Buddhist context the emphasis on non-harming may have another dimension. A number of texts teach that this practice may lead to a favourable future birth. The implication is clearly that harming results in rebirth in an unfavourable destiny (*gati*). Perhaps someone who has committed acts of cruelty to animals will become an animal, a ghost or even a denizen of hell. In this sense, an act of cruelty contaminates the person who commits the deed – as a result he or she becomes impure. This impurity is viewed as dragging the person down to a lower level of existence after death. If this interpretation is accepted, then there is something to be said for the view that non-injury (*ahiṃsā*) was regarded in a positive light as much for its purificatory role in a person's spiritual development as it was for its effects on animal and human welfare.

The case of vegetarianism brings this contrast to prominence (cf. Harvey, 2000, pp. 157–65). It is often assumed that the Buddha taught vegetarianism. This certainly seems to follow logically from the doctrine of non-injury. In fact, examination of the relevant sources reveals a rather more complicated situation. The Pāli Canon reveals that the Buddha was himself occasionally to be found eating meat. Not only that, but, under certain conditions, he gave members of the *saṅgha* permission to eat meat. The only requirement for a monk is that the meat should be properly cooked and pure. In other words, the monk should neither see, hear nor suspect that the meat has been prepared specifically for him. A final proviso is that the monk should refrain from eating ten kinds of meat, e.g., the flesh of the snake, lion, elephant, dog, etc. It has been convincingly argued, by Ruegg (1980) and others, that strict vegetarianism only became a coherent position in Mahāyāna Buddhism, at a pretty late stage in the history of the tradition. We should bear two factors in mind here. In the first place, vegetarianism is not a necessary condition for concern for the environment. In the second, compassion for the fate of individual members of the animal kingdom is not the same as the more general concern for the destiny of species characteristic of much environmentalist literature.

LOVING-KINDNESS

In order to expand on the foregoing discussion, let us now turn to an aspect of Buddhist meditational practice. This is the cultivation of loving-kindness (*mettā*). A frequently recommended series of meditational subjects are the four divine abidings (*brahma-vihāras*).

Concentration on the *brahma-vihāras* (i.e., loving-kindness, *mettā*; compassion, *karuṇā*; sympathetic joy, *muditā*; and equanimity, *upekkhā*) is believed to form an important preliminary in the Buddhist system of mental cultivation. Of the four, the meditation on loving-kindness is perhaps the most widely practised. By extending *mettā* towards others, goodwill is promoted and the heart becomes filled with love. However, in a discussion of this practice in his influential work on meditation, called the Path of Purification (*Visuddhimagga*), Buddhaghosa mentions eleven advantages which accrue to the practitioners themselves. Strangely, no advantages are listed for the recipient of the *mettā*. At another point in the discussion, we are told to avoid the directing of *mettā* towards animals. It is thought to be better, in order to attain the deepest level of meditation, to confine one's attention to a human object.

In the Pāli texts, the Buddha is occasionally described as extending *mettā* towards animals. However, when the context of these occurrences is examined, it is clear that the Buddha does this for a very specific purpose. It is done to calm an enraged animal. A good example of this is the occasion when an attempt was made on the Buddha's life. A mad elephant is set loose to trample him and his entourage, but, through the Buddha's defensive use of *mettā*, this dangerous situation is diffused. Clearly *mettā* practice is an important feature of the Buddhist path, but when we look into its rationale we are forced to draw surprising conclusions. In general, the highlighted advantages of the practice are felt by the practitioner not by the living being to whom it is directed. In particular, successful practice is believed to result in rebirth in one of the divine realms. Non-human focuses of *mettā* are only infrequently met with in the scriptures, and even when they are, the objective of the practitioner is to render a potential threat harmless. A good example of this is to be found in the chanting of a portion of one of the Buddha's sermons (*Aṅguttara Nikāya*, II.72 *Khandha Paritta*) as a charm to ward off dangerous snakes.

I have argued (Harris, 1991) that, when seen in this light, the Buddhist attitude towards animals is essentially instrumental.[5] Its essential function is to aid the practitioner in his search for spiritual perfection, and any good done to the being to whom *mettā* is extended is merely a happy side-effect. This fact is actually recognized by the tradition itself, for the scriptures accept that the cultivation of the *brahma-vihāras* does not lead directly to *nirvāṇa*. Since the practice is directed towards beings within the world, the results are held to be basically mundane (*lokiya*). In effect, the attitudes of mind reflected by the practice express our highest ethical ideals, and these ideals can be applied only within the realm of conditioned things. It is important to emphasize the fact that these ideals do not in themselves bring about any supramundane achievement.[6] They are not uniquely Buddhist ideals but refer to actions which are viewed in a positive light by society as a whole. Actually the scriptures acknowledge that *brahma-vihāra* practice does not originate within the Buddhist tradition. It was employed by the sages of old and merely preserved by the Buddha. The Buddha was quite prepared to accept these ideals, particularly since they perform a clear role in the maintenance of civilized values and in the meditative cultivation of the heart, but he stressed that one must accept their fundamentally provisional nature.

In view of what has been said above, it seems clear that kindness and the avoidance of cruelty are civilized forms of behaviour endorsed by the Buddhist tradition. In accordance with this principle, the Buddha recommended that his lay followers should take the welfare of their domestic animals seriously. For instance, cowherds are warned not to milk their herds dry. It is a common custom in Buddhist regions of South and Southeast Asia, even today, to release animals, and particularly birds, from captivity. This practice probably derives from the Buddha's command that monks should free animals caught in hunters' traps.

ANIMALS

However, there is little doubt that, for Buddhism, animals belong some way down the hierarchy of beings. They occupy one of the three unfavourable destinies (*gatis*). They are less wise than humans and cannot make effective progress on the Buddhist path. They cannot, therefore, be admitted as members of the *saṅgha*, for their presence within the monastic community would be deleterious. In the literature of monastic discipline, the Buddha regularly lists animals, for certain purposes, alongside hermaphrodites, thieves, parent-killers and, most significantly, those guilty of other heinous crimes: murderers of an *arahat* or injurers of a *buddha*.

There are plenty of incidents within the canon (particularly the

Jātaka) in which animals behave impeccably, and in many respects better than the average human, but nevertheless the animal realm is in general something to be wary of. Animals are thought to be more vicious than humans. The forest-dwelling monk is particularly prone to the dangers represented by wild animals. He may be attacked by tigers or snakes. Hence the importance of the practice of *mettā* as a protective mechanism. Looked at from another perspective, he is subject to the depredations of many small creatures. Their cumulative effect is to make his existence in the forest distinctly uncomfortable. Insects, rats and the like are continually attacking his limited range of possessions. Now, though this may be inconvenient on one level, the monk can turn this to his advantage. The activity of the animal kingdom is an example, on the grand scale, of the process of decay which affects all conditioned things. Meditation on this fact can develop a deeper understanding of the impermanence, insubstantiality and suffering associated with the world. As a result, the monk's desires for worldly things diminish. In fact, the perception of danger may itself be utilized on the spiritual quest. Fear is a particularly strong emotional state. Its strength and associated physical effects may become meditational objects. Investigation of fear in this manner may lead to important insights into the functioning of the mental processes, and this in turn may lead to greater insight into the *Dhamma*. Certainly this practice is recommended by some meditation teachers in Thailand today. It is said to have a powerful therapeutic value.

Before moving on, let us summarize the conclusions of this section. Kindness towards animals is encouraged by Buddhism. Such kindness is in accordance with worldly conventions. On this level the Buddha had no argument with the ethics of his day and indeed extended them. However, Buddhism ultimately expects to move further than such considerations, for the tradition ideally represents an attempt to escape from the restrictions imposed on us by our position as beings within the world. Active concern for the animal kingdom is compatible with Buddhism but does not arise naturally from its central insights into the nature of reality. It can happily be taken along as baggage on the path to perfection, but at some stage it must be abandoned. In actual fact, many of the practices which seem, at one level, to be targeted at the welfare of animals, have as their ultimate aim the spiritual development of the practitioner. The Buddhist ethic in this area is essentially instrumental.

The natural environment and Buddhism

If Max Weber was correct, and there is some evidence to suggest that he was, then it looks likely that Buddhism has its origins in the growing urban centres of northern India some 500 years before Christ. Tradition holds that the Buddha's favourite residing places were parks and pleasure groves which came into the possession of the early *saṅgha* as gifts from wealthy lay followers. These were clearly convenient places for the reception of alms from surrounding residents, and from such suburban locations the Buddha was well poised to extend his influence. A life spent in the heart of the jungle would hardly have been as useful in this respect. The Pāli Canon indicates that the laying out of such areas was thought to be a highly 'meritorious' action, but it is important to note that these locations are essentially artificial. They are made by humans.

In the *Cakkavatti-sihānada Sutta*, an early Pāli text, a description of the far future, in which conditions have improved greatly on the present, is given (Walshe, 1987, pp. 395–406). At that time, humans can expect a lifespan of approximately 80,000 years. However, cities then will have grown to such an extent that the countryside will have all but disappeared. Surprisingly, the text gives no hint that this will be an undesirable state of affairs. On the contrary, the wilderness will have been tamed, and this is portrayed as a positive advance for humanity. The text might be interpreted as evidence for the great confidence felt by early Buddhists in the superiority of urban over rural culture.

It is an acknowledged fact that Buddhist sources are rather light on glowing descriptions of the natural world. One or two passages can be identified in which the author appears to be delighting in the glories of nature, but these are few and far between.[7] There is a good reason for this. The doctrinal content of the Buddha's teaching paints the world in a rather sombre light. It is subject to corruption and intrinsically unsatisfactory. It is possible that one may be instantaneously struck with aesthetic pleasure on viewing a natural scene, but for the Buddhist this can never be more than a fleeting perception. There is no value attached to holding on to such experiences. In such a doctrinal environment it is difficult for natural mysticism to take a firm hold. This is clearly in great contrast to Christianity. For the latter tradition, the world can be read as a text revealing evidence of the divine creator's purpose. The perception of beauty can draw one closer to an appreciation of the author of such beauty. In short, nature reveals God. This is impossible with Buddhism. I do not mean by this that Buddhists themselves may not rejoice in the astonishing profusion of the natural world; there is no intentional dourness in Buddhism. But they cannot be led on from such reflections to any ultimate end.[8] Delight in the world can too easily be a stage on the way towards increased desire for more such delights, and this must eventually lead to further suffering.

FORESTS

Buddhism shares many of the characteristics of the ancient traditions of Indian renunciation. So, despite its possible urban roots, the ideal of forest-dwelling had an impact on at least a proportion of the Buddha's followers. The forest is the antithesis of the cultivated and cultured environment of the town. It is the home of a variety of wild beasts and for this reason alone it induces fear. But there is another attendant problem associated with the forest – it may also be a haven for any number of malicious spirits. As such it is seen in some texts as a place of ill-will and wickedness. It is an alien land. As a consequence, nuns are prevented from taking up abode here; they may be seduced by unwholesome beings dwelling there. Some forests are referred to by name in the Pāli texts, and we are told that they were once cleared for cultivation but became reforested as a result of the ill-will of certain sages. Lack of cultivation, then, has a certain connection with negative emotions and outright wickedness. Cultivation on the other hand is equated with righteousness.

However, the forest can be employed as a meditational device. A number of prominent Buddhist writers recommend mindfulness of the forest as a means of gaining insight into impermanence. Buddhaghosa, for instance, extols the positive consequences of attention to falling leaves, and in the Mahāyāna the forest is sometimes seen as a metaphor for *saṃsāra* itself. It is not surprising, then, to find that Buddhist literature is full of natural imagery to describe the course of spiritual progress. For instance, one is said to move from a state in which the path is not cultivated to one in which it is. One sows the seeds of 'merit' in the field of the *saṅgha*. One takes the middle path to enlightenment. Paths which wander through uncharted territory must be avoided.

PLANTS

Buddhist scriptures contain rather little to indicate how the vegetable kingdom should be treated. However, a few snippets of information may be gleaned from a reading of the texts of monastic discipline (see Harvey, 2000, pp. 174–6; Schmithausen, 1991a). Monks must avoid damage to plant life. Incurring such damage is an offence which requires expiation on the part of the monk. This seems a clear-cut matter, but on closer investigation it appears that the texts are primarily concerned with damage to crops. If this is so, then one wonders about the intention underlying the rule. Is it wrong to damage any form of plant life, or is there an offence only when cultivated produce is concerned? It is difficult to give a precise answer, but we know that monks are prohibited from engaging in agricultural activity. This ruling presumably arose for a variety of reasons. In the first place, farming is a full-time occupation and leaves little spare time for the cultivation of the spiritual life. On the other hand, agricultural activities, such as ploughing, digging, etc., lead inevitably to the accidental death of worms and insects. Perhaps the avoidance of damage to crops is a simple extension of this principle. Monks would naturally damage crops in the harvesting process; therefore, they should avoid agriculture entirely. Now this is a fairly specific regulation, and some evidence exists to suggest a more wide-ranging ethic. The Buddha is certainly said to have avoided all damage to seed and plant life. This may be interpreted as an extension of the principle of non-injury (*ahiṃsā*) to the vegetable kingdom. However, while monastic conduct may be regulated along such lines, the life of the lay Buddhist must necessarily be less exacting.

The vast majority of Buddhist populations, at all phases of the history of the tradition, have been tied to the land as a matter of life and death. The laity must ensure that adequate foodstuffs are available for their families, but they have an added responsibility: they must provide alms for members of the *saṅgha*. Under such conditions, monks would be ill-advised to demand unrealistic levels of behaviour among the ordinary people. There is a gulf, then, between the expectations imposed on monks and those thought appropriate for the laity. Monks must avoid all intentional harm to flora and fauna. Failure to observe these measures will hinder the path to *nirvāṇa*. The laity, on the other hand, is compelled, by circumstance, to inflict a moderate level of harm on the natural environment. Agriculture cannot take place without some damage. However, the undesirable consequences of agricultural activity are diminished by lay alms-giving. By making regular offering of food to the *saṅgha*, the lay-person is ensured rebirth in a favourable destiny (*gati*) after death. Weber refers to this less restrictive code practised by the Buddhist laity as an 'insufficiency ethic'. The term implies that lay activity, while it may be determined by certain moral criteria, is not sufficient in itself to bring about the ultimate goal of the tradition, i.e., *nirvāṇa*.[9]

Before leaving this section, it is necessary for us to investigate the status of plants in the Buddhist scheme of things. They are certainly not conceived of as inanimate objects. They are thought to possess the single sense of touch, though none of the other faculties is present, e.g., the hearing, taste, mind, etc., which characterize higher organisms. They can nevertheless experience pain. It is apparent from our earlier discussion that the world of plants is not one of the six destinies – we can never be reborn as a tree or piece of grass. This is noteworthy because some Hindu *dharma* texts do accept this as a possibility. For Buddhism, though, the realm of vegetable life stands apart from the sphere of beings ultimately destined for enlightenment.[10] It is part of the stage on which salvation is played, but does not itself possess the capacity for perfection. From the perspective of enlightenment, plant life shares in the purposelessness and meaninglessness of the entire realm of conditioned things. This does not mean that Buddhists may treat the vegetable kingdom with contempt. An individual's role as lay-person or monk will be a crucial factor in determining the precise manner in which responsibilities are exercised, but the principle of non-injury must always be present as the background to behaviour. The major difference is that the *saṅgha* member works with a hard interpretation of the principle, while the lay-person adopts a softer approach.

Overview

It is obvious that Buddhism starts with a very different set of priorities from those encountered in the religions of the ancient Near East. Its lack of a supreme creator, plus an insistence on the cyclical nature of the beginningless world process, stand in stark contrast to the Judaeo-Christian tradition. In its origin Buddhism is a religion whose highest goal reflects world-weariness, though this situation clearly underwent significant modification as the centuries progressed. Nevertheless, the Buddha's prime importance as a religious teacher was his identification of the world as a domain devoid of substantiality. Recognition of this fact results in non-reliance on the things of the world. In consequence, the typical follower of the Buddha in the early period is a renouncer.

In essence and theory, then, Buddhism cannot uphold a self-consciously 'environmentalist' ethic. The reason for this is straightforward. There is nothing within the sphere of nature which can be said to possess any inbuilt meaning or purpose. There can be no Buddhist justification for the fight to preserve habitats and environments *per se*; though Buddhism does advocate the avoidance of intentional harm to the individual sentient beings dwelling in any environment. Everything, without exception, is subject to decay, whether this be a particular environment or the existence of a species.

In practice, however, the situation is a little different. Since its inception Buddhism has been a missionary religion. In order to increase its influence in Asia, missionary monks have seen the sense in preserving local traditions as long as they do not come into conflict with central doctrinal concerns. The result of this activity has been that in many regions of the Buddhist world the renunciatory concerns of the early period have rested lightly on the lay population. We also know that the Buddha himself adopted an ethical outlook which drew substantially from pre-Buddhist systems of thought. From our perspective, his most important borrowing was the insistence on non-injury (*ahiṃsā*). Buddhists are expected to apply this principle in their dealings with all beings. All actions – be they bodily, verbal or mental – are to be referred back to this ideal. This is the essence of right action and speech, two of the members of the Noble Eightfold Path.

A consequence of this insistence is that animals and plants are to be respected and such respect arises naturally from the insight, provided by Buddhist cosmology, that all sentient beings are intimately interrelated. The level at which the principle of non-injury may be practised is effectively determined by a person's status in the Buddhist community. Agriculturalists must attempt to protect animal life but some injury is unavoidable, because of the nature of the work. Monks are prevented from working on the land, for the negative consequences entailed by such tasks would be harmful to the spread of the *Dhamma*. Nevertheless, one finds, for example, monks in Thailand who, amongst themselves and with lay-people, work to protect remaining areas of virgin forest and to re-forest other areas whose previous felling had led to disruption of water supply or flooding (Harvey, 2000, pp. 181–2; Batchelor and Brown, 1992, pp. 92–9).

We should not imagine that the doctrine of *ahiṃsā* was imported into Buddhism without modification. On the contrary, it had to be incorporated into a coherent vision of things. The justification for non-injury is essentially instrumental.[11] By behaving in a loving and compassionate fashion, one is ensured a favourable rebirth as a god (*deva*). This does not mean that the beings to whom love is directed will not benefit. In fact they will have their unfortunate lives enhanced, particularly if they are animals, and may in time come to a fuller understanding of the *Dhamma*.

In short, Buddhism endorses a spirit of toleration and co-operation with the natural world. It does so because this traditional mode of behaviour is given a specific sense by the tradition, and in the final analysis does not come into conflict with the ultimate goal, which is transcendence of the conditioned world. From the perspective of enlightenment, nothing may have a final purpose or essential value, but, at least in the early stages of the spiritual path, Buddhism acts as though it does. Here then is one of the many paradoxes encountered in the study of this unique religious system of thought.

Notes

1 In the sense of a conscious theory and praxis of how and why we should preserve the natural world and its diversity. This of course may be partly because it is the modern world that has developed the power to destroy much of nature. (Ed.)

2 Strictly speaking, early Buddhism did not see the world as endless, but as hugely old without any discernible beginning and as likely to continue for huge periods into the future; the question of whether it might some day end because all beings attained *nirvāṇa* was left as an open question. In the Mahāyāna, though, a time when all beings had attained *nirvāṇa* was postulated. (Ed.)

3 Though the human realm offers the possibility of transcending the conditioned realm by attaining the perfection of an *arahat*.

4 Indeed, in Buddhism, to intentionally kill one's mother or father is

counted among the most heinous acts, along with killing an *arahat*.

5 Yet one could argue that the reason that *mettā* is seen as beneficial to the practitioner of it is that it is seen as in itself the right and appropriate attitude to other suffering beings. (Ed.)

6 Though they are seen as very beneficial in preparing the mind for other practices that do. (Ed.)

7 A relatively rich source, here, is the *Theragāthā*, a text of the Pāli Canon which records verses of a number of monk *arahats* (see Harvey, 2000, pp. 154–5). A number of these are what might be called wilderness-meditators, dwelling in the mountains and forests. Mahā-Kassapa, for example, says 'With clear water and wide crags, haunted by monkeys and deer, covered with oozing moss, those rocks delight me' (v. 1070). (Ed.)

8 Yet such a view overlooks certain East Asian developments of Buddhism, particularly Zen, which came to see nature as a manifestation, or even actual appearance, of the *buddha*-nature, with arts such as the *haiku* poem seeking to convey the mysterious suchness of ultimate reality glimpsed in simple natural events. (Ed.)

9 However, the disciplinary code of monks, though more extensive than the lay ethical code, is also insufficient on its own to attain *nirvāṇa*; meditation and wisdom are also necessary. (Ed.)

10 Though in China and Japan, some held that plants had the *buddha*-nature and could attain enlightenment (Harvey, 2000, pp. 176–7). (Ed.)

11 At least in many of its explicit justifications, though these imply that non-injury has good results *because* it is in harmony with the nature of things as regards the inter-related world of suffering beings and the working of the human mind. (Ed.)

Further reading

Attfield, R. (1983) 'Western traditions and environmental ethics' in R. Eliot and A. Gane (eds) *Environmental Philosophy*. Milton Keynes: Open University Press.

Batchelor, M. and Brown, K. (eds) (1992) *Buddhism and Ecology*. London: Cassell (sponsored by the World Wide Fund for Nature).

Bowker, J. W. (1990) 'Cosmology, religion and society', *Zygon*, 25, pp. 7–23.

Callicott, J. B. and Ames, R. T. (eds) (1989) *Nature in Asian Traditions of Thought: Essays in Environmental Philosophy*. Albany: State University of New York Press.

Gethin, R. (1998) *The Foundations of Buddhism*. Oxford: Oxford University Press.

Hargrove, E. C. (1989) *Foundations of Environmental Ethics*. Englewood Cliffs, NJ: Prentice-Hall.
Harris, I. C. (1991) 'How environmentalist is Buddhism?', *Religion*, 21, pp. 101–14.
Harris, I. (1994) 'Causation and *telos*: the problem of Buddhist environmental ethics', *Journal of Buddhist Ethics* (free Internet journal: http://jbe.gold.ac.uk), 1, pp. 45–56.
Harris, I. (1995a) 'Buddhist environmental ethics and detraditionalization: the case of EcoBuddhism', *Religion*, 25, pp. 199–211.
Harris, I. (1995b) 'Getting to grips with Buddhist environmentalism: a provisional typology', *Journal of Buddhist Ethics*, 2, pp. 173–90.
Harris, I. (2000) 'Buddhism and ecology' in D. Keown (ed.) *Contemporary Buddhist Ethics*. Richmond: Curzon, pp. 113–36.
Harvey, P. (2000) *An Introduction to Buddhist Ethics: Foundations, Values and Issues*. Cambridge: Cambridge University Press, pp. 150–86.
Passmore, J. (1980) *Man's Responsibility for Nature*. London: Duckworth.
Ruegg, D. S. (1980) 'Ahimsa and vegetarianism in the history of Buddhism' in S. Balasooriya *et al.* (eds) *Buddhist Studies in Honour of Walpola Rahula*. London: Gordon Fraser.
Sandell, K. (ed.) (1987) *Buddhist Perspective on the Ecocrisis*, Wheel booklet nos 346–8. Kandy, Sri Lanka: Buddhist Publication Society.
Schmithausen, L. (1991a) *The Problem of the Sentience of Plants in Earliest Buddhism*. Tokyo: The International Institute for Buddhist Studies.
Schmithausen, L. (1991b) *Buddhism and Nature: The Lecture Delivered on the Occasion of the EXPO 1990. An Enlarged Version with Notes*. Tokyo: The International Institute for Buddhist Studies.
Schmithausen, L. (1997) 'The early Buddhist tradition and ecological ethics', *Journal of Buddhist Ethics*, 4, pp. 1–74.
Tucker, M. E. and Williams, D. R. (eds) (1997) *Buddhism and Ecology: The Interconnection of Dharma and Deeds*. Cambridge, MA: Harvard University Center for the Study of World Religions.
Waldau, P. (2000) 'Buddhism and animal rights' ecology' in D. Keown (ed.) *Contemporary Buddhist Ethics*. Richmond: Curzon, pp. 81–112.
Walshe, M. (1987) *Thus Have I Heard: The Long Discourses of the Buddha*. London: Wisdom Publications.
White, L. Jnr (1967) 'The historical roots of our ecological crisis', *Science*, 155, pp. 1204ff.

9. Cosmology, myth and symbolism

Christopher Lamb

The Buddhist idea of time and history (shared with the whole period of Indian philosophical speculation from before Buddhism to post-Buddhist Hinduism) has generally seen them as cyclic, in opposition to the Judaeo-Christian view that historical time is a unique linear process with a beginning and an end. The cyclic cosmos runs according to the so-called law of *karma*, meaning 'action' and its effects, whereas the linear cosmos is ruled according to the ordinances of a supreme Being, and, specifically, one who acts in history and who made everything that is. On the other hand, while Buddhism has no creator-God theory, it might be said to attribute the role of creator to impersonal *karma*, since it is *karma* that keeps the processes of the phenomenal world (*saṃsāra*) in operation. It is sometimes said that history is about causation, but this is predicated on the notion of individuals or selves as separate agents of causation; the ancient Indians did not emphasize this, and had relatively little interest in history. Both cultures put causation as fundamental, but the crucial difference between them lies in the way they view the self. In Buddhism the notion of a substantial self arises from fundamental ignorance, *avidyā*. Nevertheless, in early Indian culture, it was the Buddhists who had the greatest interest in history, as seen in their composition of chronicles of the history of Buddhism and Buddhist lands, such as the Theravādin *Mahāvaṃsa*, composed in Sri Lanka.

The Japanese philosopher Keiji Nishitani (1982, pp. 168–217) points out that the Buddhist conception of time is not entirely cyclical but is, after all, radically actual. He agrees with the historian Arnold Toynbee that a linear view of history has carried a positive value in that it has allowed human beings a sense that they can take control of their own destiny, but, on the negative side, has encouraged self-centredness. This has always been considered 'sinful', rooted in the *mythos* of original disobedience, and so on, resulting in separation from God. Further, notions such as 'chosen people', and 'the elect' are not only affirmed by the ideological point of departure, but are actually structural, thus helping to give rise to racism and nationalism.

However, he goes on to argue that, in fact, all religions at the level of *mythos* share the view of time as recurrent and ahistorical. For example, in the world of nature, seasonal cycles and astronomical time return to their starting point; the liturgical year is a recurring annual celebration of single historical events. (We note that the Mass is the continual offering of the sacrifice of Calvary throughout time; Christmas is not only the adaptation of the *mythos* of fertility cycles occurring at the winter solstice to the Incarnation of God in history, but it also celebrates the ahistorical generation of the Son from the Father at the heart of the Trinity.) In another sense, all religion is located in the field of history, and Nishitani reminds us of Kant's idea that evil is the start of history; so even if Buddhism has been more concerned with suffering than with evil, within it salvation is a historic event.

The status of the notion of rebirth

That said, to what extent is the Buddhist idea of the cycle of rebirths a mythic one? Certain forms of modern Western Buddhism (e.g. Batchelor, 1997) see it as purely mythic and thus a dispensable notion. Whether or not this is the case, it clearly functions at least in part as a myth, i.e. a meaning-giving story. It allows Buddhists to say, for example, that all people and animals that one meets have been close friends or relatives in some past life, and should thus be treated well. It also provides a framework of belief within which many specific stories, such as the *Jātaka*s, can be set.

As regards its status within Buddhism, the idea of rebirth is not something that was uncritically drawn in from the surrounding culture, as is sometimes said. The ideas of *karma* and rebirth were relatively new in the Buddha's day and were not yet 'givens' of Indian culture – as seen by the fact that, among the Buddha's contemporaries, the Materialists rejected both, the Sceptics were agnostic on both, and the Ājīvakas accepted rebirth but not *karma*. Moreover, early accounts of the Buddha's enlightenment include him remembering many of his past lives and seeing how others were reborn according to *karma*, these being seen as key insights. Again, both the idea of annihilation at death and that of eternal immortality after death are repeatedly criticized, as well as scepticism on what, if anything, might happen at death. Only in the case of enlightened people is their state after death seen as an unknown quantity (see pp. 102–4), at least in the Theravāda. For unenlightened beings, rebirth and *karma* are seen as part of the way things are, that can be confirmed by the meditative experience of *buddha*s and other advanced meditators. For most Buddhists, though, belief in *karma* and rebirth are matters of faith based on their trust in the Buddha and those parts of his message that they have so far been able to confirm for themselves. Besides this, it is also seen as making good sense of life, through its ability to help explain fortune and misfortune by reference to past *karma*, and as offering a framework of motivation for the whole of this life.

That said, most forms of Buddhism focus on making the best of one's present life. Indeed, the notion of 'rebirth' can also be applied on a this-life time-scale as well as a life-to-life one. That is, cycles of change and continuity are seen not only as spanning lives (and on a larger scale, world-systems), but also as occurring during life: from life-situation to life-situation, day to day, mood to mood, and indeed moment to moment. Such a view seems to be equally ancient as the life-to-life aspect of rebirth, or 'again-becoming' (*purnabbhava*). Amongst recent Theravāda teachers, the influential Thai monk Buddhadāsa criticized aspects of Buddhism that emphasized life-to-life rebirth and the pursuit of good *karma* for future lives, and emphasized it as something occurring during life, particularly each time the thought 'I' arises (Swearer, 1989). Yet to see rebirth as occurring *only* during life would seem to be another extreme that is certainly in tension with centuries of Buddhist tradition and philosophy.

Cosmology

In the early days of Buddhism, speculations about the ultimate origin and detailed nature of the universe were discouraged because their existence was only a refraction of mental processes:

> It is in this fathom-long carcase (which is) cognitive and endowed with mind, that, I declare, lies the (experienced) world, and the arising of the world, and the stopping of the world, and the course that goes to the stopping of the world. (*Samyutta Nikāya*, I.62)

Nevertheless, the Pāli *sutta*s contain scattered descriptions of our external world and its evolution, along with references to other worlds in space, and these are later systematized and elaborated on (see Gethin, 1998, pp. 112–32). The fullest and most systematic account is given in Vasubandhu's *Abhidharma-kośa-bhāṣya* (fourth century CE). This massive compendium of doctrinal and commentarial material is based on earlier Sarvāstivādin *Abhidharma* treatises and is the most highly systematized account of non-Mahāyāna Buddhist doctrine. The cosmological questions discussed concerned not only the universe as a receptacle, *bhājana-loka*, for living beings, but also the beings and their distribution within it.

The most ancient view of our world is that it consists of a single system, a disc on whose edge is a ring of iron mountains, *cakra-vāla*, and with a concentric series of golden mountains which rise from the surface of the earth. In the central ring rises the great Mount Meru, also known as Sumeru. There is a tradition observed by Northern Buddhists, Hindus, Jains and Tibetan Bon-pos that Mount Kailash in western Tibet is identifiable with Mount Meru, the vertical axis and navel of the world. The system is also called *trai-lokya-dhātu*, The Triple World (see Table 9.1). The triple nature of the world refers to the three degrees of refinement in which conscious existence can take place.

LEVEL ONE

This is the realm of sense-desire, *kāma-dhātu*, which includes, on the one hand, the destinies of woe: hells, abodes of animals, ghost-realms, and anti-god-realms, and on the other hand, the abodes of

Table 9.1 The Triple World

	4	Sphere of Neither-perception-nor-non-perception	
III Realm of Non-Form	3	Sphere of Nothingness	
ārūpya-dhātu	2	Sphere of Infinite Consciousness	
	1	Sphere of Infinite Space	

No material abodes above Akaniṣṭha – receptacle-world ends here

II Realm of Form *rūpa-dhātu*	Fourth *dhyāna*	8 Akaniṣṭha 7 Well-Seeing 6 Beautiful 5 No Heat 4 Effortless	Pure Abodes
		3 Abundant Fruit 2 Merit-Born 1 Cloudless	
	Third *dhyāna*	3 Complete Beauty 2 Immeasurable Beauty 1 Limited Beauty	
	Second *dhyāna*	3 Radiant Gods 2 Immeasurable Splendour 1 Limited Splendour	
	First *dhyāna*	3 Great Brahmās 2 Brahmā-priests 1 Retinue of Brahmā	
I Realm of Desire *kāma-dhātu*	Kāmadeva	6 Rulers over the Creations of Others 5 Those who Enjoy Creation 4 *Tuṣita* 3 *Yāma* 2 Thirty-three Gods – Meru peak 1 Four Great Kings – fourth tier Intoxicated – third tier Bearing Garlands – second tier Bowl in Hand – first tier	
	Humans Ghosts Animals Hell-beings		
	Golden Earth Circle of Water Circle of Wind Space		

(Adapted from W. R. Kloetzli (1983) *Buddhist Cosmology*. Delhi: Motilal Banarsidass, pp. 33–9)

humankind and the realms of the gods of desire; two classes of these gods dwell on terraces on the slopes of Meru leading up to Indra or Sakka, who dwells on the summit in the second heaven, that of the 'thirty-three'. The *Tuṣita* heaven, the abode of Maitreya, the Buddha-to-come, is the fourth heaven.

Buddhist 'zoology'

Beings exist throughout the five *gati*s (destinies): two of these are good and three bad. The human realm is a good destiny because only from there can the key work for enlightenment be done. The gods are also considered fortunate because they have been born in one of several sub-*gati*s through 'merit' accrued in previous lives. Such 'merit', though, is only a finite resource. There are three classes of gods distributed throughout the three *dhātu*s (realms):

1 Four completely disembodied classes of gods in the formless realm, their existence sustained solely by their rebirth. The *Abhidharma-kośa* says that highly realized persons might get powers to perceive them, but only in a form that is humanly perceivable.

2 Seventeen kinds in seventeen places in the realm of pure or elemental form.

3 Six kinds in six places in the realm of sense-desire.

The three bad (i.e. unfortunate) destinies include the animals, whose realm overlaps with the human, the hungry ghosts, who are to be found throughout the human realm but also in the realm of the god of the dead, *Yama*, below Meru (not the same as *Yāma*, one of the six kinds of gods of sense-desire), and, third, the hells, eight of which are hot and eight cold.

There seems to be no clearly assigned place for the *asura*s, anti-gods. In the Tibetan pictures of the Wheel of Life, the *asura*s occupy a sixth *gati* between humans and ghosts, but commentators on the *Abhidharma* do not give them their own *gati*. Some of these also consider that they are able to intermarry with both gods and ghosts. They inhabit the caverns of Mount Meru below sea-level, in four great towns. From there they go out to attack the 'Thirty-three gods' of Mount Meru. This has given rise to the mistaken notion that they dwell at the fourth stage of Meru. There are other assorted beings, genii, vampires (*rākṣasas*), serpents (*nāgas*), divine birds (*garuḍas*), and divine musicians (*gandharvas*), found in various realms, particularly that of the Four Great Kings, but their role seems to be ancillary.

Buddhist cosmography

The axial mountain is said to go up to the height of 84,000 *yojanas* (see pp. 240–1). A *yojana* has been said by some commentators to represent as much as nine miles, in which case the height of Meru would go beyond the stratosphere. Each face is of a different material; the eastern face is silver or crystal, the southern is sapphire or lapis lazuli, the western is ruby and the northern is golden. The sun and moon have their orbits round the peak.

The human realms overlap, of course, with the animal realms. In the exterior ocean facing the four sides of Mount Meru are the islands or continents, *dvīpas*, inhabited by different kinds of people. Thus in *Pūrvavideha*, in the east, people live to be 250 years old. To the south lies *Jambu-dvīpa*, Rose-apple land, the known world, which originally probably meant India, the land of the *buddhas*. Humans live no more than 100 years here at this point in the *kalpa* or aeon, and their faces are shaped like their continent. This is not the only correspondence between physiological and cosmic structures, and there seems to be a very ancient precedent for it. The Jains viewed the cosmos as a Great Person or Being, *mahā-puruṣa*, and later tantric practice drew correspondences between physiology and the cosmos. To the west is *Aparagodāna*, Western pasturage, where people live to be 500 years old. In the north lies *Uttarakuru*, Northern *Kuru*. There are no villages or towns here but people live for 2,000 years.

LEVEL TWO

This is the realm of form, *rūpa-dhātu*, rising in seventeen heavens, known collectively as the *brahma-loka*. These levels are also grouped into four stages of meditation, *dhyānas* (Pāli *jhānas*). Each level of consciousness is said to have a rebirth realm, or group of them, to which it corresponds, with attainment of a particular level of consciousness conducing to rebirth in the corresponding rebirth-level. Good or bad states of mind 'tune' the mind into the corresponding level of reality, such that it may be possible to become aware of the beings of that level, and then lead to rebirth at that 'waveband' of reality. In such a 'psycho-cosmology', maps of meditation-levels and rebirth-levels have many correspondences.

The compassionate god Great Brahmā in seen to live in the third level of the *brahma-loka*. At the top of the *brahma-loka*, at the seventeenth level, is the Akaniṣṭha heaven, the highest of the 'Pure Abodes'. These are only accessible to 'Non-returners': those who almost become *arahat*s while humans but then do so in one of these realms, so as never to 'return' to the realm of sense-desire.

LEVEL THREE

This is the realm of non-form, *ārūpya-dhātu*, rising as the four infinities. These are not places but non-material trance-states, described respectively as:

1 The realm of infinite space

2 The realm of infinite consciousness

3 The realm of nothingness

4 The realm of neither-perception-nor-non-perception

The orthodox sources do not consider this part of the receptacle-world, *bhājana-loka*, since the beings here are immaterial and therefore nowhere.

Cosmology of thousands

The triple-tiered world, *trai-lokya-dhātu*, of the *cakra-vāla* is possibly the most ancient Buddhist idea of our world, but even in the oldest scriptures there is an indication that the early Buddhists had a conception of a huge number of physical worlds, each developing over vast periods of time known as *kalpa*s, or eons. If not infinite, the number of worlds was huge beyond imagining. The early cosmologists had no scientific means of establishing a mathematical basis for their models; so their visions of the vastness of space could only be expressed in vast numbers; the same applies to numbers of world-systems.

Louis de la Vallée Poussin (1911, p. 137) places the multiplication of world-systems in three levels:

1 A system of a thousand worlds, a 'small chiliocosm'

2 A system of a million worlds, a thousand 'small chiliocosms'; this is the 'middle chiliocosm'

3 A system of a thousand million worlds, a 'great chiliocosm' or 'three-thousandth great-thousandth universe'

In the Mahāyāna, thought turned to the nature of the many world-systems briefly referred to in the earlier texts. It was felt that many world-systems are benighted in that they have not had a *buddha* and thus have never heard the *Dharma*. Nevertheless, in the vast universe, it was felt that *buddha*s are 'as numerous as the grains of sand on the banks of the river Ganges'. They are found in '*buddha* lands': realms where one or more *buddha* has lived through the stages of bodhisattvahood and finally reached enlightenment. Some *buddha* lands, such as our own world, are 'impure' in that they are ordinary worlds containing both good and bad rebirths. Some are paradise-like Pure Lands, truly wonderful places conjured into existence by their presiding *buddha* as ideal realms in which the *Dharma* is constantly heard. Descriptions of these realms were developed and devotion came to be focused on their *buddha*s, especially Amitābha, seen to preside over the 'Happy Land' (*Sukhāvatī*) in the 'western' part of the universe.

Cosmology of innumerables

The *Mahāvastu*, a Mahāyāna-influenced text of a pre-Mahāyāna school, and *sūtra*s of the Mahāyāna treat the *buddha* lands or *buddha* fields as innumerable (*asaṃkhyeya*). The *Mahāvastu* (I, 55) says it requires a hundred thousand *kalpa*s to win enlightenment, and later (I, 59) says that for immeasurable incalculable *kalpa*s and under a countless number of *tathāgata*s, *arahat*s, and perfect *buddha*s, those who seek perfect enlightenment in the future go on acquiring the roots of virtue.

The Mahāyāna also came to see the life-span of a heavenly *buddha* as truly huge. In chapter 16 of the *Lotus Sūtra*, Śākyamuni, the *buddha* of our world, says:

> If these world-spheres, whether an atom was deposited in them or not, were all reduced to atoms, and if each atom were a kalpa, the time since my achievement of Buddhahood would exceed even this. For a hundred thousand myriads of millions of nayutas of asaṁkhyeyakalpas I have been constantly dwelling on this Sahā world-sphere, preaching the Dharma, teaching and converting; also elsewhere, in a hundred thousand myriads of millions of nayutas of asaṁkhyeyas of realms [I have been] guiding and benefiting the beings. (Hurvitz, 1976, p. 238)

Indeed,

> At that time, Śākyamunibuddha's emanations in the eastern quarter, Buddhas of lands equal in number to the sands of a hundred thousand myriads of millions of Ganges rivers, each Buddha preaching Dharma, assembled in this place, Buddhas of ten directions all gathering in order and sitting in the eight quarters. (Hurvitz, 1976, p. 187)

The *Avataṃsaka Sūtra* (see pp. 42–3; Cleary, 1984, p. 189) develops the Mahāyāna cosmic vision into one which sees the universe as a vast network of interpenetrating worlds:

> In each atom of the lands of the cosmos
> Rest the vast oceans of worlds;
> Clouds of Buddhas equally cover them all,
> Filling every place.
>
> In each atom are many oceans of worlds,
> Their locations each different, all beautifully pure;
> Thus does infinity enter into one,
> Yet each unit's distinct, with no overlap.
>
> Within each atom are inconceivably many Buddhas
> Appearing everywhere in accord with beings' minds,
> Reaching everywhere in all oceans of worlds:
> This technique of theirs is the same for all.
>
> In each atom the Buddhas of all times
> Appear, according to inclinations;
> While their essential nature neither comes nor goes,
> By their vow power they pervade the worlds.

The shared Buddhist pantheon

In Buddhist cosmological theory, the gods of the *brahma-loka* are simply part of the world of beings, *sattva-loka*, and inhabit the receptacle-world, *bhājana-loka*.

It should be understood that the gods (Brahmā, Indra and other gods of the Hindu pantheon among them) play no part in Buddhist soteriology. They cannot save or bestow grace; nor are they immortal: they may live immensely long and blissful lives from the human perspective, but they are still subject to the general impermanence of conditioned things. The human realm is the only one in which the key work for liberation, *nirvāṇa*, may be done, because only in the human condition can the First Noble Truth be fully comprehended. The gods may play a supporting role in the drama of Buddhist eschatology. For example, after he had achieved liberation under the *bodhi*-tree, the Buddha was uncertain whether other people would understand if he tried to teach them from his new-found profound insights. The god Brahmā Sahampati appeared before him and aroused the Buddha's compassion by means of argument:

> Then Brahmā Sahampati, having arranged his upper robe over one shoulder, having stooped his right knee to the ground, having saluted the Lord with joined palms, spoke thus to the Lord: 'Lord, let the Lord teach *dhamma*, let the Well-farer teach *dhamma*; there are beings with little dust in their eyes who, not hearing *dhamma*, are decaying, (but if) they are learners of *dhamma*, they will grow.' (Horner, 1951, pp. 7–8)

Note that even before the establishment of the *saṅgha*, the *Vinaya*'s account makes Brahmā Sahampati conduct himself before the Buddha in every way like a monk. After the Buddha granted his request, he bowed down before him and passed him, respectfully keeping his right shoulder towards him.

Though Buddhism has no creator-God theory in the way the monotheistic religions have, there is a place for the pan-Indian gods in the world-system, even in ancient Buddhism. Naturally, as Buddhism moved into other lands, other gods beside the Indian ones entered the scene and complicated the cosmological picture.

The Mahāyāna pantheon

In addition to the accommodation of elements of popular religion within the Buddhist household, there was in the Mahāyāna a theoretical elaboration of the nature of buddhahood itself. These metaphysical speculations started with abstract enumerations of the aspects of buddhahood, but eventually the abstract forms were given iconographic representation into what are frequently called the Celestial or Heavenly *buddha*s and *bodhisattva*s. These figures are the iconographic representations of both the goal and the path. The goal is the state of full *nirvāṇa*, represented by fully awakened beings (*buddha*s) in the state of *samādhi*, while the dynamic state of the path is represented by the highly realized compassionate beings bound for enlightenment (advanced *bodhisattva*s).

L. A. Waddell (1895) gives what he calls a 'rough general descriptive list' of what is probably the largest pantheon in the world. The following arrangement has been adapted from the one given in his *Tibetan Buddhism* (1972, p. 327):

1 *Buddha*s – Celestial and human

2 *Bodhisattva*s – Celestial and human, including Indian saints and apotheosized Lamas

3 Tutelaries – mostly 'demoniacal' (in appearance, at least)

4 Defenders of the Faith

5 *Ḍākinī*s – female tutelary spirits

6 Indian Brahmanical gods

7 Country gods (*yul-lha*) and guardians (*srung-ma*) and local gods

8 Personal gods, household gods and familiars

This pantheon developed gradually through the Mahāyāna and Vajrayāna periods. Its first additions are key heavenly *buddha*s and *bodhisattva*s. Amitābha *buddha* (see pp. 112–13) is referred to for the first time in the *Sukhāvatī-vyūha Sūtra*, translated into Chinese between 147 and 186 CE. He later became very popular in China and Japan.

The Japanese commentator Genshin summarizes the conditions for rapid progress to buddhahood in Amitābha's Pure Land as follows:

1 Power of Amida (Amitābha) Buddha's vows to those born in his Land.

2 Constant *buddha*-light encouraging the enlightened mind.

3 Sounds of the Land's birds, leaves, bells, etc., inducing them to reflect on the Three Jewels.

4 Constant companionship of *bodhisattva*s.

5 Long Life. (Kloetzli, 1983, p. 126)

The *Lotus Sūtra* is one of the earliest sources for the cult of Avalokiteśvara, the *bodhisattva* of compassion. In all it mentions 23 celestial *buddha*s and *bodhisattva*s. Other Mahāyāna *sūtra*s mention more.

The earliest *bodhisattva* to attain cult status was no doubt Maitreya (Pāli Metteyya), the Buddha-to-come, who appears in the Pāli Canon. His name is cognate with the word *mitra*, meaning 'friend'; so he is the friendly or benevolent one. Early on, Buddhism may have come under the influence of Zoroastrianism. By the beginning of the Christian era the cult of a Buddhist 'Messiah' was widespread. Kitagawa (in Sponberg and Hardacre, 1988, p. 19) reflects some of the complexities of the meaning of Maitreya:

> In what manner does the study of Maitreya illuminate our understanding of the nature of the Buddha and bodhisattvas? Are they saviours, 'docetic' phenomena, hypostasisations of Dharmic principles? Are we to understand that 'heavenly' bodhisattvas are personalisations of the Buddha's qualities (e.g., compassion and wisdom)? Quite apart from their 'historicity', what is their 'ontological' status? Are we to assume that they have been preordained in the cosmological scheme? Or do they come into being by means of the devotee's 'visualisation' or the adept's magical powers? ... Assuming that Maitreya is an eschatological figure, how crucial is eschatology to Buddhist soteriology? ... What is the relationship between the figure of Maitreya and millenarianism? Does the 'prophecy' about Maitreya have millenarian connotations? Or did millenarian movements 'discover' Maitreya as an appropriate symbol?

Mañjuśrī, whose name means 'Gentle Glory' or 'Sweet Splendour', is called Kumārabhūta or 'Ever Young Prince Royal'. He is a kind of male Athene. He is also known as Mañjughoṣa, 'Sweet Voiced'. In China the Godai-Mountain, Wu-t'ai-shan, was his holy place known about in India in the seventh century CE. In his autobiography *The Wheel of Life* (1972, pp. 114–55), John Blofeld describes his own pilgrimage to Wu-t'ai-shan, where he witnessed the 'manifestation' of the *bodhisattva* in a display of meteorites. Mañjuśrī has pre-eminence in *sūtra*s such as the *Lotus* and the *Vimalakīrti-nirdeśa* (see pp. 43–4). In the latter, at the request of the Buddha and followed by 8,000 *bodhisattva*s, 500 disciples, many hundreds of thousands of gods and goddesses, he ventures to the house of the redoubtable Vimalakīrti to preach the *Dharma*. When Vimalakīrti gets to know who is coming, he magically transforms his house to emptiness! Mañjuśrī, as the *bodhisattva* of Wisdom, turns this into a teaching on the emptiness of all phenomena.

By the third century CE, Avalokiteśvara had become the predominant *bodhisattva* (see p. 114). He is the chief attendant of Buddha Amitābha in the Western Paradise, according to the *Sukhāvatī-vyūha Sūtra*. Many believe he can nullify *karma* and that he visits all suffering beings in all the realms. (Sometimes it is Kṣitigarbha who is depicted in all the *gati*s painted on the Wheel of Life. In the Far East he has the power to save beings during the period leading up to the coming of Maitreya, and in China he has become associated with rituals for transferring 'merit' for the welfare of ancestors.) 'Avalokiteśvara' may mean 'the Lord who looks down' (from the mountains where he lives, like the Hindu god Śiva), or 'the Lord who is seen from on high' (by Amitābha, who is often depicted above his head). He is traditionally associated with Potalaka in southern India, and it was for this reason that the palace built on the Red Mountain in Lhasa was named the Potala when Avalokiteśvara was seen to have incarnated as the Dalai Lamas of Tibet.

In China, Avalokiteśvara was represented as Kuan-yin or 'Sound Regarder'. She usually appears as a woman or as an androgynous youth. This may have something to do with the Indian ideal of manly beauty as a sixteen-year-old youth, but it is perhaps not without significance that the female *bodhisattva*, Tārā, is said to have revealed herself as an emanation of the male Avalokiteśvara by being born from the tears he wept at seeing the plight of suffering beings. Tārā herself is depicted in the lotus position but with one leg unfolded ready to step down into the world to give succour.

As Thurman (1987) sums up:

> ... the bodhisattva *par excellence* [is] the bodhisattva Ārya Avalokiteś-

vara, one of whose incarnations is among us today, His Holiness the Dalai Lama of Tibet. Just as it is a hopeless task to try to comprehensively discuss all the bodhisattvas, so is it a hopeless task to try to talk about all the manifestations and visions and magnificent activities of this bodhisattva. In some sense he is the prime example of a divine bodhisattva, a being who already got beyond Buddhahood and as a bodhisattva, is more Buddha than all the Buddhas. He is said to be the quintessence of the universal compassion of all the Buddhas. He appears in many scriptures and has at least one hundred and eight forms iconographically. He can appear as a female, in the form of Ārya Tārā, or as a female terrific such as Bhṛkuti or Śrī Devī, and he can appear in male terrific form, as Hayagrīva. His most famous forms are the two-armed thoughtful form who utters the *Heart Sūtra*, the quintessence of the *Transcendent Wisdom* teaching of selflessness and emptiness, the four-arm pacific form that dwells in his paradise in south India, Potalaka, and the thousand-armed form of the resurrected [see p. 139] Avalokiteśvara ... His Holiness the Dalai Lama is believed by Tibetan Buddhists to have a special connection with this form [the Thousand-Armed, Thousand-Eyed, Ten-Headed Lord of Great Compassion].

Reincarnating Lamas

In Tibetan, the term *sprul-sku* (pronounced *tulku*) means the 'transformation body', *nirmaṇa-kāya*, the third of the three bodies of the Buddha (see pp. 110–12). In this theory, Śākyamuni Buddha was the 'Transformation body' or manifestation of supreme buddhahood, *Dharma-kāya*. Buddhahood can have no representation of itself but can manifest in a human or celestial form, the 'Enjoyment body', *sambogha-kāya*;[1] for example, the five *jina*s (see below). The idea that a certain teacher could let his disciples know, in advance of his death, where he would be reborn probably began with the rNying-ma school. Their teacher, Padmasaṃbhava, prophesied that he or his disciples would return to earth to reveal scriptures that he had hidden (*gter-ma*s). The returning master was not part of a series, however. The institution of an unbroken lineage of reincarnated beings who hold some office goes back to the *Kar-ma-pa* Lama Dus-gsum-mkhyen-pa (1110–93), and in the sixteenth century the third Dalai Lama was given his title ('Great Ocean') by Altan Khan, and conferred it retrospectively on his two predecessors. They were regarded as a series of incarnations of the celestial *bodhisattva*

Avalokiteśvara, who had already appeared in incarnate form as the king Songtsen Gampo. The Pan-chen Lama was instituted soon after the Dalai Lama, but in this case he is seen as the incarnation of the celestial Buddha Amitābha. As an incarnate *buddha*, it may seem surprising that he does not rank above the Dalai Lama, but this is explained by the dynamic relation between the Buddha in *samādhi* (deep meditation) and his dynamic reflex, the *bodhisattva* Avalokiteśvara.

The five *jina*s of Vajrayāna Buddhism

The *maṇḍala* of the five *buddha*s (sometimes inaccurately referred to as *Dhyāni-buddha*s, but more accurately the five *tathāgata*s, or five *jina*s, 'conquerors' of mental defilement) first appears in the *Guhyasamāja-tantra*. The *buddha*s found in early Mahāyāna *sūtra*s have two more added to their number. Some authorities give an early date to the *Guhyasamāja-tantra*, about the fourth century CE, but its contents were seen as kept secret until the mid-seventh century. In the *maṇḍala*, the *buddha*s are positioned at the cardinal points and the centre of the cosmos. In tantric understanding, each of them has never been anything other than a *buddha* and has never passed through the *bodhisattva* stages.

Their colouring follows solar symbolism. Akṣobhya, dark blue, suggests the deep blue of the Indian dawn sky, Ratnasaṃbhava, yellow for the sun at noon in the south, Amitābha, red for the setting sun in the west, Amoghasiddhi, green for the Northern Lights at midnight in the north. Vairocana at the centre is white; his title is an epithet of the sun, 'Resplendent'. Sometimes the position and attributes of Vairocana and Akṣobhya are interchanged. Apart from certain features which distinguish the five *buddha*s, they are always depicted in a state of perfect meditation; all creative acts in the world are performed by one of their reflexes, the *bodhisattva*s who belong to their families. B. Bhattacharyya (1980, p. 129) supposes that the five *mudrā*s or ritual gestures ascribed to Śākyamuni Buddha and frequently represented in Buddhist iconography may have given rise to the concept of them. The tantric tradition sees them as related to the five *skandha*s (Pāli *khandha*s), or personality factors (see p. 77), and as also having correspondences with other sets of five. In one notable case, the ancient Buddhist triadic formula, body, speech and mind, has been incremented by two more: 'qualities' and 'action'. In

Tibetan Buddhism this allows for up to five incarnations of a *bodhisattva* or holy *lama* to be alive at the same time, e.g., one for the 'mind', one for the 'speech' incarnation, and so on.

The patterning into groups of five fits with a number of groups of five, for example: Śākyamuni with his three predecessors (see below) plus Maitreya, the Buddha-to-come; the five elements; five *skandha*s; the five cardinal points or regions; five senses (though in Buddhism there are six – mind counts as a sense). Each *buddha* has his consort and heads a family of *bodhisattva*s and deities. In iconography the five *jina*s first appeared as ascetics, wearing monks' robes, with or without begging bowls. Later they have adorned bodies, holding the same postures but clothed in silks and jewels and wearing crowns. In the glorified form they hint at a representation of the *Dharma-kāya*, though, strictly, it is beyond representation.

Vairocana is in the centre, coloured white. A transition from Śākyamuni to Vairocana seems to take place in the early Mahāyāna *sūtra*s; in the *Lotus Sūtra* the Buddha appears as the shining lord at the centre of existence, quite unlike the historical ascetic figure. Later *sūtra*s refer to him as Vairocana. He is shown with his hands in the same preaching *mudrā*, or sometimes turning the Wheel of the *Dharma*. Perhaps the earliest text where Vairocana appears is the *Sarva-tathāgata-tattva-saṃgraha*, which teaches the unity of all the *buddha*s.

Akṣobhya in the east is coloured blue, which represents space but is also the colour associated with wrathful aspects of *bodhisattva*s. The earliest non-historical *buddha* seems to have been Akṣobhya, or 'Imperturbable', who appears in the *Vimalakīrti-nirdeśa*. He also appears in the *Small Perfection of Wisdom Sūtra*. He holds a diamond in his left hand and makes the earth-witnessing *mudrā* with his right, reaching down to touch the earth. The *maṇḍala* is always entered from the east, where Akṣobhya at dawn sits touching the earth in witness, in the same way that Śākyamuni did at his defeat of Māra, the Evil One (see p. 120).

Transcendent though the five *jina*s are, they show a connection with the immanence of the historical Buddha. Hence there is an association with the elements – earth, water, fire, air, space – and each *buddha* has a series of associated symbols, gestures, psychological states and so on. For example, Akṣobhya is seated on an elephant throne, his family is the diamond-hard *vajra*, his seed syllable is HŪṂ. He has a female counterpart, Dhātvīśvarī, the

Table 9.2 The correspondences of the five *buddha* families

Buddha	**Vairocana**	**Akṣobhya**	**Ratnasaṃbhava**	**Amitābha**	**Amoghasiddhi**
Family	Buddha	diamond-hard sceptre	jewel	lotus	action
Position	centre	east	south	west	north
Colour	white	blue	yellow	red	green
Element	earth/ solidity	sky/ spaciousness	water/ fluidity	fire/ heat	air/ motion
Gesture (*mudrā*)	teaching	earth-witness	bestowing	meditation	fearlessness
Emblem	wheel	diamond-hard sceptre	jewel	lotus	crossed *vajra*-sceptres
Throne	lion	elephant	horse	peacock	shangshang bird
Ḍākinī	Locanā	Dhātvīśvarī	Māmakī	Pāṇḍarā	Samayatārā
Mode	body	mind	qualities	speech	action
Skandha	*rūpa* (form)	*vijñāna* (consciousness)	*vedanā* (feeling)	*saṃjñā* (perception)	*saṃskāras* (volitions)
Organ	eye	ear	nose	mouth	skin
Sense	vision	hearing	smell	taste	touch
Bodhisattva	Samantabhadra	Vajrapāṇi	Ratnapāṇi	Padmapāṇi	Viśvapāṇi
Earthly *buddha*	Krakucandra	Karnakamuni	Kāśyapa	Śākyamuni	Maitreya
Poison	sloth	anger	pride	lust	envy

Buddha	Vairocana	Akṣobhya	Ratnasaṃbhava	Amitābha	Amoghasiddhi
Neurosis	spaced-out, dull	conceptualizing	greedy, domineering	seducing	paranoid, busy
Wisdom	wisdom of all-encompassing space	mirror-like wisdom	all-enriching wisdom	wisdom of discriminating awareness	all-accomplishing wisdom
Seed syllable	OṂ	HŪṂ	TRĀṂ	HRĪ	A
Some associated deities	Mārīcī Vajravārāhī	Heruka Yamāri Ekajaṭā Nairātmā	Jambhala Vasudhāra	Avalokiteśvara Tārā Sudhanakumāra Bhṛkuṭī Hayagrīva Kurukullā	Khadiravaṇītārā Parṇaśavarī

(Adapted from K. Dowman (1984), *Sky Dancer: The Secret Life and Songs of the Lady Yeshe Tsogyel*. London: Routledge and Kegan Paul, p. 193)

'Elemental Lady'. Like the other *buddhas*, he is associated with one of the five *skandhas*, in his case *vijñāna*, consciousness; his mode is mind, his sense-organ, ear. The poison which is transformed by his divine alchemy is anger. The personality-type of this family is prone to intellectualism and must transform its over-critical conceptualizing to mirror-like wisdom. Each family has this range of symbolic and psycho-physical characteristics.

Ratnasaṃbhava, in the south, is yellow, and holds the gift-bestowing posture, right hand with open palm held out. His family is not large and he is never regarded as the *Ādi-buddha* (see below).

Amitābha, whose name means 'Unlimited Light', sits in the west, coloured red and holding a lotus on his hands held in the meditation gesture, palms upwards, placed one on the other on his lap. By repeating Amitābha Buddha's name, the devotee will be reborn in his Pure Land (see below) where there are no evil destinies and everyone is assured of only one more rebirth unless they have made the *bodhisattva* vow to remain until all sentient beings enter *nirvāṇa*. He is also seen as Amitāyus or 'Unlimited Life', the Buddha of Long Life.

Amoghasiddhi, in the north, displays the 'Fear not!' gesture, the flat palm of the right hand raised to the shoulder and facing forward.

Later a sixth *jina*, Vajrasattva, was introduced. He embodies the five *skandhas* collectively, and is depicted holding the *vajra*-sceptre and bell, one in each hand.

In the early tenth century, in the university of Nālandā, Buddhism came close to Hindu monism, not to say monotheism, with the development of the notion of a primordial *buddha* behind the five celestial *buddhas*. The *Ādi-buddha* was represented in human form by Vajradhāra, coloured blue, the complexion of space, sometimes with a consort. In his right hand he holds the *vajra*, the diamond-hard sceptre, and in his left he holds the ritual bell, with arms crossed on his chest, or, if he is with his consort, Prajñāpāramitā, Perfection of Wisdom, his arms enfold her. Other tantrists thought one of the *jinas* was the *Ādi-buddha*; some even considered that one of the celestial *bodhisattvas*, Vajrasattva, Samantabhadra or Vajrapāṇi, was the *Ādi-buddha*.

The empty nature of tantric deities

It is, no doubt, the over-arching idea in the Buddhist *tantra*s that all the deities of the pantheon are 'manifestations' of emptiness, *śūnyatā*, that allows Buddhism to deal with them. In so far as they are nothing but manifestations of *śūnyatā*, they lack ultimate existence. Advaya-vajra, a commentator who lived between 978 and 1030 CE, explains that awareness of the deities evolves through four stages: the right perception of *śūnyatā*, the utterance of the associated germ-syllable *bīja*, visualization of the icon, and the external representation. Bhattacharyya (1980, p. 110) observes:

> This statement gives a direct lie to the theory that later Buddhism was nothing but gross idolatry. It shows, on the other hand, that their conception of godhead was philosophically most profound, a parallel to which is scarcely to be found in any other Indian religion.

Like all other beings in the receptacle-world, the deities of tantric Buddhism (often referred to as the Vajrayāna or adamantine vehicle), have been given a place to reside in. This is generally thought to be at the very top of the *rūpa-dhātu* in the Akaniṣṭha heaven. However, *bodhisattva*s are never reborn here because beings never return to earth from this heaven. This is where, in the Mahāyāna, a *bodhisattva* finally becomes a *buddha*. Kamalaśīla, however, states (Bhattacharyya, 1980, p. 99) that it is beyond the Akaniṣṭha heaven, the Maheśvara abode, where the chain of consciousness of the compassionate *bodhisattva* attains omniscient Buddhahood; this is not the quiescent *nirvāṇa* of *arahat*s and *pratyekabuddha*s (Solitary Realizers). The oldest *tantra*, the *Guhyasamāja*, says that emptiness and compassion together make *bodhicitta*, the enlightenment-aspiration of the *bodhisattva* who renounces personal *nirvāṇa* in order to work for the well-being of all beings. The deities themselves are manifested from emptiness with the three constituents: emptiness, consciousness and great bliss.

The psycho-cosmic image of the human being

In the very ancient Jain cosmology, the shape of the universe looks like the rough outline of the human form. It stretches back to an idea found in the Brahmanical *Ṛg-veda* that the universe was formed from the body of the cosmic *mahā-puruṣa*, the 'Great Person'. A similar idea is found in the ancient Norse *Edda*s, where the world is made of the dismembered parts of a giant's body. In a different sense the Buddha was also known as a '*mahā-puruṣa*', so that he bore the 32 major bodily marks and 80 minor ones (see below). In Mahāyāna doctrine the development of the Three Bodies of the Buddha, *trikāya* (see pp. 110–12), with its efflorescence into the pantheon of celestial *buddha*s undoubtedly taps into the idea of the Cosmic Being of pre-Buddhist times. The *tantra*s also depend on the association between the physical body of the *yogin* and the cosmos. The spinal column is compared to Mount Meru, the axis of our world, and the whole physical organism is explained in terms of solar and lunar forces. Running through the body is the median nerve, Suṣumṇā-*nāḍī*, with two *nāḍī*s, channels, coiling about it in opposite directions. The most important, Lama Govinda (1976, p. 87) says, are:

> The pale white-coloured Iḍā starting from the left, and the red-coloured Piṅgala from the right. Iḍā is the conductor of lunar or 'moon-like' (*candra-svarūpa*) forces which have the regenerative properties and the unity of undifferentiated subconscious life as represented by the latent creativeness of seed, eggs and semen, in which all chthonic telluric cults are centred. Piṅgala is the vehicle of solar forces (*sūrya-svarūpa*, 'sun-like') which have the properties of intellectual activity, representing the conscious, differentiated, individualised life.

Along the median there are the *cakra*s, at various points, radiating centres of psychic force. The important ones are located at the perineum, navel, heart, throat and crown. The *cakra* is a solar symbol, identified with the cosmic sacrifice of the Veda. When the sun rises it does so as the universe, as the Cosmic Being (*Praśna Upaniṣad*, 1.6–8). The sun moves in his orbit in a one-wheeled car (*Mahābhārata*, 12.362.1). This is similar to the wheel of the *cakravartin*, a type of universal compassionate emperor who shares the 32 marks with a *buddha* and is the secular parallel to one.

The Buddha

While the Mahāyāna came to see the historical Buddha, Gautama, in what might be called a divinized way, it would be wrong to characterize the Theravāda as seeing him as 'simply a man' – this is the view only of a minority of modernist Theravādins (see p. 101). All traditional schools agree in seeing Gautama as the product of a *bodhisattva* training lasting many lifetimes, and as being one in a glorious line of earthly *buddhas* who appear periodically over the ages. In the Pāli Canon, the earliest listing refers to six previous *buddhas* (Walshe, 1987, pp. 199–221), while that of the *Buddha-vaṃsa* (Horner, 1975) refers to 27, seeing the fourth of these, Dīpaṅkara, as he under whom Gautama, as the ascetic Sumedha, made the vow to work as a *bodhisattva* to become a *buddha*.

The Pāli *Jātaka* collection is a set of 550 tales of former lives of the Buddha (see pp. 49–50). Each tale has a quasi-historical introduction by which the tale is yoked with some particular incident in the Buddha's life. The *Jātakas* are clearly a literary attempt to consolidate the notion of the *bodhisattva*-career. Against the context of the Indian notion of recurring cycles of history, the career of the *bodhisattva* takes a linear progression, from the vow before Dīpaṅkara to Gautama Buddha's enlightenment in the present world-age. This is one of two elements that apparently contradict the 'meaninglessness' of history. Legend also has it that Dīpaṅkara prophesied the future buddhahood of Sumedha; to this day, tantric *gurus* prophesy the buddhahood of those who take the *bodhisattva* vows before them, thereby introducing an eschatology into otherwise endless transmigrational cycles.

The traditional Theravāda view sees Gautama as having been born in his last life an extraordinary human but, once enlightened, to have transcended his human psychological limitations and developed a range of supernormal knowledges and powers, including five kinds of vision:

1 Improved human vision, so that he can see a league all round, day or night.

2 With the divine eye he can see beings dying and being reborn according to their *karma* and see many thousands of world-systems.

3 With his wisdom-eye he produces the unproduced path and attains omniscience of past, present and future events.[2]

4 With his Buddha-eye he sees the degrees of purity of all beings and knows what is needed for their liberation.

5 With his all-seeing eye there remains nothing unseen by him.

The 32 marks (*lakṣaṇas*) of a great man are delineated in the *Lakkhaṇa Sutta* of the Pāli Canon (Walshe, 1987, pp. 441–60), in the form of marks on the physical and/or psychic body that a being destined to become either a *buddha* or a *cakravartin* is born with (see p. 119), each mark being seen as the karmic product of past good deeds and a portent of good things to come. They are: (1) feet that can move evenly and be well-planted on the ground; (2) 1,000-spoked wheels on soles and palms; (3) projecting heels; (4) long fingers and toes; (5) soft hands and feet; (6) net-like hands and feet; (7) ankles like conch-shells; (8) nimble lower leg, like an antelope's; (9) ability to touch knees without bending; (10) genitals covered by a bag; (11) skin shining like gold; (12) subtle skin, to which nothing sticks; (13) one hair to each pore; (14) black body-hairs that curl in rings clockwise (the direction that the sun moves in the sky); (15) very straight frame like that of Brahmā; (16) 'outflowing places' on soles, palms, shoulders, and top of the back; (17) upper part of his body like that of a lion; (18) filled hollow between the shoulders; (19) height equal to his outstretched arms; (20) smoothly rounded shoulders; (21) beautiful taste welling up from his neck; (22) lion-like jaw; (23) 40 teeth; (24) level teeth; (25) undivided teeth; (26) very white teeth; (27) a mighty tongue; (28) a voice like Brahmā's and soft as a songbird's; (29) very blue eyes; (30) long eyelashes; (31) a filament of white hair between his eyebrows; (32) a head shaped like a royal turban. Such marks have been used as the focus of meditations to visualize a *buddha* and to explore what his spiritual body 'feels' like from the inside and hence perhaps to awaken spiritual qualities associated with each of the 'marks'.

THE TWELVE ACTS OF THE BUDDHA

Traditionally the life of the Buddha is arranged in twelve significant stages:

1 The resolve to be born.

2 The *bodhisattva* descends from *Tuṣita* heaven.

3 He enters his mother's womb.

4 The birth.

5 Accomplishments.

6 The life of pleasure.

7 The great renunciation.

8 Ascetic practices.

9 The conquest of Māra.

10 The enlightenment, i.e. attainment of both *nirvāṇa* and buddhahood.

11 The teaching ministry.

12 He passes into final *nirvāṇa*.

A mythic dimension is given even to events that we may consider historical, such as the birth, or the renunciation. At a number of them, the earth is said to shake, and news of them is spread through the divine realms. The Buddha's mother, Māyā, gave birth in a standing position, and the infant *bodhisattva* emerged from her right side. Perhaps a standing position for giving birth was a custom of the time. More remarkable is the account that the child did not emerge through the birth canal in the usual way, but from the right side. Was this a miraculous event or was the birth by some form of caesarean section? Whatever the case, Māyā died seven days later.

THE SEVEN STEPS OF THE BUDDHA

The birth narratives say that the moment the *bodhisattva* was born he placed both feet on the ground, faced the north and took seven strides, shaded by a white parasol, and scanned the four directions. Then with a voice like a bull he said: 'I am the top of the world, I am the oldest in the world; this is my last birth; I will not be reborn.' Mircea Eliade (1960, pp. 110–15) speculatively examines this mythic theme for its possible cosmological structure and metaphysical significance. The seven steps bring the Buddha (to be) to the summit of the cosmic system, passing through seven stages corresponding to the seven planetary heavens. The significance of the cosmic North is that from there the supernal lands of the Buddha are reached. The myth of the Seven Steps expresses the new-born Buddha's transcendence of the cosmos and abolition of space and time (he becomes 'highest' and 'oldest'). Further, Eliade identifies the ascension of the Buddha through cosmic stages as analogous to a recurring myth-pattern: the universe is conceived as having seven stages with the summit located in the cosmic North, or the Pole Star, or in the Empyrean. The act of transcending takes place near a 'Centre', which may be a temple, a royal city, a sacred tree, homologized with the Cosmic Tree, or the Vedic sacrificial stake (T. S. Eliot's 'axle-tree'). The cosmos was created from the summit down, so when the Buddha declared 'I am the top of the world, I am the oldest', he was returning to a transcendent state 'before the foundations of the world were laid'. Thus Eliade's interpretation, at least.

L. A. Waddell (1972, p. 346) thought of the development of the celestial *buddha*s in terms of the connection between Amitābha and Zoroastrian sun worship, but it was H. Kern who was the leading exponent of the theory that the Buddha was himself a solar myth. No one today would accept this as a viable explanation. But there is no doubt that some elements of pre-Buddhist mythology have been incorporated into historical material.

Māra: the Evil One

When one surveys the principal distinctions between the Western Judaic and the Buddhist views of history and the *mythos* associated with them, one is struck by an extraordinary parallel between them: the way that they bracket off evil. Where Hinduism allows the paradox of the evil God, the monotheistic religions make Satan the focus of evil, in dynamic opposition to God, though not equal to him in power. It is remarkable that Buddhism has personified evil as Māra the Tempter, Lord of the World (see pp. 84–5). Though Buddhism has generally been able to incorporate pre-Buddhist demonology into the general pantheon inherited from the Indian cultural milieu, the establishment of Māra, as antithetical to the religious ideal, represents a distinct departure in Indian religion.

For Buddhism, evil arises from primordial ignorance, thereby giving rise to notions of a permanent self and the three poisons of existence (greed, hatred and delusion); so there would hardly seem a place for an evil agent. Nevertheless, as Trevor Ling (1962, p. 91) points out,

> Both Māra and Satan represent a force which proves resistant to man's search for holiness. The opposing force is conceived as being so potent and so hard to overcome by man, so universally active and so malign, that it is endowed with a will and personality.

Māra is referred to in many places throughout the Pāli Canon.[3] There may be an etymological association between the name Māra and the figure *Pāpmā Mrtyuḥ* (Death the Evil One) found in the *Upaniṣads* (Ling, 1962, p. 56), thereby making an appropriate connection with the First Noble Truth of Suffering. Just as suffering (*duḥkha*) is the condition of all samsaric existence, so the sphere of Māra's activity extends to every level of the cosmos except *nirvāṇa*. Māra is, in fact, everything that is not enlightened, such as the five *skandha*s of personality (see p. 77):

> Corporality is Māra: with regard to this Māra you should overcome your longing. Feeling is Māra ... Perception is Māra ... Mental formations are Māra ... Consciousness is Māra ... with regard to this Māra you should overcome your longing. (*Saṃyutta Nikāya*, III.188–9 quoted in Ling, 1962, p. 58)

Maybe not everyone will agree with Ling's view (1962, p. 90) that 'Satan and Māra are *symbols* ... [whose principal function is] to facilitate a transition of viewpoint for those accustomed to thinking in demonic terms, rather than to embody absolute truth'. However, in Buddhism the whole of the Triple World and all it contains, including the Buddha's teachings, have only a provisional truth compared with the absolute truth of *nirvāṇa*. For Buddhists of whatever school, the absolute can be reached only through the provisional; so the pantheon of one's own school is as provisionally real as everything else.

Architecture symbolism: *stūpa*, pagoda or *chorten*

Throughout the Buddhist world, or wherever Buddhism had once been, there are to be seen distinctive monuments, known as *stūpa*s, pagodas or *chorten*s (see pp. 119, 121–2). Though the design varies from region to region, and the size ranges from something not much higher than a person to immense structures like the Great *Stūpa* of

Sāñcī which has a diameter of 120 feet and a height of 54 feet, they all broadly share the same symbolic structure.

Probably in origin they were pre-Buddhist monuments erected to great rulers. The Buddha stipulated that certain persons were worthy of a *stūpa* over their remains – enlightened ones, solitary enlightened ones, disciples of an enlightened one and *cakravartin*s, i.e., great and benevolent Universal Monarchs (*Mahā-parinibbāna Sutta*; Walshe, 1987, p. 264). In this same passage the Buddha instituted the cult of relics. This was a radical challenge to the general Brahmanical notion of the time that human remains were polluting and certainly were not to be worshipped in any way:

> A stūpa should be erected at the cross-roads for the Tathāgata. And whoever lays wreaths or puts sweet perfumes and colours there with a devout heart, will reap benefit and happiness for a long time.

As viewed from the side in its later developed form, a *stūpa* may be seen to have four, or five, parts:

1 A base which may also be stepped.

2 The mound proper, which has undergone stylization; this is called the *aṇḍa*, egg (sometimes called the *garbha*, womb) and in India it is usually a hemisphere; elsewhere it is bell-shaped, while in Tibet it looks like an upturned pot.

3 The *harmikā*, kiosk, a cube surmounting the *aṇḍa*.

4 The *htī*, spire.

5 The finial (usual in Tibet).

The *stūpa* is not simply a reminder of the dead hero but of one who has achieved or striven to achieve liberation from the cycles of life and death. As such it commemorates the transcendence of death. The earthly remains are powerful reminders of the Buddhist concept of the impermanence of all compounded things, but they have been transcended by the *tathāgata*, or Thus-gone.

The burial mound looks like the cosmic egg from which all things sprang in ancient Hindu cosmogony. That part of the *stūpa* is also known as the womb (*garbha*), perhaps indicating a connection with telluric-matriarchal ideas and ancient cults of the dead where mother Earth and mother Nature were held to be the same. Lama Govinda

(1976) argues that both lunar and solar cults are united in the structure of the *stūpa*. The base section is said to represent earth; on it is the bubble or egg of water. These are the two elements of the moon cult. As seen above, some scholars have tried to show that Buddhism represents a solar myth. Certainly, the celestial *buddha*s of the *maṇḍala*, stationed at the compass points in the colours of the dawn, noon-day, setting sun and northern lights, are reminiscent of solar deities. But the phases of the moon are very important in Buddhism – the monastic calendar is a lunar one – and if the older telluric-matriarchal cult seems to have been suppressed by the patriarchal structures of the early Buddhist *saṅgha*, it was challenged, perhaps not altogether successfully, by Mahā-Prajāpatī, the Buddha's aunt, when she and her companions sought ordination as nuns. The battle for women was won then but the victory has been eroded by time.

Above the *aṇḍa* is a cubic structure, *harmikā*, which actually contained the relics. Its similarity to a sacrificial altar has been observed, though the Buddhist sacrifice is only ever a self-sacrifice of the passions, never of animals. The symbolism of the Vedic cosmic sacrifice is not lost, however, as the axis of the *stūpa* dome is known as a *yūpa*, the term for a Vedic sacrificial post. The *harmikā* is surmounted by the spire, *htī*, which represents and sometimes looks like a ceremonial umbrella. This is a mark of royalty, the *cakravartin*, and consequently of the enlightened being. The umbrella in its turn represents the sacred tree, the tree under which the Buddha gained enlightenment, the *bodhi*-tree, below which is the place of enlightenment, the diamond seat, *vajrāsana*, the most sacred spot in the world. The spire also symbolizes Mount Meru, the axis of Indian cosmology. Lama Govinda (1976, p. 72) identifies the two upper sections of the *stūpa* with ancient solar cults: space as opposed to the lunar terrestrial, the solar year against the lunar cycle, patriarchy superimposed over matriarchy, culture, to which Lévi-Strauss says men belong, against nature, to which women belong. Plastic, mass-creating architecture, along with the greatest works of sculpture, is supposed to be found at the beginning of each civilization; as architecture develops the creation of space becomes primary.

The earliest Buddhist temples may have been cave-temples; later free-standing ones developed, particularly to house images. The first temple complex to be built in Tibet was at bSam-yas in the eighth century CE, constructed on a cosmic plan, a *maṇḍala*. Other examples of this kind of architecture are the famous Kumbum at Gyantse, built in 1440, Borobudur in Java (reckoned to have been built in the first quarter of the ninth century; it is basically a *stūpa* with elaborate terraces, covering five kilometres in all, making a *maṇḍala*), and Angkor Wat in Cambodia, built at the end of the twelfth century.

*Maṇḍala*s and *mudrā*s and their ritual use

Apart from representing the cosmos in the construction of temples and *stūpa*s, in Tibetan Buddhism the two-dimensional design of the *maṇḍala* in paint or coloured sand has become a well-observed feature of tantric ritual (see pp. 122–3). But the *maṇḍala* of the universe can be symbolized in further ways. One of these is by ritual gesture, *mudrā*, with the fingers of both hands held in a way to symbolize Meru and the Four Continents; the other is to use a ritual implement. The Tibetan *maṇḍala*-offering is, quite simply, the ritual offering of the Universe, with all its riches, to the Objects of Refuge, the Three Jewels, Buddha, *Dharma* and *Saṅgha*, as an act of veneration. The act is performed in three distinct modes, Outer, Inner and Secret, which represent ever deepening scholastic symbolism. The main consideration here is what is offered. It is a symbol in material and ritual terms, of the ancient Indian cosmos. The universe is 'constructed' using ritual implements: a metal base with three or four rings of metal, whose narrowing diameters allow them to fit inside each other, a top ornament and a heap of pure rice which has been stained yellow with saffron. Into the rice may be mixed jewels and precious coins. The metal of the *maṇḍala* instrument may be gold but it does not matter if it is just base metal; in the imagination it can be transmuted to the most precious of metals. Once built up, the *maṇḍala* of the cosmos is offered to all the *buddha*s and then allowed to collapse back into a heap of rice in the officiant's lap, signifying the ultimate emptiness of all conditioned things.

Shamanistic parallels

The contemplation of impermanence in the form of a meditation on a corpse in a cremation ground was a practice known to early Buddhists. Mircea Eliade (1960, p. 84), while recognizing that the contemplation of skulls and bones shows the 'vanity of vanity', reveals that contemplating one's own skeleton was a technique for 'going out of time' among the *shamans* of hunting and pastoral peoples, and Indo-Tibetan *yogins*. He says:

> For the former, its aim is to re-discover the ultimate source of animal life and thence to participate in Being; while, for the Indo-Tibetan monks, it is to contemplate the eternal cycles of existences ruled by *karma*; and hence to dispel the Great Illusion (*māyā*) of Cosmic Life, striving to transcend it by placing oneself in the unconditioned, symbolised by *nirvāṇa*.

On the theme of shamanistic elements in Buddhism, Eliade (1960, p. 90) points out that 'there is not a single one of these *siddhi* evoked by the Buddha that we do not meet with in the shamanic traditions; even the knowledge of previous lives, a specifically Indian "mystical exercise", has been reported among the shamans of North America'. *Siddhi* are paranormal powers, e.g., bilocation, flying, invisibility, that are the possible corollary to advanced mystical states.

By means of the technique of 'psychic heat' (Tibetan *gtum-mo*), the Tibetan *yogin*, sitting all night on a freezing Himalayan mountain-side, can cause a wet blanket to steam. Such practices of Yoga and Buddhism are identified by Eliade as 'continuations – although of course on another plane and directed to quite a different end – of the immemorial ideologies and techniques which endeavoured to change the condition of man by a change in his psychosomatic structures'.

Notes

1 Tadeusz Skorupski has pointed out to me the parallel between the notions of the 'enjoyment body' and the 'glorified body' of Jesus after the resurrection.

2 Though the Theravāda tends to see his knowledge of the future as well-based predictions of selected matters, not certain knowledge, implying the future is fixed. (Ed.)

3 For a detailed survey of the canonical coverage the reader should consult Ling's Appendix (1962, pp. 96–163).

Further reading

Batchelor, S. (1997) *Buddhism Without Beliefs*. London: Bloomsbury.

Bhattacharyya, B. (1980) *An Introduction to Buddhist Esoterism*. Delhi: Motilal Banarsidass.

Blofeld, J. (1972) *The Wheel of Life*. London: Rider.

Cleary, T. (1984) *The Flower Ornament Scripture*, vol. 1. Boston: Shambhala Publications.

de la Vallée Poussin, L. (1911) 'Cosmogony and cosmology (Buddhist)' in James Hastings (ed.) *Encyclopaedia of Religion and Ethics*, vol. 4. Edinburgh: T. & T. Clark, pp. 129–38.

Dowman, K. (1984) *Sky Dancer: The Secret Life and Songs of the Lady Yeshe Tsogyel*. London: Routledge and Kegan Paul.

Eliade, Mircea (1960) *Myths, Mysteries and Dreams*. London: Harvill Press.

Gethin, R. (1998) *The Foundations of Buddhism*. Oxford: Oxford University Press.

Lama Anagarika Govinda (1976) *Psycho-cosmic Symbolism of the Buddhist Stūpa*. Berkeley, CA: Dharma Publishing.

Horner, I. B. (1951) *The Book of the Discipline (Vinaya-piṭaka) Volume IV (Mahāvagga)*. London: Luzac & Co.

Horner, I. B. (1975) *Minor Anthologies of the Pali Canon Part III: Chronicle of Buddhas (Buddhavaṃsa) and Basket of Conduct (Cariyapiṭaka)*. London: Pali Text Society.

Hurvitz, L. (1976) *The Scripture of the Lotus Blossom of the Fine Dharma*. New York: Columbia University Press.

Kloetzli, W. R. (1983) *Buddhist Cosmology: From Single World System to Pure Land: Science and Theology in the Images of Motion and Light*. Delhi: Motilal Banarsidass.

Ling, T. O. (1962) *Buddhism and the Mythology of Evil*. London: Allen & Unwin; (1997) Oxford: One World.

Nishitani, Keiji, trans. Jan Van Bragt (1982) *Religion and Nothingness*. Berkeley, CA: University of California Press.

Schumann, H. W., trans. M. O'C. Walshe (1989) *The Historical Buddha*. London: Arkana.

Sponberg, Alan and Hardacre, Helen (eds) (1988) *Maitreya, the Future Buddha*. Cambridge: Cambridge University Press.

Swearer, D. K. (1989) *Me and Mine: Selected Essays of Buddhadāsa Bhikkhu*. Albany: State University Press of New York.

Thomas, E. J. (1975) *The Life of Buddha as Legend and History* (first pub. 1927). London: Routledge and Kegan Paul.

Thurman, R. (1987) 'The Buddhist Messiahs' in D. S. Lopez, Jr and S. C. Rockefeller (eds) *The Christ and the Bodhisattva*. Albany: State University of New York Press, pp. 65–97.

Waddell, L. A. (1972) *Tibetan Buddhism*. New York: Dover Publications. Unabridged replication of (1895) *The Buddhism of Tibet, or Lamaism*. London: W. H. Allen.

Walshe, M. (1987) *Thus Have I Heard: The Long Discourses of the Buddha*. London: Wisdom Publications.

Williams, P. (1989) *Mahāyāna Buddhism*. London: Routledge.

10. Sacred space

Martin Boord

Life, it is said, may be defined in terms of movement or growth. In India of the sixth/fifth century BCE, the era of the Buddha, spiritual growth was popularly precipitated by the act of *pravrajya*, 'going forth' from home in order to enter the religious life as a monk or wandering ascetic. The term is employed in Buddhist scriptures (e.g., *Dhammapada*, v. 388) in reference to one who has abandoned the mundane world in search of the transcendent, 'the deathless' state beyond the vicissitudes of a painful series of rebirths in *saṃsāra*, and among the earliest representations of the Buddha are those in which his presence is indicated merely by a pair of footprints. The sacred space occupied by his holy person, it was felt, could not be encompassed by any pictorial device, however sublime the symbol or skilled the artist, for the Buddha was called *Tathāgata*, 'He by whom the state of "thusness" has been reached' (see pp. 101–2).

To Buddhists of the early period, naturally, the site of supreme sacredness, towards which the home-renouncing wanderer should head forthwith, was that place where the Buddha himself was to be found. There the mendicant could expect a welcome with the words *Ehi bhikṣu*, 'Come, monk!' and thus find himself ordained within the Buddhist community.

Although the Buddha was surrounded throughout his teaching career by a large gathering of the fourfold assembly consisting of monks, nuns, laymen and laywomen, he at all times stressed the supremacy of the *Dharma* over the presence of his person. These two aspects came to be recognized as two 'bodies' (*kāya*) of the Buddha: the *Dharma-kāya* contained in his scriptural tradition to be honoured, recited and studied by the monastic community; and the *rūpa-kāya* or 'body of form' which merely served as the temporary vehicle for the transmission and explication of eternal verities inherent in the former. The superior body of the Buddha was the *Dharma-kāya* and any monk who perceived that was said to have seen the real Buddha. 'What good to you is this body of filth?', the Buddha is said to have asked. 'He who sees the *Dharma* sees me' (*Saṃyutta Nikāya*, III. 120). Indeed, his first 60 followers, each one of whom had gained supreme insight into the meaning of his teachings upon first hearing, were dismissed from the Buddha's presence and instructed to spread themselves out in all directions of the world in order to preach 'the good law' (*saddharma*) for the benefit of others. Sacredness was understood to be a quality of truth, a quality fundamental to the teachings, not a quality of time or place, teacher or retinue. Any pilgrimage undertaken by a wanderer in search of the Buddha in the outer world, therefore, could never be more than a prelude to the higher spiritual journey along the paths of meditation in search of the *buddha*-nature within.[1] The act of renouncing home and family at the outset of the spiritual quest was viewed as a means of generating 'merit' that would be helpful once the essential, inner, exploration had begun. Many aspects of the popular Hindu tradition of pilgrimage to sacred sites, as much in evidence at the time of the Buddha as it is today, were criticized by the Teacher, who perceived merely 'heedless pilgrims scattering widely the dust of their passions'.

To Buddhists of all periods, all places are potentially 'sacred' or, at least, to be treated with some respect. The sun, moon, planets and stars are each considered the homes of deities or spirits and this earth is abundant with them. Throughout the world there are to be found sacred rivers, lakes, rocks, mountains, trees and the rest, even the least of which are the abodes of life. Buddhists readily adopted the prevailing Indian notion of deities charged with the guardianship of the ten directions (the four cardinal and intermediate directions and above and below), and the Four Great Kings (see p. 261) who rule the north, south, east and west are said, even in the earliest texts, to have presented the Buddha with offerings. Indeed, the very earth itself is in some sense sacred. Personified as a golden goddess, it was she who witnessed the Buddha's defeat of Māra on the eve of his final enlightenment and each plot of earth, no matter how small, is considered to have its ruling *nāga* king with responsibility for the welfare of those who inhabit his domain, right down to the tiniest worm or insect. Monks have traditionally been forbidden to till the soil for fear of harming the creatures who dwell there and, should disturbing the earth prove unavoidable for the construction of a *vihāra*, for example, prayers should be offered for the sake of the ground's original inhabitants.

Later Buddhist architectural texts go into great detail concerning the appeasement or subjugation of the earth-dwelling *nāga* whose domain is required for human use. Marking out the desired plot of land in the form of a square aligned to the cardinal directions, astrologers then determine the position of the chthonic serpent who is thought to dwell beneath its surface. This natural 'owner of the site' is said to revolve slowly in his underground home so as to face each of the four sides in turn during the annual cycle of four seasons, and the four corners of the square, therefore, are thought to be the locations of the serpent's head at the beginning of a season. Calculating that the serpent's head travels with a regular motion along the western side of the square during the three months of spring, the northern side during the summer and so on, it is a simple matter for the architects and priests to determine the layout beneath the ground of the *nāga* on any given day of the year. Having done so, they dig into the earth at the spot calculated to correspond to 'the armpit' of the serpent and bury precious offerings there in payment for the ground in order to secure his goodwill and the future protection and welfare of the site.

Even more elaborate rites may involve summoning the Four Great Kings: Dhṛtarāṣṭra, ruler of the east; Virūḍhaka, ruler of the south; Virūpākṣa, ruler of the west; and Vaisravaṇa, ruler of the north. They may then be requested to consecrate and bless the site as sacred and to guard over it while religious works are being performed there. The ten direction protectors also, consisting of the Vedic deities, Brahmā, Indra, Yama and the rest, are often invited by Buddhists and their beneficent influence sought for the protection of the site. A more wrathful method of later times involves the demarcation of the site by sharp wooden pegs (*kīla*) which are driven into the four corners and along the boundary of the sacred area with curses to destroy all demons and their malignant power.

Building *stūpa*s

In his final injunctions to the *saṅgha*, delivered just before the time of his death and recorded in the *Mahā-parinibbāna Sutta*, the Buddha stressed once more the importance of the *Dharma* as a refuge and guide in their lives. Instructing his monks to work out their own salvation with diligence, he told them to place no faith in transitory phenomena such as the body of the Teacher, but to revere instead the doctrines and practices he had taught. The monks were 'not to hinder themselves by honouring the remains of the *Tathāgata*'. The cremation of the body and monumental interment of relics were matters to be left entirely in the hands of interested lay parties who would subsequently worship them in a fitting manner. The layfolk, it was said, would honour the funeral monument (*stūpa*) with garlands of flowers, wreaths of incense and all the traditional Indian paraphernalia of worship. They would maintain the upkeep of the shrine's superstructure and rejoice and be glad in its presence. Whereas, then, the *stūpa* of the Buddha was to be regarded as a suitable focus for the venerations of layfolk, it was not deemed fitting as a topic of interest for the ordained *saṅgha* whose minds should remain attuned to higher things.

Following the decease of the Buddha in Kuśinagara, ten *stūpa*s were constructed in the neighbouring areas in order to house and honour his mortal remains (Walshe, 1987, pp. 272–7). Relics from the cremation had been gathered together and distributed among the Mallas of Kuśinagara, King Ajātaśatru of Magadha, the Licchavis of Vaiśālī, the Śākyas of Kapilavastu, the Bulakas of Calakalpa, the Krauḍyas of Rāmagrāma, the brahmins of Viṣṇudvīpa and the Mallas of Pāpā. Drona, the brahmin who had presided over the cremation, kept the urn which had enclosed the relics and the late-arriving Mauryas of Pipphalivana claimed the ashes. It is also said that the countless gods of the heaven of the Thirty-three descended to earth at that time and each one claimed a single hair of the Blessed One's body over which was subsequently constructed a *stūpa* in heaven. The ten original *stūpa*s of the Ganges heartland are said to have been opened up, more than 100 years after they were built, by the emperor Asoka, who divided their contents among many hundreds of *stūpa*s which he caused to be constructed throughout his realm. Other monuments were built to house the Buddha's robe and bowl, clippings of his hair, his footprints and his shadow (that is, they were built on sites rendered sacred by his presence).

More than simply commemorating the master, however, by assuming possession of the relics, the emperor Asoka aligned their spiritual power with his own political authority and thereby 'legitimated' his right to rule. Tales are told of miraculous phenomena being observed in connection with these sacred traces of the Buddha, and it became an article of popular faith that their supernatural force would assist the pious king who protected them to govern his subjects with wisdom and justice.

In Sri Lanka, Buddhist kings have traditionally honoured and protected the relic of the Buddha's tooth in the belief that the security and well-being of the kingdom were dependent in no small measure upon the security and well-being of the tooth. An annual public holiday is observed in that country, during which thousands of lay-people make the pilgrimage to the temple of the tooth and witness the splendid procession of the caparisoned relic on the back of a royal elephant. Such a celebration serves primarily to unite the Sinhalese in a feeling of national pride, confirming their belief in themselves as inheritors and custodians of the Buddha's law. The atmosphere throughout that particular pilgrimage stands in marked contrast to the atmosphere of reverential devotion evident at Bodh-gayā, India, where Buddhists of every nationality lose their separate identities in common worship of an 'other-worldly' spirituality.

The cult of the *stūpa* was carried with Buddhism throughout the lands of eastern Asia, and when corporeal relics were no longer to be found, *stūpa*s were built to enclose the Buddha's image or symbol. In the *Lotus Sūtra* it is explained that a magnificent and lofty great *stūpa*, consisting of jewels, should be erected to mark the site where the *sūtra* has either been 'declared or explained or recited or copied out', and that relics of the *Tathāgata* are not required to be placed within it because the entire mass of relics is already gathered there in unison. Similarly,

> That spot of earth where this *sūtra* is revealed; that spot of earth will be worthy of worship by the whole world with its gods, men and *asura*s, that spot of earth will be worthy of respectful salutation, worthy of being honoured by circumambulation. Like a shrine will be that spot of earth. (*Vajracchedikā Prajñā-pāramitā Sūtra*, ch. 5)

In the ancient Burmese (Myanmarese) city of Pagan alone more than 2,000 monuments and temples inspired by *stūpa* prototypes were constructed, and the vast number of *stūpa*s in existence today throughout the Buddhist world can only be guessed at.

Down through the centuries, not only has the architectural form of these monuments undergone considerable change, but their symbolic significance also. *Stūpa*s no longer proclaim in simple terms merely 'The Buddha was here'; they are now understood to embody his message encoded in their structure. This change in emphasis seems to have come about, in part at least, through the close proximity of the *saṅgha* to the ever-increasing number of monuments that were built within the actual precincts of the monasteries, so that the *saṅgha* were forced into sharing responsibility for their guardianship with the layfolk. More importantly, however, because of the lack of corporeal relics, *stūpa*s ceased to function as repositories of the *rūpa-kāya* and became instead repositories of the *Dharma-kāya*. The various *Vinaya* of all but the earliest monastic orders therefore contain minor texts that treat extensively the symbolic form and mode of worship of these most characteristic of Buddhist monuments. Although the documents of the separate schools conflict in the specifics of their various interpretations, all agree the monument to consist of a terraced base, dome, upper enclosure (*harmikā*), axial pole and superimposed parasol or series of honorific discs which, by an enumeration of their parts, stand typically for the 37 factors conducive to enlightenment (*bodhi-pakṣya-dharma*).

The first step of the terraced base, then, would generally be interpreted as representing the four applications of mindfulness (*smṛty-upasthāna*): mindfulness with regard to the body, feelings, mind and all phenomena. The second terrace would be said to stand for the four right endeavours (*samyak-prahāṇa*): endeavours with regard to those moral defilements not yet born which must remain unproduced, those depravities already arisen which must be destroyed, unacquired virtues which must be generated and those virtues already acquired which must be increased. The four corners of the third terrace then indicate: a strong desire to succeed, enthusiastic perseverance on the path, thought and investigative penetration, which are the four bases of psychic (miracle) power (*ṛddhi-pāda*). The five faculties (*indriya*) of faith, enthusiasm, mindfulness, meditative absorption and insight (see pp. 125–6), and their corresponding five strengths (*bala*), would be represented by the uppermost levels of the base beneath the dome, while the dome itself would be said to represent the seven limbs of enlightenment (*bodhy-aṅga*). These consist of mindfulness, *dharma*-investigation, enthusiasm, joy, tranquillity, profound concentration and equanimity. Finally the *harmikā* would stand for the Noble Eightfold Path of right view, right aspiration, right speech, right activity, right livelihood, right effort, right mindfulness and right meditation. The pole and parasols that served to honour the structure were then taken to indicate various levels of spiritual attainment on the basis of that 37-factored path.

The *stūpa* is also understood by some to be a representation of the entire cosmos. Thus the square base stands for the world of sense-desire (*kāma-loka*), the dome for the world of form (*rūpa-loka*), while its spire and finial point the way to the uppermost world of formlessness (*ārūpya-loka*) (see p. 261).

Inner sacred space

Despite the development of elaborate rites focused upon the external world, however, the superiority of internal sacred space was never forgotten. Although the Buddha taught that the earth and its inhabitants were to be honoured at all times by his followers, whose personal demeanour he required to remain humble, he also announced:

> It is in this fathom-long carcase (which is) cognitive and endowed with mind, that, I declare, lies the (experienced) world, and the arising of the world, and the stopping of the world, and the course that goes to the stopping of the world. (*Saṃyutta Nikāya*, I.62)

This early passage sees the lived, experiential world of any person as contained in the body along with the interpreting mind. Accordingly, all forms of Buddhism have focused on understanding and improving one's perception of the world and on careful awareness of the body. There has also been a great interest in various inner worlds of non-ordinary reality and, in the Vajrayāna, a perspective on the body which saw it as the site of all sacred activity. Indeed, the Mahāyāna saw the Buddha's body as equivalent to the whole world, such that the Buddha is reported to have declared:

> All lands are in my body and so are the Buddhas living there. Watch my pores and I will show you the Buddha's realm. (*Avataṃsaka Sūtra*, IV)

The external world and the human body are, of course, each considered to be composed of the four great elements (*mahā-bhūta*) known to ancient science: earth, water, fire and air. Early Buddhist *Abhidharma* texts describe the manner in which the world comes into being as a direct manifestation of the *karma* of those sentient beings who are destined to become its inhabitants, and in the later elaborations of this theme it is said that the element of earth arises as a result of their stupidity. It is because of the oppressive weight of choking ignorance and the heavy bonds of karmic formations that this element assumes its characteristics of mass and solidity. Water is said to arise as the result of a constant flow of desire, a defilement within which so many are drowned. Hatred and anger are responsible for the fire which burns away all goodness and the free movement of air reflects the all-pervading nature of jealousy. The *rūpa-kāya* or body of a *buddha*, on the other hand, arises from no such causes. In the Mahāyāna perspective, his appearance in the world is for the sake of others, for the mental defilements considered necessary for rebirth in *saṃsāra* have all been entirely eliminated from his own mind-stream during the course of the three incalculable eons of his training. In order to manifest in a form compatible with those humans around him who are to be trained, however, the Buddha generates the solidity of earth from the unshakeable firmness of his *samādhi*, and the tears of his great compassion flow forth as water. His enthusiasm for the path of *Dharma* and his devotion to the highest good glow with the warmth of fire and his utterances of truth, his skilful acts and his prayers and muttered *mantra* give rise to the element of air. Unlike others, the body of a *buddha* also possesses the subtle element of space derived from his enlightened qualities of wisdom and bliss.

The *maṇḍala*

According to this theory, therefore, the manifestation of a *buddha* in the human realm conforms to a set of norms quite unlike the laws of physics, chemistry and biology by which humankind is governed. Although the body of a *buddha* is perceived by those around him to consist of flesh and blood, it is understood by the wise to be, in reality, an illusory play of enlightened compassion made only of light. Any appearance to the contrary derives merely from the viewer's own lack of capacity to see things in their true nature. At one time, for example, the disciple Śāriputra demanded to know why his master, the Buddha, was forced to dwell in this world of ours with its rocky paths, steep cliffs and sharp thorns when other *buddhas* were known to reside in paradise. It was explained to him then that all such impurities were merely the reflections of those impurities still lurking within his own mind and the Buddha, touching the earth with his toe, caused the entire universe to appear more splendid than any heaven. 'My *kṣetra* [Buddha Land], Śāriputra, is always as pure as this', he said (*Vimalakīrti-nirdeśa Sūtra*, I.16–17).

In the view of the later Vajrayāna school, the equation of mind and space is axiomatic. Sacred or holy space, then, cannot exist in independence of sacred or holy mind. Upon the *maṇḍala* map (see pp. 122–3 and 286) of this sacred space the central area is generally marked in blue,[2] designating the central wisdom of the *buddha*-mind which perceives the deep, space-like nature of all phenomena as boundless in potential and uncreated in fact. This wisdom of openness, free of all mental propositions, is referred to as the pristine cognition of the utterly pure expanse of reality (*suviśuddha-dharma-dhātu-jñāna*) and is one of five such pristine cognitions that designate the territory of sacred space or mind. To the east is an area marked in white which corresponds to the 'mirror-like' pristine cognition (*ādarśa-jñāna*), the enlightened capacity to perceive simultaneously all phenomena without distortion or prejudice, just as a good mirror will faithfully reflect all the objects set before it without accepting some and rejecting others. To the south, the map is marked in yellow colour, indicative of the pristine cognition of sameness (*samatā-jñāna*) which recognizes the equality of all phenomena in their being unoriginated and lacking a self. With regard to all sentient beings, this wisdom is cognisant of the fact that all beings are the same in their desire for happiness and the avoidance of suffering, and thus the southern quarter of the map marks also the impartial quality of enlightened compassion. The western quarter of the map is red. Here is located the pristine cognition of discernment (*pratyavekṣaṇa-jñāna*) which recognises the particular value and function of each individual aspect of phenomena down to the smallest detail. It knows the individual destinies of beings as well as how to discriminate between what is appropriate and what is inappropriate in the light of given circumstances and the law of cause and effect. All of this is united into a single, co-operative wisdom in the northern quarter where the pristine cognition of establishing the deeds to be done (*kṛtyānuṣṭhāna-jñāna*) is marked on the map in green. It is by means of this knowledge that the *buddhas* achieve all that is to be accomplished with regard to their aspiration for the welfare of all beings.

To that extent, then, the *maṇḍala* functions as a map of the sacred mind. Let us now examine the manner in which it charts the relationships of phenomena in the physical world. The nature of humans, according to the early Buddhist texts, is made up of five 'aggregates' (*skandha*s) which are itemized as form (*rūpa*), feeling (*vedanā*), perception (*saṃjñā*), impulses (*saṃskāra*s) and consciousness (*vijñāna*) (see p. 77). As the king of the five, consciousness is placed in the centre of the *maṇḍala* with form and the rest in the four directions beginning with the east. There they become known as the five *jina*s or five *buddha*s, supreme among the *maṇḍala* gods and progenitors of the five families of *maṇḍala* deities (cf. pp. 274–5). The sense faculties of the body then take their place within the scheme as male deities while the objects of the senses in the four directions of the surrounding world are viewed as their female consorts. The inner and outer elements are positioned on the map with water in the east, earth in the south, fire in the west and air in the north. Ruling them all is the subtle central element of space. In their esoteric form these are regarded as the consorts of the five *buddha*s, and by a gradual multiplication of correspondences the *maṇḍala* increases in significance until it can truly be said to function as a map for the entire universe of sacred space.

Perceived as operating in the ordinary external world, then, the *buddha*s are said to perform their particular functions in accordance with the *maṇḍala* plan. Thus, acts of pacification such as healing the sick, calming those who are disturbed and bringing reconciliation to embittered rivals are said to be carried out in the eastern quarter of the *maṇḍala* within a circular area, white in colour. Acts of encouragement that bring about an increase of desirable qualities are said to be performed in the south within a square area of yellow colour. Acts of control that seek to harmonize chaotic energies and establish compassionate wisdom as the dominant force take place in the west within a bow-shaped (semi-circular) area of red ground. Acts of wrath, in which totally negative forces are destroyed, are carried out in the north within a black triangular space, and these four acts in the four directions of the *maṇḍala* are all performed in accordance with a general understanding of the *maṇḍala* as a map of the sacred space of buddhahood.

Pilgrimage and the cult of traces

In the *Mahā-parinibbāna Sutta*, the Buddha validates the principle of pilgrimage by saying that the sight of four places should lead to the arousing of an uplifting spiritual quickening in the faithful: where he was born, attained enlightenment, gave his first sermon, and entered final *nirvāṇa* at death. Moreover he said:

> And any who die while making the pilgrimage to these shrines with a devout heart will, at the breaking-up of the body after death, be reborn in a heavenly world. (Walshe, 1987, p. 264)

While this only holds out a good rebirth as a result of devout pilgrimage, and the Buddha elsewhere scornfully dismissed the idea of higher expectations of ritual – 'If the waters of the Ganges could truly wash away evil then all fishes would go straight to heaven' – countless Buddhist pilgrims were to be found in all periods of Buddhist history flocking to the sacred sites in order to worship at the *stūpa*s constructed there. The emperor Asoka had his own *Dharma-yātra* or 'Journey for Truth' to Bodh-gayā, the pre-eminent site of pilgrimage where the Buddha attained enlightenment, recorded in stone – engraved on rock (edict no. 8). *Stūpa*s and shrines were constructed at every major locality connected with the Buddha's life: Lumbinī Garden near Kapilavastu[3] where he was born, Bodh-gayā (regarded by Buddhists as 'the centre of the world' and known as the indestructible or *vajra* seat of enlightenment), the Deer Park at Sārnāth where he first turned the wheel of *Dharma*, the various places where miracles were performed and important discourses delivered, and at Kuśinagara[4] and surrounding districts upon his final demise. Indeed, the biography of the Buddha as a peripatetic teacher is intimately related to topographical detail, a fact of no little interest to pilgrims.

The popularity of pilgrimage and 'the cult of traces' led to the growth in ancient India of tourism as an industry. It has been suggested, in fact, that local narratives concerning the various episodes of the Buddha's biography were collected and embellished to such an extent by tourist guides anxious to entertain and inform the pilgrims that they became the actual basis upon which the biographies themselves later came to be written. In the detailed reports of their travels kept by some of the pilgrims from China, we may read of monks and monasteries, *stūpa*s, shrines, temples and images and, in particular, of the local legends associated with innumerable sacred sites. Fa-hsien, for example, left his home in Chang-an in 399 CE in search of *Dharma*, traversing the whole of Central Asia and North India before embarking by ship for Sri Lanka and Java. By the time of his return to China in 412 CE he had documented an enormous cult of relics spread all the way across the Buddhist world, and similar reports were made by others of his countrymen in the centuries that followed. The small published guidebooks to local sites that these pilgrims collected could be strung together so as to form a complete history of Buddhism, revealing the religion as one fundamentally based upon its notion of sacred topology.

It should be noted here that the use of the word 'history' by Buddhists encompasses a broader range of meanings than generally assigned to the term in the West. Thus the sacred sites eagerly identified by the pious (promoted, no doubt, by their zealous guides) included all features of the landscape that could conceivably be associated with any Buddhist legend at all. Not only, then, did this sacred topology feature the birthplaces of saints and the sites of their demonstrations of miracles and so on, not only were the caves and forest hermitages once inhabited by great luminaries pointed out, but the sites of exploits of the *bodhisattva* during his previous births, as recorded in the books of the *Jātaka*, and the miraculous deeds of gods and *nāga*s from beyond the human realm were also identified in large numbers upon the ground.

By drawing together large numbers of pilgrims from all over the Buddhist world, the more important sites have long served as cultural melting-pots within which the divergent views and customs of the many Buddhist sects could continuously interact with one another to their mutual enrichment. A harmonizing 'cultural norm' for Buddhism has thus been maintained under their influence. The smaller, more localized sites, however, may have tended to bond culturally the few who frequented them in the customs of a particular shrine and thus have given rise to disparate local traditions.

The relevance of sacred sites as an essential ingredient of Buddhism travelled with it wherever it spread. *Stūpa*s believed to contain relics of the Buddha are to be found all over Asia, such as those at Doi Suthep near Chiang Mai in Thailand and That Luang in Vientiane, Laos. The Shwe-dāgon *stūpa* in Rangoon is said to house the staff of

Kāśyapa and the robe of Kanakamuni,[5] two *buddhas* of the past, as well as eight hairs of Śākyamuni, the *buddha* of the present. Within a reliquary in the Daḷadā Māligāwa, Kandy, Sri Lanka, is to be found one of several of the Buddha's teeth, and the faithful of that land tell apocryphal tales of the Buddha having visited their island by the meditative power of flight on three occasions, finally leaving the imprint of his foot upon the rocks of Mount Sumanakūṭa (Śrīpada) in the south. He is similarly said to have visited the western coast of India, Myanmar (Burma), north-west India, Kashmir, Central Asia and elsewhere, so that the cult of traces grew up in all of those places, and in every country in the Buddhist world the institution of pilgrimage as a viable mode of worship or accumulation of 'merit' was established.

There are sixteen especially sacred sites of pilgrimage in Sri Lanka and twelve in Thailand associated with the twelve-year calendrical cycle. Four sacred mountains in China are deemed to have associations with great *bodhisattvas* of the Mahāyāna pantheon: Mount Wu-t'ai with Mañjuśrī, Mount O-mei with Samantabhadra, Mount P'u-t'o with Avalokiteśvara and Mount Chiu-hua with Kṣitigarbha. Similar traditions are instituted in Tibet, where a large number of ritual circuits of holy sites are known. There are 33 holy places in the western provinces of Japan considered sacred to Avalokiteśvara, and another 88 temples in Shikoku associated with Kōbō Daishi (Kūkai), the ninth-century patriarch of the Shingon sect, who was born in that district. Visiting these places in turn, as prescribed by tradition, generally involves the pilgrim in an arduous ritual journey of several hundred miles (almost 750 miles in the case of the Shikoku circuit). Pilgrims in Japan used to wear wide, flat hats made of reed to protect them from the sun, and the custom arose of writing *Doko-ninin* ('two on the trip') on these hats to signify that the traveller was accompanied along the way by the Buddha.

The activity of pilgrimage is generally considered by Buddhists to be productive of great 'merit' through the arduous disciplines of body, speech and mind involved and, furthermore, the significance and worth of the pilgrimage are much enhanced if the traveller at every station on his journey has the opportunity to receive religious instruction and ritual empowerments. Auspicious timing thus constitutes a critical feature of the journey, for it is important that the devotee arrives at each sacred site just at the time of year when its particular value is being celebrated. The result of this is that large numbers of pilgrims inevitably gather together at certain sacred sites at particular times, bringing wealth and foreign news from all directions to a central place of exchange, and this is of enormous importance to local economies. An important aspect of the tradition, then, is that every local festival is as much market day as religious and social event but, however much trading and bartering are engaged in en route, it is generally true to say that pilgrimage among the Buddhists remains a genuine act of religious piety.

An entire literary genre seems to have been devoted to sacred sites since Asoka first engraved upon rock a record of his own pilgrimage to Bodh-gayā. Local pamphlets devoted to the particular legends of their area have for centuries been a traditional feature of the major sites, and these provincial materials in turn have regularly been taken and incorporated into long guidebooks covering the entire circuit route in terms of the history and significance of all that may be encountered along the way. In their treatment of such things as *stūpa*s, temples and images, these guides often prove to be valuable historical documents, while in their treatment of sacred springs, lakes, rocks, caves, mountains, trees and the rest they may also record an enormous wealth of folklore. 'Pilgrims' guides' have also been produced to such mythical sites as Śambhala, the kingdom in Central Asia within which the teachings of Kālacakra are supposed to have been preserved; Sukhāvatī, the Western Paradise of the Buddha Amitābha; the continents of Uttarakuru and so on around Mount Meru (see p. 260), as well as various heavens and hells that constitute features of early Buddhist cosmology.

Twenty-four sacred sites of the *tantra*s

With the rise in India of the tantric school of Buddhism (Vajrayāna), a series of 24 or 32 sacred places of pilgrimage were defined on the basis of the fundamental myth concerning the *buddha*s' overthrow of the demonic Rudra (Maheśvara[6]) and his hordes. In a former age, it is said, all beings were gods possessed of bodies of light and they lived in bliss. Eventually, however, because of their craving for sensation, beings began to materialize in physical form and dwell upon the earth, eating solid food.[7] The first areas to become inhabited by these *deva*s from the sky were the seats (*pīṭha*) of Pullīramalaya, Jālandhara, Oḍḍiyāna and Arbuda. Then the nearby seats (*upapīṭha*) of Godāvarī, Rāmeśvara, Devīkoṭa and Mālava were occupied by the *gandharvas* and so those eight places became known as *Khecarī*, '(inhabited by) those who move in the sky'.

After that, the fields (*kṣetra*) of Kāmarūpa and Oḍra were adopted as the homes of *yakṣas* while the nearby fields (*upakṣetras*) of Triśakuni and Kośala became the abodes of their servants. Fierce *rākṣasa* moved into the areas (*chandoha*) of Kaliṅga and Lampāka and their servants came to dwell in the *upacchandoha* of Kāñcī and the Himālaya. Because these eight places were occupied by beings from the earth they became known collectively as *Bhūcarī*, 'roaming the earth'.

Then the subterranean *nāgas* took control of the meeting places (*melāpakas*) Pretapurī and Gṛhadevatā while the nearby meeting places (*upamelāpakas*) of Saurāṣṭra and Suvarṇadvīpa became overrun with their servants. Finally, the *asuras* emerged from the dark depths of Mount Meru and occupied the charnel grounds (*śmaśānas*) of Pātaliputra and Sindhu, their servants inhabiting the nearby charnel grounds (*upaśmaśānas*) of Maru and Kulatā. These eight places subsequently became known as *Pātālavāsinīs*, '(occupied by those who) dwell beneath the ground'.

Then there arose in the world the proud spirit Maheśvara whose misuse of sacred teachings had caused him to become very powerful and dangerous. Soon he had taken complete control of the 24 places and all the gods and demons who dwell therein became his subjects. Instructing them in the ways of vicious depravity, this evil ruler encouraged his followers to prey upon human beings for food and thus throughout the world it was a time of great fear. Malicious demons were to be encountered roaming abroad both day and night. In their hands they carried sharp tridents (*khaṭvāṅgas*) and other weapons, and upon their bodies they wore human and animal skins for clothing. Adorning themselves with the shining bones of their victims, these demons wore tiaras of skulls upon their heads while around their necks hung garlands of severed heads dripping with blood. Whenever they were thirsty they would satiate themselves on human blood and at night they would cohabit with one another's wives.

Witnessing this dreadful situation upon the earth and deeply moved by the plight of suffering humanity, the *buddhas* assembled together on the peak of Mount Meru and elected from among their ranks the *bodhisattva* Vajrapāṇi to subdue the monstrous tyrant. His body having been blessed by the *Tathāgata* Vairocana, his speech by Amitābha, his mind by Akṣobhya, his attributes by Ratnasaṃbhava and his deeds by Amoghasiddhi,[8] the invincible Vajrapāṇi confronted the demon Maheśvara on the summit of Mount Malaya and overthrew him. The body of that proud spirit was cast down from the mountain with such force that his dismembered parts were scattered into the eight directions. Maheśvara's head landed in the south at a place called Body's End, his heart landed in the east at Sitavana, his intestines at Lankakuta to the west, his genitals at Padmakuta to the north, his right arm to the south-east at a place called Self-formed Mounds, his left arm at Secret Great Pleasure to the southwest, his right leg fell at Lokakuta in the north-east and his left leg at Creeping Great Laughter in the north-west. These sites subsequently became famous as 'the eight great charnel grounds' (*aṣṭa-mahā-śmaśāna*s), and thus the number of sacred places associated with this myth is raised to 32 (cf. p. 280).

With the overthrow of their lord Maheśvara, the various gods and demons who had been his subjects were converted by the power of Vajrapāṇi to the path of Buddhism. The 24 places under their control thus became incorporated into 'the kingdom of Buddhahood': the *maṇḍala* or sacred domain of the wrathful (*heruka*) *buddha*s. There can be no doubt that *yogin* devotees of this cult of wrathful *buddha*s undertook the arduous trek from site to sacred site around India as part of their devotional worship. Carrying tridents and wearing necklaces of bone, these tantric pilgrims (*kāpālika*s, 'adorned with skulls') proclaimed the defeat of Maheśvara by mimicking his attributes and visiting those very places where once he held sway. There they would gather together and celebrate the rites of enlightenment and the triumph of good over evil.

Spirit of the earth

A simpler parallel to this story is told with regard to the conversion of Tibet. That country, it is said, was under the sway of an ogress who resisted every attempt by humans to introduce to her realm the teachings of the Buddha. In this case, however, the actual landmass of the country was said to be the body of the ogress, who was finally subdued by the construction of *stūpa*s and temples upon her heart and limbs which rendered her immobile and thus incapable of further harm (Gyatso, 1989). Around the central temple upon her heart, an inner series of four constructions pegged down her shoulders and hips, an intermediate series pegged down her elbows and knees, and an outer series pegged down her wrists and ankles. Those original thirteen sites of her subjugation remain places of worship and pilgrimage to this day.

Maṇḍala-temples

As a map of the state of enlightenment, the tantric *maṇḍala* is generally square in form with the centre, marked blue, as its most sacred spot. Around this in the four directions stand the white, yellow, red and green courtyards spoken of above. These five areas comprise the floor-plan of a divine residence with four doors, before each of which stands a large triumphal archway (*toraṇa*).[9] The palace is overhung with projecting roofs from which dangle an abundant array of precious jewels and it has an upper storey with a dazzling *vajra* spire rising skyward from the centre. It rests upon a solid, unshakable, foundation and is surrounded by circular rings of lotus petals, *vajra* lattice and mountains of fire.

Many attempts have been made to represent this ideal of sacred architecture in bricks and mortar and every Vajrayāna temple is equated with the *maṇḍala* in the minds of those who worship there. The large temple complex of Samye (bSam-yas, eighth century CE), the first of its kind to be built in Tibet, was conceived outwardly as a map of the cosmos with its central and outlying buildings standing for the world-axis Mount Meru and its surrounding islands of habitation. Inwardly it was modelled on the divine architecture of the *maṇḍala* with different floors dedicated to specific deities of the Vajrayāna pantheon. Later temples at the dawn of the second wave of Buddhist traditions to enter Tibet (eleventh century CE) followed this plan even more rigorously. In western Tibet, for example, the temple at Tabo built by Rinchen Zangpo has a specially built *maṇḍala* house and at Alchi stands the three-storeyed temple called Sumtsek, both of which were purpose-built for the bestowal of Vajrayāna empowerments.

For the purposes of general assembly, however, although ideationally perfect, the *maṇḍala* with its square design and radial symmetry is ill-suited to ritual requirements. The four-doored sacred prototype is generally found inadequate to cope with the need to position the images, the offerings and ritual paraphernalia, the senior monks, the musicians and the main body of the *saṅgha*, each in prescribed hierarchical order for the performance of the rites. For temples of assembly, then, the radial symmetry of the ideal *maṇḍala* plan quickly gave way to the more practical arrangements of bilateral symmetry about a single axis leading from the main door to the high altar. The radial plan remained, however, viable for special 'initiation chambers' within which few people were expected to gather at a time, or for small shrines and other buildings not intended for human entry. It also remained perfectly acceptable to the Hindu architects of India and Nepal, who tended to construct one house as a temple for the god, into which the priest alone could crawl, and another (*maṇḍala*) for the assembly of a congregation of worshippers. Such an arrangement could not meet the special requirements of the egalitarian Buddhist *saṅgha*, however, and thus Buddhist temples in general do no more than reflect the glory of the sacred *maṇḍala* palace in the minor decorative features of their architecture. Thus the triumphal archways of the *maṇḍala* are replaced in Buddhist temples of the Kathmandu valley by decorative plaques placed over the doorways, and rows of lotus petals, and ornamental carved friezes depicting loops and tassels of jewels are incorporated within the structure of the temple walls.

With the growing influence of Vajrayāna ideas, the architectural forms of *stūpa* and *maṇḍala* began to converge. One of the earliest extant representations of the *maṇḍala* form, in fact, is the ninth-century *stūpa* of Borobudur in Java, now recognized as a depiction of the Vajradhātu *maṇḍala*. In Tibet the 'great *stūpa* of a thousand images' (*sKu 'bum mchod rten chen po*) in Gyantse deliberately sets out to recreate in architectural form a vast array of *maṇḍala*s in over 70 chapels on five storeys. Countless temples, Buddhist and Hindu, epitomize the *maṇḍala* ideal in the jungles of Cambodia and throughout southeast Asia and each one of these magnificent edifices carries the transcendent notion of sacred space to the mortal realm of humanity.

The tantric *maṇḍala*, however, is not merely to be located in the mundane, external world. As the absolute paradigm of sacred place it is considered to embody a transcendent ideal, the roots of which are to be found in the heart of wisdom. The peaceful Buddha, surrounded by his retinue of *bodhisattva* sages, is taken to be the prototype of the peaceful *maṇḍala* assembly, while the wrathful *heruka* and his conquered retinue, consisting of former acolytes of Maheśvara, is the prototypical *maṇḍala* of wrath. The essential *maṇḍala* of buddhahood, in either peaceful or wrathful form, may be contemplatively generated in the mind on any occasion, for its true nature is an archetype of manifestation beyond manifestation itself. The pillars and beams, the foundation platform and the walls and so on of the divine palace, within which the *maṇḍala* deities reside, are constructed of sacred doctrine, so that the entire edifice is a construct of truth, not of materiality. Its depiction in form, therefore, is a representation of *Dharma* in exactly the same way as the *stūpa* looked at above.

Unification of outer and inner

Taking the *maṇḍala*, then, as equivalent to all *dharma*s or aspects of realization and its path, the *yogin* contemplates the eight great charnel grounds around the sacred periphery as the eight levels of consciousness (*vijñāna*) within his own nature. Recognizing all appearances (eye consciousness), sounds (ear consciousness) and the rest as inherently perishable (*anitya*), empty (*śūnya*), unsatisfactory (*duḥkha*) and lacking a 'self' (*anātman*), he casts their impure natures out to the eight great charnel grounds and thereby purifies his perception of reality. As a pilgrim to the holy places of the external world, the *yogin* visits the *pīṭha* and is said thereby to achieve the first *bhūmi*, or stage of the *bodhisattva*'s path, called Joyous. Travelling to the *upapīṭha* he attains the Immaculate. As he reaches the *kṣetra* and *upakṣetra* he traverses, in turn, the stages called Radiant and Flaming. In similar fashion the *yogin* gains the stages called the Invincible, Manifest, Far-Reaching, Immovable, Excellent Intelligence and Cloud of *Dharma* as he continues on his pilgrimage to the *chandoha, upacchandoha, melāpaka, upamelāpaka, śmaśāna* and *upaśmaśāna*. These ten stages of the *bodhisattva*, together with the ten perfections (*daśa-pāramitā*) simultaneously accomplished on his journey, constitute the final stages of his path to perfect enlightenment (*samyak-saṃbodhi*) leaving nothing more to be achieved. By the placement of his body in sacred space the *yogin*'s mind has reached its goal, becoming liberated in the *Dharma-kāya* where the minds of all *buddha*s reside.

For the sake of the world, however, in fulfilment of his Mahāyāna vow to liberate all beings, the *yogin* should strive to perfect the internal *maṇḍala* of his form (the *rūpa-kāya*). With the help of a manuscript 'traveller's guide' he may thus undertake an internal pilgrimage to those 24 sacred places where once dwelt the beings from the sky, the earth and the regions below the earth. These groups of places and the deities attendant upon them are contemplatively to be metamorphosed by the *yogin* and integrated within the subtle system of pathways (*nāḍī*s) and energy nodes (*cakra*s) within his body where they are to be thought of as the retinues of his mind, speech and form (see p. 278).

A tantric pilgrim's guide to medieval India

Pullīramalaya in the outer world are the 'mountains of abundance' (Paurnagiri), the Malaya range on the western Ghats abounding in sandalwood trees. Within the body this site is to be equated with the forehead from where a pathway carries energy (*prāṇa*) to the fingernails, toenails and teeth. It is guarded by the wisdom *ḍākinī*[10] Pracaṇḍā and her male consort Śikhaṇḍakapālin, and the *yogin* on his pilgrimage should worship that divine couple there.

Jālandhara stands at the confluence of three rivers in the district of Kangra (Himachal Pradesh), where there are to be found sacred springs and a natural blazing of fire from the earth. The site remains popular to this day with pilgrims who go there to bathe in its holy waters (modern name Jawalamukhi). The *yogin* should contemplate this site as the 'aperture of Brahmā' upon the top of his skull where heat rises and three pathways meet. Pathways radiate from that place, the home of Caṇḍākṣī and Mahākaṅkāla, carrying energy to the hairs of the *yogin*'s head and body.

Oḍḍiyāna in the west (now Pakistan) is a triangular area in the Indus valley that has been blessed by countless *vidyādhara*s[11] and *ḍākinī*s. The people of that region are said to be possessed of great wisdom and this corresponds in the body to the right ear, the abode of Prabhāmatī and Kaṅkāla, from which pathways carry subtle energy to the pores of the skin.

According to the ancient texts, Arbuda (Taxila, also known as Vajrakūṭa) was a peaceful, prosperous area of wooded slopes abundant with cattle. The abode of Mahānāsā and Vikaṭadamṣṭrin, it corresponds in the body to the spine, from which flow pathways of energy for the flesh.

Godāvarī, across the valley to the west of the Vindhya mountains, is known as 'the place of the cow's gift'. It is said that in former times a Nepalese cowherd lost one of his cows in the hills and when he finally found the beast her udder was empty. Seeing a nearby hollow in the ground full of milk, he dug into the earth and discovered a buried Śiva *liṅga* and a black stone flask of nectar marked with the triangular sign of origination (*dharmodaya*). The correspondence of this in the body is the waxy hollow of the left ear, from which radiate pathways to the muscles and tendons. It is known as the home of Viramatī and Svaravairiṇa.

To the east of Bodh-gayā lies an area of forest where once the king Rāmeśvara had his city. There is a rock nearby the shape of which reminds one of a horse's mane, and it is said to be the abode of Kharvarī and Amitābha. Within the body it is the harmonious spot between the eyebrows, from which radiate pathways to the bones.

Devīkoṭa, the abode of the goddess, is an ancient temple of Umā built by King Deśopāla within which are to be found two images of the goddess that look like eyes. It is situated at a distance of four *krośa*s (a little over two miles) from the town of Pancapata in Bharendra and it is said that those who gaze upon the images sometimes see their own form. The abode of Laṅkeśvarī and Vajraprabha, its position in the body is the eyes, from which flows a pathway to the liver.

Mālava in central India is a district made beautiful by white flowers, said to abound with horses. It corresponds to the shoulders, the abode of Drumacchāyā and Vajradeha, from where there is a pathway that flows to the heart.

Those eight sites of the sky-travelling ones (*ḍākinī*s) are arranged in the body as a circle (*cakra*) for the mind. Now, with regard to the eight places of those who roam upon the earth, these constitute within the body a circle of speech.

In the hot place to the east known as 'the form of desire' (Kāmarūpa), there is a hollow shrine like an armpit within which the triangle of origination may sometimes be discerned upon the rock by those of much 'merit'. Airāvatī lives there, together with Aṅkurika. Its place in the body is marked by the two armpits, from which travel pathways to the eyes.

Oḍra in the kingdom of Daśaratha in the south is famous as 'the place of nourishment'. It is said that a deity once took residence there within a stone shaped like a breast and sustained the happiness and prosperity of the kingdom. Mahābhairavī and Vajrajaṭila dwell there now and their place within the body is the breasts which provide sustenance and joy. Pathways from there convey *pitta* ('bile', one of the three vital humours) to the rest of the body.

Triśakuni is the 'triple intersection' where the rivers Ganges, Indus and one of their tributaries meet. It is a most charming and agreeable place, constantly resounding with the calls of ducks, storks, geese, swans, parrots and other birds. There is a natural stone there in the form of the triangle of origination, the abode of Vāyuvegā and Mahāvīra. In the body it is located at the navel, the triple intersection of the three primary *nāḍī*s, from where a pathway flows to the lungs.

Kosala in the west of India is just one *krośa* from the kingdom of Prasenajit. In the place of meditation there, there is a symbol (*liṅga*) with the shape of a nose. The home of Surābhakṣī and Vajrahūṃkāra, its place in the body is the top of the nose, from where a pathway flows down to the garland of intestines.

Kaliṅga is in the area of Hastidhara ('having elephants', possibly Hastinapura), about twelve *yojana*s (fifty miles) from Bodh-gayā where meadow and forest meet. It is a region inhabited by *preta*s (insatiable ghosts) and the abode of Syāmādevī and Subhadraguṇa. It corresponds in the body to the mouth, from where a pathway travels all the way to the colon.

Lampāka is situated beyond the territory of Turkestan, a place inhabited by non-humans where water beats against the rocks. Its name derives from a certain neck-shaped rock in the vicinity that seems to hang down (*lamba*) from the side of the mountain. Subhadrā and Vajrabhadra live there and it corresponds in the body to the throat, from where there runs a pathway to the stomach.

Of Kāñcī the ancient guidebooks say 'At a distance of twelve *yojana*s from Turkestan is the district of Kāñcī where there is to be found a large boulder in the shape of a heart'. Current opinion, however, identifies this city with modern Kanchipuram, not far from Madras. It is said to be a place of clarity where all the people are possessed of wisdom. Hayakarṇī lives there with Mahābhairava and their abode within the body is the heart, from where a pathway moves downward for the elimination of faeces.

In the district of Himālaya there stands the sacred mountain Kailash from which the waters of our world (the Indian sub-continent) flow down. There, on the shore of Lake Anavatapta ('never warm', now identified with Manasarovar), stands the sacred Jambu tree from which our world derives its ancient name of Jambudvīpa, 'the isle of Jambu'. Among the 24 places, Mount Kailash is possibly the most famous of all, a favoured destination of pilgrims from every school. Known among Hindus as the sacred abode of Śiva, this mountain has been the site of countless legends and miraculous events as recorded in the guidebooks of Buddhists and non-Buddhists alike. From the mouth of an elephant to the south of that place is said to arise the Sutlej river which eventually joins the Indus. From the mouth of a horse to the east arises the Brahmaputra. From the mouth of a bull (or peacock) to the west arises the Karnali which joins the Gogra and ultimately the Ganges. From the mouth of a lion to the north flows the great river Indus. The *ḍākinī* Khagānanā lives there with Virūpākṣa and their abode in the body is the penis because water also flows out from there. A subtle pathway from that spot carries energy to the centre of the hairline.

Now, with regard to the eight sites formerly inhabited by those from the nether regions beneath the surface of the earth, these are to be understood within the *maṇḍala* as comprising the circle of the body.

The region of Pretapurī is a desolate and uninhabited area at the border of India and Tibet. It is very difficult to obtain food and drink there or to satisfy any desire. Mountains of rock tower ominously overhead and precipitous gorges loom beneath one's feet. The pathways are slippery and uneven and only those *yogin*s of the highest calibre venture there to meditate. It is known as the abode of Cakravegā and Mahābala and because it is a region of insatiable desire characterized by chasms it is equated in the human body with the vagina. Subtle pathways from there convey *śleṣma* ('phlegm', one of the three vital humours) to the rest of the body.

'The residence of the deity' (Gṛhadevatā) is an arbour of willow trees (or reeds) in Khotan marked by a sacred rock with the shape of a pyramid. It is the abode of Khaṇḍarohā and Ratnavajra which, in the body, is identified with the anus. Subtle pathways from that region serve to expel purulent matter from the body.

Saurāṣṭra is a place of great strength. Some identify it with Varanasi while others say that it is the city of Bumu in Turkestan. The land in that area is strong and supportive of all that is built upon it so within the body it is equated with the strong thighs that serve to carry the trunk. Sauṇḍinī and Hayagrīva live there and it is the seat of the pathways that convey blood throughout the body.

Suvarṇadvīpa (Pāli Suvaṇṇadīpa) is 'the golden island' of Sumatra that lies in the ocean to the east of India which some identify with the country of the glorious king Maṇicūḍa of China. It is said that one's prosperity greatly increases in that place. It is the home of Cakravarminī and Ākāśagarbha. Within the body it is the shanks, where the pathways of perspiration are to be found.

With regard to Nagara, some say that it is the city of the *rākṣasa*s[12] in Sri Lanka while others identify it with an area on the borders of India and Kashmir. The site is marked by an outcrop of rock resembling the five-fold hood of a *nāga* king and for this reason it is associated in the body with the five toes which project from the foot in a similar manner. Suvīrā and Marari live there and pathways from the toes convey fat.

Sindhu is the old name for the Indus valley which divides the areas of Jalandhara and Turkestan. It is famous as the abode of many *ḍākinī*s and is given as the residence of Mahābalā and Padmanarteśvara. Its place in the body is the instep of the foot, from where pathways convey tears.

Maru is an area of rocky caves situated to the north of Jalandhara. The caves particularly favoured by *yogin*s for their meditation in that place, are quite inaccessible from below and may only be reached by descending on ropes from above. It is the abode of Cakravartinī and Vairocana which, in the body, is the thumbs. Pathways from there convey watery spittle throughout the body.

Kulatā is another rocky area in the foothills around Lahoul. It is said to be a peaceful place of pleasant contact where the *yogin* should worship Mahāvīryā and Vajrasattva. In the body it is the knees, from where pathways convey mucus.

With regard to these 24 sacred places of pilgrimage, the *yogin* (*siddha*) Saraha has said: 'I have visited in my wanderings *kṣetra* and *pīṭha* and *upapīṭha* for I have not seen another place of pilgrimage blissful like my own body' (*Dohākoṣa*). 'Pilgrimage' in this context is to be understood as the movement of the subtle airs and humours along the internal pathways of the body, experienced by the *yogin* as bliss. The various *ḍākinī*s to be worshipped by Saraha at those sites are of the variety known as 'naturally' or 'simultaneously-born' (*sahaja*). Other *yogin*s on the path would conjure up those partners in their minds and worship them in the form 'generated by meditation' (*samādhi-ja*), or summon them by means of spells (*mantra-ja*), or seek them in the sacred places of pilgrimage in the external world (*kṣetra-ja*). In the light of the tantric theory of correspondences mentioned above, however, the truly enlightened *yogin*, whose residence is the central palace of the divine *maṇḍala*, moves freely within the sacred space of his own wisdom which pervades both inner and outer phenomena without distinction. There he enjoys the blissful company of the elements which are, for him, the best of consorts. Wherever he roams he remains at the epicentre of sacred space for his natural abode is always at rest at the foot of the tree of enlightenment.

In this tantric perspective then, we see a vision of outer and inner sacred space in total integration.

Notes

1 This is how a Mahāyānist might express it; a Theravādin might simply talk of exploring and developing inner spiritual qualities.
2 Note that the scheme on pp. 274–5 is according to a different tantric system.
3 Pāli Kapilavatthu.
4 Pāli Kusinārā.
5 Pāli Kassapa and Koṇāgamaṇa, respectively.
6 An epithet of the Hindu god Śiva.
7 So far, as described in the *Aggañña Sutta* of the Pāli Canon (Walshe, 1987, pp. 409–10).
8 See pp. 272–6 on these five *jina*s.
9 The term used for the gateways of early *stūpa*s: see p. 121.
10 *Ḍākinī*s are seen as wrathful female holy beings who help shock people out of spiritual complacency.
11 A *vidyādhara* is a master of tantric magic.
12 A *rākṣasa* is a demon.

Further reading

Basham, A. L. (1954) *The Wonder That Was India*. London: Sidgwick & Jackson.

Bechert, H. and Gombrich, R. (eds) (1984) *The World of Buddhism*. London: Thames and Hudson.

Berkson, C. (1986) *The Caves at Aurangabad: Early Buddhist Tantric Art in India*. New York: Mapin International.

Dahman-Dallapiccola, A. L. (ed.) (1980) *The Stūpa: Its Religious, Historical and Architectural Significance*. Wiesbaden: Franz Steiner Verlag.

Dorje, G. and Kapstein, M. (eds and trans.) (1991) *The Nyingma School of Tibetan Buddhism: Its Fundamentals and History*, by Dudjom Rinpoche. Boston: Wisdom Publications.

Dowman, K. (1987) *Power Places of Central Tibet*. London: Routledge and Kegan Paul.

Dutt, N. (1980) *The Early History of the Spread of Buddhism and the Buddhist Schools*. Delhi: Rajesh Publications.

Gomez, L. and Woodward, H. (eds) (1981) *Barabudur: History and Significance of a Buddhist Monument*. Berkeley: University of California.

Gyatso, J. (1989) 'Down with the Demoness' in J. Willis (ed.) *Feminine Ground: Essays on Women and Tibet*. Ithaca, NY: Snow Lion, pp. 33–51.

Hazra, K. (1984) *Buddhism in India as Described by the Chinese Pilgrims, CE 399–699*. Delhi: Motilal Banarsidass.

Lamotte, E., trans. Sara Boin-Webb (1988) *History of Indian Buddhism*. Louvain: Institut Orientaliste.

Pal, P. (1982) *A Buddhist Paradise, the Murals of Alchi*. Basel: Ravi Kumar.

Slusser, M. (1982) *Nepal Maṇḍala. A Cultural Study of the Kathmandu Valley* (2 vols). Princeton, NJ: Princeton University Press.

Snellgrove, D. (1987) *Indo-Tibetan Buddhism*. London: Serindia.

Strachan, P. (1989) *Pagan Art and Architecture of Old Burma*. Whiting Bay: Kiscadale.

Walshe, M. (1987) *Thus Have I Heard: The Long Discourses of the Buddha*. London: Wisdom Publications.

Index of concepts

Page numbers for primary entries are shown in **bold type**. Where terms are in languages other than Pāli or Sanskrit, this is indicated. When Pāli and Sanskrit (Skt) versions of a term differ, this is indicated. Language is also indicated where a term is common only in Pāli or Sanskrit.

Index of names

Including named historical individuals, texts, Buddhist schools and fraternities, gods, holy beings, heavens, Pure Lands, places, peoples, religions and political movements (but see Index of concepts for three main cultural areas of Buddhism and spiritual vehicles, such as the Mahāyāna). Primary entries in **bold type.**